The Marketing Customer Interface 1999–2000

The Chartered Institute of Marketing/Butterworth-Heinemann Marketing Series is the most comprehensive, widely used and important collection of books in marketing and sales currently available worldwide.

As the CIM's official publisher, Butterworth-Heinemann develops, produces and publishes the complete series in association with the CIM. We aim to provide definitive marketing books for students and practitioners that promote excellence in marketing education and practice.

The series titles are written by CIM senior examiners and leading marketing educators for professionals, students and those studying the CIM's Certificate, Advanced Certificate and Postgraduate Diploma courses. Now firmly established, these titles provide practical study support to CIM and other marketing students and to practitioners at all levels.

 The Chartered
Institute of Marketing

Formed in 1911, The Chartered Institute of Marketing is now the largest professional marketing management body in the world with over 60,000 members located worldwide. Its primary objectives are focused on the development of awareness and understanding of marketing throughout UK industry and commerce and in the raising of standards of professionalism in the education, training and practice of this key business discipline.

The Marketing Customer Interface 1999–2000

Rosemary Phipps and Craig Simmons

Published on behalf of
The Chartered Institute of Marketing

OXFORD   AUCKLAND   BOSTON   JOHANNESBURG   MELBOURNE   NEW DELHI

Butterworth-Heinemann
Linacre House, Jordan Hill, Oxford OX2 8DP
225 Wildwood Avenue, Woburn, MA 01801-2041
A division of Reed Educational and Professional Publishing Ltd

Ⓡ A member of the Reed Elsevier plc group

First published 1999

British Library Cataloguing in Publication Data
A catalogue record for this book is available from the British Library

ISBN 0 7506 4369 2

Composition by Genesis Typesetting, Laser Quay, Rochester, Kent
Printed and bound in Italy

Contents

A quick word from the Chief Examiner

I am delighted to recommend to you the new series of CIM workbooks. All of these have been written by authors involved with examining and marking for the CIM.

Preparing for the CIM Exams is hard work. These workbooks are designed to make that work as interesting and illuminating as possible, as well as providing you with the knowledge you need to pass. I wish you success.

Trevor Watkins,
CIM Chief Examiner,
Deputy Vice Chancellor,
South Bank University

Acknowledgements

Thank you to Sophie and William for their support, also to Oliver for reviving my energy in an hour of need and Kathy Brocklehurst for typing the manuscript.

A special thank you to my colleagues and fellow consultants at Oxford College of Marketing – Lisa Harris, Graham Cooper, Eric Dore, and Oxford Brookes University Staff Stuart Rookes, Daniel Ganley, Georgina Whyatt, Peter Gardner, Chris Blackburn and Aileen Harrison.

I am especially grateful to Mark Hindwall at MCB for providing me with access to the Emerald Library. Also, thanks to Louise Cox at A. C. Nielsen. I hope students will make every attempt to keep up to date by reading these publications in the future.

Rosie Phipps and Craig Simmons

How to use your CIM workbook

The authors have been careful to structure your book with the exams in mind. Each unit, therefore, covers an essential part of the syllabus. You need to work through the complete workbook systematically to ensure that you have covered everything you need to know.

This workbook is divided into twelve units each containing the following standard elements:

Objectives tell you what part of the syllabus you will be covering and what you will be expected to know having read the unit.

Study guides tell you how long the unit is and how long its activities take to do.

Questions are designed to give you practice – they will be similar to those you get in the exam.

Answers give you a suggested format for answering exam questions. *Remember* there is no such thing as a model answer – you should use these examples only as guidelines.

Activities give you the chance to put what you have learnt into practice.

Exam hints are tips from the senior examiner or examiner which are designed to help you avoid common mistakes made by previous candidates.

Definitions are used for words you must know to pass the exam.

Extending activity sections are designed to help you use your time most effectively. It is not possible for the workbook to cover *everything* you need to know to pass. What you read here needs to be supplemented by your classes, practical experience at work and day-to-day reading.

Summaries cover what you should have picked up from reading the unit.

A glossary is provided at the back of the book to help define and underpin understanding of the key terms used in each unit.

Introduction

This module is new to the Advanced Certificate in Marketing. Although some of the topics formed part of the Certificate course, Understanding Customers, this new module has been developed to focus upon the centrality of the customer, both internally and externally, to effective marketing strategies.

We are now standing at a new frontier of business. There is competition from low-cost economies using new technologies, skilled people and mobile capital; innovative product processes and services are spreading rapidly across the globe; electronic commerce is rapidly changing the way business meets customer demands. Science and knowledge are underpinning the new technologies which are developing at a faster pace. In order to remain competitive, the importance of developing a strong customer focus within organizations is stressed, and this book describes the diverse range of processes that enable this communication to take place.

Such a focus is necessary because increasing attention to customer service, creativity, innovation and the management of change demand more from marketers than ever before. The understanding marketers need to have of customers and processes within the organization, needs to go far beyond the traditional role played by the marketing department. Throughout the module it is stressed that organizations need to adopt this customer-centred focus throughout the firm so that marketing extends beyond the management of the marketing department to managing an organization that has a marketing focus.

You will discover that this workbook provides a comprehensive guide to the latest thinking as to how organizations can develop a true marketing focus. It draws upon theories and practical examples from a diverse range of industry sectors across the world. Extensive use has been made of the worldwide web to collect relevant material, and a number of websites and traditional publications are recommended for readers seeking further information about specific topics.

Macro- and micro-environmental forces driving change

❏ Be introduced to the wide range of factors that influence customer behaviour.

❏ Be introduced to some of the macro- and micro-environmental factors that are currently influencing conditions in the market.

❏ Look at the driving forces behind customer power.

❏ Understand how organizations can respond to these pressures.

❏ Look at examples of customer focused marketing in specific economic sectors.

❏ Rethink the use of the word customer.

❏ Be introduced to the concept of role and role relationships.

Study Guide

Readers are introduced to the wide range of factors that influence customer behaviour. A number of macro- and micro-environmental forces currently impacting on organizations are discussed. Forces that are making organizations fundamentally rethink existing ideas about their external adaptation and internal integration.

Specific research done by the Future Foundation has identified a new drive for a caring and liberal form of capitalism. Trust and the goodwill a company generates as a result of its contribution to society have now become the values on which some consumers will make purchases. Within this framework of values as markets mature and competitive pressures increase, organizations are discovering that customers are expecting more. Research carried out by the Institute of Customer Service outlines changes in customer behaviour, actions companies are taking in response to these changes and what they should do in the future to become more customer focused.

Examples of customer-focused marketing from different economic sectors are given. Students are advised to research and add to these examples during their course.

Students are then asked to think about the use of the word customer and to extend their ideas to the concept of role relationships.

Study Tips

Organize your study materials from the beginning of your course:

● Use file dividers to keep broad topic areas indexed and relevant materials and articles with the relevant notes.
● Look out for relevant articles and current examples, you will find these useful to illustrate examination answers.

Factors influencing customer behaviour

Managing the marketing customer interface involves understanding people, the way in which they purchase, interrelate and interact with the interface of the organization.

The following factors influence customer behaviour:

External factors

Macro-environmental factors PEST
Political influences, legal constraints, economic conditions and changes in the economy, international developments, socio-demographic changes, cultural influences, technological developments and environmental interests (otherwise known as PEST factors).

Micro-environmental factors

1 The type of market and its characteristics, market life cycle, industry structure.
2 The number of competitors, generic positioning, competitive strategy.
3 The suppliers in the supply chain.
4 The method of distribution and the distribution chain.
5 The number of customers, the way in which the market can be segmented, the degree of market segmentation, the adoption and diffusion curve.
6 Individual psychological factors such as motives, perceptions, approach to risk, attitudes, personality, unique ability, knowledge, demographic and situational factors.
7 Social factors such as roles and family influences, opinion leaders, innovators, reference groups, social classes, culture and subculture.
8 The decision-making process (DMP) and the extent of the decision making involved – extended and limited problem solving (EPS and LPS), routine response buying, impulse buying and the degree of involvement in the purchase.
9 The decision-making process within the decision-making unit (DMU).
10 The influence of stakeholders and the impact the organization has on society.
11 The defining and management of relationships.

Internal factors

1 Values and meta values (the values behind the espoused values) embodied in the vision, mission and enacted in the way the organization manages itself.
2 Objectives, strategy and policies.
3 The marketing mix and other situational factors.
4 Leadership, management and human resource management.
5 Production/operational processes.
6 Financial and resource management.
7 Outsourcing and partners.

Many of these points are discussed in this workbook, others are discussed in detail elsewhere in the syllabus.

The emergence of customer power in the new competitive climate

Driving forces for change and organizational response
Some of the principal challenges that Kashani (1996) identified in an international study of 220 marketing managers were:

- High and rising levels of competition across virtually all markets.
- Far higher levels of price competition.
- An increasing emphasis upon and need for customer service.

- The demand for higher levels of product quality.
- High rates of product innovation.
- The emergence of new market segments.
- The growing power of distribution channels.
- Growing environmental green concerns.
- Increases in government obligations.
- European integration.
- Increasing advertising and promotional costs.

The principal implications of these were seen by managers to be the need for constant improvements to product and service quality, development of new products, keeping up with customers and adding to or improving customer service.

Kashani also asked managers about the sort of changes that were most likely to affect their markets in the future. The three most significant of these proved to be:

1 The consolidation of competition as fewer but larger players emerge.
2 Changing customers and their demands.
3 The globalization of markets and competition.

In order to cope with the sort of changes he suggests that marketing needs to respond in several ways:

1 Marketing should take far more direct line responsibility within the organization, with an emphasis upon segment or product management, where the focus is upon customer segments or particular products or technologies. This would have the effect of integrating marketing thinking and action into day-to-day business decisions.
2 Marketing needs to become more strategic and less specialized so that it becomes part of a more integrated process.
3 Marketing or customer orientation needs to become far more wide-spread so that marketing would no longer be the isolated concern of a few people but of staff throughout the whole business. This would mean that marketers would need to be more skilled in strategic thinking, communication and customer sensitivity.

As marketing is part of an organization which interacts directly and immediately with the environment it is essential that marketing comes to terms with areas of growing importance.

Doyle (1994) identified the major changes that the marketing planner would be faced with as:

- The fashionization of many relatively traditional markets as model changes occur much faster, obsolescence becomes more rapid and markets become more fickle.
- The replacement of mass markets with micro markets.
- Rising expectations across virtually all markets and a reduced tolerance to accept poorer or poor performance.
- The greater pace of technological change.
- High levels of competition.
- The globalization of an even greater number of markets.
- Differentiation on the basis of service and the soft rather than the traditional hard elements of the marketing mix.
- The increased commoditization of many markets.
- Greater government and legislative constraints.

Kotler's (1997) views on the changing emphasis and priorities within marketing are broadly similar with the greatest emphasis upon:

- Quality, value and customer satisfaction.
- Relationship building and customer retention.
- Managing business processes and integrating business functions.
- Global thinking and market planning.
- Building strategic alliances and networks.

- Direct and on-line marketing.
- Services marketing.
- Ethical marketing behaviour.

As Wilson and Gilligan (1997) write:

- It is apparent there is a need for companies to adapt as the pace of change increases, the speed of anticipation and response will become ever more important and time-based competition more essential.
- As markets fragment, customization will become more necessary.
- With expectations rising quality will become one of the basic rules of competition (in other words a 'must have') rather than a basis for differentiation.
- Information and greater market knowledge will provide a powerful basis for competitive advantage.
- Sustainable competitive advantage will increasingly be based upon an organization's core competencies, the consequences of the lack of strategic focus becomes more evident and more significant.
- As market boundaries are eroded, the need to think global would become ever more necessary. In this way, the marketing planner will be able to offset temporary or permanent declines in one market against growing opportunities in another. At the same time, of course they need to recognize the strategic significance of size and scale is increasing. However, the marketing planner should not lose sight of the need for tailoring products and services to the specific demands of markets by thinking globally but acting locally.
- Differentiation will increasingly be based upon service.
- Partnerships with suppliers and distributors will become far more strategically significant.
- Strategic alliances will become more necessary as a means of entry and operating within markets, partly because they offer the advantage of access to greater or shared knowledge, but also because of the sharing of costs and risks.
- A far greater emphasis upon product/service and process innovation.
- The need to recognize the greater number and complexity of stake-holder expectations.

Doyle identifies the ten most obvious of these being the need to:

1 Break hierarchies and reorganize around flatter structures.
2 Organize around small/smaller business units.
3 Develop self managing teams.
4 Reengineer.
5 Focus upon developing networks and alliances.
6 Move towards transactional forms of organization.
7 Become a true learning organization.
8 Emphasize account management in order to integrate specialist expertise across the organization for the benefit of the customer.
9 Recognize the importance of expeditionary marketing (instead of focusing upon what Hamel and Prahalad refer to as 'Blockbuster innovation' designed to get it right first time). The organization concentrates upon developing a stream of low-cost, fast-paced innovative products.
10 Rethink the way in which the board of directors operates so that it is focused to a far greater extent upon strategic direction rather than control and day-to-day management.

As Wolfgang E. Grulke, Chief Executive, FutureWorld writes, the computer and telecommunications revolution has taken the business world by storm, and has been a critical contributor to the forces that are creating a fundamentally new economy on the planet – the service or information economy.

Over the past decade we have begun to realize that the 'old' industrial economy has entered the end of its life cycle. In the USA less than 30 per cent of employment is now in the traditional industrial businesses. Analysts estimate that more than 90 per cent of the US GDP this year will come from information and service businesses. We see similar shifts worldwide.

With the advent of GATT and other similar agreements the world is becoming a global supermarket of products – all sourced globally. The customer chooses on quality, cost and convenience. Time and distance no longer appear to add cost. Customers only judge on value.

Furthermore, almost every global product is in itself the product of many different countries – perhaps manufactured in Malaysia, by a Japanese company with capital provided by a German bank!

The world has already become a global supermarket of products – and it is also *fast becoming a global supermarket of services and ideas*. That transformation is of vital importance to your industry.

A new infrastructure for global capitalism
The internet currently links an estimated user community of more than 60 million people. Also, the number of users is growing at an exponential rate, doubling every year. The growth of information on the internet is even more explosive, typically doubling every four to five months! At the beginning of 1991 there was not a single business using the internet. Today, hundreds of thousands of businesses are operational on the internet. At the current rate of growth, 125 per cent of the world's population will be connected by 2003! Clearly this rate of growth cannot continue and will tail off. Whatever happens in the future, the internet is already an integral part of the nervous system of global capitalism.

New trade routes for a new economy
The trade routes for the new information economy are the electronic networks that span the globe – the telephone, television and computer networks that together make up the much-vaunted information highway.

The traditional value chain, the process of how your product or service gets into the hands of the customer, is being devastated by the drivers of the new economy. In the past the complete value chain was directly under your own control, sequential and somewhat constant and predictable. Today the value chain is fragmenting. The pressure to be competitive by global standards is forcing companies to outsource key components of the value chain to best-of-breed suppliers – wherever in the world they are – with information and communication technologies taking time, distance and cost right out of the equation. The traditional predictable *value chain* has become a chaotic instantaneous *value network*, the *marketplace* has transformed into a virtual *marketspace*.

Today small companies can have access to global networks for a few hundred dollars a month – something that would have cost millions of dollars just a few years ago and would have been available only to the largest of businesses. In future 'size' alone will be less and less of a competitive advantage.

As the physical, geographic *marketplace* moves to being a virtual, global and paperless *marketspace*, the nature of competitiveness is changing fundamentally. National boundaries become almost irrelevant – no more than a nuisance. *The primary limits to business performance are those that exist in our minds*.

(Published with permission of Wolfgang Grulke. For further articles contact www.futureworld.co.za)

Changing cultural values

Recent research carried out by the Future Foundation (future@netco-muk.co.uk) says that the impact of globalization on individual economies and working practices has been one of the key influences on the development of a new political economy.

The steady deregulation of world trade is forcing businesses in all sectors to become more competitive in the face of a greater choice of goods and services in previously protected home markets. Thus in most market sectors there is a growing need to sustain and create a competitive advantage through focusing on core competence, building strong and valued brands and keeping costs under control. This is having a major impact on employment and working practices. Downsizing and the restructuring of corporations has resulted in ever more functions being contracted out. Not surprisingly, employees' perceptions of their own job security have plummeted as a result.

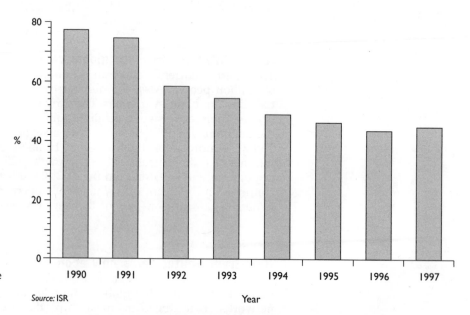

Figure 1.1
Employment security – percentage saying they felt secure in their employment

Source: ISR

Year

Globalization has been critical in the development of a new political economy. The reality and seeming inevitability of global competition has forced governments of all political persuasions to adapt their economic and social policies. At the same time, it has increased job insecurity and income polarization and threatened social cohesion and hence has fed the need for a more caring focus.

This reflects the two poles of a new political economy: full hearted acceptance of the global market economy while at the same time searching for mechanisms to protect individual citizens from the ravages of it. This has driven the search for the so-called 'third way' of politics – or social capitalism as the Future Foundation has labelled it.

An evolving hierarchy of responsibility

Maslow suggested that as societies develop so people move up a hierarchy from the basic sustenance required just to live in primitive societies through security to socialization, and then through self-esteem to self-actualization. The stage of self-esteem is associated with lifestyles focusing on status driven consumption ('what I have'). Self-actualization is less concerned with appearance and more with personal development and quality of life ('how I am').

The Future Foundation argue that there is a similar process in organizations which matches the needs of individuals in society – after all, organizations are collections of individuals. Thus, in a less developed society, a company's first priority is to provide basic products that people can afford. As society develops, the company takes more notice of its employees, helping to provide security of employment where possible. In

UK history, this would be reflected in both the development of labour regulations and paternalistic employers.

As society moves into the socialization phase, companies begin to produce products and brands that express a feeling of being part of society – in effect the mass-market brands of the 1950s and 1960s. The search for status and the development of positional consumption is consistent with the development of designer labels and upmarket brands – arguably, most typified by the UK in the 1980s. The movement to self-actualization – which society is currently engaged in – points to companies, products and brands having a wider perspective, adding to people's personal development and quality of life.

In a sense then we can map the individual's hierarchy of needs with the corporate hierarchy of responsibilities as they have developed in the UK over the last century.

Corporate hierarchy of responsibilities

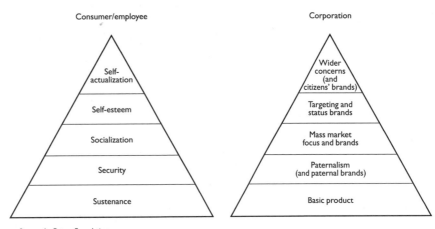

Figure 1.2

Source: the Future Foundation

How does this translate into a company's role? First it re-emphasizes that a company's wider role and responsibilities in society are likely to grow in importance. Second, it suggests a clear hierarchy of responsibilities and tasks a company needs to embrace:

1 Getting the basic offer right in terms of price, quality and service.
2 Getting the right employee focus – an issue that is becoming more important in the less secure job environment, as we discuss below.
3 Getting the right customer focus.
4 Considering and responding to other stakeholders.
5 Assessing responsibilities to the wider society.

Companies need to decide where they are positioned on this hierarchy and where they should be to satisfy their stakeholders and maximize their commercial potential (given that, effectively, the Future Foundation argue that being higher up the hierarchy is likely to be 'good for business'). Those companies wishing to lead the world must aspire to being at the very top of the hierarchy.

In this the Future Foundation add that each level is, on the whole, dependent on the level before. You need to get each one right before moving up the scale.

Customers expect more

Within this changing environmental framework as markets mature and competitive pressures increase organizations are discovering that customers are expecting more. As competitors catch up with the leaders, customers have a greater range of choices, they react to the homogenization of alternatives by becoming more price sensitive and less loyal.

Customer service demands have increased dramatically over the past five years
Customers have come to expect more and more from the companies selling them products or services.

According to a survey carried out for the Institute of Customer Service by Bain and Co., customers now:

- Demand more access time – customers often demand 24-hour service, seven days a week.
- Are less willing to wait – in one organization the average time callers wait on hold before they hang up has fallen in two years from 130 seconds to just thirty seconds.
- Demand faster responses – customers now expect the person who answers the telephone to be able to deal with their request or query, there and then.
- Want more information – they want it delivered directly, and they are less willing to wait to receive something in the post.
- Have less patience with broken service promises – if roadside recovery is promised in thirty minutes, customers ring if the engineer hasn't arrived in twenty-five minutes. If the water is off for ten minutes longer than customers were told it would be, customers ring – and water companies only recently told them how long they would have to wait.
- Complain more and more, and are more aggressive in their telephone manner – UK consumers are no longer frightened to complain, and are quicker to demand to speak to the manager, to demand compensation, and to threaten action in the small claims court.

The stereotypical consumer who will wait in silence as they are repeatedly ignored is fast disappearing. And this trend will continue

Respondents in the survey felt that customer expectations will continue to increase. Some point out that consumers are travelling more and more, and are exposed to the best that the world has to offer. These experiences influence their service expectations from domestic suppliers.

Service advances in one sector now affect other sectors
Service improvements made in one sector influence customer expectations in other sectors. A number of survey respondents point to leading retailers who, by the improvements they have made within their own organizations and industry, have raised expectations in all other sectors.

Retailers entering financial services complain that, although they believe that their service levels are better than those provided by any existing players, they risk upsetting customers if standards don't reach what they expect from their retail brand.

A number of companies are attempting to use service to differentiate themselves from competitors.

Getting the right customer focus
Organizations are responding to these challenges in different ways!

Loyalty enhancing service
Many recent academic texts, and the work of consulting firms such as Bain & Company, have made organizations more aware of the service profit cycle and the financial impact of loyalty-enhancing service (Figure 1.3).

There is therefore a basis for believing that investments in improved customer service will lead to higher levels of profitability. But given the never-ending supply of investment opportunities to improve service, the challenge for companies will be to identify which will yield the greatest return.

Companies must be able to rate the company's performance against each of these values, and to rate the performance of their competitors and of a variety of leading service firms. What they have yet to do is to relate these 'soft' measures to the 'hard' measure of customer retention.

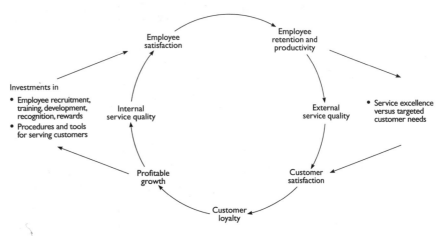

Figure 1.3
Service profit cycle

Source: The Loyalty Effect (Reichheld), Harvard Business Review, Bain & Company

It is not enough to track customer loyalty. Customer satisfaction measures may not be an accurate indicator of customer behaviour. The real measure of customer value is customer loyalty.

Sophisticated analysis
Better performing companies appear to have more sophisticated customer techniques.

In research carried out for the Institute of Customer Service, those companies that told the Institute of Customer Service they earn over 15 per cent return on capital (ROC) use annual and lifetime customer profitability calculations, measure customer loyalty and use this information in investment decisions more than other respondents.

Investment in people and technology
If companies are to keep pace with rising customer demands, they need to make significant investments in both people and technology. Before they do this they must understand their customer base:

- Carry out a needs analysis.
- Determine their segment profitability.
- Measure retention.

Technology will be the key to delivering superior service at lower cost. In research done by the Institute of Customer Service, 80 per cent of UK respondents recognize the importance of technology and 72 per cent of respondents felt technology will be vital when it comes to reducing the costs of service. But most organizations surveyed felt they have a problem with the way they use technology. Only 31 per cent of UK respondents consider their use of technology to be good or state of the art in its support of customer service. Systems were described as 'out-of-date', 'completely inadequate', and 'unsatisfactory'. Historic rates of return from IT investments are seen as poor

The ultimate indictment is the relatively poor rate of return that survey respondents feel they have obtained from IT. Only 23 per cent of UK respondents feel their returns have been good or excellent. It is viewed as an investment black hole. Don't be fooled into thinking that technology alone will solve the people issues.

Despite the far-reaching applications for advanced technology, respondents felt strongly that it will not allow them to use lesser-skilled customer service employees. Companies hope to use technology to simplify processes and practices – 'to put the science on the computer'. This will allow staff to spend more time interacting with customers, particularly on value-added activities. In no way will technology replace the personal touch – which is generally the key differentiator in the consumer experience. The trick is to use technology to create even higher levels of consumer intimacy – via customer prompt screens, for example.

The use of technology is also allowing greater use of multi-skilling. This gives employees more interesting jobs, and means that customers are more likely to be offered solutions with a single call – but it also implies that staff have enough business judgement to take responsibility for a broad range of commercial decisions. The image that technology will completely replace people in the provision of service appears unlikely.

Market segmentation

Understand the profitability of the segments in your customer base. Different types of customers will have different needs, and will be of differential value to an organization. It is therefore very important to understand how much different segments of the customer base contribute towards profitability, to allow prioritization of investment.

Although more than 80 per cent of UK companies surveyed by the Institute of Customer Service segment their customer base, only 40 per cent of them calculate annual profitability by segment, and even fewer – 22 per cent – measure lifetime profitability.

The Institute of Customer Service say that only around 40 per cent of respondents identify customer needs by segment 'to a fair degree/in great detail', and set service standards according to those needs. Without understanding needs and profitability by segment, it is difficult to prioritize service investments. How do you know whether to invest in next-day delivery or same-day delivery if you don't know if your customers value it and will pay for it. Some respondents use service standard categories such as gold, silver and bronze customers (but often these were fairly crude).

Track customer satisfaction

Customer satisfaction is measured by nearly 90 per cent of UK and US respondents. A variety of means were mentioned:

- Random customer surveys.
- Customer focus groups.
- Mystery shoppers.
- Complaints analysis.
- Operational measures such as, on-time delivery.
- Abandoned call rates.
- Time to turn-round correspondence.

Value analysis

One technology company speaks of the 'value analysis' that they recently embarked upon. They used research to identify customer needs by segment – such as technical advice, speed of response, price and so on – and the relative importance of each need in determining customer value.

Managing people

Respondents see people issues as fundamental to their future success. And it is in this area of employee policies that managers are most passionate about. They understand that customer service staff are not just based in the call centre but spread throughout the organization.

Organizations are now recognizing that customer service must be delivered by all staff who have frequent contact with customers, and this requires a significant shift in attitude, culture and approach.

Recruitment

The front-line staff of tomorrow need excellent interpersonal skills, numerical and verbal reasoning, IT competency and general commercial awareness. They must be able to resolve customer problems as they arise – which means they need the self-confidence, latitude and knowledge to do so. This suggests that organizations will have to think very differently about their recruitment and training strategies.

Typical annual staff turnover rates in call centres in the UK are in the region of 30 per cent. But one UK company managed to reduce theirs from 20 per cent to 2 per cent over a two-year period by systematically rethinking the way it ran its centres. They did this by:

- Hiring staff with a different skill and personality set.
- Reducing the management hierarchy and adopting self-managed teams.
- Providing more and different training for staff, giving them more responsibility for problem solving.
- Implementing a revised reward structure linked to customer service measures.

Employees found they had more interesting and rewarding jobs with better pay. Employee attrition fell and customer service improved at the same time. The challenge for most organizations will be to replicate this success with their own operation.

Given the demanding specification for tomorrow's front-line staff, the Institute of Customer Service believes there will be a shortage of candidates. This, combining with the high cost of recruiting the wrong people (e.g. cost of training, poor productivity and lost customers) will make it critical that companies adapt their recruiting practices to attract the right sort of people. They will need to investigate new sources for employees (including universities in more technical sectors) and they will need to be sure that their package of job responsibility, training, compensation, and development opportunities will offer potential recruits the most compelling career prospects.

Commercial awareness
'Employees will need a better understanding of business operations, and an appreciation of the financial implications of actions. Staff will need to be empowered to do their job – which means resolving customer issues and making decisions. They'll need training for this.'

'Employees will need to be less functional. They'll need broader product knowledge and more cross-training.'

Team working
'Project management skills are important, to facilitate cross-functional working. They need to know how to run a meeting.'

'We will see more self-managed teams – with each employee having a wider span of control.'

Interpersonal skills
When managers were questioned on the types of skills that were needed they gave the following replies:

Customer care skills – soft skills as well as functional skills.

How to provide customer advice, and how to communicate.

Selling skills.

How to keep customers happy, and increase customer loyalty.

How to deal with the difficult customer.

Managers are struggling with the rapid development of in-house training programmes to address these varied needs – with existing programmes having focused primarily on functional skills. Enhancing interpersonal skills is particularly difficult, and companies tend to rely on on-the-job coaching and role-playing exercises. It is likely we will see a rise in the provision of third-party training programmes to improve softer skills, and in significant investment in the development of tailored in-house programmes.

Training

There will be a dramatic increase in the training needs of staff if their latent motivation and capabilities are to be unlocked. The status of front-line staff will need to be raised, and measures and incentives will change.

In many organizations the Institute of Customer Services talked to, it appears as if front-line customer service staff are sometimes seen as second-class citizens. Given the increasing importance of service and the need for more highly skilled people in service roles this must change. How? Firstly, through better recognition:

> Immediate recognition by line management is important, as well as very top management recognition.

> Recognition is critical – through career development and job enrichment opportunities.

> One-off awards can be used to recognize the exceptional achievement. There shouldn't though be specific incentives for customer service itself – that should simply be the 'way things are done around here'.

> The link between variable pay and operating performance and customer satisfaction must be increased.

> Bonuses will be set on service improvement targets.

> Everyone's compensation must be linked to service performance and, in particular, to customer retention.

In one call centre, employees are eligible for a bonus of up to 20 per cent of their total compensation each month. Their performance is measured in terms of:

- Customer satisfaction – every tenth call automatically triggers the mailing of a customer feedback form.
- Abandoned call rate – for the team of which they are a member.
- Amount of time that they are available to speak to customers.

The bonus is big enough to influence employees' behaviour, and the performance dimensions are clearly measurable. The customer services director in the same organization is also eligible for a 20 per cent bonus – dependent upon customer satisfaction, employee satisfaction and profitability.

Companies will be employing new model, high-flier customer service managers

It is not just the front-line staff whose job descriptions are changing. The survey respondents highlight the important and changing role of front-line managers.

> We need 'balanced' managers – result-focused, driven, high-energy commercial champions, yet approachable team workers.

> First-line managers must be able to manage in dynamic environments, and they must be empowered to take responsibility and to make things happen.

> They must be commercially astute, totally customer focused, with excellent management and communication skills.

> They must be able to take a more strategic view – not just deal with irate customers.

> They need to be coaches, team developers and performance monitors – not merely supervisors.

Managers will need to exhibit all the characteristics of good customer service staff, but they will also need a deep understanding of the economies of the business and be able to take balanced decisions rapidly. At the same time, they will need to act as coaches and mentors to ensure high levels of employee satisfaction and retention, particularly while cultural changes in customer service are implemented. Companies will be demanding more and more from these managers – these are tomorrow's high-fliers.

Taking the customer focused approach does not mean just putting a smile on the face of people who are dealing with customers. Yes, it is important for people to be pleasant, and yes, it is important for the environment to be pleasant. However, organizations must put their concentration on the organizational factors necessary that will enable the whole organization to become more responsive.

Examples of customer orientation

National Health Service

Research done by Burns, 1992 shows that what bothers patients is not about medical treatment, quality of equipment or general administrative efficiency. What bothers them is that they are kept hanging around and the doctor does not explain what is wrong with them.

This is a classic example of an organization not understanding about customers and their needs.

Local authority

Work by Hall, 1992 adapted from Burns, 1992 shows that in a comparative study of two borough councils in two affluent middle-class suburbs in the UK (Solihull in the West Midlands and the London Borough of Richmond) customers were more satisfied with Solihull than with Richmond. What emerged was that although Richmond provided more superior services, Solihull treated customers more sensitively.

British Airways

Before British Airways launched its 'Customer First' campaign they carried out a survey whose objectives were to understand how they compared with their major competitors and what factors customers thought were most important when travelling by air. Concern and problem solving, after the above were the top four factors. Customers valued staff being able to break out of routine systems in order to accommodate their individual needs and also to recover after a mistake has been made.

Car industry

Research by Lewis, 1994 showed that the fleet owners put a higher value on after-sales service. Ford then put in motion what it called 'Ford business solutions'. This covered a number of separately linked initiatives which were aimed at improving customer service and thereby differentiating it from its competitors. Fleet operators were given one point of contact and not shoved from pillar to post.

Exam hint	Students should actively seek out examples of customer orientation in profit and not-for-profit organizations.

Service initiatives

Service offerings
- A retailer responds to customer demands by introducing a 'one in front' checkout guarantee, customer service desks, open gates, and a customer call centre.
- An airline offering full-service arrival lounges – including message retrieval, shower facilities, breakfast – for their business and first-class passengers flying long-haul routes, at no additional cost.
- An internet provider increasing its call centre service hours from six days a week for twelve hours a day to seven days a week for twenty-four hours a day.
- A retailer setting different service standards at different times of the day, based on customer research that identified the different needs of morning shoppers, lunch-time shoppers and afternoon shoppers.

- A food manufacturer targeting 98.5 per cent service performance, defined as delivery of the right product, in the right amount, at the right time and to the right place – while competitors and retailers tend to use only volume measures, or only record service failures above certain levels.

Employee training and empowerment
- A retailer with more than 10,000 outlets conducting face-to-face training for employees in each and every outlet over a two-year period.
- An insurance company developing in-house a specialized series of training programmes for employees recruited into a new dedicated unit serving all customers won since January 1998.
- A hotel chain authorizing employees to spend up to £1250 to correct a problem affecting customer service.

Feedback
- A telecommunications company conducting over 10,000 interviews a month with customers who have asked for a service or fault repair, made a request or a complaint.
- A building society carrying out regular customer surveys, focus groups, and encouraging complaints as well as compliments. Surveys are simple to understand and kept to one page, and the home telephone number of the CEO is at the bottom of the page. Every customer who completes a survey is telephoned (over 35,000 customers a year), either to thank them or to apologise.
- A life insurance provider using a dedicated team to contact clients when they ask to cash in their policy, laying out alternative options. As a result 55 to 60 per cent of policies stay in force.
- An airline investing in customer relations to increase its approachability, through easy availability of postage-paid comment cards, customer forums, and a programme allowing customer relations staff to fly with customers to experience problems firsthand. Retention rates of customers who complained to customer relations more than doubled, to 80 per cent.

Leadership
- The CEO who is so personally passionately committed to service excellence that he does roadshows, and says 'I'll sack you if you consistently give poor customer service'.
- The CEO who measures his managers in terms of their 'impact on society', namely the extent to which they increase the service performance hurdle rates for others.

(Supplied by the Institute of Customer Service)

Discussion on the use of the word customer

Traditionally the word 'customer' was used to define people whom the organization dealt with externally. Today it is used more broadly to include people working within the organization as well.

The Conservatives, when they were last in power, introduced the idea of 'consumers' into schools (John Bazalgette, Grubb Institute). They did this by drawing upon their idea that the 'market' provides the most efficient way of organizing activities of all kinds. Schools were thought of in terms of delivering services to consumers, they were a kind of shop or supermarket. Teachers were traders, parents and employers 'consumers', pupils the product. They used the idea that Marks & Spencer provided – an organizational model of how a nationwide chain should be run.

The Grubb Institute predicted at the time that this idea would be communicated to pupils within the school system where they would learn to be 'consumers' rather than citizens. The Secretary for State for Education at the time (Kenneth Baker) said that was exactly what the government wanted: people who were more like consumers and who knew how to get what they wanted in the market-place, just as the effective shopper does. As the Grubb Institute said at the time, 'the problem with confusing the two terms is that individual consumers do not take responsibility for the overall quality or type of product; all they need to concern themselves with is their own purchases'. People are social beings, each person participates in society's evolution and is moulded by its features – to function well in a society means a whole hearted involvement in society. If people do not involve themselves in society they will be isolated from society. Society and organizations are there to achieve a purpose and organizations and institutions provide roles in order for this to take place. To be a social being either at work or in society entails one to take on a role and to take on formal and informal responsibilities to other people. The 'customer' role does not allow for this dual responsibility – it is a one way process.

As predicted by the Grubb Institute the use of the word consumer and customer has entered overall use and is broadly used by society to describe any and every exchange. It has provided a model we use to guide our behaviour irrespective of circumstance. However, if we reintroduce the idea of role and role relationships, in which an exchange is taking place and value is being created we need to think about a number of additional aspects. This is now particularly important as marketing as a discipline has entered the not for profit, government, public and religious institutions and the professional relationships these organizations engage in extend beyond customer and consumer terminology. But before we do this, let us consider the use of the word role, and to think about it as the idea one has in one's mind that helps us to manage our behaviour in different circumstances.

Role and role relationships

Role relationships

If one starts to look at customer relationships based on role relationships in which an exchange is taking place and value is being created, we need to think about the following:

1 Role.
2 Role relationship.
3 Role expectations.
4 The creation of value in the exchange.
5 The measurement of value.
6 The evaluation of value.

We will discuss some of these ideas briefly now, but they will be referred to throughout the book.

Role

Taking a role is about behaving in relation to one's inner understanding of the situation; about monitoring and tuning that behaviour so as to bring about and/or contribute to the aims or purpose of the enterprise from the particular position one is in – as a nurse, doctor, secretary, salesperson, customer care manager.

The role is made up of the components shown in Figure 1.4.

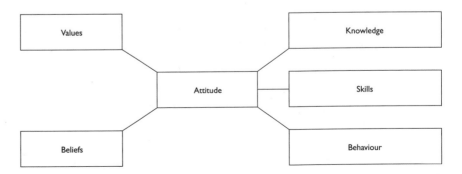

Figure 1.4

Taking on a role does not mean you leave your feelings and values at the door. The role acts as a showcase in which the five components of the individual can be displayed.

Role relationships

As an example of a role relationship, let us take the example of a nurse giving an injection. The ability to perform the nurse role will depend on a number of aspects

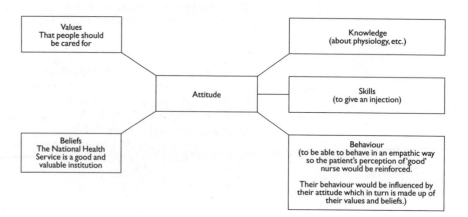

Figure 1.5
Nurse role

Similarly, if we look at front-line staff as people who are in contact with customers, we would expect them to have different sets of knowledge and skills and behave in a way in which the customer's idea of a 'good' encounter would be reinforced. Their ability to do this would be determined by their attitudes, which is made up of their values and their beliefs

This idea of role relationship also brings into consideration the behaviour of the person on whom the service is being carried out. The role relationship is interactive.

The patient should have some idea about how to behave as a patient. Similarly, a customer should have some idea on how to behave as a customer. This is especially important on airlines, trains, and buses, where the passenger role can affect the safety of other people.

The word client is used by accountants, lawyers, psychotherapists and social services. The word client implies a professional role relationship where personal and professional ethics are of prime consideration. Equally, the role responsibilities of both parties need to be considered where disclosure of important facts may be key to ensuring quality and legality.

Role expectations

If one assumes that one is dealing with a 'reasonable' sort of person who understands how to behave, a customer's understanding of the role being performed well, will be determined by their previous experience and any 'ideal idea' they may be carrying in their own mind about what to expect.

When role expectations are not met, or just meet or fall below expectation, there is a gap. When people experience this gap they can feel frustrated, disappointed and angry. Dissonance is created. Part of the success in managing customer relationships is to understand how to manage this gap. It can be done by:

- Understanding what the expectations are in the first place.
- Creating the correct offer and expectation and ensuring they match.
- Being able to manage the disappointment people feel when they go wrong.
- Exceeding the expectation they have and creating excess delight so that dissonance is not experienced.

Ensuring the creation of value in the exchange
The creation of value in the exchange is dealt with in the sections covering quality, management, dealing with organizational barriers and so on.

Measurement of value and evaluation of value
The measurement of value and evaluation of value is dealt with in the section on market research.

The customer is king

Yes, the customer is king/queen if you want to keep their business. And you can take the customer from their throne if you want to and if circumstances allow you to.

Not all customers are kings/queens. Some don't deserve the obsequious behaviour they demand, nor are some of them profitable.

Some customers need to have their role defined. Recent stories about passengers' unruly behaviour on airlines make this imperative.

David Armstrong writes:

> Taking up the pupil role does not mean knowing the ropes, the rules of the system, what behaviour is expected and who is to do what and when. It refers to what happens when one is able to form some idea of the aim and task of the institution, what it stands for, what it seeks to do, to which I can relate my behaviour as a member from my own particular position. A role in this sense is an organizing principle in my mind, which may need continual revision in the light of my experience, through which I can manage my own behaviour to make a contribution to the task of the system of which the role is a part. (*New Directions in Pastoral Care*, Blackwell, 1985)

Enabling this to take place

In order to understand and enable this process to take place we would first have to understand how people conceive their role. Secondly, we would need to understand the way they relate to the role the institution actually offers. For example, is the role experienced in terms of expectations and rules of others standing over their own wishes?

The ability to take a role is a two-way process. It is not a one-way process which the word customer implies and can be beligerent, demanding, self satisfying and violent. Extending this idea puts a new light on the contribution 'customers' need to make in enabling and contributing to organizational and institutional tasks.

Use of the word customer in the public sector

In relating the word customer to the public sector (government departments and authorities responsible for the administration of local/municipal affairs) the following factors need to be taken into consideration.

The public sector provides a number of services. In some services the word customer is appropriate, for example where there is a choice between using social housing or housing provided or managed by the private sector.

Citizens pay taxes and in some cases are users of the services provided for by the state. They do not have a choice in deciding which services to purchase or not, and they are unable to choose an alternative provider of these services, for example, social benefits. The public sector also markets social causes. For example, stop smoking and birth control. Here they are attempting to make a behavioural change for the overall improvement of society.

In many other aspects the word customer should in fact be replaced by the word citizen. Citizens have a relationship to the overall community. Customers seek to please themselves. The word customer erodes this sense of responsibility and detracts from the role of public service delivery – equity and the cure of social problems. Citizens do however have the opportunity to contribute to the democratic process which decides which political group will manage those services, and although they can vote, they cannot vote with their feet because there is no choice. The adaption of the word customer is an attempt to convince citizens on their primacy. One has to ask the question – are citizens being fooled by this?

The political group in power reflect the culture, values and belief(s) of the society. As such in many cases they are marketing an ideology and taking certain aspects of the marketing mix and marketing terminology in order to carry this out. The development in certain political campaigns confirm this.

The policy decided on by the political managers of the public sector will determine the need and the level and extent of the services that are provided. Individual citizens are unable to do this. The selection and extent of the overall services provided have in effect to sell themselves otherwise the political group will be removed.

In marketing there is an integrated use of the marketing mix, in politics very often the election promises have little or no bearing on what the citizens receive. Is government, in using the word customer, trying to create a form of voter (customer) brand loyalty to the prevailing ideology, consumers of government reform? Or is the government in its drive to privatization getting control of the public sector by giving itself more choice so that they become the customers, and can choose whom they give the taxpayers money to?

On a practical and interpersonal level, the way in which the public sector carries out its tasks has to be done in the light of public opinion and the relationships formed in the day-to-day carrying out of these services. The needs of citizens (people) have to be taken into consideration and their right to demand certain standards needs to be encouraged. This puts a pressure on the providers of these services to maintain the level of service citizens have come to expect because of their previous experience of the customer role. This in many cases has led to a situation where citizens behave like the worst type of customer – greedy, belligerent and dependent. Citizens have a responsibility to contribute to society, to look after the resources, not 'consume' them inappropriately. The word customer is inappropriate and can encourage infantile behaviour in certain situations.

Citizens may also have different ideas of the public sector's primary task – the task they must perform in order to continue their existence. For example, the prison service has three tasks:

1 To punish offenders.
2 To contain offenders.
3 To reform offenders.

The manner in which each of these three tasks are carried out, and the priority given to each of them will determine whether citizens needs are satisfied. It is a political decision as to how the users of the service, the prisoners, should be treated. Very often it does not match what the more punitively minded citizens require.

Policy making

The policy which guides the public sector is made by political groups whose judgements reflect the values and beliefs of the country. This is done on a macro- and a micro-scale depending on political judgement as to need.

Quantification of those needs must be carried out in order to establish demand and provision, equity and social reform. Market research needs to be carried out in order to assess whether the needs are being met in an adequate way – for example in the provision of public housing, the collection of waste and so on.

Pressure group activity and votes influence political judgement. The various charters help to make citizens aware of the standards they can expect from the providers of these services and their right to be treated as individual people when they use them and in some cases to compensate the users for a fall in standard or provision.

The word customer appears to have been substituted for citizen, and the right people have to be treated politely and with due consideration. The word customer has been used to change the culture of these organizations and has enabled the paternalism of we 'know what is best for you' to be overcome. However, citizens have responsibilities as well and these need to be defined as well.

Use of the word customer in internal organizational role relations

The word customer is also used to denote the role relationships defined by the job description that exist in organizations. A role has specific responsibilities attached to it, the casual use of the word customer detracts from this but on the other hand creates a certain pressure in terms of creating a sense of demand, urgency and standards. As in all role relationships standards are set and role holders need to be made aware of them so that standards can be monitored, evaluated and reviewed. We have role relationships with our colleagues, the term customer does not strictly apply but will be used as a term in this book as it is now used in the literature.

Use of the word customer in charity marketing

The users (recipients of charity) of these services are not customers. They are the recipients of a service which may or may not be asked for.

The donors to these services do so for a number of different reasons. They can be divided into two groups, individual donors and corporate donors. Both of these groups give for their own reasons.

To this extent the range and number of different charities that exist could be looked upon as a cultural reflection of social concern and prevailing values and beliefs. They can be analysed and segmented using the different systems of segmentation to ensure that the 'psychological needs' of the individual donors and those influencing which charities receive donations are also satisfied.

Some corporate donors may decide to contribute on the basis of recognition of need, or they may wish to tie their donation into a high profile activity reflecting the organization's social concern and sense of altruism for the recipients of a particular charity. This may be seen as good business practice and form part of their desire to become proactive socially. It may also meet the needs of their employees who wish to work for a socially responsible organization.

The plight of the recipients is used to raise money for charities. In some cases this is possible as the charity is able to use the recipients to promote their own cause. In other cases such as child sexual abuse it is more difficult as it is not possible to use the recipients to promote their own cause and care has to be taken to protect them.

The word customer when applied to the third sector would apply to the extent that donor and corporate needs are satisfied.

Rethinking the word customer

It is time that marketers began to rethink the word customer. They need to approach it more flexibly and think in terms of roles and role relationships. Some 'customers' in markets need to have their roles defined, for example, passengers, patients, citizens, students and pupils. In many cases they need their roles defined for them so they understand how they can contribute to the institutional and/or organization's task. Colleagues are colleagues – they are not customers, their role is defined by a job description and consists of tasks that contribute to the organizational mission. Role expectations also need to be clarified and opened out for discussion.

Summary

In this unit we have noted the range of factors influencing customer behaviour and some of the macro- and micro-environmental factors currently influencing organizations. Readers have seen a variety of ideas organizations are developing in order to provide superior customer service. The use of the term customer and the idea of role and role relationships has been introduced.

We will now go on to discuss the classification of goods and services, the decision-making unit, market segmentation, mass customization, one-to-one marketing.

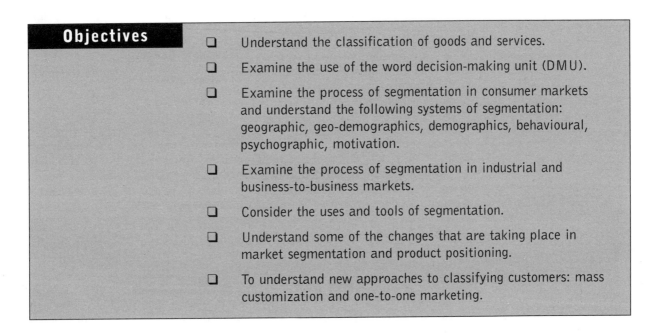

Unit 2   Market segmentation – classifying customers for competitive advantage

Objectives

❑   Understand the classification of goods and services.

❑   Examine the use of the word decision-making unit (DMU).

❑   Examine the process of segmentation in consumer markets and understand the following systems of segmentation: geographic, geo-demographics, demographics, behavioural, psychographic, motivation.

❑   Examine the process of segmentation in industrial and business-to-business markets.

❑   Consider the uses and tools of segmentation.

❑   Understand some of the changes that are taking place in market segmentation and product positioning.

❑   To understand new approaches to classifying customers: mass customization and one-to-one marketing.

This unit introduces readers to the range of variables that effect the buyer decision process and industrial situations. A classification of products and services is then given so that students are able to understand that the type of goods and services that are being supplied will effect the way in which people make their purchasing decision and as a result influence the way in which marketers approach their use of the marketing mix. The concepts of extended problem solving (EPS) and limited problem solving (LPS) are introduced later in the workbook.

Students are then asked to link their knowledge of the product life cycle, market life cycle and the adoption and diffusion curve to the process of market segmentation.

Traditional methods of market segmentation, target marketing and positioning are then considered for both consumer and industrial/business-to-business marketing.

Changes currently taking place in market segmentation and product positioning are then discussed and readers are then introduced to the ideas of mass customization and one-to-one marketing.

Product/service classification

To establish marketing strategies for individual products, marketers have developed different classification schemes based on the characteristics of the products.

Purchases are traditionally classified into three groups:

1 *Non-durable goods* – these are tangible and consumed quickly (cold drinks, washing powder, etc.).
2 *Durable goods* – these are tangible and last a long time (washing machines, clothes, etc.).
3 *Services* – these are intangible and can last a long or a short time (accountancy, education, etc.).

A mix of tangibility and services

It is useful to view products and services as a mix of tangibility and intangibility:

- A pure tangible good which has no service attached to it.
- A tangible good with accompanying services to enhance its consumer appeal.
- A service with accompanying goods and services.
- A pure service.

Services are traditionally thought of as being different from products in that they are intangible, heterogeneous, unable to be stored, and simultaneously consumed and produced.

Services

Kotler defines a service as 'any activity of benefit that one party can offer to another that is essentially intangible and does not result in the ownership of anything. Its production may or may not be tied to a physical product.'

A key phrase that encapsulates the essence of a service is that a service does not result in the ownership of *anything*. You will receive a certificate of motor insurance, which is tangible, but you have bought intangible protection. You have been helped to feel really good by the chef but you don't own the ingredients he bought at the same market you visited that morning. The nurse dresses your wound but any ownership of the bandages is only loosely peripheral to the service provided.

Gummesson feels that apart from the simultaneous production and consumption the other three differences do not hold true. Airlines are classified as a service but the aircraft, food and drinks are very tangible. The physical evidence surrounding a service makes it tangible. Services and goods alike can be standardized and produced and still contain customized elements. The pizzeria and the bank offer highly standardized services. However, management consultants, lawyers and architects are highly customized (although they contain standardized modules). Gummesson feels that the claim that services cannot be stored is nonsense. Services are stored in systems, buildings, machines, knowledge and people. The ATM is a store of standardized cash withdrawals. The emergency clinic a store of skilled people, equipment and procedures. However, he does feel that the simultaneous production and consumption process, the presence of the customer, and the customer's role as co-producer form the distinguishing properties between goods and services. These are also the salient features in total relationship marketing and the new service economy. They require interaction in a customer–provider relationship, sometimes also in a customer–customer relationship. The interaction can be face to face, but it can also take place via IT and other equipment.

Industrial and consumer goods

The classification is further developed by a distinction being made between consumer and industrial goods. Industrial goods are bought by organizations for use in their business or for processing. Consumer goods are bought for their own use.

It is on this basis that the following classification is made for consumer goods; industrial goods are considered later on.

Consumer goods

Consumer goods can be divided into convenience goods, shopping goods, specialist goods and unsought goods.

Convenience goods

These are items that are purchased regularly with a minimum of comparison and buying effort (matches, bread, soap, etc.). Manufacturers attempt to predetermine the purchasing decisions by promoting them as branded products, so the consumer looks for a certain brand rather than a generic (non-branded) product. Convenience goods are also further classified into staple, impulse and emergency purchases.

- Staple goods are consumed on a regular basis (fruit and vegetables, tomato sauce, baked beans) and product differentiation tends to be minimal.
- Impulse purchases are not pre-planned (magazines and sweets at a supermarket checkout counter).
- Emergency goods are needed at short notice (shovels in a snow storm, umbrellas at an open air concert, etc.).

Shopping goods

These include major durable or semi-durable items which are bought less frequently (hi-fi, clothes, washing machines, etc.). The consumer compares price, quality, style, and suitability. Much pre-planning goes into the purchase. Branding strategies aim to simplify the decision process for consumers. Shopping goods can be further classified as homogenous or heterogeneous.

- Homogeneous goods are broadly similar to each other in technical performance and price, examples are refrigerators and washing machines. Certain brands attempt to differentiate themselves through image or technical or design superiority. Generally price is a major influence on the purchasing decision.
- Heterogeneous goods tend to be non-standard, and price is often of secondary importance. Behavioural factors play an important role in the purchasing decision. A wide range to satisfy individual tastes is important.

Speciality goods

Items which have a unique character (branded clothing, a Porsche). Their purchase is characterized by an extensive search and a reluctance to accept substitutes. Consumers are usually prepared to pay a premium price and it is important to create and preserve the correct image. Customers rarely compare speciality goods.

Unsought goods

Those goods the customer has not considered buying before being made aware of them such as smoke detectors and compact discs, insurance, double glazing. Unsought goods often satisfy a genuine need that the consumer did not recognize existed.

As you have seen a product's characteristics will have a major effect on the decision-making process and the marketing strategy and techniques used to sell it.

Consumer goods can be divided into convenience goods, shopping goods, speciality goods and unsought goods. How would this distinction help you to decide on the decision-making process and the use of the appropriate marketing mix. Give examples.

Industrial goods

Industrial goods are divided into capital items, materials and parts and supplies and services.

Capital items

These include installations and accessory equipment.

Installations consist of buildings (factories, offices) and fixed equipment. They are expensive and critical to the long-term success of a company. Purchase is often the result of a very extensive search. Price factors must be viewed as important in such a decision, however it is rarely the single deciding factor. Much emphasis is placed on the quality of sales support and advice, and subsequent technical support and after-sales service. The producers have to be willing to design to specification. They use advertising, but much less so than personal selling. Personal selling is more important than advertising.

Accessories include portable factory equipment (ancillary plant and machinery, office equipment and office furniture) and are usually less expensive than installations. They have a shorter life than installations, but a longer life than operating supplies. Quality, features, price and service determine how suppliers are selected. Middlemen are used as the market tends to be geographically spread. Buyers are numerous and orders are quite small.

Materials and parts

These include raw materials and manufactured materials and parts.

Raw materials (farm products such as wheat, cotton, livestock etc., and natural products such as fish, lumber, crude petroleum, iron ore, etc.). Farm products are supplied by many different producers to marketing intermediaries who process and sell them. Quality, consistency of supply, service, price and delivery are important. The uniformity of natural materials limits demand creation. They are rarely advertised and promoted. Grower groups promote their own products in campaigns (e.g. potatoes, oranges, milk, eggs). Some brand their goods (e.g. Outspan oranges).

Manufactured materials and parts include component materials (iron, cement, etc.) which are usually processed further, component parts (small motors, adhesives, etc.), and replacement and maintenance items for manufacturing which enter the finished product with no further changes in form. Most manufactured materials and parts are sold directly to the industrial users. Price and service are the major marketing factors and advertising is less important.

Supplies and services

These are industrial goods that do not enter the finished product at all.

Supplies are sometimes called the convenience goods of industrial requirements as they are bought without much effort or comparison, their purchase is routine and undertaken by less senior employees. They include operating supplies (lubricants, stationery, etc.) and maintenance and repair items (paint, nails, brooms, etc.). They have a low unit value, are marketed through resellers and there are a large number of customers who are spread geographically. Price and service are important because of the similarity between suppliers and brand preference is not high.

Business services (also called industrial services) include business advisory services (advertising, legal, professional consulting) and maintenance and repair services (window cleaning, office equipment repair).

Generally these services are carried out under contract although some original equipment suppliers include maintenance and repair as an ongoing aspect of their services. Business advisory services are often new-task buying situations.

Business-to-business services can be thought of as tradable services and support services. Figure 2.1 classifies services into a six-cell matrix.

Importance of service

Focus of service	LOW	HIGH
Property	*Facility support* Laundry Janitorial Waste disposal	*Equipment* Repairs Maintenance Product testing
People	*Employee support* Food service Plant security Temporary personnel	*Employee development* Training Education Medical care
Process	*Facilitator* Book keeping Travel agent Packaged software	*Professional* Advertising Public relations Legal

Figure 2.1
A taxonomy for purchasing business services. *Source:* Fitzsimmons, Noh and Thies (1998), Purchasing Business Services, *Journal of Business and Industrial Marketing*, **13**

As the focus moves from property to people to process the following takes place:

- The difficulty of evaluating the service increases.
- The seniority of people involved in the decision making increases.
- The decision process becomes dominated by surrogate measures like past performance and professional certification.
- It becomes more difficult to decide the criteria for purchase in an objective manner.
- As the time taken to assess the final outcome of the service increases, the perceived risk and risk handling behaviour increases.
- Personal service and sources become more important in deciding purchasing criteria.
- As the service becomes more important the need for the supplier to be physically near decreases.
- Where importance of service is low, purchasing may be more driven by cost considerations.
- The more important the service, the more important non-cost factors such as twenty-four hour service may be in securing business.

The decision-making unit (DMU)

What is a customer?

Although it is useful to use the word 'customer' as a single unit, it is important from the start to understand that purchases are made both by individuals and groups of people involved in the decision-making process. In the commercial world the term 'customers' is appropriate but marketers need to give consideration to the word 'customer' and how it is now applied in other sectors, sometimes in not a wholly appropriate way.

Definition 2.1

The term customer refers to the purchaser of a product or service. They may or may not be the consumer. The term consumer refers to the end user of a product or service.

The term DMU refers to the decision-making unit, that is the group of people who decide whether to buy a product/service.

Internal customers

People working within the same organization are also referred to as customers. This is not strictly correct, internal customers are actually users.

The DMU ensures that the marketer makes a distinction between the people who are actually buying/paying for the product/service from the people who are using it – the users – and not to confuse the two (although in some cases the user, decider and buyer/payer are the same person).

Autonomous purchase

Example: individual purchase – face cream
User: the woman
Decider: the woman
Payer/buyer: the woman who pays for it and gets it from the shop
Influencer: a friend

Family purchase

Example: a child's purchase – toy
User: child
Influencer: child's friends
Decider: parents
Payer/buyer: one or both parents who pay for the product and get it from the shop

Organizational purchase

Example: a photocopier
Starter/initiator of the buying process: the person who first suggested the idea
User who is likely to operate the product or service being bought: typist, general office staff, anyone who is the ultimate user
Advisor: supplies technical and/or professional assistance
Influencer: anyone who stimulates, informs or persuades at any stage of the buying process
Decider: purchasing committee or people who actually take the purchase decision
Buyer/purchaser of the product or service: could be the buying department
Gatekeeper: receptionist, secretaries who control the flow of information and are between the purchaser and the product/service source
Financier: supplies the necessary resources, or who reports on their availability and, if necessary, on the mechanisms by which the resources can be acquired

The concept of 'payer' is explored by Jagdish N. Sheth, Banwari Mittal and Bruce I. Newman (*Customer Behaviour: Consumer Behaviour and Beyond*, Harcourt Brace 1999). They say that there are three customer roles – user, payer and buyer. The user is the person who consumes or uses the product or receives the benefits of the service. The payer is the person who finances the purchase. The buyer is the person who participates in the procurement of the product from the marketplace. Role specialization occurs when the user lacks expertise, time, buying power or access. It also happens when the product/service is unaffordable and the user then becomes dependent on whatever services are supplied; or it is subsidized and choice is therefore restricted; or where it is free and the user is not the same as the purchaser, for example, library books.

As the examples show a decision-making unit identifies the number of people who are involved in the decision-making process and ascribes a role to them. Each person will have their own concerns, motivations and interests in determining the outcome. These need to be considered when carrying out market segmentation and designing the information carried in promotional material.

Life cycle and the adoption and diffusion curve

The concept of market life cycle, product life cycle and the adoption and diffusion curve (page 122) are particularly important to marketers. They need to consider these three ideas alongside the concept of market segmentation. As markets and product/services mature new people will be drawn into the market. This means that the needs of the market and the market segmentation will change. Organizations need to be continually updating their offers, and creating new ones so that they are continuously matching the developing needs of their customers and also by developing new offers, bringing in new innovators and opinion leaders into the cycle. When markets mature, marketers should look at innovation and improved service, and message modification, not use price in an attempt to retain market share. Otherwise they collectively run the risk of commoditizing the market and ruining profitability.

You will find a number of ways in which market segmentation is defined:

> The process of dividing large heterogeneous markets into smaller, homogeneous subsets of people or businesses with similar needs and/or responsiveness to marketing mix offerings.
>
> Kinnear, Thomas C. and Bernhardt, Kenneth L. (1990)
> *Principles of Marketing*. 3rd edn, Scott Foresman/Little Brown

> To segment is to divide into parts. In the marketing context these parts may be groups of consumers with like requirements or groups of products/services with like attributes.
>
> Crimp, Margaret (1990) *The Marketing Research Process*, Prentice Hall

Market research

A market researcher is likely to approach the design of a segmentation study from one or two angles:

1 *Consumer typology* – clustering consumers
   Data will be collected and analysed to sort consumers and group them homogeneously according to geographic, geodemographic, demographic, psychographic and buyer behaviour factors.
2 *Product differentiation* – clustering products
   Data relating to the products/services/brands is collected and analysed with a view to sorting products into groups which in the eyes of the consumer have similar attributes.

Exam Hint

The examiners may well use the terms 'target marketing' and 'market segmentation' interchangeably. In this unit we have seen that in fact market segmentation is only one step in the target marketing process. The terms product or market positioning are also used interchangeably.

Although many marketers can see the rationale of segmentation, many are dissatisfied with it as a concept. They often find it difficult to apply to certain markets. It is therefore important to remember that:

- it is a creative tool
- it is different for every situation
- the majority of markets can be segmented in a variety of different ways
- there is no one right way to segment a market
- it is not a one-off exercise and needs constant monitoring to maintain its usefulness.

The marketer has to try different segmentation variables to find the best market view.

Value of segmentation

For the customer
- provides greater choice of products/services
- products/services should more closely match the needs of consumers.

For the organization
- better marketing planning as reactions to marketing activities can be predicted
- it helps organizations to identify prospects who are most likely to buy
- marketers will get to know their customers better so that they can provide a better service
- budgets can be more closely allocated on the basis of the investment and return needed from different segments
- smaller segments may be easier to dominate
- marketing and sales activity will be closely focused, leading to more sales, lower costs and higher profitability.

Geographic techniques

This is the simplest technique and simply involves dividing markets into different geographical units such as nations, states, regions, counties, cities. The marketer then chooses to operate in a few or all of the areas. The marketing mix will change to take into account any regional differences.

Culture

Culture refers to a complex set of values, beliefs and attitudes that help individuals to communicate, interpret and evaluate members of a given society. It has three important features:

1 It includes both abstract (values, beliefs, attitudes, symbols, rituals) and material elements (art, music, literature, buildings).
2 It is socially transmitted and learned.
3 It influences human behaviour.

Since consumption involves behaviour, culture is an important influence. You will need to refer to cultural affinity zones and cultural affinity classes, which are covered later.

Geodemographic techniques

Geodemographics is an extension of geographic techniques in which recognition is given to the fact that, broadly speaking, people with similar economic, social and lifestyle characteristics tend to congregate in particular neighbourhoods and can be considered as micro-cultures.

This technique is useful in identifying new retail sites and the stock they should carry, selecting sales territories, allocating marketing resources, leaflet distribution and direct marketing.

However, in market research, geodemographic systems can only tell the marketer:

- what type of area a brand is doing well or badly in
- where further research can be carried out once the target has been defined

Unless the geodemographic technique is linked to attitudinal, behavioural or motivation studies, they do not tell the marketer:

- how to define the target segment in terms of consumer behaviour
- the consumer attitudes which help to explain that behaviour

Residential neighbourhood classifications

Every one of the postcodes in the country has been analysed according to the type of housing it represents and classified into a neighbourhood group. Each of these neighbourhood groups now has its own detailed lifestyle profile which lists every type of behaviour from typical marriage and employment patterns, to car ownership and holidays abroad.

One of the best known classifications is ACORN, standing for A Classification of Residential Neighbourhoods (Figure 2.2). This was developed by Richard Weber in 1973, who applied techniques of cluster analysis to 38 separate neighbourhood types, each of which was different in terms of its housing, population and socio-economic characteristics. Kenneth Baker (1982) of the British Market Research Bureau saw how useful it could be and it was used for supervising the field work of the bureau's Target Group Index. Later Richard Weber joined Consolidated Analysis Centres Inc. (CACI) and developed his ideas. See Figure 2.2 for the ACORN classification.

More sophisticated approaches have been developed including CCNs MOSAIC, CDMSs SUPERPROFILES, Infolink's DEFINE and PINPOINT Analysis's PiN and FiNPiN.

ACORN Types		% of households in GB	ACORN Groups
ACORN Category A: THRIVING			
1.1	Wealthy Suburbs, Large Detached Houses	2.2%	1 Wealthy Achievers, Suburban Areas
1.2	Villages with Wealthy Commuters	2.8%	
1.3	Mature Affluent Home Owning Areas	2.7%	
1.4	Affluent Suburbs, Older Families	3.4%	
1.5	Mature, Well-Off Suburbs	2.9%	
2.6	Agricultural Villages, Home Based Workers	1.5%	2 Affluent Greys, Rural Communities
2.7	Holiday Retreats, Older People, Home Based Workers	0.7%	
3.8	Home Owning Areas, Well-Off Older Residents	1.5%	3 Prosperous Pensioners, Retirement Areas
3.9	Private Flats, Elderly People	1.3%	
ACORN Category B: EXPANDING			
4.10	Affluent Working Families with Mortgages	1.8%	4 Affluent Executives, Family Areas
4.11	Affluent Working Couples with Mortgages, New Homes	1.3%	
4.12	Transient Workforces, Living at their Place of Work	0.3%	
5.13	Home Owning Family Areas	2.5%	5 Well-Off Workers, Family Areas
5.14	Home Owning Family Areas, Older Children	2.6%	
5.15	Families with Mortgages, Younger Children	1.9%	
ACORN Category C: RISING			
6.16	Well-Off Town & City Areas	1.1%	6 Affluent Urbanites, Town & City Areas
6.17	Flats & Mortgages, Singles & Young Working Couples	0.9%	
6.18	Furnished Flats & Bedsits, Younger Single People	0.5%	
7.19	Apartments, Young Professional Singles & Couples	1.4%	7 Prosperous Professionals, Metropolitan Areas
7.20	Gentrified Multi-Ethnic Areas	1.1%	
8.21	Prosperous Enclaves, Highly Qualified Executives	0.9%	8 Better-Off Executives, Inner City Areas
8.22	Academic Centres, Students & Young Professionals	0.6%	
8.23	Affluent City Centre Areas, Tenements & Flats	0.7%	
8.24	Partially Gentrified Multi-Ethnic Areas	0.8%	
8.25	Converted Flats & Bedsits, Single People	1.0%	
ACORN Category D: SETTLING			
9.26	Mature Established Home Owning Areas	3.4%	9 Comfortable Middle Agers, Mature Home Owning Areas
9.27	Rural Areas, Mixed Occupations	3.4%	
9.28	Established Home Owning Areas	3.9%	
9.29	Home Owning Areas, Council Tenants, Retired People	3.0%	
10.30	Established Home Owning Areas, Skilled Workers	4.3%	10 Skilled Workers, Home Owning Areas
10.31	Home Owners in Older Properties, Younger Workers	3.2%	
10.32	Home Owning Areas with Skilled Workers	3.3%	
ACORN Category E: ASPIRING			
11.33	Council Areas, Some New Home Owners	3.7%	11 New Home Owners, Mature Communities
11.34	Mature Home Owning Areas, Skilled Workers	3.3%	
11.35	Low Rise Estates, Older Workers, New Home Owners	2.9%	
12.36	Home Owning Multi-Ethnic Areas, Young Families	1.0%	12 White Collar Workers, Better-Off Multi-Ethnic Areas
12.37	Multi-Occupied Town Centres, Mixed Occupations	2.0%	
12.38	Multi-Ethnic Areas, White Collar Workers	1.0%	
ACORN Category F: STRIVING			
13.39	Home Owners, Small Council Flats, Single Pensioners	2.3%	13 Older People, Less Prosperous Areas
13.40	Council Areas, Older People, Health Problems	2.1%	
14.41	Better-Off Council Areas, New Home Owners	2.0%	14 Council Estate Residents, Better-Off Homes
14.42	Council Areas, Young Families, Some New Home Owners	2.7%	
14.43	Council Areas, Young Families, Many Lone Parents	1.6%	
14.44	Multi-Occupied Terraces, Multi-Ethnic Areas	0.7%	
14.45	Low Rise Council Housing, Less Well-Off Families	1.8%	
14.46	Council Areas, Residents with Health Problems	2.1%	
15.47	Estates with High Unemployment	1.3%	15 Council Estate Residents, High Unemployment
15.48	Council Flats, Elderly People, Health Problems	1.1%	
15.49	Council Flats, Very High Unemployment, Singles	1.2%	
16.50	Council Areas, High Unemployment, Lone Parents	1.5%	16 Council Estate Residents, Greatest Hardship
16.51	Council Flats, Greatest Hardship, Many Lone Parents	0.9%	
17.52	Multi-Ethnic, Large Families, Overcrowding	0.5%	17 People in Multi-Ethnic, Low-Income Areas
17.53	Multi-Ethnic, Severe Unemployment, Lone Parent	1.0%	
17.54	Multi-Ethnic, High Unemployment, Overcrowding	0.3%	

Figure 2.2
CACI ACORN profile of Great Britian

The common element in all geodemographic systems is their use of census enumeration district (ED) data. Other systems are broadly similar although each uses a variety of other variables. MOSAIC for example includes housing data similar to the Acorn system but also includes:

- financial data (county court judgments, finance house/credit card searches)
- socio-economic census data (occupations and car ownership)
- census data (ownership, facilities and size of household, number and ages of residents)
- demographics (people who have moved house)

Extending Knowledge

You have been given the task of arranging a direct mail shot to potential customers. Write to ACORN and CCNs MOSAIC, CDMSs SUPER-PROFILES, Infolink's DEFINE, and PINPOINT Analysis's PiN and FiNPiN and get some more information about them.

Geographic modelling
GMAP University of Leeds
Geographic modelling is different from residential neighbourhood classification systems because it is based on using catchment areas, demographic data within those areas, with information from market research on patterns of behaviour and competitor information. Geographical models then simulate the interaction between supply and demand.

Extending Knowledge

Find out more about GMAP from the University of Leeds.

Demographic techniques
Demography studies the measurable aspects of society such as: age, gender, education, occupation, social grade, religion, race, culture, nationality, family size and family life cycle. Most secondary data is expressed in demographic terms and the information helps marketers to:

- provide an understanding of market structure and potential customer segments
- identify potential for sales
- identify trends in population
- locate a target market.

Data is easy to get hold of, and compared to other segmentation methods it isn't too expensive.

Social class and status
Two of the most commonly used terms in segmentation are class and status.

Social class is the most heavily used segmentation technique used in the UK because it relies on an existing class system and provides an objective measure for classifying people.

Social class gives a hierarchical classification in which each group is stratified into strata or classes. The technique relies heavily on a combination of:

- occupation
- income
- educational attainment.

The idea of class is complex but some of the key ideas are as follows:

1 The notion of hierarchical distinction which is also expressed in ideas such as social stratification – upper class, middle class, lower class, working class.
2 The use of census data to provide descriptive categories such as those used by the Registrar General in dividing the population of the United Kingdom.
3 The use of occupations to identify socio-economic status groups such as manual and non-manual, or white collar and blue collar.
4 The description of a society in terms of the degree of social mobility. This leads directly to classifications such as open societies (social mobility and movement from one class to another being possible) and closed societies (social class being defined and fixed at (and by) birth as in a caste system).
5 The ideas of Marx which centre on ownership and non-ownership of property and resources and which give rise to the classification of bourgeoisie and proletariat as the dominant classes in capitalistic societies.
6 Weber's use of similar analysis focused on the subdivisions of property, including ideas such as knowledge or education.

Source: Rice, C. (1993) *Consumer Behaviour,* Butterworth-Heinnemann.

Social grade	Social status	Occupation
A	Upper middle class	Higher managerial, administrative or professional
B	Middle class	Intermediate managerial, administrative or professional
C1	Lower middle class	Supervisory or clerical, and junior managerial, administrative or professional
C2	Skilled working class	Skilled manual workers
D	Working class	Semi and unskilled manual workers
E	Those at lowest level of subsistence	State pensioners or widows (no other earner), casual or lowest-grade workers

Figure 2.3
NRS Social Grade definitions

These are the standard social grade classifications using definitions agreed between Research Services Ltd and NRS. A JICNARS publication *Social Grading on the National Readership Survey* and National Readership Survey Appendix E describe the definitions and methodology used.

Definition 2.2

Class is used by the marketer to identify groups of people of similar status to share beliefs, aspirations and values. It is an objective way of classifying people according to such criteria as occupation, education, lifestyle, place of residence and income. It implies an awareness of class consciousness within the group, a degree of uniformity of lifestyle, and social interaction.

Rice, C. (1993) *Consumer Behaviour,* Butterworth-Heinemann

Activity 2.1

1 What class are you? On what basis do you make that judgement?
2 Do your colleagues agree with you?
3 What class are the other people living in your neighbourhood?

Allocation to social class categories
Allocating people to a particular category usually involves one of three approaches:

1 The *subjective* approach where participants are asked to decide their own social class.
2 The *reputational* approach where individuals are asked to determine the social class of others in the community.
3 The *objective* approach where non-participants allocate individuals on the basis of pre-determined factors (e.g. occupation, education, income and wealth, lifestyle).

In 1990, the Market Research Society published an up-to-date guide to socio-economic status. The guide defines the pecking order of 1500 jobs and is based not on earnings, but on qualifications and responsibilities.

Activity 2.2

Look at Figure 2.4. Do you agree with the classifications?

Status

Status is a subjective phenomenon which is a result of the judgement of the social position the person occupies. Here the distinction from class becomes somewhat blurred as the judgement is usually also based on factors such as power, wealth and occupation.

It is possible to identify three forms of status:

1 *Ascribed status* – this is similar to the ideas of ascribed groups. Individuals have little control over this as it covers the status accorded by society to classifications such as gender (male/female) and race/colour.
2 *Achieved status* – in contrast, is that which has been acquired by individuals through occupation, place of residence and lifestyle.
3 *Desired status* – this is the social status an individual wishes to attain. Here the analogy is with the aspirational group.

Social grade/class

The social grades, class, occupation and percentage of the UK population has already been outlined in Figure 2.3.

Criticisms of social class

The major criticism of class being used is that it is too restrictive and may not reflect the changing nature of UK society. It is also too narrow – six categories cannot possibly provide an accurate reflection of 55 million people. In addition, nearly a third of those earning over £21,000 are C2DE and half those earning £15,000–£21,000 are C2DE. The correlation between social grade and income no longer exists.

People find it difficult to define themselves and most people believe themselves to be a different class. Some people like and cling to the idea of being working class, even though objective data proves this belief to be incorrect.

Head of the household categories don't take into consideration what is happening in society. Women now return to work, and many households have two earners.

Access to education has removed many class barriers.

Although values, attitudes, beliefs and purchasing habits don't change overnight, unemployment has reduced the spending power of many middle class managers. However, class is still reflected in certain types of behaviour, for example eating habits reflect class structure. In a recent survey of 7000 British households, it was convincingly shown that our eating habits are affected not just by our income, but also by class, gender and age ('social class and change in eating habits', *British Food Journal*, 95(1), 1993).

Question 2.2

1 What are the differences between social class and status? Of what value are these concepts to the marketer?
2 What criticisms have been made about using social class as a segmentation variable?

A: admiral, advocate, air marshal, ambassador, archbishop, attorney, bank manager, bishop, brigadier, chemist shop manager (more than 25 staff); chief constable, chief engineer, chief fire officer, chief rabbi, chiropodist (more than five staff); national orchestra conductor, coroner, university dean, dental surgeon with own practice, chartered estate agent, self-employed farmer (more than 10 staff), financier, general practitioner (own practice/partner), school head-teacher (more than 750 pupils), homoeopath, insurance underwriter, magistrate, hospital matron, judge, MP, professor and town clerk.

B: advertising account director, archdeacon, area sales manager, ballistics expert, qualified brewer, bursar, church canon, chef (more than 25 staff), police chief inspector, computer programmer, stock exchange dealer, deputy power station manager, drawing office manager, fund manager, master mariner, orchestra leader, parish priest, parson, prison governor, probation officer, rabbi, senior buyer, senior engineer, qualified social worker, secondary-school teacher, television newscaster, lecturer and nursing sister.

C1: advertising account executive, accounts clerk, announcer (television, radio or station platform), art buyer, articled clerk, athlete, band master, bank cashier, boxer, bus inspector, calligrapher, campanologist, telephone canvasser, cardiographer, cartographer, chef (five to 24 staff), chemist dispenser, chorister, chorus girl, clown, sports coach, coastguard, computer operator, skilled cook, police constable, advertising copywriter, travel courier, curate, cricketer, dancer, dental hygienist, private detective, dietician, driving examiner/instructor, estate agent (not chartered), fashion model, film projectionist, golfer, hospital houseman, book illustrator, disc jockey, juggler, domestic loss adjuster, magician, maitre d'hotel, masseur/masseuse, midwife, monk, nun, staff nurse, non-manual office worker, pawnbroker, plant breeder, RSPCA inspector, receptionist, secretary, telephone operator, sports umpire, youth worker.

C2: AA patrolman, self-employed antique dealer, boat builder, bus driver, shoemaker, bricklayer, carpenter, chimney sweep, bespoke tailoring cutter, deep-sea diver, dog handler, hairdresser, skilled electrician, fireman, thatcher, train driver, Rolls-Royce trained chauffeur, skilled miner.

D: au pair, bingo caller, dustman, bodyguard, bus conductor, chauffeur, croupier, dog breeder, lumberjack, unskilled miner, nursemaid and ratcatcher.

E: anyone brave enough to admit it.

Figure 2.4
Some examples from the Market Research Society's occupation groupings. *Source:* MRS (1990)

Sex

Changes in society brought about by the change in women's role has resulted in a number of marketing campaigns being directed at women (cigarettes, cars, hotels).

Income

Generally income provides a useful guide to the capacity to purchase goods, but other factors such as lifestyle, life cycle, cultural values will determine how it is spent.

Age

Age is a useful discriminator in many consumer markets.

Family life cycle

The idea of family life cycle is that as people progress through their lives their membership of the family and lifestyle will change. These changes will then have an effect on the economic character of the household as well

	Stages in the family life cycle	*Buying patterns*
1	Bachelor stage: young, single people living at home.	Few financial commitments. Recreation and fashion orientated. Buy: cars, entertainment items, holidays.
2	Newly married couples: young, no children.	Better off financially than they are likely to be in the near future. High purchase rate of consumer desirables. Buy: cars, white goods, furniture.
3	Full nest 1: youngest child under six.	House buying is at a peak Liquid assets are low. Dissatisfied with level of savings and financial position generally. Buy: medicines, toys, baby food, white goods.
4	Full nest 2: youngest child six or over.	Financial position is improving. A higher proportion of wives are working. Buy: wider variety of foods, bicycles, pianos.
5	Full nest 3: older married couples with dependent children.	Financial position is improving yet further. A greater proportion of wives work and some children get jobs. Increasing purchase of desirables. Buy: better furniture, unnecessary appliances and more luxury goods.
6	Empty nest 1: older married couples, no children at home, head of household still in the workforce.	Home ownership is at a peak. The financial situation has improved and savings have increased. Interested in travel, recreation and self-educanon. Not interested in new products. Buy: holidays, luxuries and home improvements.
7	Empty nest 2: older married, no children living at home, head of household retired.	Substantial reduction in income. Buy: medical products and appliances that aid health, sleep and digestion.
8	Solitary survivor in the workforce.	Income still high but may sell home.
9	Solitary survivor, retired.	Same medical and product needs as group 7. Substantial cut in income. Need for attention and security.

Figure 2.5
The family life cycle and its implications for buying behaviour. *Source:* Adapted from Wells and Gubar (1966); Wilson and Gilligan with Pearson (1993), *Strategic Marketing Management,* Butterworth-Heinemann

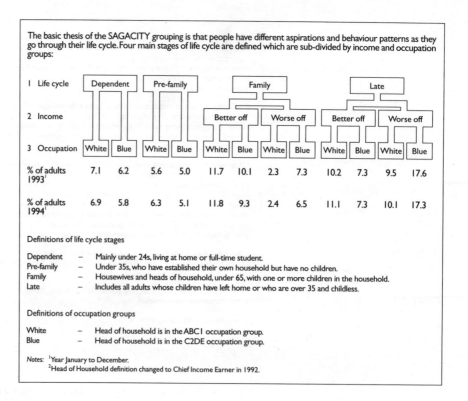

The basic thesis of the SAGACITY grouping is that people have different aspirations and behaviour patterns as they go through their life cycle. Four main stages of life cycle are defined which are sub-divided by income and occupation groups:

1 Life cycle	Dependent		Pre-family		Family				Late			
2 Income					Better off		Worse off		Better off		Worse off	
3 Occupation	White	Blue	White	Blue	White	Blue	White	Blue	White	Blue	White	Blue
% of adults 1993[1]	7.1	6.2	5.6	5.0	11.7	10.1	2.3	7.3	10.2	7.3	9.5	17.6
% of adults 1994[1]	6.9	5.8	6.3	5.1	11.8	9.3	2.4	6.5	11.1	7.3	10.1	17.3

Definitions of life cycle stages

Dependent	–	Mainly under 24s, living at home or full-time student.
Pre-family	–	Under 35s, who have established their own household but have no children.
Family	–	Housewives and heads of household, under 65, with one or more children in the household.
Late	–	Includes all adults whose children have left home or who are over 35 and childless.

Definitions of occupation groups

White	–	Head of household is in the ABC1 occupation group.
Blue	–	Head of household is in the C2DE occupation group.

Notes: [1]Year January to December.
[2]Head of Household definition changed to Chief Income Earner in 1992.

Figure 2.6
The SAGACITY life cycle groupings. *Source:* RSL (Research Services Ltd) and NRS Ltd

as income and household expenditure. There are various models used (see Figure 2.5 and Figure 2.6).

The family life cycle (FLC) has been criticized because the changes taking place in society are not reflected in the basic FLC models. Women's roles have changed, there is also a high divorce rate and a large number of single parent families, many couples are childless and remain so, many marriages take place much later, if at all. The labour market has changed and many families have dual income earners, some are out of work, or retire early.

> There is however a distinctive life time pattern to saving and spending. When we are in our twenties and thirties – getting married, buying houses, having children – we borrow and spend. When we are old and retired, we 'dissave' and spend. In middle age, therefore, we have to save to repay debts and build up capital for our old age.

> Reading (1988)

Activity 2.3

You have now read through the section on life cycle. Which markets do you think you could usefully apply it to?

Question 2.3

In what way could a portfolio of products for an insurance company be designed for consumers using life cycle segmentation as an approach?

Behaviour in the product field

This method is based on a series of behavioural measures including:

- Attitudes to the product/service – positive, indifferent, negative etc.
- Knowledge – aware, unaware, interested, intending to buy
- Benefits sought – apply to product/service
- User status – non-user, ex-user, potential user, first time user, regular user

- Usage rate – light, medium, heavy
- Loyalty status – none, medium, strong, absolute
- Purchase occasion – regular, special occasion, critical event
- Adoption process

A few of these are discussed in more detail, others are fairly self-evident.

Benefit segmentation
Marketers focus on selecting the major benefit on which the unique selling proposition (USP) can be based.

Marketers can however use more than one benefit to position a product/service (see positioning further down).

- User status – non-users, ex-users, potential users, first-time users and regular users. First-time users and regular users can also be considered in terms of the rate of usage – heavy, medium, light. This segmentation variable can be used in formulating strategy. For example: a company with a high market share will focus on converting potential users into actual users. A company with a smaller or lower market share will often concentrate on persuading users of competitive brands to switch brands.
- Loyalty status can also be used to segment a market – hard-core loyals, soft-core loyals, shifting loyals and switchers. If consumers are very loyal to a product it is unlikely that they will switch.
- The adoption process could also be used to segment a market – innovators, early adopters, early majority, late majority and laggards.

> The US fitness market can be broken into three market segments, comprising 50 per cent of US families:
>
> **Winners** who recognize the need to get fit and equate it with their desire to achieve generally; **Dieters** who perceive fitness as a way of controlling their weight; and **Self-improvers** who perceive fitness as a necessary part of their sense of well-being.
>
> These three segments can be easily targeted by marketers working in health services marketing, such as hospital marketing managers.
>
> *Source:* 'Benefit segmentation of the fitness market, *Health Marketing Quarterly,* **9**, 1992.

Motivation, psychographics and social value groups
For a detailed description of how motivation theory is applied to marketing see page 166.

What is psychographics?
Psychographics is not the same as demographic analysis as it tends to include qualitative data on motives, attitudes and values.

Although psychographics includes qualitative factors, like motivation, its findings are presented as quantified, statistical data in tabular format. It is different from motivation research as it relies on less intensive techniques like self-administered questionnaires and inventories (ordered listing or catalogue of items that assesses traits, opinions, beliefs, behaviours, etc.).

The technique of measuring lifestyles is known as psychographics. In the classification shown below the word psychographic has come to cover personality, lifestyle and various other systems of classification.

The term psychographic segmentation is given to the main way in which lifestyle analysis is carried out. It is commonly called AIO analysis and it focuses primarily on developing personality inventories based on attitudes when discussing:

- The relevant activities which are usually observable, measurable and objective and relate to how people spend their time: work, hobbies, social events, shopping habits, sports, entertainment, reading, holidays, club membership.
- Interests which imply all or some of the following: attention, curiosity, motivation, focus, concern, goal-directedness, awareness, worthiness and desire related to – topics, events, subjects, family, home, achievements, food, media, recreation, fashion, community.
- Opinions – where people stand on product related issues. It is a term used to describe something that is intellectually held and based on expectations, evaluations and interpretations about objects, events, people, social issues, or topics such as politics, business, education.

Activities, interests and opinions are different from beliefs where there is an emotional component, and from attitudes which can also be thought of as something internal.

Lifestyle

Lifestyle is the way in which a person tries to achieve their desired self-concept.

The term lifestyle was introduced to marketing in 1963 by William Lazer with the idea that a systematic relationship exists between consumption and lifestyles of a social group. It is important to remember that people in the same demographic group can have very different psychographic profiles.

Max Weber thought of lifestyle as a mark of status which enabled the person to be recognized as belonging to a group and helps them to become socially integrated.

Alfred Adler used the same term but thought of lifestyle as the way in which the individual adapts psychologically to society.

Lifestyle can therefore be looked at in two ways, either as a reflection of personality and motivation (inwardly driven), or a sign of social stereotyping (externally driven).

Lifestyle analysis starts with individual motivation using techniques of group discussion and depth interview, and then links it to groups of people. Once the groups have been defined the marketer is then able to decide on the group and create a stereotype at which the advertising message is to be targeted.

Social value groups

Social value groups are founded on shared values and beliefs but the members of each group also share distinct patterns of behaviour.

Examples of social value groups

The VALS System (SRI International)   The VALS system was developed in the USA by Arnold Mitchell of the Stanford Research Institute.

1 The uninvolved

Very low interest or involvement with car or with motoring. This group seldom tinkers with the car and does very few repairs; does a low mileage, has little technical ability, and gets little satisfaction from maintaining the car.

Likely to be older white collar; this group includes most women motorists. This group relies heavily on the garage and will follow the dealer's advice in the choice of motor oil.

2 The enthusiast

A high degree of interest and involvement with the car and with driving and working on it. This is almost the reverse of the uninvolved group. These people do many repairs, have high technical ability and obtain much satisfaction from maintenance. They have many accessories on their cars, enjoy talking about cars, and are interested in motor sport. Nearly all are male and an above-average proportion, about half, are working class. They have a high level of driving experience, and likely to own an older second-hand car.

Nearly all change and top up the oil themselves and have strong opinions about brands. Have a strong tendency to buy from non-garage outlets, especially motorist accessory shops.

3 The professionals

These are highly involved with driving and with the car, but only as a necessary part of the working life. Mainly use the car for business, do high mileage, but do little of the servicing or repairs themselves.

Likely to be male and white collar, driving relatively new car – often a company car.

4 The tinkerer

Through a combination of economic necessity and enthusiasm, are more involved in working on the car than in driving it. Much the reverse of the professional group, they get much satisfaction from maintenance work and tinkering, but although they do many repairs they have low mileage.

Tend to be male and working class, very often skilled. Car likely to be old, second-hand, used mainly for pleasure and driving to work.

They do most of the minor work on the car but may leave bigger jobs to the garage. Tend to top up and change oil themselves, but are brand-conscious.

5 The collector

An enthusiasm for collecting trading stamps is the distinguishing characteristic of this group, which tends to be normal in most other respects. They tend to be young and inexperienced.

Figure 2.7
The five types of motorist. *Source:* England, Grosse and Associates (1969). Margaret Crimp (1990), *The Marketing Research Process*, Prentice Hall

The VALS framework used the answers of 2713 respondents to 800 questions to classify the American public into nine value lifestyle groups. This framework shows that individuals pass through various stages of development, each of which influences attitudes, behaviour and psychological needs. They move from being driven by needs (survivors and sustainers) to an outwardly directed hierarchy (belongers, emulators and achievers) to an inner directed hierarchy (I-am-me, experientials, societally conscious).

These nine groups, together with estimates of the percentage of the US population within each group are:

1 Survivors who are generally disadvantaged and who tend to be depressed, withdrawn and despairing (4%).
2 Sustainers who are again disadvantaged but who are fighting hard to escape poverty (7%).
3 Belongers who tend to be conventional, nostalgic, conservative and generally reluctant to experiment with new products or ideas (33%).
4 Emulators who are status conscious, ambitious and upwardly mobile (10%).
5 Achievers who make things happen, and enjoy life (23%).
6 I-am-me who are self-engrossed, respond to whims and generally young (5%).
7 Experientials who want to experience a wide variety of what life can offer (7%).
8 Societally conscious people with a marked sense of social responsibility and who want to improve the condition of society (9%).
9 Integrateds who are psychologically fully mature and who combine the best elements of inner and outer directedness (2%).

The bottom group do not represent much of a market, and neither do the top group. The top group is important for setting trends and is growing. The needs-driven group is getting smaller. The middle group remain the main market for consumption and are staying the same.

Other models have been developed over the years from the insights offered by lifestyle analysis such as Young and Rubicam's 4Cs and Taylor Nelson's Monitor and Stanford Research Institute's life ways.

Monitor (Taylor Nelson) This typology has the following framework and is rather similar to VALS.

1 Sustenance-driven. Motivated by material security, they are sub-divided into:
   (a) aimless, who include young unemployed and elderly drifters and comprise 5% of the population;
   (b) survivors, traditionally-minded working class people who comprise 16% of the population;
   (c) belongers, these conservative family-oriented people form 18% of the population, but only half of them are sustenance driven.
2 Outer-directed. Those who are mainly motivated by the desire for status, they are divided into:
   (a) belongers
   (b) conspicuous consumers (19%)
3 Inner-directed. These are subdivided into:
   (a) social resisters who are caring and often doctrinaire (11%)
   (b) experimentalist, who are hedonistic and individualistic (14%)
   (c) self explorers, who are less doctrinaire than social resisters and less materialistic than experimentalist.

Young and Rubicam 4Cs
This is a Cross-Cultural Consumer Characterization based on the following framework:

1 the constrained:
   (a) the resigned poor
   (b) the struggling poor
2 the middle majority:
   (a) mainstreamers
   (b) aspirers
   (c) succeeders
3 the innovators:
   (a) the transitionals
   (b) reformers

The 4Cs define the individual and group motivations and needs. Young and Rubicam have used this to develop marketing and advertising campaigns both domestically and internationally. The British Gas 'Tell Sid' shares campaign and Legal and General's 'Umbrella Campaign' were based on this analysis.

The terms Yuppie (young upwardly mobile professional) and Bumps (borrowed-to-the-hilt, upwardly mobile professional show-off) have been used to illustrate a particular style of life.

The Stanford Research Institute's life ways cover the relationship between people and society and suggest that people fall into one of six groups. Kotler (1988) summarized them as follows:

- *Makers* Makers are those who make the system work. They are the leaders and up-and-comers. They are involved in worldly affairs, generally prosperous and ambitious. They are found in the professions and include the managers and proprietors of business.
- *Preservers* Preservers are people who are at ease with the familiar and are proud of tradition.
- *Takers* Takers take what they can from the system. They are attracted to bureaucracies and tenured posts.
- *Changers* Changers tend to be answer-havers; they commonly wish to change things to conform with their views. They are critics, protestors, radicals, advocates and complainers.
- *Seekers* Seekers are the ones who search for a better grasp, a deeper understanding, a richer experience, a universal view. They often originate and promulgate new ideas.
- *Escapers* Escapers have a drive to escape, to get away from it all. Escape takes many forms from dropping out, to addiction, to mental illness, to mysticism.

These life groups differ in many ways and need to be seen as market segments with specific material and symbolic needs.

Practical application of market research

You will remember that the market researcher is likely to approach the design of a segmentation study from one of two angles:

1 Consumer typology – clustering consumers.
2 Product differentiation – clustering products.

However, in practice many marketers face a situation where they do not have the information to do this in any depth and a general 'thumb nail' approach is shown to you below under method one. The second approach, where the objective is to cluster products, is shown to you under method two.

Method one – a thumb nail sketch clustering consumers

Sometimes students get the target marketing process confused with the marketing mix. So, in order to get these out of the way, first think about the product/service, the place (channels of distribution) and the price. Then think about the target marketing process and follow these steps:

Target marketing process

1 Market segmentation
   Using the segmentation systems explained to you above – geographic, geodemographic, demographic, behavioural and psychographic – think about dividing the market into distinct groups of buyers who might call for separate products or marketing mixes.
   Then see if any natural segments already exist. The most important ones will show you the basic structure of the market.
2 Market targeting
   After the different ways in which a market can be segmented are identified the marketer develops different profiles of the market segments. These are then evaluated and a decision is made on which market segment/s to enter.
3 Market positioning
   The third step is market positioning which involves deciding on the competitive position for the product/service.
4 Designing the marketing mix
   After this has been carried out the marketing mix is designed – product, price, place and promotion.

Example:

Historic site publications

Product features:	photography, illustration, map, postcards, writing style and design, quantity of information, size of publication, language
Price:	a range – low, medium and high price
Place of purchase:	on-site shop, off-site shops

Target marketing process

1 Market segmentation

Geographical:	UK, Europe, USA, historic site
Demographic:	family life cycle (child, adult, family), income, language group (home or visitor from abroad), school, class
Behavioural:	purchase occasion – one-off purchase, could be a collector of a series benefits sought – memento, record of history, entertainment, curriculum related activities
Psychographic:	? no information available

39

The main segmentation variable here in the UK would be for overseas or home visitor use. Segmentation on home visitor use would be life cycle and schools use. There would therefore be three primary segments – overseas visitors, home visitors and schools.

2   Market target
These will need to be assessed using the criteria explained to you above in market targeting – how to choose (a) usable market segment/s.

For example: this information could then be related to other information such as the number of visitors (with or without children), foreign language visitors, schools coming to a site and an estimate of the potential market and market segments made on the basis of an analysis of these figures and the target market/s chosen.

3   Product positioning (this is discussed in more detail below)
The product would be positioned on:
- price
- quality
- product features

4   Marketing mix
Once you have decided on your segments you will need to develop the appropriate marketing mix. You may decide to use:
- one marketing mix for the whole market (undifferentiated marketing strategy)
- a number of marketing mixes designed to meet the needs of each market segment (differentiated marketing strategy)
- choose a market segment that is your major market segment and allow the mix to filter through to the rest (concentrated marketing strategy)

To help you decide which method to use it is often helpful to lay out the following grid:

Home market – family life cycle

	Segment one Child	Segment two Adult	Segment three Family
Product	Illustration	Photography	Illustration and photography
	Stickers Postcards Poster	Map	Map Postcards Poster
Number of pages (rough guide)	12	30/100/200 (3 products)	30
Price	£1	£3/£10/£20	£2
Promotion Sales promotion Public relations Selling	possible trade deals press release only sales visits to outlets		
Place	on-site and immediate surrounds of site		

Schools and foreign language publications developed separately.

Method two – product differentiation – clustering products
Here the focus would be on consumer use and perception of types of product or service and, more especially, brands.

In this method the marketer works backwards from the position the product occupies in the marketplace in relation to the competition. They would think about the sequence of variables which consumers may consider when they make a purchase. This information is then related to other geographic, geodemographic, demographic, behavioural and psychographic information.

This could be done by: creating a perceptual map on two (or more) dimensions; or creating a brand map by using attributes.

Creating a perceptual map on two dimensions

The thread that runs through all this is the need for the marketer to understand the structure of the market. This is most commonly done by focusing on three areas:

1. Develop a spatial map of consumers' perceptions of brands within a given market sector.
2. Identify how consumers see existing products/services in relation to this map and put the names of competitors' brands onto this map. You will then be able to use the map either to spot a gap or develop an ideal position for your brand.
3. From this map you will then be able to develop a model which will help you to predict consumer responses to new and modified products/services.

Example:

Here the wine market is positioned on two dimensions – type of drinker, and usage occasion.

```
                          Formal occasion
                                │
Harvey's Claret                 │              Blue Nun
Mouton Cadet                    │              Black Tower
Quality generics                │              Mateus
                                │              Lutomer
                                │
More experienced  ─ ─ ─ ─ ─ ─ ─ ┼ ─ ─ ─ ─ ─ ─  Less experienced
heavy drinkers                  │              heavy drinkers
                                │
Own-label                       │              Hirondelle
Cheap (Vin de Table)            │              Nicolas
generics                        │              Don Cortez
                                │
                          Informal occasion
```

From this map the advertising agency, Abbott Mead Vickers, was able to examine the duplication of brand usage among wine drinkers and establish the degree of overlap between the different brands. By doing this, clusters of brands emerged according to usage and provided the agency strategist with an understanding of the market's structure, the existence of any gaps, the nature and intensity of the competition, and the type of marketing mix needed to establish or support a brand.

This sort of picture of the market can then be taken a step further by superimposing a second map illustrating in greater detail consumer profiles. This might typically include sex (male versus female), age (young/middle-aged, old), income group (high earners versus low earners), and marital status (married versus single).

Source: Wilson and Gilligan with Pearson (1993),
Strategic Marketing Management,
Butterworth-Heinemann

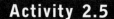

Think about the textbooks that you're using on this course and fill in the names of the publisher and titles of the books.

Academic approach
(facts only).

Low price – – – – – – – – – – – – –|– – – – – – – – – High price

Practical approach
(facts and how to apply the facts)

Ask yourself: Are your needs being met? Is there a gap in the market?

Creating a brand map by using attributes

Another way of doing it is to list the attributes and put them into a hierarchy.

Example:

Initial perceptions of instant coffee brands

Expensive .... Cheap

Gold Blend Blend 37	Nescafe Maxwell House	Red Mountain	Own label
The best instants	Popular	Cheaper	Cheap and nasty
Special Expensive When one has people around Christmas	Everyday Reliable The standard Frequent use Old favourites Ordinary	Not as classy Middle of the road Cheap and cheerful	Weak Bitter Lack flavour

Source: Feldwick, (1990) p. 210

These perceptions led to qualitative research in which the perceptions of Red Mountain elicited the image and personality as being:

Outdoor, rugged, working class, eccentric, ordinary, scruffy, lumberjack, macho, farmer, normal, dull, boring, rough and ready, strange, untidy, basic.

From these findings the product was repositioned not to compete directly with Gold Blend but at the market occupied by Nescafe and Maxwell House. The brand proposition that was decided on was 'Ground coffee taste without the grind'.

Source: Advertising Works 5, Holt, Rinehart Winston, 1990.

Perceptual maps can be used to:

1 Establish the bases for segmentation.
2 Identify gaps in the market.
3 Identify which brands are perceived to be similar to your own brands.
4 Assess your strengths and weaknesses.
5 Reposition yourself in the marketplace.

Although these methods show the underlying process, the marketer will also have to decide between 'a priori' and 'post hoc' methods. Both methods have their place.

A priori methods
Segmenting in advance – for example where you know who is purchasing from you, it is then possible to tailor the marketing strategy to the needs and expectations of each group.

The examples of historic site publications, wine and coffee are a priori methods. Other a priori examples, using method one, are given to you in the worked answers.

Post hoc methods
Segmenting the market on the basis of research findings. Where the market is new, the marketer has no experience of it, or the market is changing or there are no natural segments, a more formal procedure is needed. Segmentation, targeting and positioning are based on information from the analysis.

The method is shown to you below.

Seven steps in market segmentation, targeting and positioning

Market segmentation

1 At an individual level identify what the needs are through informal interviews and focus groups.
2 Based on their needs profile, group the customers into homogeneous subgroups or segments.
3 Based on these findings prepare a formal questionnaire that is administered to a sample of consumers to collect data on:

- attributes, and their rating
- brand awareness and brand ratings
- product usage patterns
- attitudes towards the product
- demographics, psychographics and mediagraphics

The needs-based subgroups will then be identified with *other characteristics* that will enable you to reach the segment with your promotional mix.

Market targeting

4 Cluster analysis will then allow you to create a number of different segments (internally homogeneous and externally different). The potential of each segment can be evaluated and the segment selected that will give you the greatest opportunity – this is your target market (see below how to choose a usable market segment).
5 Choose which segment/s you will target.

Market positioning

6 The product/service will then need to be positioned within the selected segment/s.
7 Develop the right marketing mix for each target segment.

Market targeting: how to choose a usable market segment/s

Ideally segmentation bases should allow us to reveal segments that have the following characteristics:

- *Measurable* The segments should be measurable. In many markets it can be more difficult to do if there is a lack of specific published data.
- *Accessible* The marketers should be able to reach the segments with promotion.
- *Substantial* The segments revealed should be large enough to serve profitably. This decision is relative because what one organization may consider as being appropriate for them, another may not. Ford may not be interested in custom-built cars whereas a smaller company may be able to target this segment.
- *Stable* Ideally it should be possible to predict how the segment will behave in the future and that it will exist long enough to warrant the time and cost of development.
- *Appropriate* The segment should be chosen so that there is a fit between it and the organization's objectives and resources.
- *Unique* The segment should be distinguishable from other market segments and show clear variations in market behaviour in comparison with other segments.

Question 2.4

On what basis would you choose a market segment?

Positioning

- positioning refers to the way in which a product/service is defined by the consumer in their minds relative to that of the competition.
- positioning is carried out after market segmentation.
- the message should be distinctive and the customer should understand it as the basis for their buying decisions.
- positioning should take into account the position of a market leader, follower or challenger – followers should not position themselves too close to or directly against the market leader.

A smaller firm should be able to find its own customers and position in the marketplace.

Positioning strategies can be related to:

- the product attributes
- the benefits they offer
- the price
- the quality
- the application – extending cornflakes from a breakfast cereal to something that can be eaten all day
- the users – extending the eating of cornflakes to adults
- by product class – against another product class (margarine tastes like butter) or with another product class (soap that acts like a moisturizer)
- by competitor – against a competitor (products are compared with a competitor), or away from a competitor (we are not the same we are different)

Very often there is an overlap between the original market segmentation and the positioning, this can cause some confusion as the same ideas are repeated and one gets lost between thinking – is it segmentation I am doing or is it positioning?

Try doing these examples without looking at the answers below. You may or may not agree with the worked examples as they have not been done with any of the added benefits of research. Think about how you would extend or change what has been suggested to you. A question mark has been put in where there is not enough information available.

Remember

It is not always possible to fill all the information into the segmentation systems, either because not enough is known about the market, or the category does not apply.

- look for natural segments
- most marketers will segment a market in more than one way and use two or more demographic variables
- try and think of which method will be most suited to the particular product/service
- not all the ways in which a market can be segmented are covered in the classifications shown to you above, so use them as a guide
- segmentation is a creative exercise and must be related to the market with which you are dealing.

1 Clothes washing market.
2 Analgesic market.
3 Vitamin market.
4 Air travel.
5 Greeting cards.

First think about the product/service, the place (channels of distribution) and the price in order to get them out of the way so you do not get them confused with market segmentation. They can also be helpful when you consider market positioning and the marketing mix.

Target marketing process

1 Market segmentation
   Using the segmentation systems explained to you above (geographic, geodemographic, demographic, behavioural and psychographic) think about dividing the market into distinct groups of buyers who might call for separate products or marketing mixes.
2 Market target
   These will need to be assessed using the criteria explained to you above in market targeting – how to choose a usable market segment/s.
3 Market positioning
   Now think about the sequence of variables which consumers may consider when they make a purchase, how you think the product would be positioned within that market segment in relation to the competition.
4 Marketing mix
   The marketing mix would be designed on the basis of the above information.

Answers

Clothes washing market

Target marketing process

1 Market segmentation
   Geographic: US
   Demographic: age, male, female
   Behavioural: benefits and different mixes of benefits – extra action, hot, warm, cold water, enzyme, non-enzyme, concentrated, less suds, fabric softener, mild and

gentle, with bleach, with special ingredients (pro-teins, borax, detergent to get out stains), scented, unscented, extra-scented, liquid/powder, concentrated/unconcentrated (based on Kotler) – can you think of any more?

Psychographic: ? no information available – would need research
Motivation: clean clothes, good mothering/fathering

2 Market positioning
Market positioning would take place on one of these benefits.

Analgesic market

Product ingredients: aspirin, paracetamol, codeine, etc.
Product features: size of tablet, shape of tablet, colour of tablet, container size
Place of purchase: chemist or general distribution
Price: a range

Target marketing process

1 Market segmentation
Geographic: UK
Demographic: age of user, male, female
Behavioural: purchase occasion: regular, special
benefits sought: speed of treatment, safety, ease of swallow, frequency of dosage
user status: non-user, ex-user, potential user, first-time user, regular
loyalty status: none, medium, strong, absolute
the usage: type of ailment (head, period, arthritis, cold, flu, hangover, migraine)
the usage rate: light, medium, heavy
usage time: morning, day, evening
Psychographic: ? no information available – would need research
Motivation: pain relief

The main segmentation variables would be the usage (type of ailment), benefits sought. Other demographic information related to this would be age of user and sex. This information should reveal the basic market structure.

2 Market positioning
Market positioning would be done on using a selection/combination of these points:

Product features
Product ingredients
Benefits sought
Price
Against a competitor

Vitamin market

Product ingredients: ?
Place of purchase: chemist, general distribution
Price: ?

Target marketing process

1 Market segmentation
Geographic: UK
Demographic: age
Behavioural: needs/benefits related to each age group
Psychographic: ? no information available – would need research
Motivation: health, vitality

The main segmentation variables would be the needs/benefits related to each age group.

2 Market positioning
Market positioning would be done on using a selection/combination of these points:

    Product features
    Benefits
    Price
    Quality

Air travel – air passenger market

Target marketing process

1 Market segmentation

Geographic:	international
Demographic:	age, occupation, male, female, cultural differences
Behavioural:	purchase occasion – journey purpose: business – corporate, independent, conference and incentive travel
	leisure – holiday, visiting friends and relatives
	length of journey – long haul, short haul
	benefits sought – excess baggage, schedule convenience, in-flight amenities, status recognition, safety, status of airline, type of aircraft, punctuality, flexibility
	usage rate – light, medium, heavy (frequent flier)
	loyalty status – none, medium, strong, absolute (also relate this to country of origin loyalty)
	critical event – sudden illness, or emergency back home
Psychographic:	no information on psychographics
Motivation:	safety, comfort, reliability

The main segmentation variable would be business or leisure. Further development of this would involve looking at all the other variables shown above. This should reveal distinct groups of buyers who might call for separate products or marketing mixes.

2 Market positioning
The product would be positioned within those segments using a combination of these points.

    Product features
    Benefits
    Price
    Quality
    Against a competitor (better than)
    Against a product class (train, road, ship)

Greeting cards

Product features: humour, romantic, cartoon, classic artwork, photography, stickers, badges, electronic music and so on
Place of purchase: corner shop, greeting shop, garage, giftshop, etc.
Price: under £1, over £1 etc.

Target marketing process

1 Market segmentation

Geographic:	UK
Demographic:	age, class, sex
Behavioural:	type of occasion – Christmas, Easter, birth, birthday, Valentine, Mother's Day, bereavement, thank you just to say hello, remember me, miss you, love you, and so on.
Psychographic:	? no information available – would need research
Motivation:	just to say hello, remember me, miss you, love you, and so on

The major segmentation variables would be on the type of occasion and benefits sought. This would be related to other segmentation variables such as social class, age, sex, race.

2 Market positioning
The product would be positioned within those segments using a combination of:

Product attributes
Price
Quality

Activity 2.6

Now carry out the same exercise on your own organization.
Are there any gaps in the information available to you?
What can you do to acquire the information that you need?

Exam Hints

1 You must be able to tell the difference between the overall process – target marketing – and the steps involved in carrying this out, which are – market segmentation, market targeting and market positioning.
2 The marketing mix (product, price, promotion, place, and in the case of services, people, process and physical evidence) is designed after this process has been carried out. Not before.

Market segmentation and product positioning have recently undergone several changes:

- Increased emphasis on segmentation criteria that represent softer data such as attitudes and needs.
- Increased awareness that the basis of segmentation depend on its purpose. For example, the same bank customers could be segmented by account ownership profiles, attitudes towards risk taking and socio-economic variables. Each segmentation could be useful for a different purpose, such as product cross selling, preparation of advertising messages and media selection.
- Greater use of hybrid segmentation methods. For example, a beer producer might first segment consumers according to a favourite brand. Then, within each brand group, consumers could be further segmented according to similarities in attitude towards beer drinking, occasions where beer is consumed and so on.
- Research on dynamic segment models that consider the possibility of competitive retaliation. Such models examine a company's vulnerability to competitive reactions over the short term and choose segment combinations that are most resistant to competitive encroachment.
- A move towards letting the data speak for itself and finding segments through the detection of patterns in survey or in-house data. So called data mining methods have become much more versatile.

Segmenting industrial markets

Much of the work done on consumer market segmentation can be applied to industrial markets – such as usage rates, benefits sought, geographical location, etc. Other factors which would affect the buying situation would be:

1 Buying situation – new buy, modified rebuy or new task.
2 Type of product and the degree of standardization.

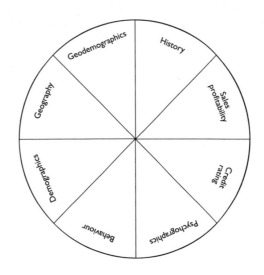

Figure 2.8

3 Significance of the purchase to the buying organization.
4 Degree of risk and uncertainty involved for the buying organization.
5 Source loyalty.

Another approach is to look at the major industrial market segmentation variables. A summary of these questions in declining order of importance is shown below.

Demographic

- *Industry* – on which industries that use this product should we concentrate?
- *Company* – on which size of company should we concentrate?
- *Location* – in which geographical areas should we concentrate our efforts?

Operating variables

- *Technology* – which customers' technologies are of greatest interest to us?
- *User status* – on which types of user (heavy, medium, light, non-user) should we concentrate?
- *Customer capabilities* – should we concentrate on customers with a broad or a narrow range of needs?

Purchasing approaches

- *Buying criteria* – should we concentrate on customers seeking quality, service or price?
- *Buying policies* – should we concentrate on companies that prefer leasing systems, systems purchases, or sealed bids?
- *Current relationships* – should we concentrate on existing or new customers?

Situational factors

- *Urgency* – should we concentrate on customers with sudden delivery needs?
- *Size of order* – should we concentrate on large or small orders?
- *Applications* – should we concentrate on general or specific applications of our product?

Personal characteristics

- *Loyalty* – should we concentrate on customers who exhibit high or low levels of loyalty?
- *Attitudes to risk* – should we concentrate on risk taking or risk avoiding customers?

From Bonoma and Shapiro (1983); Wilson and Gilligan with Pearson (1993), *Strategic Marketing Management*, Butterworth-Heinemann

The decision-making unit is a useful tool for deciding on segmentation variables within the industrial market. People within the unit can be grouped in various ways according to the size of their business and response to variables such as new purchase, attitude to risk, size of order, etc.

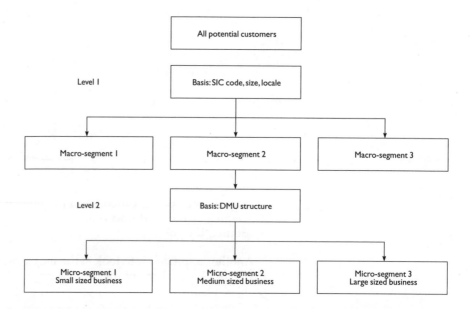

Figure 2.9

One-to-one marketing and mass customization

As markets become increasingly competitive, marketers are turning to methods that will make them increasingly less vulnerable. Companies are focusing on a technique that they hope will satisfy customers so much the price will become irrelevant. The approach is to first differentiate and then focus on target groups of customers with customized products. The next step is to focus on keeping your current customers by providing them with better customer service, better communications and ongoing product differentiation. This technique of one-to-one marketing aims at customizing a product so carefully that it fits the customer perfectly.

Products can be customized in different ways:

1   'Core' mass customization where products are customized on a mass basis using modular designs and fast, flexible, modular production processes as enabling individual products to be delivered directly to the customer. For example, Motorola has twenty-nine million variations of hand-held pagers. Customization can take place by:
    ● combinational assembly – customize by assembly;
    ● in-house processing – customize by process machining, painting;
    ● information content – customize by onboard software.
2   'Post-product' customization where standard products are manu-factured on a mass basis and customized by having unique services wrapped around the common core. For example, customized software solutions.
3   Mass 'retail' customization where standard products are manufactured on a mass basis and customized at the point of sale or delivery. For example, quick response high street opticians Vision Express where 90 per cent of all glasses are made in house.
4   'Self' customizing products where the manufacturer, through the use of design and technology capabilities, includes options within the mass-produced product so that the customer may personalize the product at the point of receipt or during the use of the product. For example, personal computers which can be configured to the users choice of screen layout. Vacuum cleaners that can adapt to unique household flooring and carpets.

Why customize? – the drivers

There are various reasons, Panasonic did it because of downward price pressures, inventory obsolescence, reduced plc, increased competition, cheap imports and segmentation complexity. Raleigh did it because of the demand from customers and dealers for specials, which inconvenienced manufacturing whose business processes and IT systems were designed for large batch production.

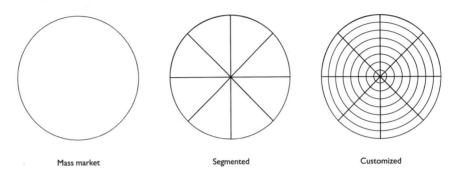

Mass market   Segmented   Customized

Figure 2.10

Imperatives to achieve mass customization are:

- Lean production involving the use of JIT, short set-up times for equipment, minimal work-in-progress inventories.
- Modularity of products and processes.
- Successfully integrated IT to cope with the explosion of complexity which mass customization brings.
- A paranoiac customer focus.
- Supplier partnerships to ensure flexible response to the demands of customization.

(Foundation for Manufacturing and Industry. Department of Trade and Industry. IBM Consulting Group. 1997.)

One-to-one marketing and mass customization are the extension of traditional target marketing and product differentiation, the only difference is that it tries to fit the customer's needs more perfectly. In order to do business in this way there is a need to change how the business is organized. Information technology is the element which makes this possible and the organization, in order to mass customize, must be able to track large volumes of data.

Levi, Strauss and Co. is making mass customization an instrument of customer satisfaction. They take a woman's measurements, transmit them electronically to the factory and use them to customize a pair of jeans.

One-to-one relationships and mass customization have two different requirements. The first deals with knowing what the customer wants and building a relationship. The second involves providing a mass-customized product and will therefore rely heavily on manufacturing technology.

Marketing one-to-one requires commitment and a culture that is dedicated to treating each customer as the complete focus of the company.

There are four basic steps to go through:

1 Identify customers – identify your heavy, medium, light and non-users of your products. It is no use spending money and effort to try and win the wrong customers over.
2 Differentiate each customer – identify what they want and treat them differently.
3 Interact with each customer – every contact that you have with the customer will give the opportunity to learn more about their needs and their potential value to the organization.
4 Customize products/services for each customer – this step is only possible if you have carried out the last three steps and have already identified what the customer wants. It is possible to do this if you

51

integrated production process with the firm's customer feedback. This will in effect create a barrier of entry as a customer will have to re-invent another relationship with another business in order to get this level of service.

To be able to do this you will need:

- A proper database.
- People working for the organization capable of personal interaction.
- Interactive media.
- Systems that support mass customization.

Individualization doesn't mean adding a layer variety of products which customers can now choose, it is about getting product and services exactly right for those individual customers within the target segment and user group with whom the organization has decided to do business.

M	T	C	I	Unique level 4
M	T	C	Different level 3	
M	T	Similar level 2		
M	Common level I			

M = Mass, T = Targeted, C = Customized, I = Individualized

Figure 2.11
Reconfiguring the market. *Source*: Sanda Vandemerve, John Wiley & Sons, 1996

Summary

In this unit you have been introduced to the classification of goods and services and will understand how these need to be considered in customer behaviour, market segmentation and the marketing mix.

You have also looked at the decision-making unit and adoption and diffusion curve and been asked to consider them in your market segmentation process.

Traditional methods of market segmentation have been discussed and you have been introduced to the idea of:

- How the whole objective of segmentation is to identify groups of people within the broader market who have needs which are broadly similar to each other and who respond in a similar way to the promotion methods and the rest of the marketing mix.

- How the concept of segmentation is related to consumer and industrial markets and is one of the main cornerstones of marketing.

  1 Segmenting consumer markets
    - Geographic
    - Geodemographic
    - Demographic
    - Behaviour in the product field
    - Motivation, psychographics and social value groups
  2 Segmenting industrial markets
    - Demographics
    - Operating variables
    - Purchasing approaches
    - Situational factors
    - Personal characteristics

- That the market researcher is likely to approach the design of a segmentation study in two ways – by collecting data in order to cluster consumers or by collecting data to cluster products.

- That the process of target marketing calls for four different steps:

  1 *Market segmentation* The first is market segmentation which calls for dividing a market into distinct groups of buyers who might call for separate products or marketing mixes.
  2 *Market targeting* After the different ways in which a market can be segmented are identified, the marketer develops different profiles of the market segments. These are then evaluated and a decision is made on which market segment/s to enter.
  3 *Market positioning* The third step is market positioning which involves deciding on the competitive position for the product/ service.
  4 *Designing the marketing mix.*

- You have also considered the limitations of some of the methods that can be used. The importance of mass customization and one-to-one marketing has been shown as being the way forward for certain types of business.

Strategy and methods to produce customer focused behaviour

❑ To understand the need for marketing strategy to be aligned with human resource management strategy.

❑ To understand the range of options that enable organizations to become customer focused.

Study Guide

The unit introduces students to the link that needs to be made between marketing strategy and human resource management strategy in order to meet customer needs. The framework of thinking has been extended from the traditional marketing audit to the use of the 7S McKinsey framework and extended to the customer care audit. The customer care audit and the EFQM excellence model take into consideration aspects of the external and internal environment that need to be considered in order for a diagnosis to be made. This allows the organization to decide what it needs to do in order to improve. Following the diagnosis a range or menu of different ideas are presented on the methods that organizations have used to encourage quality, and customer focused behaviour.

The unit is structured so that readers can see the following linkages between analysis, identification of core competencies, business philosophy, structure, technique and integration.

1 Analysis – marketing audit, 7S McKinsey framework, customer care audit, EFQM excellence model, success models, balanced scorecard.
2 Identification of core competencies, recruitment, performance management, training and development, rewards and recognition (see Unit 4 Additional management techniques for mobilizing performance).
3 Philosophy – vision and leadership, culture, marketing, Kaizen, total quality management (TQM), relationship marketing (RM) (see Unit 8 Relationship marketing).
4 Structure – business process reengineering, value chain analysis, customer activity cycle (CAC).
5 Techniques – benchmark, ISO 9000, just-in-time (JIT), IIP, MBO, empowerment, learning, 360-degree feedback, self-directed teams, Ishikawa.

Strategy

All organizations are in an interdependent relationship with their environments, and it is through the strategic planning process that an organization comes to understand what adaptations it should make in order to stay in business. Organizations need to consider the realities of both the external environment and the internal organizational environment and the way they interrelate.

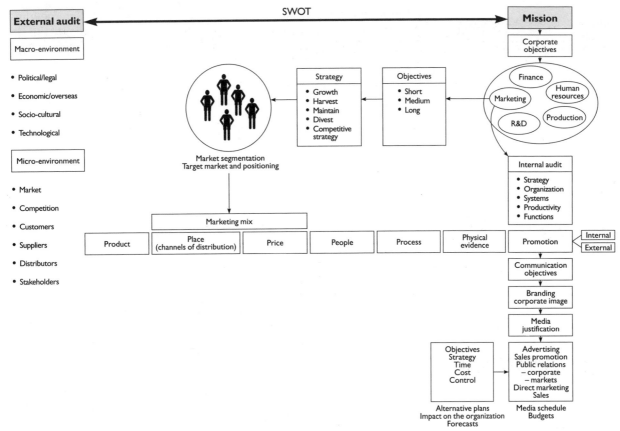

Figure 3.1 Strategic and tactical framework illustrating the aspects considered in marketing planning. Oxford College of Marketing

The development of services, technology, globalization, homogenization of markets, increased competition, mass customization and one-to-one marketing, and the advent of the more demanding customer, have meant that the discipline of marketing now needs to understand and develop new skills to enable the organization to manage the interface between itself and the external environment.

Creating strategy traditionally consists first of auditing the macro-environment, the micro-environment and the internal environment of the organizations' marketing department.

Components of the audit

Within the general framework of the external and internal audits, Kotler et al. (1989) suggest there are six specific dimensions that are of direct interest to the auditor. These are:

1   The marketing environment audit, which involves an analysis of the major macro- and micro-economic forces and trends within the organization's task environment. This includes PEST factors and markets, customers, competitors, distributors, dealers, and suppliers.
2   The marketing strategy audit, which focuses upon a review of the organization's marketing objectives and strategy, with a view to determining how well suited they are to the current and forecasted market environment.
3   The marketing organization audit. This aspect of the audit follows on from the previous point, and is concerned specifically with an evaluation of the structural capability of the organization and its suitability for implementing the strategy needed for the developing environment.
4   The marketing systems audit, which covers the quality of the organization's systems for analysis, planning and control.
5   The marketing productivity audit, which examines the profitability of different aspects of the marketing programme and the cost effectiveness of various levels of marketing expenditure.
6   The marketing functions audit, involving a detailed evaluation of each of the elements of the marketing mix – the 7Ps outlined below.

55

Information from the audit is then analysed into the SWOT framework. From this analysis the process of matching organizational strengths to the market place and overcoming weaknesses takes place. The objectives are then set, strategies decided and the relevant marketing mix consisting of the 7Ps is put into place:

- Product/service
- Price
- Place (distribution channel)
- Promotion
- People
- Process
- Physical evidence

This analytical framework is covered in the *Marketing Operations 1990–2000* workbook.

The traditional marketing audit touches only a limited number of organizational aspects mostly related to the marketing department. However, we now need to extend our thinking outside the marketing department into the whole organization and into the relationships surrounding it so that we create not only a market-focused marketing department, but also a market-focused organization.

Marketing needs to take a broader view and, as suggested by Christopher, Payne and Ballantyne, the 7S McKinsey framework can provide a model on which this view could be based.

The 7S McKinsey framework

Drawing on their work at McKinsey & Co., Waterman, Peters and Phillips (1981) argue that effective organizational change depends on the effective assignment of seven variables that have come to be known as the 7Ss, or 7S McKinsey framework. These are:

- Structure.
- Strategy.
- Systems (and procedures).
- Style (management style).
- Staff (people).
- Skills (corporate strengths and skills).
- Shared values/superordinate goals.

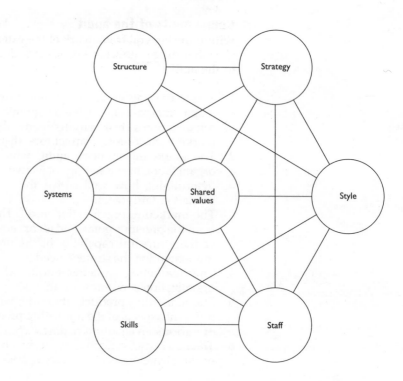

Figure 3.2
7S McKinsey framework

56

The strategic and tactical dimension of market planning can be covered in the traditional framework illustrated in Figure 3.2. However, the 7S framework can be adapted to take into account the variables that need to be aligned to create a model that extends beyond the management of marketing to managing an organization that has a marketing focus.

Customer care audit

It is suggested that the specific elements outlined in the McKinsey framework cover shared values, structure, style, staff, skills training and systems that could be used as the basic structure for conducting a customer care audit.

This audit needs to take place within the context of the external environment – macro- and micro-, so that an understanding of how environmental pressures and various relationships can affect the feelings, behaviour and the effectiveness of the people working within the organization.

The difference between this audit and the traditional marketing audit is that it focuses mainly on the factors that can effect processes and positive feelings within the organization that may ultimately impact on customers and operational effectiveness. It takes marketing out of the box of the 7Ps and puts it firmly into the centre of the organizational strategy.

The presenting problem – customer complaints

When an organization has a problem with customer care it needs to look at the whole organization. It is no use at all to go in for a mere facelift or trying to put a smile on Tutenkamun by redoing the corporate image!

Loss of customers and customer complaints must be treated as the presenting symptoms, and in order to carry out a proper diagnosis a proper audit needs to be done.

From the text below it can be seen it is necessary to approach the organization in a number of ways.

External environmental macro- and micro-factors affecting the organization

Macro-environment

Political
Political groups reflect the values and beliefs of the people they represent. What is happening politically that will affect the way in which people expect to be treated in their role as customers, citizens, passengers, patients, employees and so on? How do these dominant values and beliefs influence the way in which the organization conducts itself in the wider environment? For example, what do people feel that government should be doing more of? Does your organization need to think in terms of helping to create local job schemes, supporting charity, supporting housing, a disabled scheme, etc?

Legal
What laws are being enacted that will affect people's legal rights as customers and as employees? For example, what is happening with pollution control, equal opportunity, disability and anything else related to the way in which the organization conducts itself internally that will influence the way it is perceived in the wider environment and affect the way employees feel about their own organizational practices?

Economic
What effect is the economy having on customers in terms of their mood and a propensity to spend? How does the mood of the country affect the way in which they treat front-line staff? What effect is high/low unemployment having on employees' morale?

Overseas

What effect is global competition having on the organization and how are employees reacting to an increasingly competitive environment? Is the organization thinking globally? Is management creating some understanding in the workplace about the external environment and the need to adapt and integrate their work practices in a different way? How will the process of change affect people?

Socio demographic/cultural

What effect is a multi-cultural company having on different national groups and the way in which they are managed? How is cultural difference dealt with in the organization? Does the organizational culture override the national culture?

How does culture affect front-line staff? Are front-line staff aware of how to behave in different circumstances? Are front-line staff aware of how their own projections and tendency to stereotype can interfere in a genuine role relationship? Is the organization training staff to reflect and understand their own reactions to customer behaviour? Is the organization adapting its HR policies to match the needs, values and lifestyle of younger employees?

Technology

What changes are there in technology? How is the company approaching the use of technology? How will technology affect the working of groups? What effect is this having on staff and are there any behavioural changes that they need to adopt while dealing with customers? What new skills need to be learned? What action is the organization taking to create this understanding?

Environmental concerns

What concerns are there about the environment? What effect are environmental practices within the organization having on staff? How is the company responding to this, and to the wider environmental concerns of staff? What action is the organization taking to improve its own work practices? Do their employees feel proud of what they are doing? What action is the organization taking to ensure this?

Micro-environment

Market

- What effect are conditions in the market having on employees?
- How do employees handle themselves in a new market as opposed to a mature market? If the market is depressed what effect is this having on employees and does this mood communicate itself to customers and affect their buying?
- Are employees aware of the position their organization holds in the market and what they need to do in order to increase income and reduce costs? How does this understanding affect them?
- What action is being taken by the organization to bring some understanding of the market place to employees?

Competition

- Does the organization know what the competition is doing? What is it doing to bring this knowledge to its employees, so that they can discuss what they need to do in order to become more competitive, especially in relation to customer retention? Can competition be defined globally?
- What effect are the organization's own competitive strategies and tactics having on its employees? How do they feel about the way in which their organization behaves?

Customers

- Does the organization understand the needs and wants of its target market?
- Does the organization create its products and services from the customer's point of view?

- Does the organization develop customer relationships and retain the loyalty of existing customers?
- Is market research related to customer care ongoing – customer care questionnaires, monitoring of complaints, focus groups, random customer surveys, mystery shopper, complaint analysis, operational measures such as time deliveries, abandoned callouts, time to turn round correspondence, etc. Is this information fed back into the organization to the people who look after customers, and acted upon?
- Are standards specified to customers so they know what to expect?
- How do front-line staff respond to customers' needs and buying processes?
- Are there any particular behavioural skills that staff need to know about in order to cope competently with their customer group? What training is the organization giving staff to help them do this?
- What ongoing support does management give staff who have to deal with difficult or unpleasant situations?

Suppliers

- How do suppliers behave towards the organization?
- What sort of relationship does the organization seek to have with its suppliers and vice versa?
- Are they treated as adversaries or are they seen as part of the whole quality system?
- Are relationships long term?
- How committed are suppliers to the organization?
- What actions has the organization taken to establish long-term relationships with its suppliers?

Distributors

- How do distributors behave towards the organization and vice versa?
- Is there any inter-group conflict within the distribution channel?
- How is conflict managed and resolved?
- Are customer needs being met within the distribution chain?
- What action has the organization taken to establish long-term relationships with its distributors?

Stakeholders

- Which stakeholders present particular opportunities or problems for the organization?
- What steps has the organization taken to satisfy their concerns?
- What effect is the behaviour of stakeholders having on employees?

Internal analysis of the organization

The approach to internal factors is based on the use of the 7S McKinsey framework as an analytical model.

Shared values

Mission statement

- Does the mission statement have values and behaviour written into it that relate to customer care? Is marketing and the principle of meeting customer's needs accepted as a business philosophy?
- Is the mission statement something that employees can visualize, articulate and internalize so that it gives them a sense of purpose and an expectation of success?
- Does each job description carry the mission statement with its customer care objectives outlined in such a way that employees are able to translate it into clear actions? Can the success of these actions be quantified and be of use in the appraisal process.

Culture

- Is there a philosophy within the organization of putting customer needs first?
- Is there a culture of innovation and learning?
- Is this culture embodied in policy, routines and rituals?
- What sorts of stories circulate around the organization about its treatment of customers – are they positive or negative?

Corporate image

- Is there any conflict between the image the organization presents and the way employees perceive it to be? How does this dissonance affect them?
- How are other symbols used to link a customer-focused culture with customer perception and employees' perception?

Structure

Organizational structure

- Does the organization have an agile, simple structure that will help it to follow up or disband opportunities?
- Are the marketing positions market segment or key account manager?
- Is the structure able to give fast support to customers?
- Does the work process (value chain) support the needs of the customers' value chain?
- Are roles within the organization interlinked to facilitate a customer-centred focus?
- Does the structure make it easy to get in touch with decision makers?

Style

Leadership

- Does the CEO spend time with customers?
- Does the CEO champion customer care?
- Does the CEO and management create a climate of high morale?
- Is customer service represented at top management level?
- Does the CEO view products as part of an integrated product and service offering?
- Does the CEO ensure that non-marketing staff are rotated through the organization to customer contact points?

Management

- Does management make any provision to help employees discuss and come to terms with any stress and anxiety that can arise from customer contact? Are employees encouraged to admit to such stress?
- Does attending to customers' needs and employees' well being take priority in the internal running of the organization?
- Do managers have the skills to manage people (motivation, empowerment, discipline, coaching, facilitating, counselling etc.)?

Systems

Recruitment and induction

- Are recruitment practices geared towards acquiring people who understand about marketing and customer care?
- When people join the company does the induction process reinforce the climate and culture the organization wishes to perpetuate?

Appraisal and reward

- Is the appraisal process linked to key performance indicators and other customer care issues?
- Is the reward system linked to customer retention, customer care and other key performance indicators?

Information, communication, decision making and financial

- Are systems for information, communication and decision making focused to enable the meeting of customers' needs?
- Are these systems used to formulate marketing strategy?

Skills

- Has the organization identified its core competencies?
- Is training in place that enables employees to perform well in a customer-focused way?
- Is marketing and customer care (assertiveness, conflict management, negotiation, etc.) training given?
- Are staff trained to expand their role and empower themselves in a manner in line with the organizational objectives?
- Are managers trained to delegate and empower front-line staff? Are they doing it, not just talking about it?

Staff

Interfunctional relationships – inter group

- Is there harmony between groups?
- Are there any interfunctional conflicts that are affecting customer care?
- Are groups given the opportunity to mix and meet professionally and socially?
- Do cross-functional groups work well together?

Group – intra group

- Is there a good atmosphere in front-line teams?
- Do they understand how to work in a team?
- Do they all share the same understanding of what it means to be successful as an individual and as a team member?
- Are people told how they are doing so they can know what they are achieving?
- Are customer complaints fed back to the team so they can learn from experience?
- Is any role conflict within the team discussed so that jobs are not left undone?

Individual employees

- Do employees working directly with customers enjoy their work?
- Are employees empowered and trained to be able to deal with customers flexibly?
- Does the job description carry specific and measurable customer care objectives?
- Is the mission statement translated into actionable tasks?
- Do employees understand what they need to do in order to be successful within the organization and with customers?
- Are employees encouraged to think about their customer care relationships in order to improve their ability to relate to customers?
- Do all employees understand that customer care is the responsibility of the whole organization?
- Do employees understand that customer care takes precedence over the internal needs of the business?
- Do people agree on what they must do in order to keep customers satisfied?
- Is there any intra-role-conflict (for example, employees being asked to carry out policies with which they disagree)?
- Are individuals empowered to expand their role?
- Are employees motivated and skilled so that they continually improve their processes, quality and response times?

Once the audit is carried out the marketer will become aware of the organizational fit, and the internal linkages that enable an organization to become more effective to meet the needs of the customers. The organization will then be able to view its products and services not only in terms of the behavioural aspects discussed in the customer care audit and look after its intangible assets, but also in terms of understanding the new capabilities it needs to develop in order to be successful. **Strategy is dealt with in the marketing plan and is covered by the questions asked in the traditional marketing audit.**

The EFQM excellence model (previously the EFQM business excellence model)

A core approach to analysing organizational performance is the model designed by the European Foundation for Quality Management: The EFQM excellence model has become best practice in leading organizations and helps you to understand the cause of change and effect within the business and that matters if you are the managing director or a newly appointed sales assistant.

This model provides a framework for assessment and continuous improvement for all organizations, whatever their size or type, and whether they are in the public, private or voluntary sectors. It focuses on a number of performance measures which range from financial and operational areas to the following commonly accepted factors of measuring business excellence. These are leadership, people management, policy and strategy, partnerships and resources, business processes, customer satisfaction, people satisfaction, impact on society, and key performance business results. The data collected involves both qualitative and quantitative measures of performance, giving a comprehensive initial analysis of an organization's situation. Information about the model can be obtained directly from http://efqm.org and your local Business Link.

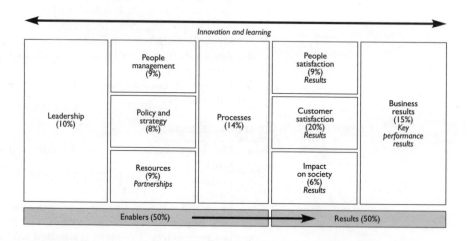

Figure 3.3
EFQM excellence model. For further information: http://efqm.org

Self assessment can be taken by a whole organization, or by a department or division or operational unit. It allows an organization to identify both its strengths and those areas in which improvement can be made. It provides an effective means to coordinate and integrate an organization's quality initiatives.

The benefits of self assessment against the excellence model can include:

- More focused leadership.
- Development of concise action plans.
- Greater motivation of people.
- Identification of process improvement opportunities.
- Direct input to the business planning process.
- More integrated policy and strategy development.
- Quantification of the impact of improved customer satisfaction on your organizational performance.

There are various ways to undertake self assessment and the method you adopt will depend on the culture and objectives of your organization. There is a range of software and paper-based products. The foundation runs workshops, conferences and seminars to help choose the best way for each organization to take.

There is a questionnaire (available from EFQM consultants) and the data from it allows you to come up with an analysis of the organization. This will enable you to pinpoint areas that need to be improved. The relevant techniques can then be used in order to improve performance.

Example

0 ———— 20 ———— 40 ———— 60 ———— 80 ———— 100

Leadership

People management

Policy and strategy

Resource management

Processes

Customer satisfaction

Impact on society

Business results

Success models – improving the quality and performance of businesses

Background

The term 'success model' comes from the RSA inquiry report, *Tomorrow's Company* and is central to their definition of 'inclusivity' – their vision for how organizations will sustain competitive success in the future. Tomorrow's company 'uses its stated purpose and values, and the understanding of the importance of each [Stakeholder] relationship to develop its own Success Model from which it can generate a meaningful framework for performance management'.

What is the success model approach?

Essentially the success model approach is a diagnostic which attempts to help managers to more deeply understand an organization or a team so as to plan *effective* change. In particular to identify:

- The business agenda – what matters and why?
- The people agenda – what value is added and by whom (internal and external)?
- The culture – how does the organization make decisions, learn and change?

The outputs from the diagnostic are:

- A diagrammatic framework showing all the relationships, interdependent activities and how these link to the desired outcome (vision/ mission?).
- A scorecard which captures the key measurements necessary to plot that the right value is being added in every part – in order to aid learning.

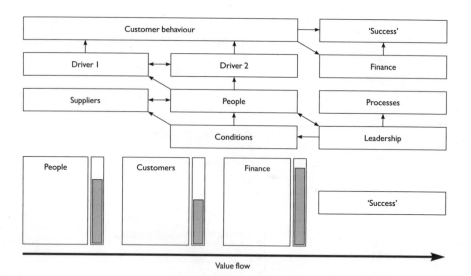

Figure 3.4
The Oxford Group's Success Model

The success model approach helps clients to focus on and identify more definite and measured change and improvement in:

- Commercial performance (sales and productivity).
- Internal/external customer ratings (and loyalty).
- People commitment and capability.

In particular the use of the success model has helped to identify and accelerate the implementation of real learning and change (e-mail: nigelp@oxfordgroup.co.uk).

The balanced scorecard

The balanced scorecard was developed by Robert S. Kaplan and David P. Norton (Harvard Business School Press). The balanced scorecard is a management system that can channel the energies, abilities and specific knowledge held by people throughout the organization toward achieving long-term strategic goals.

The balanced scorecard guides performance and shows how to measure in four categories – financial performance, customer knowledge, internal business processes, and learning and growth – to align individual, organizational, and cross-departmental initiatives and to identify new processes for meeting customer and shareholder objectives.

The balance scorecard emphasizes that financial and non-financial measures must be part of the information system for employees at all levels of the organization. Front-line employees must understand the financial consequences of their decisions and actions; senior executives must understand the drivers of long-term financial success.

The objectives and measures for the balanced scorecard are derived from the top-down process driven by the mission and strategy of the business unit and it translates mission and strategy into tangible objectives and measures.

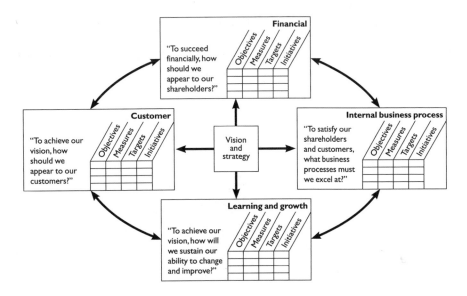

Figure 3.5
Source: Robert S. Kaplan and
David P. Norton, 'Using the
Balanced Scorecard as a Strategic
Management System', *Harvard
Business Review* (January–
February 1996): 76. Reprinted
with permission

As you can see from Figure 3.5 the balanced scorecard provides a framework to translate a strategy into operational terms. It can then be used to:

- Clarify strategy.
- Gain consensus.
- Communicate strategy to the organization.
- Align departmental and personal goals to the strategy.
- Link strategic objectives to long-term targets and annual budgets.
- Identify and align strategic initiatives.
- Perform periodic and systematic strategic reviews.
- Obtain feedback to learn about and improve strategy.

Cause and effect relationships
The balanced scorecard enables an organization to see causal relationships. Figure 3.6 illusrates this perspective.

Customer measures are shown in Figure 3.7.

The need for a performance management system in the public sector
Best value has placed authorities in the position of having to implement some form of performance management system. The millennium will see the introduction of legislation which will require authorities to adopt a performance measurement framework which will necessitate a continuing need to undertake fundamental performance reviews (FPRs) for all services.

For further information see www.barony.co.uk or e-mail barry.hill @barony.co.uk

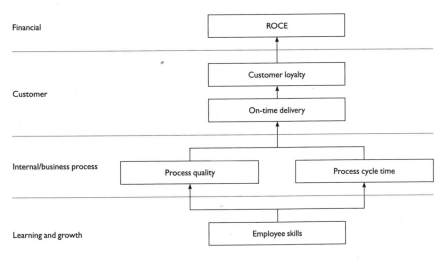

Figure 3.6

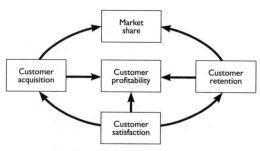

Market share	Reflects the proportion of business in a given market (in terms of number of customers, dollars spent, or unit volume sold) that a business unit sells.
Customer acquisition	Measures, in absolute or relative terms, the rate at which a business unit attracts or wins new customers or business.
Customer retention	Tracks, in absolute or relative terms, the rate at which a business unit retains or maintains ongoing relationships with its customers.
Customer satisfaction	Assesses the satisfaction level of customers along specific performance criteria within the value proposition.
Customer profitability	Measures the net profit of a customer, or a segement, after allowing for the unique expenses required to support that customer.

Figure 3.7
The customer perspective – core measures. *Source*: The Balanced Scorecard, Kaplan and Norton, Harvard Business School Press, 1996

Financial perspective How should we appear to those who fund the services?		Customer perspective How should we appear to our stakeholders who receive the service?	
Actions	Performance measures	Actions	Performance measures
Continuous improvement perspective How can we sustain our ability to grow and improve?		Internal business perspective What service delivery processes must we excel at?	
Actions	Performance measures	Actions	Performance measures

Figure 3.8

Review

Marketing audits, SWOT analysis, EFQM, success models and the balanced scorecard allow us to take a systematic, critically unbiased review of the basic objectives and policies of the company, the marketing function, the organization, the finance methods, procedures and personnel employed to implement those policies and to achieve those objectives.

The objectives of the analysis are as follows:

1 Know where we are now.
2 Understand our own strengths and weaknesses.
3 Appreciate what opportunities and threats exist.
4 Determine whether we can improve our existing business by rectifying weaknesses and capitalizing on strengths, taking advantage of opportunities and preparing for threats.

The remedies that are taken will depend on what the organization believes and understands to be effective for its particular business.

In their new book McKinsey consultants John Hagel III and Marc Singer (*Net Worth*, Harvard Business Press, 1999) argue that different firms have a different economic logic. There are customer relationship businesses, which focus on building and maintaining relationships with customers. There are infrastructure management businesses, which focus on managing assets such as factories to minimize costs and maximize revenues where economies of scale are vital. There are product innovation and commercialization businesses, where the focus is innovation and where being first is the essence.

Transaction marketing with its short time focus on immediate sales is being questioned as companies are now beginning to understand that it costs more to acquire a new customer than it does to keep an old one.

Activity based costing, in which all the activities directed at acquiring and maintaining a customer are separately costed, makes this distinction clear. Heskett introduced the concept of market economies, by which he means achieving results by understanding the customers instead of by concentrating on developing scale economies. Reichald gives an example of this: 'At MBNA (in the credit card business in the USA), a 5 per cent increase in retention grows the company's profit by 60 per cent by the fifth year' (Christian Gronroos, MCB University Press, *From Marketing to Relationship Marketing – towards a paradigm shift in marketing*). The questions that businesses must now ask are the following:

1 Which customers do I want to do business with?
2 With which ones can I make a profit?
3 How do I protect my profit?
4 Which tasks am I going to carry out myself and which ones will I outsource or work with a business partner?

The marketing mix is recognized as having limitations especially in service sectors where work systems have to be more directly responsive to customers, and non-routine decision making has to be given to front-line staff in order to maintain flexibility.

Service, quality and the management of costs are key strategic issues on which to establish competitiveness and maintain differentiation in the market place.

Matching business strategies, employee role behaviour and HRM policies

Human resource strategy involves deciding on the way in which the people in the organization are managed. These ideas are then translated into policies and procedures that are integrated with the business strategy. Porter (1974) defines three generic business strategies – and each generic strategy implies different skills and requirements for success. These would translate into different organizational structures and cultures. Schuler and Jackson summarize (1987) these approaches below:

Environment
Human Resource strategy also needs to be placed within the context of the external environment, and display an understanding of what is happening within the macro- and micro-environments. It also needs to be considered in relation to situational factors within the organization. Figure 3.9 illustrates this process.

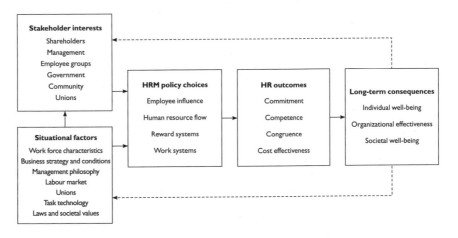

Figure 3.9
The Harvard Framework for human resource management. *Managing Human Assets* by Michael Beer, Bert Spector, Paul R. Lawrence, D. Quinn Mills, Richard E. Walton. The Free Press, 1984

Table 3.1 Business strategies, and associated employee role behaviour and HRM policies

Strategy	Employee role behaviour	HRM policies
1 Innovation	A high degree of creative behaviour	Jobs that require close interaction and coordination among groups of individuals
	Long-term focus	Performance appraisals that are more likely to reflect longer-term and group-based achievements
	A relatively high level of cooperative, interdependent behaviour	Jobs that allow employees to develop skills that can be used in other positions in the firm
		Compensation systems that emphasize internal equity rather than external or market-based equity
	A moderate concern for quality	Pay rates that tend to be low, but that allow employees to be stockholders and have more freedom to choose the mix of components that make up their pay package
	A moderate concern for quantity; and equal degree of concern for processes and results	Broad career paths to reinforce the development of a broad range of skills
	A greater degree of risk-taking; a higher tolerance of ambiguity and unpredictability	
2 Quality enhancement	Relatively repetitive and predictable behaviours	Relatively fixed and explicit job descriptions
	A more long-term or intermediate focus	High levels of employee participation in decisions relevant to immediate work conditions and the job itself
	A moderate amount of cooperative, interdependent behaviour	A mix of individual and group criteria for performance appraisal that is mostly short term and result oriented
	A high concern for quality	A relatively egalitarian treatment of employees and some guarantees of employment security
	A modest concern for quantity of output	Extensive and continuous training and development of employees
	High concern for process; low risk-taking activity; commitment to the goals of the organization	
3 Cost reduction	Relatively repetitive and predictable behaviour	Relatively fixed and explicit job descriptions that allow little room for ambiguity
	A rather short-term focus	Narrowly designed jobs and narrowly defined career paths that encourage specialization, expertise and efficiency
	Primarily autonomous or individual activity	Short-term results-oriented performance appraisals
	Modern concern for quality	Close monitoring of market pay levels for use in making compensation decisions
	High concern for quantity of output	Minimal levels of employee training and development
	Primary concern for results; low risk-taking activity; relatively high degree of comfort with stability	

Following on from the analysis of the organization's strength and weaknesses using a combination of the marketing audit, customer care audit and EFQM excellence model, the organization would think about its human resource policies in relation to its competitive positioning and its core competencies (core competencies are covered in Unit 4).

The organization would then consider its guiding philosophy and structure and then decide on the relevant techniques to stimulate customer-focused behaviour.

Before discussing these philosophies and techniques we will first need to place the development of management ideas into an historical context.

Historical development of ideas – the search for quality
Since the early days of industrialization and mass production there has been a struggle between making the most of mechanized production and technology and creating jobs which enrich human experience.

Economic pressure and the culture in which we live have allowed technology and machines to dominate at work, so that very many workers have no opportunity to use all their abilities and gain very little satisfaction from their work. However, the growth of service industries is forcing businesses to look at the way in which they have been influenced by the ideas of organizing labour in mechanized production, and to rethink and create new ways of dealing with people at work and of improving quality.

Customer satisfaction
The determining of strategy, especially a competitive one, requires an understanding of what customers value, or might value, and at what price. Costs, quality and price are inextricably linked. Quality is the means by which a firm sustains its position among competing offers over time and it is quality that gains uniqueness and value in the eyes of the customer.

In an increasingly competitive world, the distinguishing factor between organizations is often the service they provide for their customers or clients. This not only affects retail and sales outlets, but every aspect of industry and institutional life. All members of an organization, not only staff in direct contact with customers, have a part to play in improving standards of quality.

Organizational efficiency
The question of creating organizational efficiency can be considered in different ways as this brief history shows.

We often talk about organizations as if they were machines – efficient, reliable and predictable. But they are not, and with the development on the emphasis of service and relationships within the area of business, it would be foolish to think they are.

Until the nineteenth century craftspeople understood and carried out their tasks in different environments, but with the industrial revolution there was an increasing trend towards bureaucratization and routinization of life generally. The diversity, complexity and size of operations meant that tasks were splintered and knowledge was channelled into specific tasks – to match the efficiency of machines and maximize profits. Changes were made to the design and control of work so that people no longer organized their own work, and the discretion of the workers was reduced in favour of control by their machines and supervisors. The whole shift was to take responsibility for the organization of work, from the worker, to the managers, who would do all the thinking and then train the worker to do it effectively; workers would then be monitored.

The most famous of these management gurus was Taylor (1856–1917) and he was fond of telling his workers 'You are not supposed to think – there are other people paid for thinking around here'. This method of working splits the worker and separates the hand from the brain. What was lost was the idea that people have a natural ability to work and manage their own resources, that hand and brain are able to work together and should be encouraged to do so. The whole thrust of many of the management theories of the time was that organizations can and should be rational, efficient systems – little attention was given to the human aspects.

Organizations where people are treated as machines have the following limitations (Gareth Morgan, *Images of Organizations*, Sage):

- They have difficulty adapting.
- Workers are forced into mindless unquestioning attitudes.
- Personal interests take precedence over organizational goals.
- They can have a detrimental effect on the workforce, especially those in the lower levels of the hierarchy.

However, if the work environment is stable, the task simple and repetitive precision is required, a mechanistic approach can work efficiently – provided that the human machine parts are willing to do as they are told. Management must also live with the consequences. There are some organizations where knowledge and process skill is protected and delivered successfully as these examples show but in different ways!

Asda
Archie Norman, chairman of Asda, believes that good relations with customers depend on good relations with employees. In his business he says 'it means bringing back those old craft skills to which we can all relate and which are fulfilling and are challenging. Being a master baker is a really difficult thing – colleagues are entitled to enrich themselves in their work and to make it more interesting and varied' Director, Annual Convention 1998.

McDonald's – developing and transferring best practices
Jonathan D. Day and James C. Wendler (1998) Best practice and beyond: knowledge strategies, *The McKinsey Quarterly*, **1**, 19–25, http://www.mckinseyquarterly.com

In many service industries, the ability to identify best practices and spread them across a dispersed network of locations is a key driver of value. Such a strategy can create powerful brands that are continually refreshed as knowledge about how to serve customers better travels across the network. In these circumstances, it may be all but impossible to tell whether value has been created by the brand or by knowledge. The two are inseparable. How much does McDonald's brand depend on, say, network-wide knowledge of how best to cook French fries?

The thoroughness of McDonald's best practice approach is legendary. By the time restaurant managers attend Hamburger University in Illinois, they will have received between 1500 and 3000 hours of regional training.

The company also gets comparable outlets to work together to benchmark performance, set aspirations, and make product mix and service decisions. These peer groups are supported by a real-time information system that transmits sales to headquarters hourly. Thanks to this system, the location of group members is immaterial; one group could include branches in Warsaw and Rio de Janeiro. At the same time, the system enables corporate headquarters to keep a tight grip on the valuable knowledge that links its outlets.

However, McDonald's is pursuing an essentially centralist model in which the corporation defines rigid standards not only for its products but for the processes that deliver them. The company's recent squabbles with franchisees over the introduction of the Arch Deluxe product and the 55 cent sandwich promotion illustrates the degree to which this formula can conflict with entrepreneurialism. Recent moves suggest that McDonald's may devolve more decision making to franchisees and seek to learn more from them, particularly about new business development.

Traditional wisdom maintained that knowledge is held implicitly in the management role and tasks such as analysing, planning and organizing, controlling output and measuring effectiveness can only be done by managers. Current thinking, with its emphasis on relationship management and empowerment places many of these tasks at the front line. Isabel Menzies Lythe says 'rather like a football team – the manager is not on the field passing the ball, the captain and the team are. However, time framework is an important decider. Traditional management relates to a different time framework. The football team has to do it now'.

Many franchising systems have used the Tayloristic approach, and scientific methods to determine how work should be performed with manuals that set standards providing a recipe for success, provided the service or product can be controlled in this way. Surgical wards, courier firms, organizations in which precision, safety and clear accountability are at a premium, are often able to implement mechanistic approaches successfully, at least in certain aspects of their operations (Gareth Morgan).

However, when circumstances keep changing and flexibility and creativity are valued, a different type of response will be needed. Standardized procedures and bureaucratic hierarchies are not the best way to deal with an environment that is constantly changing and where responsiveness is valued.

Taylor's scientific management came under criticism and the Human Relations School suggested that workers should be involved in decision making and could carry out work without close supervision because they could become self-motivated.

The 1960s brought job enrichment, the 1970s an interest in industrial democracy and legislative backing (though not in the UK) and the 1980s emphasized quality circles, team briefing and profit sharing. The 1980s also heralded the dawn of the enterprise culture and theorists such as Peters encouraged businesses to involve everyone in everything and to lead by empowering people. *In Search of Excellence* (Peters and Waterman, 1982) emphasized autonomy and entrepreneurship and he told managers to trust and involve employees. The end of hierarchy was heralded; delayering and decentralization became the thing to do. In the meantime an interest in the Japanese Kaizen, and total quality management approach introduced ideas of bottom-up identification of problems and TQM began to empower by delegating aspects of the managerial role to employees and giving them responsibility for quality control. Managers became facilitators, team work and participation were encouraged. Responsibility and accountability were delegated and pride, job satisfaction and quality were said to improve.

Human resource management now stands between a range of options that have been developed over the years. Risk strategies control the worker to perform and strategies encourage the worker through a process of self-engagement and development to meet with the customer at both a functional and feeling level to provide superior service and create customer delight. Continuous relationship marketing (where applicable) seeks to embed these relationships so they are ongoing.

The challenge to increase productivity, lower costs and improve quality within a global framework of increased competition needs a workforce who can enable an organization to differentiate on quality and add value by providing superior service. Organizations if they choose to go along this route will need to build organizational cultures that are flexible, built on trust, cooperation and a commitment to organizational goals. Organizations that follow another model can choose to minimize costs by exploiting insecurity over employment so that the balance of power lies within the hands of the managers and changes to working practices can be more easily implemented. Other approaches could include:

- Lowering wages in order to become more competitive.
- Laying staff off.
- Speeding up work processes.

- Investing in technology so as to increase output and reduce labour costs.
- Relocating plant to a country where wages are low, labour unorganized and passive and workplace standards low (and leave the government and local community in the home country to pick up the pieces).
- Rewarding employees so what they earn is related to output (piecework, speeding up the assembly line, profit share or share ownership).
- Introducing a market model into the workplace so people in the same organization are pitted against each other.

Atkinson's flexible firm model provides a dual labour market approach with the distinction between 'core' (primary) and 'peripheral' (secondary) groups of workers. These ideas have been challenged on ideological and empirical grounds (Williams, 1993). But the fact remains – if you are a core worker with the relevant skills and knowledge and are in high demand, life may be good. Peripheral workers will face a life that is less secure.

There are a number of strategic themes that run through the various approaches used by organizations to create customer-focused behaviour. Many are interlinked and organizations will choose and use what they need in order to fulfil their objectives.

They include:

- Philosophies:
  - Vision and leadership;
  - Culture;
  - Kaizen;
  - Total quality management (TQM);
  - The marketing philosophy that puts customer needs at the heart of the business is not discussed here;
  - The learning organization;
  - Relationship marketing (see Unit 8 Relationship marketing).
- Structure:
  - Business process re-engineering (BPR);
  - Value chain;
  - Customer activity cycle.
- Techniques:
  - Benchmarking;
  - ISO 9000;
  - Just-in-time production and distribution systems;
  - Investors in People (IIP);
  - Flexibility;
  - 360° feedback systems;
  - Self-directed teams;
  - MBO – see Unit 4;
  - Employee empowerment;
  - Time-based competition, lean production/lean enterprise, and activity-based cost management.

Most of these ideas are discussed in the remainder of this unit, but it is important to understand that although some are applicable to all organizations, others may not be suitable in another. Many organizations have more than one initiative running at a time. The organization decides on its core competencies, its philosophy and then uses the most suitable measurements and technique to ensure that it is achieving relevant results. Organizational structure, the role of the manager and many other aspects of organizational life are contextual. Do not be lulled into uncritically accepting what you read.

Philosophy

Vision and leadership

As you can see from Figure 3.22 at the end of the unit the role of the leader is key to creating any organization. The leader chooses markets, decides on roles (which are then structured), decides on the systems throughout the organization and recruits people. This then begins to create the culture. The vision the leader has of the organization, and which stakeholders then carry in their minds, will provide a guiding sense of the organizational purpose. We only need to think of the Body Shop and Virgin, for example, to understand how such vision has entered our culture and can embody certain values both in society and in the people who work for these organizations.

Culture

Organizational culture can be broadly thought of as the way in which people working within an organization learn to cope with adapting to their environment. This includes the problems that arise from the external environment and also the way in which the organization integrates its activities internally. New members of the organization are taught that the way in which the organization operates is correct. In a customer-focused organization people come to believe that meeting customer needs is essential. Culture is a learned product of group experience and is discovered, invented and developed by members of the organization as it develops over time. One of the tasks of leadership is to create and also manage culture. Any change in culture needs to be led by management. The recruitment, induction, appraisal and reward systems support it.

Culture is therefore a product of:

- The context – macro- (PEST factors) and micro- (markets, competitors, customers, suppliers, distributors, stakeholders) environments.
- The structures and functions found within an organization – for example, a centralized organization will have a different culture from a decentralized one, marketing has a different culture from sales, finance and production and so on.
- People's attitudes to their work and the individual and occupational role defences developed by them to protect them from undue stress.
- The individual's psychological contract with the organization – people are attracted to jobs which fit their personalities, in which they can implement their self-concepts and from which they can obtain the outcomes they desire, both conscious and unconscious. Individuals are in a process of self-selection when they choose an organization and organizations tend to choose people who mirror their own self-concepts.
- Leadership – leaders choose markets, they structure organizations, recruit staff and act as behavioural models for employees to follow. They organize the adaptation to the external environment and internal integration.

Marketing creates some of the symbols of culture:

- Corporate image.
- Promotional material and branding.
- Customer philosophy, market orientation, strategic thinking, marketing research belief in planning and evaluation.
- An understanding that marketing activities need to be carried out within the context of the wider social/cultural environment and as such reflect its concerns.

Marketing also guides the organization on its external adaptation – its strategy and marketing mix; and internal integration – structure, systems and design of the value chain necessary to meet customer needs and value chain, and create a competitive advantage.

Culture is an important ingredient in the service delivery process. It is 'the way we do things around here'. The following points outline what customers expect from a service-oriented culture:

- No buck passing, people are responsible and flexible.
- It is an open, non-defensive culture in which people can admit mistakes.
- You can expect the same level of service from everyone in the organization; employees know what standards they are working to.

- Common values and beliefs underline the attitudes of employees.
- Customers are asked how they feel and their feelings are acted upon.
- Managers are exhibiting the behaviour they wish others to follow.
- Employees are friendly to the customers and make them feel welcome.

Kaizen

Kaizen is a system of business thinking and behaviour developed by the Japanese and is based on ten principles (Patricia Wellington, 1996, *Kaizen Strategies for Customer Care*, Pitman Publishing):

1 *Focus on customers.* It is everyone's responsibility in the company to meet customer needs.
2 *Make improvement continuously.* A Kaizen company always looks for improvements. Once found they are built into the formal performance standards immediately.
3 *Acknowledge problems openly.* Problems can only be dealt with in the open if the organization fosters a supportive, constructive, non-confrontational and non-recriminatory culture.
4 *Promote openess.* As Patricia Wellington says, there tends to be less functional compartmentalization or ringfencing in a Kaizen company than in a Western counterpart. Similarly working areas are more open plan in Japan (only the most senior executives will have individual offices), the usual symbols of rank or status are rarely seen and communality is favoured – all of which reinforce leadership visibility and communication.
5 *Create work teams.* All employees belong to a work team and are managed by a team leader. They also belong to a year group (people who joined at the same time), a quality circle and cross-functional teams. This draws people into the life of the organization.
6 *Manage projects through cross functional teams.*
7 *Nurture the right relationship process.* They look for harmony.
8 *Expect employees to develop self-discipline.*
9 *Inform every employee about what is going on.* This covers mission, culture, values, plans and practices. Employees are then given the skills and the opportunity to apply the information they have been given.
10 *Enable every employee.* Kaizen employees are empowered to influence materially their own and their organization's affairs. They encourage employees to multi skill, give access to data and budgets, and encourage decision making.

The difference between a Kaizen, a total quality management and an ordinary organization
The change from a conventional Western organizational model to a Kaizen one can be significant as Table 3.2 shows.

This model throws up a number of differences, how would you feel about them? And what sort of problems do you anticipate having at work in order to change the way in which the organization manages itself?

Many of the new western practices such as total quality management are based on Kaizen – other TQM programmes are called, as Patricia Wellington says, by many names:

- Continuous improvement;
- Working together;
- Our contribution counts;
- Total involvement;
- Focus on quality;
- Focus on customers;
- Putting customers first;
- 560 brands are better than one;
- Customer first;
- We all make the difference.

Table 3.2 Comparing Western culture and management to Kaizen. *Source:*
Patricia Wellington (1996) *Kaizen Strategies for Customer Care*, Pitman Publishing.

Western culture	→	*Kaizen culture*
Self	→	Team
Own department	→	Company
Immediate profit	→	Long-term gains
Short-term RoI	→	Market share
Stasis	→	Change
Making do	→	Continual improvement
Results	→	Process
Introspection	→	Customer satisfaction
Imposed discipline	→	Self-regulation
Annual appraisal	→	Continuous performance management
Proprietorial information	→	Information sharing
Them and us	→	Harmony
Rigidity	→	Flexibility
Western management		*Kaizen management*
Unitary leadership	→	Delegation Participation Consensus
Authoritarian decision making	→	Democratic decision approving
Support for and promotion of individual high fliers	→	Support for and promotion of teams
One-way communication	→	Two-way communication
Focus on implementation and outcomes	→	Focus on planning, preparation and process
Individual and territorial specialism	→	Cross-functional collaboration
Acceptance of certain margin of error and subsequent corrective action as the norm	→	Striving for continuous improvement to produce error-free outputs, and doing things right first time

Total quality management

The best-known quality management philosophy is total quality management (TQM) because it is concerned with all work processes and the way they can be improved to meet customers' needs more effectively.

The TQM approach involves the following:

1   Understanding what customers want.
2   Having detailed specification of what customers want and being able to deliver it to them.
3   Understanding and managing the processes of manufacture/service delivery so variation can be traced.
4   Keeping records so that it is possible to rectify the variables.

It is important to remember that when people want changes any quality system that only conforms to expectations could soon run out of steam. An organization can only maintain its differentiation if it constantly seeks to add value to what the customer says is important. The question is how to create a quality system that has the flexibility to constantly exceed expectations. However, Deming (one of the original quality gurus) said that formal performance measurement could actually produce bad quality because people who feel they are judged by others may not give of their best. He adds that measurement systems sometimes measure the wrong things.

The importance of quality has been reflected in the growth of TQM and the ability to think about organizations and their internal and external relationships as one system.

The core of TQM is the customer–supplier relationship, where the process must be managed. The 'soft' outcomes of TQM – culture, communications and commitment – provide the foundations of the TQM model. The process core must be surrounded by the 'hard' management necessities of systems, tools and teams.

In order to achieve this, attitudes to work and skills have to be changed so that the culture of the organization becomes one of preventing failure – doing the right things, first time, every time.

TQM means achieving total quality through management's ability in gaining everyone's commitment and involvement and ensuring that a continual effort is made towards improvement. This will result in a reduction of total costs as waste is avoided by eliminating errors, and value is added to what is being produced because actions are carried out which add value to the production process.

TQM involves training people to understand customer–supplier relationships (the role relationships), not buying on price alone, managing systems improvement, modern supervision and training, managing processes through teamwork and improved communication, elimination of barriers and fear, constant education and expert development, and a systematic approach to TQM implementation.

The role of marketing

The TQM process starts with marketing and forms part of the foundation framework. Marketing must take the lead in establishing the true requirements of a product or service. This must be communicated properly throughout the organization in the form of a specification. It also calls for market research and the ongoing assessment of customer satisfaction.

The main pillars of TQM are:

1 The foundation framework:
    (a) A customer focus;
    (b) Quality chains;
    (c) Quality design and conformance to design;
    (d) Process understanding;
    (e) Working together with suppliers and customers;
    (f) Leadership and commitment to TQM;
    (g) Empowerment.
2 A quality system.
3 The tools and the improvement cycle.
4 Organization and team work.
5 Implementation.

The learning organization

The creation of the learning organization is another philosophy enabling customer-focused behaviour and continuous improvement to take place. There are many different approaches to describing the characteristics of a learning organization. Pedlar, Burgoyne and Boydell (1991) identified eleven characteristics:

1 The formulation of strategy, implementation, evaluation and improvement are structured as in learning experiences. Feedback loops enable the organization to see how they can improve.
2 Participative policy making. Everyone is involved in creating policy, differences are aired and the participation process opens things out so that customers and supplies save involvement.
3 Informing technology is used to empower and inform employees.
4 Formative accounting and control. Accounting, budgeting and reporting systems are designed to assist learning.
5 Internal exchange. All internal units see themselves as customers and suppliers of each other.

6 The rewarding of flexibility.

7 Enabling structures. Roles need to be structured in relation to the needs of internal customers and suppliers so that personal growth and experimentation are encouraged.

8 Boundary workers as environmental scanners. Employees in contact with suppliers, customers and neighbours of the organization need to collect data and feed it back.

9 Inter-company learning. Employees join with customers and suppliers for training, job exchanges, research and development. Benchmarking is also used.

10 Learning climate. New ideas are tried out, everything is questioned, mistakes are allowed and the importance of continuous improvement is emphasized. Feedback is requested and acted upon.

11 Self development opportunities for all. Individual learning is encouraged at all levels – coaching, mentoring, counselling, peer support and feedback all support this.

Further reading Argyris (1992), *On Organizational Learning*, Blackwell Publishers.

Difficulties of implementation

People may need to be helped in dealing with the implementation of TQM and relationship marketing. The expansion of role and responsibility and the increased expectation that colleagues may have regarding their role as 'customers', may create additional stress within the organization. Increased contact with external customers may also create anxiety. 'Industrial intimacy' is not everyone's cup of tea.

Role development leads to a situation where people can be empowered to take authority for themselves. The concept of empowerment is fundamental to the development of TQM and relationship marketing and the ethos of the customer-centred organization. Good management should help and not hinder this process and managers may need to learn new skills as facilitators to enable people to take more responsibility for themselves.

Activity 3.1

1 Identify your internal customer–supplier chain so that you can look at your role and role relationships.

2 Write down the tasks you are expected to carry out. Think about the expectations other people have about the way you behave and carry out your work.

3 Now think about your own ideas about your own role. You may want to use your job description as a starting point.

4 When you have done this, concentrate on:

• What helps you to perform your role;
• What stops you from carrying out, or expanding your role.

Are these constraints external, or do they merely exist in your own mind? Have you developed any ways of protecting yourself from the anxiety or stress that comes from carrying out your role? Is the way you have protected yourself (by creating a role defence) stopping you from carrying out your work more effectively? Are the defences you are using the same as those used by everyone in the organization? What constraints are coming from the organization and the external environment.

5 Once you have carried out this exercise, think about how it made you feel. Did you feel comfortable or uncomfortable? How do you think your colleagues would feel if they carried out a similar exercise?

6 What effect is the way you perform your role having on the customer supply chain?

Management of sub-cultures and sentient systems

Many different cultures often co-exist in an organization. Some examples of sub-cultures would include:

- Managerial cultures.
- Occupationally-based cultures.
- Group cultures based on geographical proximity.
- Worker cultures based on shared hierarchical experiences.
- Unions.

These sub-groups very often have different objectives, different concepts about time, different ideas about what is important to them, different values, attitudes and beliefs about themselves, they often share secrets, and share cared for rooms and possessions. They are groups of people to which an individual feels they belong, to which loyalty is shown and in which they feel to some degree at home. These sub-cultures are also called sentient systems – groups that people invest feeling or sentiment in.

Leadership or management of any organization entails identifying its constituent task and sentient systems and understanding the relations between them. When a sentient system is threatened by change its defences will increase. Sometimes there is a conflict between a sub-culture and the objectives of the organization. For example, loyalty to a union can often outweigh loyalty to the organization itself.

These sentient groups exist within the organization and also extend outside it. For example, an organization may find an unexpected resistance to change coming from other stakeholders. Management has to manage the individual sentient groups, as well as the relationships between them, the overall organization and the outside groups that feel they have a relationship with the activities of the organization itself. Public relations and other methods of communication play a part in this by recognizing the interests of consumer and pressure groups and other 'relationships'. Other barriers to role change and organizational change are discussed throughout the book.

Intergroup behaviour

Groups feel and believe that they have a relationship with each other. Individuals tend to idealize the groups that are important to them. Very often this means suppressing less satisfactory aspects. Some groups may be treated with suspicion, others are treated neutrally. Individuals in the group build up pictures of other groups from hearsay, guesswork and projected aspects of their own minds. When the task systems of different groups have different priorities, groups may find that they are at odds with each other.

Envy

The success of one department may not always be encouraged or supported by another that is less successful. This envy operates like a hidden spanner in the works. It can manifest itself by active sabotage or by actively (or unconsciously) withholding necessary cooperation.

The effective group is one that is in contact with reality and knows the boundary between what is inside the group and what is outside it. Individuals also need to know the boundaries between themselves and the outside world. In the same way that individuals use projection as a defence against anxiety, so do groups.

Application

The marketing concept tries to blend everything in the organization towards meeting customers' needs. However, other departments can sometimes put more importance on their own tasks. An understanding of their priorities will help marketing go some way to understanding their internal customers a little more.

Table 3.3 Interdepartmental conflicts. Adapted from Kotler (1980), *Principles of Marketing*, Prentice Hall International Inc.

Research and development wants	*Marketing wants*
• Product quality • Research for its own sake • Plenty of time in which to develop their ideas	• Customer perceptions to lead the definition of quality • Ideas that can be applied • Products that have features that add value to them and differentiate them from their competitors
Manufacturing wants	*Marketing wants*
• Plenty of time • Long runs • Only a few models • Orders that are standard • Average quality control • Few changes	• Short lead times • Short runs • A variety of models • Custom made orders • Tight quality control • Changes made when they need them
Finance, accounting and credit wants	*Marketing wants*
• Standard transactions • Few standard reports • Fixed budgets • Pricing to cover costs • Low credit risks • Controlled and tough credit terms • Strict procedure for collecting money • Strict reasons for spending • Full financial disclosure by customers	• Special terms and discounts to suit different customers' needs • Many reports tailored for specific information needs • Flexible budgets so plans can be changed to suit developments in the market place • Prices that will help them to develop the market • Easy terms of credit • Methods of examining credit that will not upset customers • Procedures for collecting money that will not upset customers
Purchasing and inventory wants	*Marketing wants*
• Narrow product lines • Standard parts • Material that is bought on price, not necessarily quality • Lot sizes that are economical • Purchasing at infrequent intervals	• Broad product lines so that customers can have variety and products can be delivered that will suit each customers' needs • Non-standard parts • Material that will meet customers perceptions of quality and add value to the product • Large lot sizes and a high level of stock so that nothing runs out • Purchasing that can be carried out in relation to customers' needs

---

Activity 3.2

1 What interdepartmental barriers or conflicts exist in your own organization?
2 Which of these impact specifically on the marketing department?
3 How do they affect your ability to satisfy your external customers' needs?
4 What do you do to help other departments understand customers' needs in order to help things go more smoothly?

John Macdonald (TQM, does it always work? Some reasons for disappointment, *Managing Service Quality*, **6**(5), www.emerald-library.com) says that many companies have been disappointed with the results of their drive for quality improvement. He outlines the principal reasons for disappointment. These are:

1 Lack of management commitment, all talk and no action.
2 Lack of vision and planning-people apparently become 'born again' quality managers and this clouds their vision.

79

3 Satisfaction with the quick fix – the quick fix mentality dashes off and puts in quality circles, customer care programmes and empowers the people. As John Macdonald says, 'each of these approaches is valid and can be powerful contributors to an overall process, but only if the operating environment is conductive to their success'.
4 The process becomes tool bound – people become so involved in collecting statistics they have no time to do the real work.
5 Quality is too constraining – TQM addresses the whole organization and the way in which it is organized. Managers do not see it as a strategic imperative but delegate it to a department.
6 Complacency with customer satisfaction – Macdonald gives the example of IBM who was so concerned about customer surveys on product and service quality and satisfaction they missed out that customers wanted something else – small computers.
7 Culture change versus project approach – Macdonald points out that it is important to take a whole view approach.
8 Quality management institutionalized – people who initiate TQM as a process to achieve continuous improvement should not remain responsible for it. It should subsequently be absorbed by the whole organization.
9 People do not really get involved.
10 Lack of real business manageables – aspects of the TQM process not being measured in a meaningful way.

Structure

From an everyday point of view the way in which an organization develops is mainly determined by the product it produces and the technology it uses. But from a psychological point of view the culture, the structure and the way in which it functions are determined by the psychological needs of the management and staff.

In a customer-centred organization the way in which the organization structures itself should be determined by the needs of customers and the market in which it operates. Creating this balance between two needs – those of customers and those of employees is the challenge organizations now face.

There is no one way to structure an organization but structure and strategy influences the way in which people work and also the way in which they are managed. Human beings are the product of social structures but they may also form them. Flatter structures have advantages as decisions are taken more quickly and performance can be more related to rewards. Organizations that are very large tend to behave more slowly and can demotivate people who are in contact with customers and so work within a different time framework of flexibility and quick decision making. It is not that certain types of structures are wrong; it is the way people behave in them.

Structure and hierarchy
(Adapted from E. Jacques, *In Praise of Hierarchy*)

It is important to remember that hierarchies exist internally to:

- Separate out jobs that have different complexity.
- Separate out jobs that have different types of mental activity.
- Ensure that people are accountable for what they do.
- Add real value to work as it moves through the organization through the various layers.
- Provide a structure in which evaluation and coaching are done by people who are genuinely perceived as being above those they evaluate and coach.

Without these factors in mind over-layering can create difficulties like too much passing of problems up and down, bypassing, poor task setting, frustrated subordinates, anxious managers, inadequate performance appraisals and personality problems.

In trying to create flatter structures and give employees that face the customer more responsibility managers need to understand that people will have to be able to do the following:

- Carry out more complex jobs and use different types of mental activity.
- Become more personally responsible and accountable and manage themselves.
- Create real value to their jobs rather than passing it up the hierarchy.
- Work in different frameworks of time.

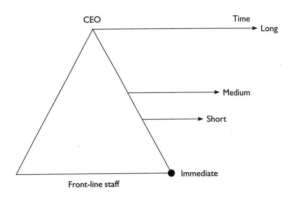

Figure 3.10

In a flatter structure senior managers will be responsible for coaching, training and evaluation. There will be less promotion, giving employees a sense of not knowing where their career will lead to next, and senior managers will become much closer to the customer.

This means that organizations adopting flatter structures will have to think about the following:

- Creating a learning organization that grows and empowers its own staff and develops and multiskills people to take on a variety of roles.
- Ensuring that people take professional exams, go on secondments and carry out on-the-job training.
- Encouraging people to manage their own career portfolios, to develop wider portfolios and also to get experience in outside roles, for example with charities, when the organization itself is not in a position to help the person get that experience (people need more than one group, one 'organizational basket', so to speak, to identify with – obviously there needs to be a balance in terms of prioritizing individual needs and organizational need).
- Making sure that its bonus structures are geared to multi-skilling and not managerial grades and that the acquisition of new skills is rewarded.

Structure is the extension of culture. It is merely a working relationship that has arisen out of the idea of how an organization should be organized in the process of adaptation to the external environment and internal integration. It is as much a construction as it is a symbolic form. Take, for example, a management organization where the belief is that the managers are the sole depositaries of decision making. The form arises from the ideas leaders have about themselves and about other people. It is important that the culture and the structure that it produces can respond to the needs of the customers and the market, and at the same time take into account the hierarchical systems within the organization that allow it to function effectively within different frameworks of time and complexity.

81

Organizations can be structured by function, product, territory or market sector and customer segment. There is no one best method. Formal structures are also influenced by the:

- Size of the business.
- Location of the business.
- Type of staff, abilities and skills.
- Age of the organization.
- Type of technology.
- Type of market – stable or unstable.
- Current fashion in managerial thinking – downsizing, flatter structures, matrix organization etc.
- Leader and managerial cultures – see Charles Handy, *Gods of Management* – Apollo, Zeus, Dionysus and Athena.

Business process re-engineering (BPR)

BPR is a method that strips away the hierarchical structure of a company and looks at the way in which processes flow. The company then allows the new processes to define how it should be structured. Michael Hammer, co-author of *Re-engineering the Corporation and the Re-engineering Revolution* is among the acknowledged experts of process re-engineering. On the Booz Allen & Hamilton website (www.strategy-business.com/casestudy) you can read about a case study that Dr Hammer carried out at GTE Telephone Operations.

Value chain

Porter (1985) introduced the value chain as a way of breaking down strategically relevant activities in order to understand the behaviour of costs and the sources of differentiation as alternative approaches to securing competitive advantage.

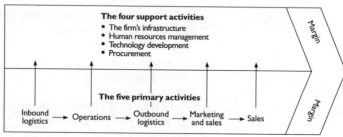

Figure 3.11

Source: Adapted from Porter, M. E. (1985), *Competitive Advantage*

The traditional value chain starts with the company and moves to the customers. The customer-centred value chain begins with the customer so that customer priorities drive the business.

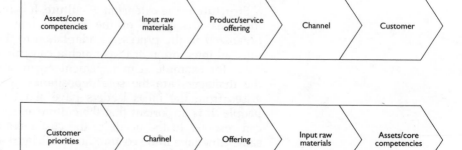

Figure 3.12
Traditional value chain

Figure 3.13
The customer-centred value chain

This can be extended further to look like Figure 3.14.

The value chain of the organization should be designed to meet the customers value-chain.

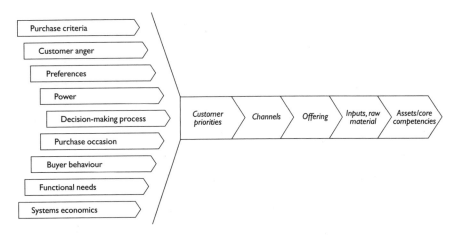

Figure 3.14
The modern value chain. *Source*: Slywotzky and Morrison, *The Profit Zone*, Times Books

Cross-functional work flows

If you were working on your own there would be no need for any structure or functional differentiation within your organization because the whole organization would be integrated into your head. However, once an organization grows, controls come in and work then has to be integrated between people and across departments. When one person's activities are not matched with another person's needs there is a quality gap. These gaps can occur between departments and within departments and contributes to increasing costs, delays, and quality failures along the firm's value chain.

If tasks are put on a flow chart, these links or gaps can be studied and can give organizations a real opportunity to improve their quality. By carefully defining the way in which customers use what the organization is offering, modifications can be made within the firm in terms of designing jobs, working environments, word processors and training, to name a few areas.

The customer activity cycle (CAC)

In her book, *The Eleventh Commandment* (John Wiley and Sons, 1996), Sandra Vandermerwe says that the transformation to 'owning customers' (customer loyalty) is more important than restructuring of the organization into new neat categories. She feels that no amount of traditional restructuring will lead to the fundamental deep changes in mindset that will lead to the notion of 'owning customers'. This involves boundaryless-ness and an active sharing of ideas.

This statement of hers is quite true. However, rather like the difficulties encountered in TQM, readers are pointed to acquiring a real under-standing of role, role defences and institutionalized organizational defences (these topics are discussed elsewhere in this book).

She mentions Paul Allaire, CFO of Rank Xerox as saying, 'there is a formal structure and then there's the way the company really works. You have to change the way it really works'. Vandermerwe warns against restructuring at the start of a customer transformation process as it takes energy and resources at a crucial time.

Building new processes involves:

- Identifying what you do now and how you can do it better by understanding what your customer wants – start from the customer activity cycle (see below) and work backwards. Imagine you are starting from scratch, and don't graft improvements onto existing processes.

- Learning how to improve on an ongoing basis and build in new processes all the time.
- Involving people who are in contact with customers as early as possible and letting them tell you how to do it differently.
- Looking at key request areas and ensuring that people are really doing what they were employed to do in the first place.
- Helping people identify what they need to do differently on an ongoing basis.

Sandra Vandermerve's methodology provides a general framework which begins with end-users. The CAC methodology serves different purposes:

1 People see the difference between what they have been doing and what is now needed.
2 As an educational tool, it forces people into the customer's space and provides a common view and tool to see what customer value really means and what it would take to add to this.

Figure 3.15
The customer activity cycle (CAC) tool

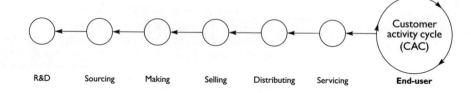

Figure 3.16
The CAC as the starting point for creating value internally

The Customer Activity Cycle (CAC) Tool

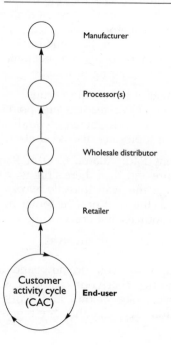

Figure 3.17
The CAC as the starting point for creating value externally

Example
This is the basic model used to analyse the CAC cycle for Citibank

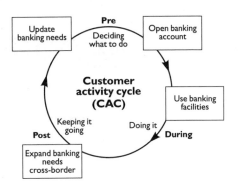

Figure 3.18
Customer activity cycle: Citibank global customer (simplified)

Figure 3.19 shows some of the value adds Citibank has developed at each of these critical points.

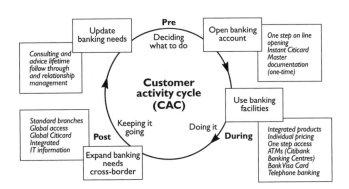

Figure 3.19
Value adds on customer activity cycle: Citibank (simplified)

The Fishbone or Ishikowa diagram
The fishbone structures work processes by mapping all the problem cause and effect relationships into a simple diagram. It can be used for analysing problems and for finding solutions.

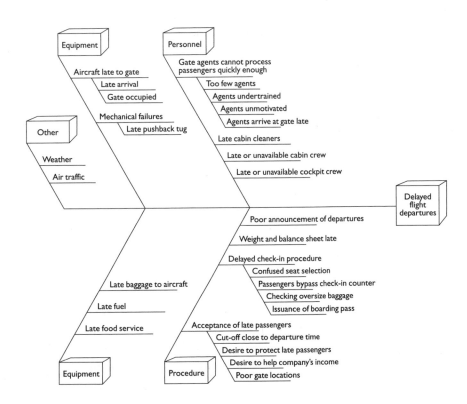

Figure 3.20
Causes of flight departure delays.
Source: Wyckhoff, D. (1984) *New tools for achieving service quality*

Once the system of service delivery is understood standards can be set and the service monitored. Standards need to be looked at in terms of the pre-transaction, the transaction and the post-transaction demand.

Techniques

Benchmarking

Benchmarking is an analytical process organizations use in order to compare their performance with that of their competitors. It is used to:

- Identify key performance measures for each business function.
- Measure the organizational performance as well as that of competitors.
- Identify areas of competitive advantage/disadvantage by comparing respective performance levels.
- Improve key issues.

Benchmarking can be divided into five stages:

1 Determining what to benchmark.
2 Forming a benchmarking team.
3 Identifying benchmarking partners.
4 Collecting and analysing benchmarking information.
5 Taking action.

The features of service include intangibles and people-oriented factors which make quality improvement more elusive and difficult to achieve.

Services need to be analysed and benchmarked in the following ways:

Front-stage and back-stage operations: the back stage refers to the system which supports front-stage operations, including systems of decision support, physical support, and management support. The front stage is characterised by customer contacts.

Key elements of service operations: although front-stage and back-stage operations may differ in content, they are both intimately concerned with people, time, place, tangibles and intangibles in the service system. These five elements are interrelated and exert an overriding influence on customers' perception of the service quality of the entire system and should be the major concern of benchmarking.

1 People: 'people' refers to both customers and service providers. Their behaviour, appearance and attitude often influence the perception of service quality. Because of their close contact with customers during the entire servicing process, a service provider should be concerned with not only the results but also the service delivery process.
2 Time: this element concerns whether the time of service offering is convenient for customers; and whether a given waiting time is acceptable.
3 Place: such factors as the location, environment, décor, temperature, lighting, and atmosphere of the service environment.
4 Tangibles (physical evidence): goods provided in the service delivery. Goods are received during service transactions, e.g. meals in McDonald's restaurants and clothes in a department store. Tangibles include name cards, business brochures, server's dress and certificates used to support service transactions. As with place, the quality of these tangibles may be identified with service quality.
5 Intangibles: comprise the essential functions of service processes, for example, the diagnosis and treatment of patients in a hospital, the legal consultation in a lawyer's office, the teaching programmes in school, and purchase transactions in a department store.

These above five elements highlight the crucial matters that need to be investigated for quality improvement in service systems. Parasuraman et al. (1985) conducted an exploratory investigation and concluded that service quality comprised the following ten dimensions:

1 Reliability.
2 Responsiveness.
3 Competency.
4 Access.
5 Courtesy.
6 Communication.
7 Credibility.
8 Security.
9 Understanding.
10 Tangibles.

The quality level of a service is a function of the gap between a customer's expectations and the perceived service. Parasuraman et al. (1988) subsequently developed a quality measuring instrument SERVQUAL and reduced the ten dimensions into five factors: tangibles, reliability, responsiveness, assurance, and empathy.

Marketing quality assurance (MQA)
MQA is a third-party organization specializing in:

- Providing assessment services to organizations wishing to develop quality systems for their marketing, sales and customer service activities.
- Assessing companies in the service sector to the ISO 9000 series of quality systems standards. Developing third-party certification guidelines for specific areas, such as public relations (see Figure 3.21).

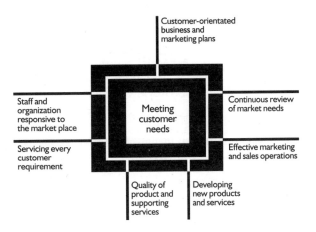

Figure 3.21

ISO 9000 series
The market need for accredited quality programmes increases. As Japanese manufacturing rose many Western companies became interested in quality management, and total quality management (TQM) as a philosophy for continually improving quality and getting the commitment of employees began to grab people's attention. As the interest in TQM grew the International Organization for Standardisation (ISO) developed an internationally recognized standard of quality management ISO 9000 (originally based on the British System BS 45750).

ISO 9000 is based on the idea of quality by inspection. It controls people's performance by controlling their activity. ISO starts with a view of the organization compared to a set of requirements and then decides that if the requirements are met they will have a beneficial impact on performance. Documentation of activities then becomes the method of monitoring performance. It is a method of control which ensures consistency of output. Critics of ISO 9000 say that because it starts from an attitude of control it demotivates, introduces bureaucratization and suboptimization of standards – people do what counts towards ISO not what doesn't. Critics believe that ISO 9000 reinforces the idea that work is divided into management and worker roles and that control is now maintained by adherence to procedures, budgets, targets and standards.

Evidence suggests that it adds to costs, makes customers unhappy and demoralizes staff, but most of all it prevents organizations taking opportunities to improve performance which they might otherwise have seen, 'blinding' them to the means for improvement.

Just-in-time production and distribution systems (JIT)

The ability to deliver defect-free components exactly when they are required provides the edge needed in this new competitive environment. For any supplier who can become an effective supplier to a JIT customer, the impact is significant – a possible single-source position in a long-term relationship in which the supplier is viewed as an extension of the customer's company.

Investors in people

According to Investors in People UK (the organization responsible for the administration of IIP) the standard

> provides a framework for improving business performance and competitiveness, through a planned approach to setting and communicating business objectives and developing people to meet these objectives. . . . [It] draws on the experience of some of the UK's most successful organizations both large and small [and] therefore provides a comprehensive benchmark of best practice against which an organization can audit its policies and practice in the development of people. (Investors in People UK, 1994)

Organizations achieve recognition through a process similar to that of BS EN ISO 9000, involving documentary and auditing assessment, in this case by their local Training Enterprise Council (TEC). The standard is based on the four key principles that an investor in people should:

1 Make a public commitment from the top to develop all employees to achieve its business objectives.
2 Review training and development needs of all employees.

Table 3.4 Comparison of traditional manufacturing operations to JIT systems

Elements	How the elements are viewed in:	
	A traditional manufacturing system	A JIT manufacturing system
Inventory	Seen as an asset. Insures against errors, late delivery	Seen as liability and indicates operational problems. Seen as unnecessary
Production steps	Set-up time is long and value is placed on maximum output	A critical goal is to reduce set-up time to the absolute minimum
Suppliers	Multiple sources of supply for 'protection' of relationships often adversial	Suppliers are partners and one or only a very few are used and incorporated into the quality standards
Quality	Toleration of small percentage of rejects and scrap	Quality expected to be 100 per cent
Equipment	Maintenance reactive; inventory kept and breakdowns occur	Maintenance proactive; strict maintenance schedules are followed and breakdowns are tolerated
Lead times	Long lead times are built in to compensate for problems	Short lead times
Workers	Managers control	Emphasis is on management by consensus; workers have a say and proprietary interest in the firm's operation

3 Take action to train and develop individuals on recruitment and throughout their employment.

4 Evaluate investment in training and development to assess achievement and improve future effectiveness.

In order to carry this out they will need a business and training plan. For further reading see Simon Down and David Smith (1998), It pays to be nice to people. Investors in People: the search for measurable benefits, *Personnel Review*, **27**(2), www.emerald-library.com

Employee empowerment

In the rapidly changing business world the process of defining strategies for the development of the workforce is becoming ever more important. One such strategy that is being used is the move from control to empowerment and learning.

Empowerment cannot be looked at on its own but needs to be seen as a way of introducing a new type of contract into the organization. Charles Handy talks about the psychological contract that individuals make when they join an organization. 'Empowerment' is the cornerstone for motivating people to take a new approach to their work so that the competitiveness of their organization can be maintained. Empowerment can be seen within the context of society and developing political and cultural values, and also within the context of what has been happening in businesses where a focus on cost-cutting and efficiency has resulted in downsizing and restructuring, and where the employment contract changed from loyalty and long service to an emphasis on knowledge and skills – multiskilling. This has resulted in a greater choice and freedom for some employees in the market place but it has also created an atmosphere of job insecurity and lack of trust.

Conger and Kanungo define empowerment as 'a process of enhancing feelings of self-efficacy among organizational members through the identification of conditions that foster powerlessness and through their removal by both formal organizational practices and informal techniques of providing efficacy information'.

Wellins proposes that an organization empowers people when it enables employees to take on more responsibility and to make use of what they know and can learn.

Randolph defines it as 'recognizing and releasing into the organization the power that people already have in their wealth of useful knowledge and internal motivation'.

Burke states 'to empower implies the granting of power – delegation of authority'.

Geroy, Wright and Anderson define empowerment as 'the process of providing employees with the necessary guidance and skills, to enable autonomous decision making (including accountability and the responsibility) for making these decisions within acceptable parameters, that are part of an organizational structure'.

Vogt defined empowerment as the act of giving people the opportunity to make workplace decisions by expanding their autonomy in decision making.

Empowerment can therefore be seen as a two-way process – as both coming from the organization and also enabling employees to make use of the power they already possess. It is also influenced by employees' perception as to whether they indeed feel empowered to take actions that they have defined and recognized as empowering, and which are also recognized externally by the organization and peer group.

Empowerment will therefore be situational and defined by the organization and the contextual environment. It will also be relative to what employees already have experience of and their ability to reach beyond self-limiting attitudes – some of whom may not want to.

The extent to which empowerment takes place within an organization will also relate to the overall structure of the organization and the way in which power is perceived and has been historically distributed.

Empowerment in a customer service environment

Cook and Macaulay (1997), Empowered customer service, *Empowerment in Organizations*, **5**(1), found at www.emerald-library.com gives the following example of empowerment.

A customer went into a food store to buy some ingredients for a special meal she was preparing that evening. On returning home from the store she discovered that the cream which she had just purchased was sour, although the sell-buy date on the packaging indicated it should still be fresh.

The customer telephoned the store and explained her predicament. She was too late to go back and still prepare the meal she had intended as the cream was a vital ingredient. The customer complained that the store should ensure in future that the cream was fresh.

Imagine the customer's surprise when, twenty minutes after telephoning, she opened the door to the member of staff who had answered her call. He had decided to make an apology in person on behalf of the store and also to bring the customer two replacement cartons of fresh cream so her dinner party could go ahead.

This is a true story and one which epitomizes empowered behaviour: an employee has the authority and takes the responsibility to do what is necessary to satisfy the customer.

Empowerment is a change-management tool which helps organizations create an environment where every individual can use their abilities and energies to satisfy the customer. It is a method of developing an environment where customers' needs and concerns are addressed and satisfied as quickly as possible at the point of customer contact. Staff are free to take opportunities to exceed customer expectations without referring upwards or fearing repercussions from their manager.

In an empowered company people share responsibility for problems and are proactive in their response to the customer. The customer recognizes empowerment through the way they are treated in the course of doing business with the organization and experiences its positive, proactive, innovative attitude through:

- The ability of employees to provide information and make decisions.
- The speed of problem resolution.
- An increase in creative new ideas and improvements.
- Standards being set and maintained by self-discipline, not centralized enforcement.
- Being dealt with by staff who listen actively and show willingness to understand the customer's point of view.
- Being greeted with enthusiasm and a positive attitude by members of staff.
- Seeing evidence of teamwork and the willingness of staff members to support each other to service the customer.

Empowerment, therefore, will be visible to the customers through employee behaviour, their attitudes and the values which underlie them. Examples of empowerment can be found across a wide range of organizations. At the AA, for example, customer interfacing staff are empowered to deal with members' complaints and difficulties in the best way they see fit. If, for example, a customer experiences a delay in the arrival of a patrol and the customer is a woman on her own, the call operator may suggest that she goes into the nearest café or restaurant and buys a meal at the AA's expense while waiting.

Characteristics of an empowered organization are:

- Shared vision and values.
- Customer-focused strategy.
- Leadership – where everyone has a chance to be leader in their areas of responsibility.

- Structure – where there are as few as possible layers between the organization and the customer, processes are simple and customer-focused and information is readily accessible.
- Teamwork.
- Learning – where opportunities are given to grow, mistakes can be acknowledged and managers do not pretend they know everything.

Mohammed Rafiq and Pervaiz K. Ahmed 1998, A customer-oriented framework for empowering service employees, *The Journal of Services Marketing*, **12**(5) say that the special nature of services, and in particular the simultaneity of production and consumption, is one of the major reasons that many services marketers argue that contact employees should be allowed a degree of discretion when dealing with customers. For instance, Grönroos (1990) argues that the interactive nature of services provides empowered employees with an opportunity to rectify mistakes and increase sales.

> Ideally, the front-line employee should have the authority to make prompt decisions. Otherwise, sales opportunities and opportunities to correct quality mistakes and avoid quality problems in these moments of truth are not used intelligently, and become truly wasted moments of opportunity to correct mistakes, recover critical situations and achieve re-sales and cross-sales. (Grönroos, 1990, p. 9)

However, other authors argue that service employees should have little or no discretion. For instance, Smith and Houston (1983) propose a 'script based' approach to managing customer and employee behaviour, to control behaviour and process compliance. That is, they envisage little or no room for participation by employees. Levitt (1972, 1976) forcefully argues for a 'production line' approach and the 'industrialization' of services if their productivity is to be improved. One of the key elements in this approach to services is that it leaves little room for discretion for service employees.

Mills (1995) argues that the degree of management control over service employees (or conversely the degree of employee empowerment) should depend on the structure of the service system. For low-contact, standardized services behaviour can be controlled by mechanistic means such as rules and regulations. For high-contact, highly divergent services (that is those requiring a high degree of customization) Mills (1985) suggests that employee self-management and peer-reference techniques are more successful. Even Grönroos (1990) recognizes that not all decision making can or should be decentralized as 'chaos may follow in an organization if strategic decisions, for example, concerning overall strategies, business missions and service concepts, are not made centrally' (Grönroos, 1990, p. 10).

The above suggests that the approach to participation is a contingent one.

Interestingly, the move towards empowerment is reflected in the increasing way that the government, with its use of focus groups, has become not so much a leader as a follower of group opinion. Similarly, the same process is reflected in organizations where empowerment and 360° appraisal now give those lower down the hierarchy some measure of control. The managing of change in political power in an organization needs to be thought through, otherwise lip service may be paid to new words that ultimately in practice have no meaning at all.

Flexibility

Many organizations are trying to build flexibility into their organizations. Flexibility can be looked at in a number of ways. Blyton and Morris (1992) concentrate on four key types of flexibility.

1 *Task or functional flexibility.* Where employees may be multi-skilled and involved in a wide range of tasks, with fewer boundaries between jobs. This type of flexibility encourages team working practice, and in its ultimate form removes the distinction between cost and operator jobs and tasks.

2 *Numerical flexibility.* Where the labour supply is made flexible by the use of different types of employment contracts and subcontracting.

3 *Temporal flexibility.* Where the number and timing of hours worked can be varied to meet organizational needs.

4 *Wage flexibility.* Where wages offered are individualized rather than standardized.

360° feedback systems

Simon Hurley (1998), Application of team-based 360° feedback systems, *Team Performance Management*, **4**(5) www.emerald-library.com, explains that the term '360° feedback' is actually a registered trademark of TEAMS, Inc, a company that did some pioneering work on the theory and its application (Edwards and Ewen, 1996). The term 360° appraisal can also be applied to a similar process; however, 360° feedback implies that not only is assessment performed, but the results are shared with the individual being assessed/rated (the ratee). Multi-rater assessments are used and information on an individual and their performance is gathered from more than one source or person. The individuals who perform the rating have some degree of familiarity with the person being rated – they know the ratee, interact with them frequently and are qualified to assess their performance. In most cases the ratings are multi-directional – they can come from the ratee's supervisors and co-workers (peer assessment), internal and external customers (customer assessment), and/or sub-ordinates (upward assessment). When used effectively, 360° feedback can improve leadership and management abilities, increase communication and learning and assist employee and organizational development, productivity and efficiency (Edwards and Ewen, 1996; Yukl and Lepsinger, 1995). When performed correctly, it is also efficient (about fifteen minutes per survey to complete), equitable, balanced, and participative (Edwards and Ewen, 1996).

Self-directed teams

Downsizing has stripped middle layers from business organizations. These positions, created as coordinating and integrating roles, have been lost where middle managers became defenders of functional perspectives and criteria. Now the operating core in many organizations is expected to produce with less supervisory coordination. Executives hope self-regulating teams are a solution to overheads and a mechanism to push accountability down, to focus decision making at the grass roots of the organization.

A self-directed work team is a structure in which members regulate their work around a relatively whole task. The team design is around a whole task of interdependent activities rather than individual jobs. Another characteristic is that the control of the task is located within the work group rather than externally to it. This allows the overall task integration and permits quick responses and flexibility to achieve goals.

What is known about self-directed work teams is an outgrowth of two basic premises about work. The first premise is that work groups accomplish tasks through a joint operating system, called a socio-technical system. Work performance requires both a technology made up of tools, techniques and methods, and a social structure which relates people to both technology and each other. The second premise is that effective groups must be open to influence from the environment and must maintain an environmental relationship to work so that they can improve. This requires learning the system properties needed to relate to an environment.

The following principles should be observed:

- *Responsibility.* If you want a system where the people assume responsibility, then people have to be involved responsibly in creating the work system.
- *Delegation.* Decisions must be made by the people involved. They decide the vision and management fixes as little as possible.
- *Solving problems.* Effective teams need to find out where things go wrong and to deal with problems themselves, not export them.

- *Clear goals and flexible strategies.* Employees need to know where they are going and be able to adapt.
- *Boundary location and control.* The consistent, social-technical message is that if there are supervisors, they manage the boundaries as a group resource, ensuring the group has adequate resources, coordinating activities with other groups and foreseeing coming changes. More and more these resource positions are disappearing as groups become more self regulating.
- *Information flow.* Teams need information for self-direction.
- *Goals, reward and support systems.* These need to be aligned and consistent.
- *Values, both design and human.* Design must address variation and meaning in work – continuous learning, involvement in decision making, help and support between colleagues, meaningful relationships between work and outside society and a desirable future in the organization.
- *Review.* Ongoing review and learning are necessary prerequisites to managing change.

Summary

This unit has covered an extensive range of issues which need to be considered in the context of developing a true customer orientation. There

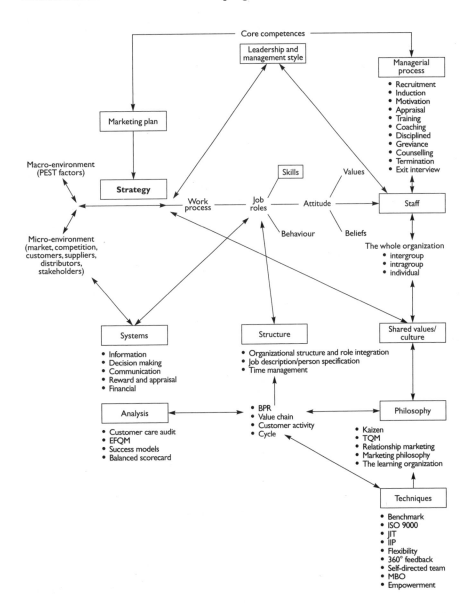

Figure 3.22

are downsides and upsides to all these methods and the balance and interest conflict between capital and labour, and the observation of it in organizational life, need to be considered. Conflict resulting in lack of competitiveness, low performance, low quality, and lack of motivation, loyalty and commitment is a problem with which most organizations are beset.

An understanding of role, role defences, institutionalized organizational defences and other unconscious processes enable us to understand what is going on. It takes skilled management and special skills to be able to work with them and create a new organizational reality.

Figure 3.22 illustrate the organization's relationship to the environment, not in terms of a marketing plan but in terms of how it organizes itself in relation to the market place in order to create a customer focus and illustrates how the philosophy, structure and techniques we have been discussing link into an overall framework.

As Charles Handy says leaders decide on markets, create roles, system, structure and recruit people. Once the people are in place culture is created. Culture is then both a product of the social and technical environment as it is of the organization, which in its process of adaptation, chooses to integrate its activities in a specific way.

In the following unit we will consider additional managerial techniques to mobilize performance.

Additional techniques for mobilizing performance

❑ To understand core competencies and relate them to culture, recruitment, training and development, appraisal, reward and recognition.

❑ Think about motivation, empowerment and the setting of objectives.

❑ To be able to reflect on job design for front-line customers and reflect on the balance between decision autonomy versus standardization of response.

❑ Understand and criticize the use of internal service level agreements.

Study Guide

A customer centric organization aligns all aspects of the organization with the customer's needs and expectations. Business success is customer satisfaction and customer referrals. In order to maximize the corporate benefits from the organization/customer interface information competence must be identified. Recruitment, performance management, training and development, and rewards and recognition are the four pillars of human resource strategy. You will also learn about motivation and accountability and internal service level agreement. The recruitment process is covered in the Effective Management for Marketing module.

Marketing working with HR

An article in *People Management*, 13 August 1998, which draws on the ideas of David Ulrich, the world's foremost thinker on people management, says that Ulrich uses concepts from marketing to draw a more direct link between the competitiveness of companies and their HR policies.

The objective of any business is to build a brand that customers are loyal to – because they think of you as delivering high quality, keen prices, good design or whatever. But increasingly, he says, brands are becoming focused not on individual products or services (which change so fast), but on firms themselves. At this level, a brand is the identity that a company projects.

It follows that organizational culture is crucial to this type of brand. The attitudes and behaviour of managers when they make key decisions, and of employees in their everyday dealings with customers, could do a lot either to strengthen or weaken the brand. A vital role for HR is to ensure that they strengthen it.

'Marketing people may build the organization's brand identity, but translating that into company behaviours and employee practices needs HR people', Ulrich told *People Management*. It is up to personnel professionals to work out what that identity means in terms of recruitment, pay, training and so on.

Sooner or later, traditional forms of competitiveness – cost, technology, distribution, manufacturing and product features – can be copied. They have become table stakes. You must have them to be a player, but they do not guarantee you will be a winner.

'Winning will spring from organizational capabilities such as speed, responsiveness, agility, learning capacity and employee competence. Successful organizations will be those that are able to quickly turn strategy into action; to manage processes intelligently and efficiently; to maximise employee contribution and commitment; and to create the conditions for seamless change.'

Key factors in maximizing the corporate benefits from the organization/customer interface are information technology, people management, value chain efficiencies and sustained leadership.

Once the business has been understood in terms of the linkages that exist between enablers, processes and results, as outlined for example in the EFQM model, they can reach an understanding of where they are now. This needs to be put in the context of their capability, environment and culture. Everyone is different. The organization can then decide where it wants to be.

Nigel Purse (The Oxford Training Group) says that the senior team must have a clear vision, mission and values that can be expressed in a competency model (or framework) that provides a language for describing people's behaviour and their characteristics. Once this has been done the key pillars of human resource strategy can be constructed. These are:

1   Recruitment (internal and external).
2   Performance management.
3   Training and development.
4   Rewards and recognition.

The competency framework will then be designed and managers trained to bring them to life.

Recruitment

Behavioural interviewing

The best predictor is behaviour as behaviour tends not to change over time. If an organization has a language to describe behaviour they can use the selection process to acquire information to gain evidence of the behaviour in a job. For example, the ability to listen, innovate and measure outcomes.

It may be necessary for interviewing skills to be changed from hypothetical questions of what would you do if . . ., to tell me about your most recent experience of . . ., what did you do? Behavioural interviewing, gathering evidence of how they have dealt with is an important skill to learn.

Use of simulation

Behavioural interviewing followed by a simulation exercise of what it would be like is the second most important aspect. For example, if a person is being interviewed for a call centre they should be asked to make an outbound call, take an inbound call, and a team exercise should be simulated so that the person can be observed working in a team. These sort of exercise need to be custom designed. Assessors would be line managers in the business who are trained to observe, record and classify the behaviour the person is demonstrating against competences defined for that role.

Use of tests

Test are used after behavioural interviewing and simulation. They can be used to assess personality, skills and aptitude. Tests complement the process, they should not be used on their own.

Performance management

This term appears to mean different things to different people. On one side there is the performance related pay philosophy where everything is just fine if we give big bonuses for high performance. The other side is about coaching and setting people up for success. The elements that need to be considered here are as follows:

Objectives and clarity

People need to have a clarity about what is expected from them, they should have objectives (management by objectives). Managers use coaching to help staff understand what is expected from them. It is the process of coaching that provides this clarity.

How to do it

Objectives need to be SMART and objectives need to be linked to the business success model. Staff need to understand the drivers of customer behaviour and what they can do to cause customers to deepen their relationship with the business. They also need to know how to behave.

Measures of performance

Measures of performance are there to help people learn. The measures are self-measurement and self-monitoring. Not measures that punish people. Feedback, both qualitative and quantitative is used for learning.

Reviewing performance

Performance is reviewed so that staff understand how to learn and how to improve. Managers use a coaching style to help people to understand what is successful and why things went well or badly. This process can be supported by paperwork in the appraisal and performance review records.

Training and development

Many organizations have resources for training such as libraries, open learning and their own programme of courses. What they don't have generally is a gateway that enables people in the organization to access resources and make the most of them. A learning philosophy is about raising self awareness so people know what they want in the way of knowledge, skills and behavioural training.

Self awareness raising such as 360° assessment can be used, but also psychometric tests and development training and simulations. For example, to change sales behaviour and enable sales people to move to a more consultative style, an event could be run simulating how customers in the future would prefer to be treated, and what it would be like for them to behave differently. They can then be given feedback so they can see what they need to do and why it mattered.

Principles of effective training

1 Most effective training experiences come from doing rather than being lectured at. It is participative and practical.
2 Training needs to be designed around three components – knowledge, behaviour and skills.
3 People need to be able to prepare to learn. They need the opportunity before an event to think about why they are coming to a course.
4 Training needs to be reinforced and followed up afterwards by a telephone call, focus group, self-help group or involvement with a line manager.

Rewards and recognition

Money is not a motivator but lack of fairness in reward and recognition can be a demotivator. Reward systems must be seen to be fair. Pay should reflect the contribution people make to a business. Line managers should be asked to make judgements about peoples' pay. They need to look at the relative position of the employee within the salary band and relate what they have achieved back to the performance management system.

Core competences

The definition of core competence and core values
In their article, Is your core competence a mirage? Kevin P. Coyne, Stephen J. D. Hall, and Patricia Gorman Clifford. *The McKinsey Quarterly*, 1997, **1**,pp. 40–54 say 'A core competence is a combination of complementary skills and knowledge bases embedded in a group or team that results in the ability to execute one or more critical processes to a world-class standard'.

Such a definition excludes many skills or properties often cited by organizations as core competencies. Patents, brands, products and technologies do not qualify; neither do broad management capabilities such as strategic planning, flexibility and teamwork; nor do high-level corporate themes like quality, productivity and customer satisfaction.

They say that core competences so defined can be grouped into two categories.

Insight/foresight competences
These enable a company to discover or learn facts or patterns that create first-mover advantages. Such insights might derive from:

- Technical or scientific knowledge that produces a string of inventions.
- Proprietary data.
- Information derived from having the largest share.
- Pure creative flair in inventing successful products.
- Superior analysis and influence.

What distinguishes this kind of competence is that value ultimately derives from the insight itself. A company may have to go to great lengths to exploit it, but others could do so just as effectively if they had access to it.

Frontline execution competences
These arise in cases where the quality of an end product or service can vary appreciably according to the activities of front-line personnel.

Insight/foresight and front-line execution competences can coexist in the same company, but each will require its own managerial focus. McDonald's, for instance, uses its front-line execution competence to engineer the food delivery system at individual restaurants and its insight/foresight to identify winning sites for outlets.

How to evaluate core competences with front-line execution:

1 Establish what your competency is. You can do this through market research and benchmarking. Find out what you are valued for and if it matches your customers value chain where you stand in relation to your competitors.
2 Establish how easily you could be imitated by the competition. Remember, to change cultural value, train personnel, change policies and create the type of front-line environment in which customer care is the core value can take a long time.
3 Analyse the economic value of front-line competence (output).
4 Find out if the competence matches your existing position differentiation in the market place and ascertain the gap.

How to create core competences

Coyne, Hall, Gorman Clifford say that:

1 A world-class competence must steer the power structure in a company. The keeper of the skill drives all the companies major decisions, even in unrelated functions. At Proctor & Gamble, for instance, the core consumer marketing skill resides in the advertising department (the company's name for brand management). Brand managers exert a dominant influence on all decisions throughout the company. And at Wachovia Bank, even relatively new credit officers routinely block loans proposed by experienced senior line officers.
2 A core competence strategy must be chosen by the CEO, not by department heads acting independently.

There are three distinct routes to developing a core competence.

1 Evolution, where a company attempts to build skill at the same time as the individuals involved perform their tasks.
2 Incubation, where a separate group is formed to focus exclusively on the chosen competence.
3 Acquisition, where one company purchases another to obtain the skills it needs.

Recruiting the right person

If one thinks about customer service as being the ability to 'satisfy customer needs (real and perceived) in a dependable manner'. An ideal front-line person would have the following profile (Martin, W. and Fritz, E. (1989), *Managing Quality Customer Service*, Crisp):

- A genuine liking for people.
- An enjoyment of working for and servicing others.
- A sharing social need.
- An ability to feel comfortable among strangers.
- A sense of belonging to a group or place.
- An ability to control feelings.
- A sensitivity towards people and ability to show compassion and empathy.
- A general sense of trusting others.
- A high record of competence.

Choosing a test

There are many tests and in most selection processes systematic selection is essential to reduce numbers to a manageable level. Most selection is about elimination, not by choice.

Some tests are more reliable than others and it is a good idea to contact a reputable company and to take their guidance on the most appropriate methods. However before a test can be chosen you will need to have a clear idea of the range of qualities of characteristics required for the job to be performed well. Details of the work to be done are put together in a job description, while the qualities and characteristics required to perform the job form part of a person's specification. The tests are not described here.

Psychological tests

Psychological tests fall into two different categories (*Source: Psychological Testing*, Institute of Personnel Management):

1 *Psychometric tests*. These determine performance such as tests of general intelligence and special aptitude or, ability, verbal, spatial, diagnostic, mechanical, manual dexterity, clerical speed and accuracy, word processor aptitude, computer aptitude, language aptitude
2 *Personality assessment and psychometric questionnaires*. Personality is defined here as the way in which an individual's behaviour is

organized and coordinated when they react with the environment – characteristics which are assessed would include emotional adjustment, motivation, social relations, interests, values and attitudes. These factors are relevant to occupational assessment. Some cognitive (intelligent) scales are included in some questionnaires as some psychologists believe these need to be taken into account.

Personality profiling can help organizations understand and manage their staff. Use the web to find out more:

- http://managementtech.com/personalysis.html (services)
- http://www.opusmarketing.com/24reasns.htm (general)
- http://www.massprofiles.com/page2.html (general)
- email: info/thomas.co.uk and ask for the free personal profile analysis, Martin Reed the MD has made this special offer to CIM students.

Customer Care training programme management

Training can be structured in the following ways:

1 It can grouped by hierarchy.
2 It can be grouped by customer supply chain.
3 A vertical slice can be taken of the hierarchy or the customer supply chain.
4 Or a combination of the above may be used.

Training group size

Organizations tend to arrange for large groups (80–150) to be at each session so that employees can see themselves within the context of the whole organization and also to understand how their own actions impact on other people. Smaller groups are used after this for training in particular skills. Group dynamic change in different group sizes, these groups are small groups 10–12, medium groups 18–25, and larger groups. The size of the group should be suited to the training event.

Planning

Customer care training should be planned so that it is ongoing and retraining arranged well into the future. Internal marketing should be used to keep interest in customer care alive, with up-to-date research provided on customer feedback, ongoing developments on innovations and improvements generally. Some of the techniques described in Unit 3 could be used as new initiatives to keep the idea of customer service alive. Benchmarking could also be used.

Organization

Analysis
From the analysis discussed in Unit 3 it will be clear where some of the weaknesses within the organization lie. Attitude surveys held with customers and with employees will enable the organization to pinpoint where they need to improve. An understanding of the core competences will clarify this further.

The setting of objectives
The setting of training objectives will then enable the organization to decide what they need to achieve. What they need to do in practice may well fit into the philosophy, structure, and techniques they have decided to use (see Unit 3).

Discussion groups
Discussions will then need to take place at a senior level as to how the achievement of these objectives then fit into the job descriptions, recruitment, induction, reward, appraisal and promotion procedures; as well as the specific training programmes.

Middle management will also need to be involved and the results from the analysis and attitude surveys relayed. Barriers to change will have to be overcome and managers may have to be trained in many of the techniques discussed in Unit 3 – leadership, team building, delegation and empowerment and the encouragement of innovation.

Implementation

Action plans for change will need to be drawn up and the outcome of these decisions will have to be marketed internally so that the rest of the staff are prepared for change. Ideas on how to become involved need to be promoted so that they are able to integrate the ideas, identify with them and ultimately own them.

Internal marketing

Internal marketing could also include promotional material such as newsletters outlining the benefits, badges (the programme could be branded), posters and so on. Workshops could be held to enable employees in direct contact with customers to understand why this training programme is being undertaken. Results from the analysis and attitude surveys can be relayed back, core competences explained, performance standards clarified, the linkages into the recruitment, appraisal, reward and promotion systems explained. The training programmes could then be outlined, for example, verbal and non-verbal skills training, complaint handling and so on. Personal action plans could also be used.

What can go wrong?

Introducing new ideas into organizations is not easy. As Ted Johns, the Senior Examiner says in his book *Perfect Customer Care* (Arrow books):

1 Complacency and arrogance about studying the competition and understanding the need for strategy and training.
2 Conservatism and the lack of receptiveness to new ideas.
3 Production orientation and suspicions about marketing.
4 Inter departmental rivalries and tight boundaries.
5 Status and seniority of high-ranking employees held in awe and company cars thought to be more important.
6 Secretive closed attitudes to information and excessive confidentiality.
7 Tolerance of inadequate achievement.
8 Scepticism about people as managers think that organizational effectiveness has nothing to do with staff, their commitment, or their involvement.
9 Rules and procedures treated as ends in themselves with strict job descriptions.
10 Lip service paid to equal opportunity.
11 Customers seen as the enemy and the organization exists for the benefit of its members.
12 Lack of support from senior management and managers too involved in the day-to-day work of the organization.
13 Staff cynical.
14 Results take time.
15 Training seen as a once-off exercise.
16 Attention put on external customers but internal relationships remain the same.
17 Quality improvement teams bogged down in detail.
18 Absence of performance feedback.

Ted Johns feels that the CEO must provide a role model, be personally visible and convey the message in company newsletters, posters, manuals and so on. The CEO should personally look for customer feedback and be involved in the recruitment, promotion and training policies. The role should be used for showmanship and symbolism

Training covers activities such as:

- Courses, workshops, seminars.
- Planned personal development.
- Management development.
- Team building.
- On-job instruction.
- Induction.

On- or off-the-job training

The decision to have on-the-job or off-the-job training will need to be taken – it does not necessarily mean an either/or situation.

There are advantages and disadvantages to both. On-the-job training has the advantages of:

- It is totally related to the workplace and therefore real – costs can be measured.
- It would be supervised.

Off-the-job training has the advantages of:

- As it is reviewed people may feel more protected and able to experiment.
- Trainers may be more able to instruct.
- Other people may be there who share the same problems.

Coaching skills

There are three principal reasons for coaching:

1 Correction of weakness.
2 Short-term development.
3 Long-term development.

The benefits of coaching to team members are numerous:

- They know where they stand.
- They know what is expected.
- They know they are valued.
- They are challenged.
- They are supported.
- They know where they are going.
- They are given feedback on progress.

Coaching can be used to help team members:

- Perform a new task.
- Improve performance.
- Develop a skill.
- Solve a problem.
- Build confidence.

In order for coaching to be effective it must take place in an atmosphere of mutual trust and support. This atmosphere must be created so that to seek help is not viewed as being weak or wrong.

The process must be learner centred. The sessions are designed to meet the needs of the learner, and this must be kept in thought. The benefits of the coaching may be useful to the coach but the process should be conducted in order to develop the learner.

Abilities, experience, goals and values, energy and rewards all affect an individual's behaviour. Abilities and experience indicate how the person is likely to perform. Goals and values will channel the person's behaviour in particular ways.

Table 4.1 Training or coaching?

	Training	*Coaching*
Focus of learning	Task	The results of the job
Timeframe	1–5 days	A month to a year
Approach to activity	'Show and tell', supervised experience	Explore problems together and set up opportunities to try out new skills
Associated tasks	Analysing task, clear instruction, supervise practise and give feedback immediately	Jointly identify the problem. Create and develop opportunities and review
Ownership	Instructor	Shared
Benefits to the company	Standard, accurate, performance	Goal directed performance, a process of continuous development and creative problem solving

Front-line staff interact with customers and their ability to interact will be determined by their abilities, experience, goals and values.

Customer care is a by-product of internal relationships and culture. Training should therefore start at the top and courses designed for the outcome that is required at each level.

Training from the top down requires that the organization understands its core competences and has some strategic vision of the market place, its customers and its positioning.

In order to implement a customer-focused training programme the following steps need to be taken:

1 Strategic vision and definition of core competences and core value and where they relate in the customers' value chain and the organization's value chain.
2 Understand the operational and managerial behavioural requirements needed to support the core competences and core values.
3 Implementing relevant managerial training such as coaching, facilitating, consulting, changes in managerial style, empowering, delegation, etc.
4 Analyse the gap between what the organization wants in the way of the customer-focused behaviour and what it is getting.
5 Deciding on standards and training.
6 Motivating staff to take part.
7 Internal marketing to ensure continuous communication takes place.
8 Identifying how success will be measured.

Staff training is as much about attitudes as it is about skills and leadership and management need to be able to show their commitment so that the relevant modelling of behaviour can take place.

In the same way as recruitment is tailored to the needs of the market in order to ensure core competences and values are maintained the type of training needs to be specific to the market and to the organization so that core competences and values are protected. Market research can then be carried out in relation to these skills and appropriate training given if standards are seen to fall. The example from Yellow Pages illustrates the process

Roles outside the organization
Smaller, leaner organizations with flatter structures may mean that employees are unable to use all their skills at work, or indeed be given the opportunity to develop new ones.

It is also a good idea if employees are encouraged to use roles in organizations in the voluntary sector to gain experience or develop new skills.

This will need balancing as the interests of the voluntary sector role may take more energy from the employee than good sense should allow. Psychologically it is healthier emotionally for individuals not to put all their eggs/ambitions into one 'organizational egg basket'.

Counselling – when training is not the solution

Counselling is a useful skill and can be learned but how can counselling help at work? People face problems such as the following at work:

- *Poor job fit.* A poor promotion, secondment or placement decision can lead to a person being placed in a job to which their skills, abilities or motivation are not well suited. The symptoms may be poor performance but the cause may be that the person is being asked to perform in areas where they lack competence or interest.
- *Role defences.* Very often these may interfere with the behavioural requirements of the role and counselling may enable the person to reflect on these aspects.
- *Poor job design.* A poorly designed job can ask the person to meet inconsistent or conflicting demands. Counselling – an external person may bring these problems to light.
- *Relationships.* Relationship problems with the boss may be centred on the boss's inadequacy or incompetence. Maladaptive behaviour in the client may be a coping response, i.e. breaking rules seeking to disprove the boss's viewpoint.
- *Insufficient training.* Again the symptoms are likely to be poor performance but the lack of the necessary education or training could be the cause. In this case it is important to establish that potential exists before reaching a judgement that training is the solution.
- *Adaptation.* To new work methods, people, systems, type of work.
- *Job stress.* The pressures in the job may be too great for one person to sustain. Poor relationships (through irritability) or poor work performance may be symptoms.
- *Personal life stress.* Problems at home, for example marital or financial, can have a very direct effect on performance and relationships at work. A change in performance for no apparent reason is usually a good indicator.

The role of counselling

Although the real root of the problem may lie outside the employee's control, i.e. job design, the employee nevertheless has to live with the consequences. Counselling is therefore concerned with developing ways of helping them to cope with the situation and to find means of changing the circumstances if possible. The focus should be particularly strong on organizational contacts and resources that can be exploited

---

Background

The point of Sale Satisfaction Monitor has been set up to provide an ongoing measure of customer satisfaction with the behaviour and effectiveness of Yellow Pages sales people. The research is conducted through an independent Market Research Agency. Over a six-month period sufficient interviews are carried out to provide each salesperson with an individual customer satisfaction rating. The sample for each salesperson is carefully monitored to ensure the balance of advertiser types within each score is equal. These ratings are sequentially combined to provide measures for sales teams, sales areas, sales regions and finally, national figures.

Attributes that are used in the Monitor have been identified through qualitative research amongst Yellow Pages' customers to determine specifically what it is they want, in terms of service, from Yellow Pages' salespeople. A total of fourteen attributes are included in the survey, ranging from 'is courteous in their dealings with you' through to 'is knowledgeable about your business and industry' and, of course, 'effectiveness in writing/designing your advertisement'.

Feedback to salespeople is conducted regularly through regionally based news-sheets containing positive comments that have been made about individual (named) salespeople. A national newsletter is planned that will provide more detail on the progress of the research and how it is contributing to the overall improvement in customer service. This newsletter will also include a 'bouquets' section to recognise those salespeople who understand the importance of their work and the benefits of providing good customer service.

Finally. On a regular basis there are what we call 'hot e-mails' where a customer may have a particular concern that requires immediate contact from Yellow Pages. With the customer's permission their name and phone number, along with the details of their concern, are transmitted back to the relevant sales manager and, if necessary, another Yellow Pages department, for action. This action takes place within 48 hours of the date of the interview.

Feedback on the actual ratings achieved by salespeople is provided on a six monthly basis through the Regional and Area managers' regular meetings. Managers will then take their teams' ratings and discuss these with their individual salespeople. The figures will track performance over time as each new period is completed, generating performance over league tables for each of the seven sales channels within each of the regions. Awards will be given both to those achieving the highest results and those who realise the greatest improvement in results over time. Those who do not improve will have the opportunity to identify training and development needs to help them improve in the future. Throughout the introduction and launch of the Monitor it has been stressed that its overall purpose is to help the Company improve customer satisfaction.

Yellow Pages – Point of Sales Satisfaction Monitor 98/99, ©Anne Wolfe, Yellow Pages. March 1999.

Questionnaire summary

Overall

Q1   In general terms how would you rate the quality of service you received overall from them (the salesperson you had dealings with)?

Attributes

How would you rate the salesperson for:

A   listening to and understanding your needs and concerns
B   being prepared to work hard to try and help your business succeed
C   giving you enough time to make your own decisions
D   giving their time to you, but understanding your time is valuable
E   communicating well with other support staff to deliver what they promised
F   having good creative ability to help design and write your advertisement
G   being courteous in all their dealing with you
H   inspiring confidence that they are experienced and know what they are doing
I   knowing your previous history with YP – your pattern of advertising or problems you may have had
J   effectively explaining the policies and actions of YP

K   being knowledgeable about your business and industry
L*   having the correct balance of business talk and friendly conversation
M*   the level of cheerfulness they showed during the call
N*   the degree of enthusiasm they showed during the call

Combined – Q1a–Q1k – average of attributes

Q2   Keeping (all) appointments/turn up on time/checking time convenient

Q3   how confident are you that you could reach the rep or another member of YP

Q4   did they promise to do anything. . .have they done it

Q5 – IF NOT ADVERTISE: why not

*Tele contacts only

Yellow Pages – Point of Sales Satisfaction Monitor 98/99, ©Critical Research. March 1999

Types of training

Empowerment training

Empowerment from a service perspective, gives employees the authority to make decisions regarding customer service. True empowerment means that the employees can bend and break rules to do whatever is necessary (within reason) to take care of the customer. There are three variables that need to be considered:

1   Coaching and mentioning.
2   Peer and supervisor modelling.
3   Career path development and strategies must be present to provide employees with the guidance and skill necessary to become empowered employees.

The main skills that customer service personnel need are understanding role behaviour, telephone skills, telemarketing, the use of technology, customer service and customer retention, problem solving and maintaining customer satisfaction.

Anne J. Broderick (1998), Role theory, role management and service performance. *The Journal of Sales Marketing*, **12**(5) www.emerald-library.com

Role training

Role theory draws on a behavioural perspective by focusing on explanations of social interaction as behaviours associated with specific social positions (Biddle, 1979). Role theory would argue that the social interaction which occurs between two people in an exchange is principally determined by the roles which each adopts (Goffman 1959; 1967), thus leading to a role script within the encounter. By identifying the dramaturgical aspects within social encounters, it offers an opportunity to examine how role behaviours and choices within the role script can enourage positive service encounter experiences.

Role analysis and planning

Within the internal service process, the efficiency of internal role sets can be identified through an analysis of a role commitment within service teams, the identification of role discrepancies between service providers doing the same job and a comparison of how service providers evaluate their own role performance.

A useful application of role analysis is evident in the training approach at Imperial Hotel Tokyo. Part of the service role training at this hotel focuses on the etiquette and psychology of guest contact, where role playing is used as a preparation tool. Guest psychology such as guests anticipating a level of prestige, feeling possessive about the hotel's facilities and requiring warmth in interactions are considered carefully. Demonstrations of appropriate non-verbal communication and body language are a standard part of the service role preparation. What the management engage in is a meticulous analysis, planning and preparation for desired behavioural outcomes in service roles. The training specified the improved interaction with customers which was sought, identified some verbal and non-verbal role interactions designed to achieve this and addressed these in both the internal service process and at the client interface. In addition, they had a clear idea of the role outcomes to be achieved by employees and how to monitor them.

A practical mechanism for this is through self-assessment and group role analysis (similar in format to quality circles). Similarly, role analysis within the service encounter is useful for specification of role learning needs on the part of client and service provider. Adaptation of the role script can lead to improved customer retention.

Role management during the service life cycle and issues of role identity, appropriate role development and role preparation are important considerations in the management of service life cycles.

Role consistency and service performance
The personal approach of service providers needs coordination, demanding role consistency throughout the service delivery cycle to underline good successive service experiences.

Role outcome measures
These three areas of role management: role analysis and planning, adaptation of role script and role management/role consistency in service performance (during the service life cycle) require some clear measurement criteria, both qualitatively and quantitatively determined.

Telephone skills
Most contact with customers takes place over the telephone. Operators must be able to greet, listen effectively, ask questions, address people, manage objectives, negotiate, manage different types of behaviour and end the conversation.

Telemarketing
Very often contact with a customer offers the opportunity to sell other products. Staff must be able to use these opportunities proactively.

Customer service and customer retention and problem solving
Customer service is not about complaint handling, it is about proactively engaging with customers. For example, finding out if they are happy with a service, ensuring that they know if anything goes wrong they are able to bring back goods for replacement. Problem solving and being able to answer questions, alternatively knowing who to involve so the problem can be solved and ensuring it has been attended to is an important aspect of proactively relating to customers.

Other types of training for front-line staff could include assertiveness training, handling aggression and conflict management, counselling skills, negotiation and sales skills, stress management and personal organization.

This is especially important for new technology which requires constant learning on the job as workers need to keep up with specific skills, but also have a need for general education.

Motivational issues and job design for front-line staff

The ongoing debate about work very much depends on the assumptions people make about the nature of man. Two views that have helped to support the idea that organizations should be made for people and not the other way around have been those of Maslow and Herzberg.

The ideas of Maslow and Herzberg are represented in Figure 4.1. Maslow suggested that various needs need to be satisfied in order to move on to the satisfaction of higher needs. Herzberg developed Maslow's ideas into what he called the motivation-hygiene theory. Here he said that men have two sets of needs which they continually try to satisfy. The need to avoid pain and discomfort and the need to grow and develop psychologically. The need to avoid pain and discomfort is satisfied by organizational factors such as policy, supervision, salary, inter-personal relations and working conditions – these are called hygiene factors and must be avoided if they are to give any long-term feelings of satisfaction. But they do not motivate people to work well. In order to do this people need to grow and develop psychologically. These needs are met by factors such as achievement, recognition, responsibility, advancement and the work itself. It is these motivators that result in positive long-term feelings of satisfaction. Leadership and empowerment are key skills in enabling this process to take place.

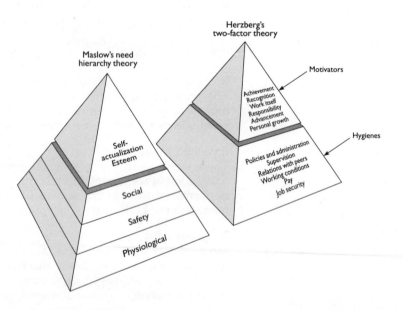

Figure 4.1

Herzberg has listed job disassatisfiers, also known as maintenance factors. These include physical conditions such as not enough to do, shift systems, hours of work, rota duties, overtime, holidays, heating, lighting, ventilation, arrangement of plant and office layout, car parks and protective clothing. There are ones that affect security such as inadequate technical supervision, unfair supervisors, unfair promotion policies, unhappy working groups, unhappy relationships with supervisor, the conditions of employment, the length of notice, redundancy policies, sick pay, pension scheme, profits sharing and social opportunities. There are economic factors like pay rises, bonuses, piece work, the use of flat rates, increments, fringe benefits, lunches, housing and cars. There may be other factors such as the duplication of effort, struggles for power, waste and inefficiency, company policy and administration. There are also job satisfiers. These might include ones that give a sense of achievement, perhaps by encouraging workers to feel a sense of pride in their work, or allowing all to get on with the job they have been allotted, giving freedom to plan work as they think best, setting achievable goals in consultation with those who have to perform them, creating positive projects which are examined and, where necessary, implemented, delegating responsibility and rewarding enterprise, giving encouragement where assignments are difficult and praise when successful, showing understanding and assisting projects to success, while making each subordinate feel that their contribution has been largely instrumental in reaching a goal. Recognition is another satisfier. This involves giving each employee self respect, confidence in themselves and their role in the company and making all tasks, including mundane operations, truly important in the eyes of all members of your organization and saying so in public. It also includes granting status to all those deserving it (clothing, tools, sick pay, pensions, merit pay) and showing appreciation for loyalty and long service and difficult tasks accomplished by public acclaim. Participation is another satisfier. This means you recognize that all members of your staff are an essential part of the team with a distinctive role to play, keeping a flow of information up/down, consulting wherever possible, explaining tasks to be tackled, giving real roles to all, which seem to be fair and being available when needed and when help is required. The last satisfier is growth. This might mean providing opportunities for individual initiative, giving opportunity for self-development within the present job, planning man-power development and providing opportunities for promotion and making this known to all members of the group, developing and showing interest in each member of your staff according to their capabilities and appraising performance and setting new goals.

Management can satisfy the needs in Maslow's hierarchy. Self-fulfilment can be encouraged by providing growth, career opportunities, training and development and encouraging creativity and empowerment. Self-esteem can be helped by managers praising high performance, publicizing individual achievement, giving feedback, providing appraisal and giving greater responsibility. Social recognition can come through a manager who provides for working in groups, where there is interaction at different levels or the chance for social/social events, or where a manager encourages participation in informal structures. Safety is enhanced by the provision of safe working conditions, job security and a manager who treats employees equally and fairly. On the physiological front a manager needs to pay fair wages, provide reasonable working conditions and provide rest breaks.

Other theories
There are many other theories about motivation, for example:

- Roethlisberger and Dickson add on the need for justice, fair treatment and dependence–independence.
- McClelland emphasizes power affiliation and achievement.
- Ardery draws attention to identify, security and stimulation.

You could well add to these lists. The most important point to remember is that each person has their own list and these may differ widely and change as their life develops. Their needs are also influenced by their background, early environment, education, the person's self-concept and experience. Motivation of a person needs to be put into the context of the organization and environment they are working in. Also, the role the person has defined for them by the organization and the 'role idea' carried in their minds will determine how they carry out their work.

If you want to find out about people you must talk to them to find out how they feel about themselves and their work.

Maslow's theory is said to not apply outside western, industrialized economies and cultures and the hierarchy has been criticized. Herzberg (1987) argues his theory holds up in diverse cultures and that there are some common characteristics among workers throughout the world.

Role analysis
Before looking at how to motivate a person one needs to understand the concept of 'role'. The role being the way in which people organize their behaviour in relation to a specific situation. This definition makes the taking up of a role into something that is internally determined – the role is in the mind.

The subjective aspects of the role rely on:

1 The person's ability to understand what the job is in terms of the work to be done.
2 The person's understanding of where they are within a given organizational system – the role relationships.
3 Their realization of how people expect them to behave.

4 The understanding of the environmental considerations that impact on an organization externally.

5 The reality of the pressures that impact on them from within the organization itself.

6 An understanding of any intra-role conflict.

7 An understanding of inter-role conflict.

The role idea which individuals carry in their mind and which motivates them, and relates them to some inner meaning which helps them to manage their behaviour, is affected by:

- The individual's own view of their relationship with other people (e.g. if a person feels threatened they will define their role more tightly and vice versa).
- The individual's own assessment of their performance – if they think they are doing well they will expand their role.
- A change in working environment or a new colleague could be threatening and cause them to redefine the role.
- A change in the macro-environment, micro-environment, mission or primary task may frighten the individual and inhibit them from performing the role.

It is therefore important to always speak to the person to find out about how they view themselves in their role. Some people feel in order to carry the role they need to leave their feelings and personality at the door of the office. This is not the case and if it is the *role idea* that people are using to guide their behaviour, their ideas of how to behave will need to be reassessed. Taking on a role does not mean people have to become stereotypical imitations.

Motivating individuals

Four suggestions to motivate your staff are:

1 Get to know them.
2 Help them to achieve success.
3 Give them a feeling of control over their work.
4 Build their self-esteem.

As a manager one of your first tasks should be to get to know the individual members of your team. Make the effort to find out. Ask the right questions. How do they see their jobs? Where are they in their lives? What aspirations do they have? What do they expect of you? What problems do they have at work? Don't sit in your office, pondering on the answers to these questions. Observe your staff; talk to them; listen to what they have to say.

Vroom's expectancy theory

Motives = Behaviour = Goals

Vroom's theory is also concerned with the complex process of behaviour.

Whether a person will be motivated to achieve a goal is dependent on their *expectations* of the effect their *effort* will have on their *performance* and of the *reward* to be obtained.

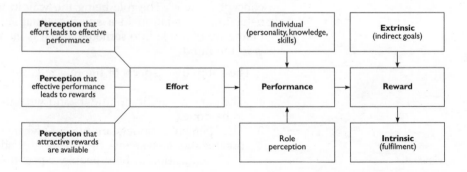

Figure 4.2

110

Rewards can be:

- *Extrinsic* – can be short term or fail to live up to expectations, e.g. pay rise.
- *Intrinsic* – are more fulfilling, e.g. responsibility, challenge, feedback, autonomy, variety and interaction (Torrington, 1987, p. 358).

An individual's perception of the process will depend on what their 'unsatisfied needs' are. Does the reward satisfy the need?

Summary

1 Vroom takes a wide view of the motivational process.
2 Individuals are motivated when they perceive their behaviour will lead to the desired outcomes.
3 The individual's perception of reality is crucial.
4 Good performance = job satisfaction (not the other way round).
5 Concentration on intrinsic rewards is needed because extrinsic rewards are short lived (Cole 1990).

As you can see from Vroom's expectancy theory shown in Figure 4.2 individuals are motivated when they perceive their behaviour will lead to what they want. Therefore, the individual's perception of reality, what they want, is absolutely crucial. If a person performs well they will be satisfied. Therefore, the more enabled a person is to be able to do a better job, the more satisfied they will become with their own achievements. The more positive feedback they get the more satisfied they will be. Part of this is empowering people, giving them challenges and so on. But one of the most important things is for them to know what they are trying to achieve. This goes back to proper objectives so that the person understands what they are there to do.

If people understand what they are there to do the inability to carry out the task then needs to be thought about in different ways. If they can't do the job, you need to sort out if it is due to ability or motivation. . .

Is the lack of ability due to:

- Lack of resources?
- Lack of training?
- Inadequate aptitude?

Is the lack of motivation due to:

- Poorly understood or unrealistic expectations?
- Rewards not being linked to the job or unfairly distributed?
- Rewards not salient to this person?
- Role defences?

Enhancing performance

It is important to remember that when you consider role performance that it is part of a 'role threesome' – knowledge, skills and behaviour (Figure 4.3).

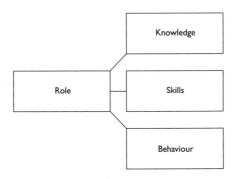

Figure 4.3

111

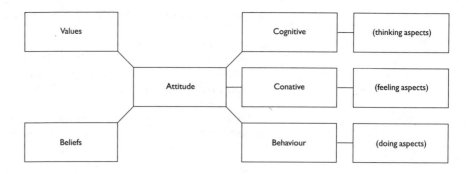

Figure 4.4

Behaviour is based on attitudes which in themselves consist of different components (Figure 4.4).

This model allows us to look at enhancing role performance in a number of different ways. It also enables market research around role performance to be linked in specific ways:

1. Values.
2. Beliefs.
3. Attitude.
4. Behaviour:
   - knowledge (cognative);
   - feeling (conative);
   - behaviour (doing).

The recruitment process can also be built around this process as values, beliefs and attitudes leading to the behavioural side are powerful determinants of organizational culture.

How to enhance role performance

Key guidelines for enhancing role performance and creating a motivating work environment are:

1. Clearly defined acceptable performance of behavioural objectives must be decided by the person (management by objectives). Everyone must know where they are going so that *success* is clearly defined – without understanding what constitutes success you will have an unhappy person. The actions that people take in order to carry out a task must link into the overall mission.
2. The person must be able to internalize these objectives (key result areas) and will have to work on their own self improvement in order to get better.
3. The organization must remove barriers in the organization that will prevent the person doing their job and make sure that the person has resources and support from their colleagues in order to do their job properly. Unless frustration is removed the person will find it difficult to do their job.
4. If people lack the knowledge, skills and can't behave in the required way, they must be given education, training, mentoring and coaching, to be able to acquire them.
5. They must be given direct feedback from customer research so that they can personally become involved with what customers say and how they are feeling.
   For example, in teaching the results of student feedback are given to the teacher so that they can personally take on board what they need to do in order to improve. In most cases they do this themselves and read what is said – feedback is immediate and reflection immediate.
   This is a sensitive process and the person will need to understand how their own defences will come up in order to protect themselves from the emotional pain of criticism. If this process is not understood and talked about openly there is the likelihood of a 'name and blame', 'them and us' culture growing. This type of climate is not conducive to positive customer relations.

6 Rewards must be linked to achieving objectives. People are in fact being 'conditioned' to behave in a certain way.
7 Appraisal and ongoing reflection are used as a learning method to encourage self-discipline. By helping people to identify problems themselves and getting them to explain how they should improve their own selves they will be able to internalize what is needed to make things better. This is in line with the principle of self-actualization outlined by Maslow.
8 Rewards must again be linked to each level of improvement – these do not have to be monetary.

Self actualization and empowerment

The whole idea of self-actualization and empowerment is based on the individual doing it themselves – systems are then structured into the organization to facilitate this enabling progress to take place.

Design of jobs

Job design for customer-facing roles can be thought about in two different ways:

Fragmentation

Taylor's ideas (called the 'Enemy of the American Working Man') would be to fragment a job into different tasks and employees would be trained to carry out the fragmented task in precisely the manner determined best. This method achieves control, a one-task job can be proficiently done, very little skill is needed, the worker remains unskilled so low pay can be given. However, for the worker it is repetitive, boring, the individual's part in the organization is almost meaningless, people get dissatisfied and careless and the person remains undeveloped and unable to progress.

Whole tasks

Whole tasks, on the other hand, allow the person to conceive the job and experience the outcome of their actions. This means that:

- Individuals can be given autonomy in their work instead of allocating aspects of it to supervisors.
- Contact with customers and feedback from customer questionnaires can be given to them so they know how well they are doing and can provide a basis for improvement.
- Meaningful sequences of work will increase the significance of the job and create more job satisfaction.

Managing by objectives

Setting objectives

It is obvious that everybody at work should know what objectives they are working towards and have some measure of knowing how successful they are. It is quite simple – if you do not know what you are supposed to be achieving how will you ever get a feeling of satisfaction about doing a good job? How will you ever be happy with yourself? How will other people know how good you are at your job? How can they praise and reward you.

Objectives are in the main defined by the employee, and not imposed from above, so that there is an implicit democratic and participative element. Thus, hopefully, the employee's wishes in the development of their own future and realization of personal aims are integrated with the organization's need to clarify and achieve its goals of profitability or social unity in relationship with their customers.

By setting objectives that are jointly determined you will be setting a scene in which individuals will be able to motivate themselves because they have been given responsibility and the opportunity to develop themselves. Control is therefore given to the individual over themselves and is not imposed on them from the outside. The person is in fact treated as a grown-up and is doing something because they want to do it, not because someone has told them how to do it.

Five dimensions of empowerment

1 *Self-efficacy.*   A feeling that you possess the capability and competence to perform a task successfully.
2 *Self determination.*   A feeling of choice, you have the ability to initiate your own actions and processes.
3 *Personal control.*   A belief in your ability to effect change.
4 *Meaning.*   A belief in the value of the goals which you are pursuing.
5 *Trust.*   A belief that you will be treated fairly and equitably.

This approach treats human beings as human beings, not as mechanistic robots.

How to do it

The first step of the organization is to understand where it is going. This may be specific or be expressed as a general aim. Within this organizational plan, function/department will construct their own plan.

Key results/areas need to be identified which will reflect the success of the department. In order to do this, go back and look at job descriptions. The job description should list five to six key areas which will define what the person is there to do. These need to be checked and updated. They can also be linked to time management so people understand what they should be spending their time on.

Each team member can then work out a job improvement plan. This will consist of:

- Objectives they have for the period under review (normally one year).
- Improvements they can make.
- Actions they need to take to achieve them.
- Constraints under which they have to work.

This is all taken to the manager, discussed and agreed. It is important that the manager does not interfere in establishing performance levels if they think they are too low. The essence of MBO is that the person has set their own objectives. The manager, sometimes with a consultant, may help to clarify the person's thinking, and can fairly insist they keep within the overall aims of the organization but must as a general principle give way in cases of disagreement. If the manager is right it will become apparent later.

At the end of the period under question to be determined, the person meets their manager and together they look at the performance of the department, the extent to which the targets were achieved, reasons why some were not, ways in which this can be rectified, and on the basis of all this, the person (not the manager) rewrites his job improvement plan for the next twelve months.

However at any time in the twelve months person and manager can meet to amend the plan if it is proving inappropriate to the situation. So the stages can be represented as shown in Figure 4.5.

To see how this works out in practice we might take a few short examples as shown in Figure 4.6.

There are numerous problems if MBO is applied incorrectly but if it is instituted correctly then the main problem is that it takes up a lot of time, particularly in the collaborative process of working out each individual's management plan, but the results will speak for themselves.

Reflection and review

Reflection and review are critical aspects of following the path towards empowering staff – being able to give and take constructive feedback is a necessary part of this process.

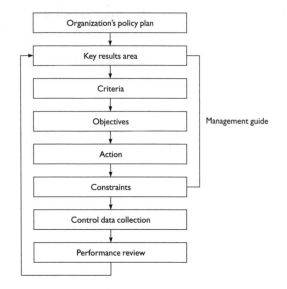

Figure 4.5

Position	Front-line staff in a retail outlet
Key area	To achieve sales by delivering a high level customer service
Criteria	• Sales from area • Returns • Customer opinion • Shrinkage
Objectives	a) £x January–June per month b) £x July–October per month c) £x November–December per month d) Zero customer complaints e) Shrinkage reduced by _____ f) Returns reduced by _____
Action	a) Analyse sales per category b) Analyse returns per category c) Analyse shrinkage per category
Control data	Quantitative a) Sales by day, week, month, period b) Shrinkage c) Returns Qualitative a) Customer complaints b) Customer satisfaction c) Customer retention

Position	Regional Sales Manager
Key area	To achieve gross profit and sales volume targets in the region
Criteria	• Gross profit as against sales value per customer • Regional selling expenses • Volume of regional sales • Ratio of order to quotation • Customer satisfaction/retention
Objectives	a) £x January–June per month b) £x July–October per month c) £x November–December per month d) Zero customer complaints
Action	a) Analyse costs, compare with other regions and make recommendations by January b) Institute new customer campaign aiming at 25 new customers per sales territory by August – ongoing c) Carry out customer satisfaction survey by June
Control data	Quantitative a) Monthly regional accounts b) Daily invoiced sales returns c) Statistical analysis monthly sales by salesman/by customer d) Cost of gaining new customers e) Cost of retention f) Number of referrals Qualitative a) Customer complaints b) Customer satisfaction c) Customer retention

Figure 4.6

Constructive feedback

Feedback is a way of learning more about ourselves and the effect of our behaviour on others. Constructive feedback increases our self-awareness, offers options and encourages development; it is important to learn to give and receive it. Constructive feedback does not mean only positive feedback. Negative feedback, given skilfully, can be very important and useful.

Appraisal

Organizations are increasingly setting staff performance standards based on customer care indicators and appraising staff against these.

The balance between looking at performance as an outcome of work systems and an outcome of team performance rather than the difference in performance between different staff needs to be argued. For example, how does teamwork balance the personalization the 'empowered' worker is expected to give customers?

Data used for appraising employees is gathered in a number of ways:

- Customer survey such as customer focus group, telephone surveys, postal surveys and complaints.
- Electronic surveillance such as taping telephone conversations.
- Direct encounter with a mystery shopper.

Some organizations are also using internal service level agreements.

Service level agreements

Service level agreements are used by organizations internally and externally. Many of the characteristics, benefits and dangers of external service level agreements can be applied to those used externally. Visit Naomi Karten's site www.nkarten.com to find out about external service level agreement.

Internal service level agreements

A service level agreement helps to identify responsibilities between a service provider and its customers. It is an agreement between departments that is aimed at:

1 Giving both sides the opportunity to identify their needs and priorities and expectations.
2 By creating an understanding that is shared by both sides it hopes to reduce conflict.
3 As it is a written document it gives people the opportunity to communicate its content to other people.
4 It provides an objective way to monitor and review progress.

It should not be used as a way to stifle progress, procrastinate about updating and changing, get what you want by improving standards or service deliverers. It will take time to develop as both parties need to get together in order to formulate it. Used flexibly they can increase understanding, used inflexibly they build delay into the system.

Transfer pricing

The concept of transfer pricing is that, within an organization one department is transferring its output to another. This should be regarded as a sale and there should be a definite policy on setting the selling price. The most usual methods of transfer pricing – cost, cost plus, market price and dual pricing need to be evaluated.

The human resource model

Gijis Houtzagers (Houtzagers, G. (1999), Business models for the human resource management discipline, a key instrument for selection, implementation and optimizing your HRM system, *Empowerment in organizations*, **6**(7).) has designed a model to capture the processes of the organization that administers and manages the HR components of the workforce. The model is referred to as the 'Employee and Organization Management Model'. This human resource management information system (HRMIS) defines eight components:

1 Organization – its staffing, position related responsibilities, compensation and benefits linked to positions, performance appraisal structure and the company policies.
2 Human resource logistics – budget authorization, establishing position recruitment and selection methods, maintaining applicant data, facilitating the necessary interview scheduling and documentation processes and negotiating the process.
3 Compensation and benefits.
4 Employability – this supports the ongoing development of the active workforce.
5 Relations – this covers internal and external relations such as communication, collective bargaining, procedural justice communication structure, subjects, definition of internal target groups, communications with external agents and relations between defined organizational entities.
6 Health, safety and environment.
7 Information strategies.
8 Employee administration.

The model outlined in this paper provides the following benefits:

1 It provides a tool for bridging the gap between IT and HR.
2 Reduces consultancy support as the model offers a picture of what customers want to implement and guidelines for how data is administered.
3 Training can be tracked more easily and related to all kinds of legislative and tax rulings.
4 It can provide a best practice guide for the selection process.
5 The centralization enables self service and less data maintenance.

Summary

This unit has discussed some of the managerial implications of adopting a customer orientation. It is essential that all staff are consulted and customer focused if such strategies are to succeed. This will require managers to be active to ensure staff are motivated to perform at the best level of their ability. However the organization cannot stand still as the best applications of a customer focus will become eroded over time. The next unit looks at the issues of innovation and the need for continual improvement, if competitive advantage is to be sustainable.

Innovation and the culture of continuous improvement

❑ To understand the concept of innovation.

❑ To understand some of the barriers to creating an innovative and continuously improving culture.

Study Guide

Innovation is a process whereby new ideas are developed and applied. Innovative products, processes and services are spreading rapidly across the globe and in order to remain competitive organizations need to understand and consider themselves within the context of the external and internal environment. Innovations need to be introduced into the marketplace in a manner that reduces customer barriers and they also need to ensure that strategy, leadership, rewards and mission, recognition, soft organizational feeling issues, structure, culture, role and organizational barriers are addressed.

Innovation and conservatism in customer behaviour

Definition 5.1

An innovation is any new idea, product, or service which is perceived, by the receiver of communication concerning its existence, to be new.

The definition of *innovation* has several important implications:

1 An innovation can be anything – from a novel type of paper clip to a new postal delivery service to a truly genuine response to a customer's need.
2 The innovation is in the eye of the receiver:
   • The 'innovation' does not have to be novel to the sender of the communication;
   • The 'innovation' does not have to be new, it may have existed for some time before the receiver became aware of its existence.

In customer focused organizations innovation can take place within the continuous interactions between front-line staff and their customers. Creativity and flexiblity need to be built into the very finger tips of the organizational culture.

Diffusion of innovations

The process of diffusion is concerned with how innovations spread within a market. There are four main parts to the diffusion process:

1 The innovation.
2 The time taken for the innovation to be adopted.
3 The channels of communication through which information about the innovation spreads.
4 The social systems involved.

Most writers refer to the receiver of the innovation as the 'adopter'. A simple 'one-step' communication is illustrated in Figure 5.1.

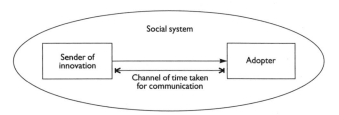

Figure 5.1
An illustration of a simple diffusion process

Adoption stages

The consumer does not adopt an innovation immediately. They may, indeed, not adopt the innovation at all. Rogers, in his book *Diffusion of Innovations*, identified the following stages in the adoption process:

- *Awareness* – the consumer is aware of the innovation but little is known about it.
- *Interest* – the consumer becomes aware that the innovation may satisfy a need.
- *Evaluation* – the consumer forms an attitude about the innovation which may be positive or negative. On the basis of this, they decide whether they are going to try it or reject it.
- *Trial* – if a trial is possible, and wanted, then the product is tried by the consumer.
- *Adoption* – the innovation is accepted or rejected. If accepted, the consumer becomes committed to the innovation (if it is a product – then this usually means purchase).

Types of innovation

There are generally acknowledged to be three types of product innovation:

1 *Continuous* – the product is being continuously upgraded in small increments. 'New' products in this case are actually only slight modification on existing products. The use of the product changes little, the consumer does not have to adapt, or modify in any substantial way, their use of the product. Examples include 'new improved' washing powders, new versions of established software.
2 *Dynamically continuous* – the product innovation is more disruptive on consumer usage patterns but does still not substantially alter them. Examples include disposable nappies, cordless telephones.
3 *Discontinuous* – the product requires the consumer to adopt new behaviour patterns entirely. Examples include the introduction of video recorders and computers.

119

How would you classify each of the following innovations — continuous, dynamically continuous or discontinuous?:

1   Petrol car → electric car
2   Toothbrush → electric toothbrush
3   Telephone → mobile telephone
4   Matches → pocket lighter
5   Video player → video camera
6   Television → remote control television

What makes an innovation successful?

According to Rogers and Shoemaker, the following characteristics of the innovation influence the speed and extent of adoption:

- *Relative advantage* – the degree to which the innovation is seen as being superior to any comparable predecessor. Of course, some discontinuous innovations (such as the video camera) may have no single, or obvious, comparator.
- *Compatibility* – the degree to which the innovation is compatible with existing culture. Products which are not compatible with existing practices (the use of chopsticks in the UK for example) are likely to take longer.
- *Complexity* – the more complex the innovation, the longer it will take to adopt. A simple to understand innovation (such as the pump-action toothpaste tube) will be more rapidly adopted.
- *Trialability* – if it is possible to sample an innovation it is more likely to be adopted rapidly. Free samples of a whole range of products and services are provided on this basis.
- *Observability* – products which are highly visible in the society in which the diffusion is taking place will be adopted more rapidly.

Thus, a continuous innovation, which is compatible with the culture, can be trialed, yet is simple and observable, is most likely to get broadly adopted most rapidly. Table 5.1 rates several innovations on these criteria. It is important to realize that these are perceived values. One person might, for example find the complexity of a particular pocket calculator 'high' whilst another might find it 'low'.

Multiplicative innovation adoption (MIA) model

The authors propose the following theoretical model of innovation adoption which is based on the Roger and Shoemaker criteria. It assumes that each of the criterion makes an equal contribution to the success, or otherwise, of the innovation. It also assumes that they combine in such a way that the presence of positive ratings on more than one criterion has a multiplicative effect on success.

Table 5.1 Rating of innovations based on Rogers and Shoemaker criteria

Innovation	Relative advantage	Compatibility	Complexity	Trialability	Observability
Compact discs	High	Low	Low	High	Medium
Sinclair C5	Low	Low	High	Low	High
Pocket calculator	High	High	Medium	High	Medium
Post-it notes	High	High	Low	High	Medium
Ford Sierra	Low	High	Medium	Medium	High

To assess an innovation using the Simmons and Phipps MIA model it is first necessary to rate the innovation on the Rogers and Shoemaker criteria using the following scheme:

- *Relative advantage* – rate the innovation with a 3 if the relative advantage is high, 2 if it is judged to be medium and 1 if it is low. This rating is referred to as RA.
- *Compatibility* – rate the innovation with a 3 if the compatibility is high, 2 if it is judged to be medium and 1 if it is low. This rating is referred to as CT.
- *Complexity* – rate the innovation with a 3 if it is simple, 2 if it is judged to be of medium complexity and 1 if it is judged to be highly complex. This rating is referred to as CL.
- *Trialability* – rate the innovation with a 3 if the opportunity to trial is high, 2 if it is judged to be medium and 1 if it is low. This rating is referred to as TR.
- *Observability* – rate the innovation with a 3 if the observability is high, 2 if it is judged to be medium and 1 if it is low. This rating is referred to as OB.

The ratings for each innovation are then multiplied together to obtain an overall prediction of the speed and extent (SE) to which the innovation will be adopted:

$$\text{Speed and extent (SE) rating} = RA \times CT \times CL \times TR \times OB$$

Referring back to Table 5.1 and using the MIA rating scheme, we obtain the SE ratings seen in Table 5.2. The higher the SE rating, the higher the predicted success of the innovation.

Table 5.2 Speed and extent (SE) ratings using the Simmons and Phipps MIA model, Oxford College of Marketing

Innovation	Speed and extent (SE) rating
Compact discs	$3 \times 1 \times 3 \times 3 \times 2 = 54$
Sinclair C5	$1 \times 1 \times 1 \times 1 \times 3 = 3$
Pocket calculator	$3 \times 3 \times 2 \times 3 \times 2 = 108$
Post-it notes	$3 \times 3 \times 3 \times 3 \times 2 = 162$
Ford Sierra	$1 \times 3 \times 2 \times 2 \times 3 = 36$

Based on the example ratings provided, it is predicted that the most successful innovation would be post-it notes and the least the Sinclair C5.

Assessment of success criteria and MIA model

Success is a difficult concept to define and thus any criteria or model is open to criticism on the basis that what they attempt to describe is itself vague. To one person it might be high sales figures, to another high profit margins, high public profile or something else. For example, one-off designer label clothes may not sell in high volumes but may be valuable in that they build up the reputation of the designer. In a sense, they are therefore a success. We could redefine success as meeting the aims that the originator of the innovation themselves set. However, this risks diluting the concept and it is probably best to accept a general definition based on cultural expectations.

The MIA model presented is theoretical and requires validation. Tools do not yet exist to measure the five criteria but could no doubt be simply constructed.

The model and criteria are powerful in that they are based on perceived characteristics. Thus, different individuals could rate the same innovation in a variety of ways. This would make the application of the technique particularly suitable for target marketing.

121

Rate the following innovations using the MIA model:

1   Electric car
2   Electric toothbrush
3   Mobile telephone
4   Pocket lighter
5   Video camera
6   Remote control television

On the basis of your analysis which would you have predicted was most likely to succeed? Does this match your current perceptions of these products in the market place?

Categories of adopters

Research on the diffusion process (by Rogers) has found that adoption follows a bell-shaped curve of normal distribution amongst adopters. This is illustrated in Figure 5.2. Initially, only a very few people adopt an innovation but the numbers steadily, then dramatically increase until they reach a peak. The number of people adopting over time then declines. This normal distribution has been approximately divided into five categories (see Table 5.3).

This information can be most useful in targeting new product campaigns. It also forms a critical basis for understanding the product life cycle and market segmentation.

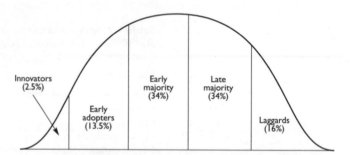

Figure 5.2
Adoption curve

Table 5.3 Categories of adopters

	Population (%)	Characteristics of group
Innovators	2.5	Risk-takers, more adventurous, more spending power, take most publications
Early adopters	13.5	Highest proportion of opinion leaders, above average education, tend to be younger than later adopters, well-respected, have greatest contact with sales people
Early majority	34	Slightly above average age, education, social status, and income. Rely on informal sources of information
Late majority	34	Above average age but below average education, social status and income. Rely on informal sources of information
Laggards	16	Lowest group with respect to education, income, and social status. Are the oldest group

Opinion leaders

As we can see from the characteristics of the adopter groups, opinion leaders are crucial in the diffusion of innovations.

Opinion leaders are those individuals who are instrumental in changing the consumer behaviour of others. If there were no opinion leaders then behaviour would stagnate with no new fashions, ideas or attitudes emerging. Marketers are interested in targeting opinion leaders as, once these are convinced of the benefits of a new product or service, the rest of the adopters will then follow.

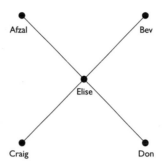

Figure 5.3
Sociogram of flow of information concerning recommendation of book

In the example shown in Figure 5.3, Elise was the opinion leader. Her knowledge of the book led to the purchase of four further copies. Obviously, you do not always buy everything that is recommended to you, the source of the recommendation must possess other qualities. Research has shown that opinion leaders generally possess certain similar characteristics:

- *Personality traits* – Opinion leaders tend to be self-confident individuals. They are confident about their own decisions and opinions and are thus more able to convince others. Leaders are also sociable, indeed they must be to enable the network of acquaintances required for communication.
- *Demographic characteristics* – Not surprisingly, people tend to seek information from those whom they perceive to be most knowledgeable in a particular subject matter and who have similar demographic characteristics. Thus, if you were buying a computer you might seek the advice of a computer-literate friend.
- *Social class* – Most commonly the opinion leader is of the same social class as the people they are influencing. This may be because advice from those of a similar status is more valued or simply that we more regularly communicate with persons in our class.

Activity 5.3	What demographic characteristics would you imagine an opinion leader in the following purchasing decisions might possess?

1 Who would you consult about purchasing Top 10 chart music?
2 Who would you consult about purchasing a violin?
3 Who would you consult about purchasing a sewing machine?

Shiffman and Kanuk (1994) present a multi-step model of how an opinion leader receives and disseminates information (Figure 5.4). Most importantly it shows that some consumers receive information directly from mass media rather than 'consulting' an opinion leader. Note also that the communication between opinion leader and consumer is two way, accurately demonstrating that opinion leaders are themselves open to influence from other sources.

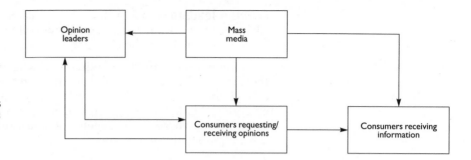

Figure 5.4
Communication path from the mass media to different consumer groups via opinion leaders. Adapted from Shiffman and Kanuk (1994) *Consumer Behaviour*

Persuasive communication

We have seen in this unit, and earlier, how communication occurs between members in a group. We will now consider what affects the persuasiveness of that communication. For instance, if a lecturer told you to keep quiet in class you (probably) would. However, if a classmate told you – would you be as likely to obey?

If a persuasive message is successful it leads to an attitude change. For attitude change to occur, a persuasive message on its own is not enough. During the early 1950s a social psychologist called Carl Hovland undertook a large volume of research in this area. With his colleagues he devised the process model shown in Figure 5.5 which shows the stages required for a message to lead to attitude change.

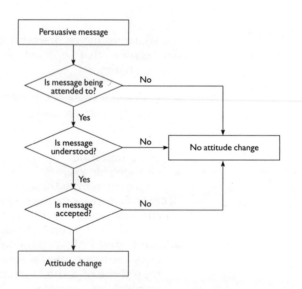

Figure 5.5
Hovland model of attitude change. Adapted from Deaux, Dane and Wrightsman (1993), *Social Psychology in the 90s*, Brooks/Cole

Persuasive message

Figure 5.6 shows a communication model where a referent, one or more members from a reference group (possibly an opinion leader), is trying to influence a consumer. The content of the communication is the message with the whole discourse taking place within a particular context. You will notice the similarity with the earlier model of diffusion (Figure 5.1) which is, essentially, the same communication process.

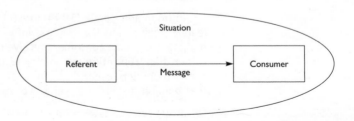

Figure 5.6
Communication model

124

The persuasiveness of the communication can be affected by the characteristics of all those elements shown in Figure 5.6:

- *Referent* – known as the source of the communication, the person trying to persuade.
- *Message* – the content of the communication.
- *Consumer* – known as the recipient of the communication, the person who is being persuaded.
- *Situation* – the immediate context within which the communication is taking place.

Source of communication
The following characteristics of the source affect its persuasiveness:

- *Status and credibility* – if the source is perceived as an expert then they are more persuasive. Thus stories in 'reputable' newspapers are more likely to be believed, as are endorsements from professionals in the topic being communicated. Experiments have shown a 'sleeper effect'. The difference between high credibility and low credibility sources is forgotten over time. However, when the recipient is reminded of source the original status effect returns.
- *Attractiveness* – the more attractive, charming, humorous the source the more persuasive (generally) they are likely to be. Of course, these characteristics are as perceived by the recipient.
- *Trustworthiness* – the more trustworthy the source is perceived to be the more persuasive they are. The trustworthiness is assessed on the basis of the perceived intentions and motives of the source.
- *Non-verbal behaviour* – non-verbal behaviour relates to trust. A 'shifty' disposition, for instance, does not instill trust.
- *Similarity with recipient* – if the source is perceived as being of a similar culture and social status as the recipient, then this can increase the persuasive power of the message.

Advertisers make use of all of these beneficial characteristics when formulating their advertisements. As we have already seen, certain individuals are used as experts or aspirational figures to gain appeal, as are people from the same ethnic or social grouping as those in the target audience.

Content of communication (the message)
The following characteristics of the message affect its persuasiveness:

- *Non-verbal aspects* – Face to face communication is more effective than mass media. In this situation the source can react to the recipient (via eye contact, body posture, etc.) and is thus able to anticipate and modify their message accordingly.
- *Implicit or explicit* – This is concerned with whether the recipient is left to draw their own conclusion from the information provided (implicit) or presented with a conclusion by the source (explicit). Thus, advertising aimed at people of high intelligence should not dictate choice but provide information for the recipient to make their own mind up.
- *Emotional appeal* – Emotions, such as fear, humour, sympathy and, of course, sex can be used to increase the persuasiveness of a communication. Experiments with smokers, concerning the danger of cancer, has shown that, somewhat surprisingly, 'high fear' messages are not the most effective way of persuasion. Scaring a smoker into thinking they are 'going to die' (high fear) is less likely to persuade them to stop smoking than a message with a lower fear content (such as 'smoking puts you at a high risk of cancer'). It appears that recipients 'switch off' when presented with high fear messages but are more receptive to messages where the fear content is more regulated.
- *One-sided versus two-sided arguments* – Whether a communication should make any reference to the competition (two-sided communication) seems to depend on the recipient.

- *Primacy-recency* – The order in which information is presented can affect its persuasiveness. The first and last slots in an advert break are the most sought after as research has shown that they are more likely to be remembered.

Recipient

The following characteristics of recipients effect the persuasiveness of the communication:

- *Level of education* – The more educated respond better to more complex arguments.
- *Resistance to persuasion* – Resistance to persuasion is strongest when counter-arguments are available and weakest when they are not.
- *Latitude of acceptance and rejection* – It is easier to persuade people where large shifts in their existing attitudes are *not* required.
- *Compatibility with self-concept* – Related to the above, if we have a certain self-concept (that is we believe we possess certain attributes or characteristics) then messages which support our self-concept are more likely to be accepted.
- *Individual differences* – Opinions differ, but some psychologists believe that there is a personality factor which equates to 'persuadability' thus some people are, inherently, more difficult to persuade than others.

Situations

The following aspects of the situation affect the effectiveness of the persuasive communication:

- *Informal situations* – These are generally more effective than formal ones for persuasion. The example of 'Tupperware parties' and other home shopping is one common way in which communication is made less formal and thus more persuasive.
- *Role-playing* – Trying to put the recipient in the 'shoes' of the source can increase persuasion.
- *Small groups* – As we have seen people are more likely to be persuaded if they are part of a small group that already shares these norms and values.
- *Public commitment* – Making a public commitment is more likely to lead to attitude change. Political parties make good use of this at election time.

Activity 5.4

Think of a recent purchase you have made. What influencing factors can you identify from amongst those listed? Were there other influencing factors as well? List them.

Similarly, can you remember any occasion when you resisted persuasion? What went wrong in the persuasive process? List the factors involved.

Customer barriers to innovation

Customers do not necessarily resist a particular innovation because they dislike it, but rather because they do not like change and disruption. It is therefore important to understand what disruptions are caused so that the innovation or change can be directed with minimal interruption to existing practices and values. Sheth and Ram identify five areas of customer concern; they can be grouped into two categories – functional (usage pattern, economic value and risks), and psychological (cultural tradition and image).

Functional barriers

Usage barrier

It takes time for innovations to be accepted by customers as they need to absorb them into their daily lives. The service sector also faces usage barriers and Sheth and Ram cite video teleconferencing and car pooling as examples which disrupt our workflow. They say that these barriers can be overcome by thinking about the following:

- *The whole system* – the whole system needs to be considered so that the new offering fits into and interacts with what is already there (e.g. dishwashers into kitchens).
- *Integration* – rather than sell to an end user a solution would be to integrate the innovation into the preceding activity or product (e.g. car telephones to car makers).
- *Force* – make usage mandatory through government legislation (e.g. seat belts, lead-free petrol, smoke detectors).

The value barrier

Sheth and Ram say innovation, must offer greater value in that products or services must have better performance; a better price, or be positioned against a different competition.

The risk barrier

Purchasing a product or service always entails a degree of risk – there is economic risk, physical risk, performance risk and psychological risk. Marketers, in order to overcome these risks, can offer free trials, present testimonials, or introduce the offer as a component in a system so that the end user does not, or cannot, evaluate it. Examples include selling independent services under a well-known brand name, or introducing medical supplies into a hospital where people have no opportunity to choose treatments.

Psychological barriers

The tradition barrier

Sheth and Ram say that an innovation is resisted when it requires making changes in the traditions established by the corporate or societal culture. They say 'as the US economy becomes more and more service-oriented, we see more evidence of customers erecting cultural or tradition-based barriers to the increasing number of innovative services'.

They give as examples advertising for a spouse, singles bars, eating alone, co-ed health spas, the use of surrogate mothers, adoption of interracial children, organ transplants and other socially integrative medical practices.

Time erodes traditional barriers but changes to traditions must be approached with the right attitude. Understanding and respect, education and the use of change agents are required.

The image barrier

Image barriers may be associated with the origins of a product or service – product class, industry and country can create unfavourable stereotypes. Ways around this are to make fun of the image, create a unique image, or to associate the product/service with something or someone who has a positive image.

Innovation and the culture of continuous improvement

Innovation is a process whereby new ideas are developed and applied. An innovating organization must be able to:

1 Reflect on what it is doing and seek feedback.
2 Acquire new ideas.
3 Be open to change.
4 Implement new ideas.

Avenues to customer-focused innovations

Innovation can come from a number of avenues and the marketer needs to be constantly looking for:

- New forms of segmentation, reaching the target market and positioning.
- New types of product or service linked to providing solutions to customers' problems.
- New mechanisms for product or service delivery.
- New techniques for creating supplier to customer continuity.
- New ways of increasing the perceived value.
- New ways of ensuring operational excellence.
- New ways of motivating front-line staff.

An innovating organization needs to take the whole system into account. It needs to consider what it is doing within the context of the external and the internal environments of the organization and how the component parts work together and influence each other. Everything is interdependent and, as Gummesson says, an organization needs to think of itself as both interacting with the environment and being integrated with it.

External environment

Understanding the market

Innovation is systemic and linked with the macro-environment (PEST factors). It is also linked to an understanding of the micro-environment (markets, competition, suppliers, distributors, customers, stakeholders).

When an organization is open to influence from the environment and staff are seen as integrated into it there will be positive relationships with suppliers, buyers, customers – even competitors – and there will be a two-way flow of ideas and feelings between these different networks of people. This openness stops an organization becoming stale and enables it to remain boundaryless. Exchanges can be facilitated in different ways: focus groups, customer feedback forms, joint meetings with professional associations and other specialists in the field, benchmarking, think tanks, brainstorming and so on. An integrated communication plan that regards communication as a two-way process is fundamental to establishing this type of feedback.

Internal environment

There is no one way of creating an innovating customer-focused organization. However, there are some aspects that can be broadly identified as contributing to the process. These include the following.

Framework of thinking

The framework of thinking with which a marketer approaches this task will depend on there being a conceptual understanding of the marketers' role. This is changing from marketing management to the management of an organization with a marketing focus. This extension of thinking means that marketers need to think of the organization as a whole, not just what the marketing department is doing. When the whole organization is thinking marketing, innovation and improvement are likely to follow.

Vision and mission

A different vision now drives a customer-centric organization. This focus requires a new integrity, it has a greater urgency and is related to providing real service and value that customers and employees can relate to.

As much as the way as customers carry a product/service idea in their minds, within an organization individuals carry both a 'role idea' and an 'organization idea'. The vision which individuals carry in their minds of the organization helps them to manage their behaviour. The organization in the mind is not a replication of the hierarchical structures we are familiar with. However, it is as much of a reality as any organizational chart and may well create a different sense of organizational purpose for each and every member belonging to it. Internal realities, because they exist in people's minds, are difficult to change.

It is largely because organizations develop to satisfy the needs of the people working within them that very often it is difficult to change the people within an organization without first structurally changing the organization itself or indeed finding new members.

Leadership vision, commitment and internal marketing are essential to creating a focus on which this 'idea in the mind' can be developed into a mental picture that inspires and guides customer-focused behaviours.

The gap between strategic intent and reality

Many marketing activities fail to get off the ground because the organization suffers from inertia and has no energy; there is no time to do anything, and the strategy is not aligned around a central guiding idea.

The central guiding idea that helps to define what the organization does and how it goes about its business is a mission statement. The mission statement and an understanding of core competences creates a mindset that links the interests of customers, shareholders, and staff together into a network of relationships.

In an innovating organization that seeks constant improvement, these values, like those that guide the core competences, need to be articulated and marketed internally.

The mission statement needs to be translated into actionable points in each person's job description so that they know what they need to do in order to contribute to the organization's objectives. Similarly, if the philosophy is that of a learning organization ongoing learning objectives must be treated in the same way. Other relevant policies and procedures will then support these values.

Leaders

Gummeson (*Total Relationship Marketing*, p. 128) says that consumers and companies need a basic level of security. Security is associated with words such as:

- Promises.
- Honesty.
- Trust.
- Reliability.
- Predictability.
- Stability.
- Fear of being swindled or let down.
- Reduction of uncertainty or risk.

Leaders need to embody the values of a customer-centric organization. They must be able to model the right behaviour so that their colleagues understand in their bones the key values of customer-focused behaviour. Leaders also need to support and be supported by shareholders in changing the focus of the organization. Their support is pivotal to creating this vision.

Rewards and the mission

The mission determines what values are to drive the imagination and behaviour of employees. It lies behind the objectives, the strategy, the tactics and the job descriptions of the organization. If the mission is to be thin and lean one would imagine that the organization would be concerned with costs. If the mission is to be customer driven, statements on customer care and fulfilling customer needs should be the driving idea behind the jobs that people carry out. Similarly, if the organization values innovation this should be reflected. Rewards need to be linked to what people achieve on behalf of the organization and hence to what the organization values.

Organizations place a value on different aspects of their activities:

- Market share.
- Profit.
- Sales turnover.
- Cost reduction.
- Training.
- Customer satisfaction.
- Customer loyalty.
- Initiative.
- Entrepreneurial spirit.
- Team working.

People join organizations because they encompass values that match their aims (the Body Shop) or in other cases give them the opportunity to carry out a professional task. When the mission and values of an organization change this can create resistance or stress. For example, when the National Health Service changed to a market model, people whose values centred around patient care had to absorb the idea of a 'financial transaction' into their understanding of their role – this transition has created a lot of stress.

Recognition and happiness

When rewards are linked to the organizational purpose, recognition can be given. When people are recognized for their contribution they will feel successful – this in turn will breed further success.

Soft issues

The customer-care audit focuses on the soft organizational issues – feelings of trust, commitment, support, concern, envy, anger and resentment. These are all relationship issues that must be addressed alongside the harder issues of IT, profitability, market segmentation, branding, etc.

Structure, training and skilling

Structures may need to be developed that respond to change and structural issues addressed so that people in the front line are able to be innovative and imaginative in satisfying customer needs (not only the needs of the managerial hierarchy). Before organizations restructure they need to think about factors such as:

- Empowering front-line staff.
- Multiskilling and training.
- Ensuring rewards are related to the right values and tasks.
- Being able to manage the change in balance of power from middle management to front-line staff.

Developing new ideas

If an organization wants to develop new ideas it may be helpful for sub-systems, differentiated from routine work, to come together to focus on new ideas. These could include project teams and network structures; which may need to be developed in order to get the mix of specialists necessary to develop new ideas.

Every part of the organization has an effect on every other part. It is no good just looking at the departments who are in touch with customers directly or in charge of innovation strategy. The beliefs and values of every department in the organization will either support or hinder the process of customer focus and innovation. Innovation and customer focus affect all the interests that various stakeholders may have in an organization. These interests need to be thought about and taken into account. People may need training to be able to negotiate, become more creative, and handle conflict and differences of opinion, so people are able to participate in the process and not just cut themselves off because it feels too dangerous to step outside what everybody else is doing.

130

Organizational culture

Organizational culture can be broadly thought of as the way in which the people working within an organization learn to cope with adapting to their environment. This includes the problems that arise from the external environment as well as the way in which the organization integrates its activities internally. New members to the organization are taught that the way in which the organization operates is correct. Culture is therefore a learned product of group experience and is discovered, invented or developed by members of an organization as the organization develops over time. One of the tasks of leadership is to create and also manage this culture. Any change in culture needs to be implemented by management – this is why management must lead any change and training process. The recruitment, induction process, reward systems and appraisal process support this.

The culture in these new customer-focused organizations is different from a bureaucratic hiearchy. The rules for getting along have changed. People may have to learn them if they are not naturally born team players.

Organizational culture as a defence against anxiety

The term organizational defence is used to describe the way in which the members of an organization protect themselves from anxiety. They are built up from the individual role defences.

Once organizational culture and working methods are in place it is very difficult to get the members of an organization to adapt to changes brought about by the macro- and micro-environments. Very often working methods are created to protect people carrying out the work from the anxiety and stress that is inherent in the work itself. Resistance to change does not only happen with individuals and departments, it can also affect the whole organization. It can also create a 'them and us' situation when dealing with customers.

As Isabel Menzies Lyth says:

> The members of an organization use culture, structure and operating methods to create working methods that help them to deal with any struggles they have in coping with the stresses that can arise from carrying out the job itself; and changes in, and threats from, the environment. New members to the organization will either quickly fit into the existing work practices or find themselves out on a limb. Some may even leave. (Menzies Lyth, I. (1988). *Containing Anxiety in Organizations*, Free Association Books.)

Creating a customer-focused innovational culture in which there is an attitude towards continuous improvement will involve looking at the way in which the organization protects itself from stress and anxiety. Innovation is not linear, it muddles through, people have to struggle with themselves to adapt to change and half-baked ideas as people struggle to formulate them. If the organizational culture and management style does not allow for this, people will feel unsafe. Managers have to be able to facilitate creative problem solving. They need to be able to use coaching skills. If this is contrary to the way in which they normally behave (directive and controlling) they may need training.

Sheth and Ram (*Bringing Innovation to Market*, John Wiley & Sons) identify five major barriers to innovation that are inherent in the structure of many organizations. The specialization trap tends to lead to rigidity because it reinforces the expertise barrier and the operations barrier. Barriers associated with the environment are identified as the resource barrier, the regulation barrier and the market access barrier. Before choosing the organization will need to consider the advantages and disadvantages of the different methods:

1 *The expertise barrier.* People with a highly vested interest in a highly specialized technology tend to be unable or unwilling to disrupt established procedures radically enough to produce truly market-driven innovations. Peters & Waterman suggest they should be put into an autonomous task force called 'Skunk Works' where they can be free

to experiment outside established corporate behaviour. It is also common to form strategic research alliances. Acquisitions and mergers are another way forward but it is important that they do not provide new barriers to implementing change.

2   *The operations barrier.* Operational barriers will also prevent change. For example, resistance to changing work processes such as marketing products that are operationally continuous rather than market driven and customer focused. Ways of overcoming these barriers could include starting afresh with a new and separate facility, modifying procedures as the industry updates itself with the use of new technology. Selective modification is another alternative.

3   *The resource barrier.* If acquiring funds could be a problem there are other ways to break through this barrier including:
    - License agreements and franchising;
    - Consortiums;
    - Venture capital.

4   *The regulation barrier.* Regulations – both industry self-regulation relating to codes of business practice, and also government regulations – control various aspects of a business. Regulations can sometimes be changed by effective lobbying. Alternatively, organizations can avoid legislation by marketing in another area, or by reorganizing the holding company so it is free to offer product or service innovations not allowed in the regulated entity.

5   *Market-access barrier.* This type of barrier includes factors as various as access to shelf space and difficulties for customers switching to new products because technology is embedded in their existing products. Porter discusses all sorts of barriers that organizations use to prevent new market centres. International trade barriers also keep competition out. Sheth and Ram suggest the following solutions:
    - Forming alliances with the dominant vendor;
    - Developing an in-house distribution system;
    - Jumping the barrier by marketing directly to the customers.

Role

Innovation requires an expansion of role. People in the organization must be able to take personal responsibility for organizational problems. This is the organizational equivalent of good citizenship – people take responsibility for themselves and society. This means they must be able to expand the role idea that helps them to manage their behaviour. For this to occur they will need to feel safe so they do not spend time defending themselves and protecting their backs. They may also need training on how to help them think about what prevents them from expanding their role. There could be personal, organizational and environmental factors – the three are interrelated.

Mixed role teams

Create teams with mixed roles and you avoid the trap of recruiting people who all think the same way. This approach to recruitment encourages diversity in which difference is accepted. Belbin identified eight team roles – people are naturally stronger in some roles than others. Using this approach to selecting team players, people are enabled to identify their strengths and weaknesses, and these can be taken into account, dismissed and 'difference' allowed for and managed.

Belbin identified nine team roles:

1   *The shaper* – this individual plays the role of a task-oriented leader, concerned to influence or shape the cause of events through getting their own way – often seen as autocratic in style.

2   *The coordinator* – also a leader but one who succeeds by drawing out the ideas of others, rather than imposing their own views.

3   *The plant* – is the individual who has plenty of ideas and enables the team to become more imaginative.

4   *The resource investor* – also gets ideas but from outside the team, the resource investigator is not a technical type but a creative, social type – a Mr or Mrs Fixit.

5 *The team worker* – This individual keeps the team in harmony.
6 *The implementor* – The individual who carries things through.
7 *The monitor and evaluator* – This individual is good at helping the team evaluate less suitable ideas that emerge within the group from shapers and plants.
8 *The completer finisher* – This very necessary individual enables teams to carry through on implementation and detail.
9 *The specialist* – Whose presence in the team is confined to the supply of technical/professional guidance.

Other factors that need to be considered

Resources and expertise

Acquiring and/or having people and allowing them to have access to resources and technology is fundamental to this process. Resources could be time, money, equipment, libraries, training, access to the internet and so on.

Openness and permeability

Organizations need to understand that customer-focused behaviour means engaging with other human beings at a feeling level. This must be embodied in policies and procedures throughout the whole organization. For a customer to be met with 'we don't give out names' is an affront. People in contact with customers need to be recruited who have this ability to engage with people.

Integrated marketing

Marketing must be able to move closer to the front line. Marketers have to develop new skills and be able to relate to wider organizational issues that involve quality and human resource management and operational aspects. Marketing has to come out of the 4Ps (product, price, place, promotion) and enter the fray of the additional 3Ps (people, processes, physical evidence) of a service driven business. Marketing has to be able to integrate its customer-focused philosophy into the whole organization. Internal marketing and the support of top management will be essential for this to take place.

Information technology

IT is essential to driving customer relationships along. It must be able to link customer contacts wherever they may occur so that an integrated communication strategy can be operated and strategic and tactical issues can be addressed. Marketing and IT should work more closely together. Other information systems, communication systems, decision making systems and reward systems need to be in place in order to allow the process of innovation and continuous improvement to take place. The organization also needs to look at creating electronic and human networks that extend outside it so that people can be kept in touch with new ideas and be encouraged to network.

Speed

Yesterday customers waited, now they go elsewhere. Organizations need to speed up their processes and decision making. Shorter life cycles and more competition make this essential.

The action list

Here is a short 'to-do' list for managers. It is not a comprehensive list, because such a list does not exist. If someone could find a way of 'bottling' continuous improvement, it would have already been done.

- Establish a clear vision and a way of measuring when you have got there.
- Spend time each day talking to people about your vision. Listen to them. Show them that you care about them through your words and actions.

- Insist on a career development plan for everybody. Do performance appraisals at least once per year. Involve your human resources function in these activities, but make them a line-management responsibility.
- Teach people customer focus. Everybody should know that the customer comes first, second and third. Nothing should be done that does not in some way serve a customer.
- Start a training schedule for teaching teamwork. Establish a team structure.
- Encourage people to improve their own education in any subjects they like.
- Teach everybody how to make good presentations. It is a great confidence builder.
- Teach project organization skills.
- Insist that top management are teachers, coaches and trainers in the various training events for at least one week each year. There is no better way of learning something than having to teach it to somebody else.
- Build people-oriented communication procedures so people know what is going on and what the management activities are.
- Build a recognition system but do not forget to say 'thank you' as often as appropriate.
- Find out how good you are through self-assessment, starting in the boardroom. For example, use the Malcolm Baldrige Quality Award or the European Quality Award criteria.
- Benchmark. Find out what other organizations are doing. Attend seminars as a student and speaker. It is not necessary to reinvent the wheel.
- For facilitators of continuous improvement, hammer on the boardroom door until they listen to your message of 'people are an asset, not a cost'. This may take more courage than most of us possess!
- Adopt a structured process of continuous improvement as your complete method of managing the enterprise.
- And, above all, make a plan of action before you start. The method should be 'ready-aim-fire' not 'ready-fire-aim'.

(John Gilbert (1998), 'A job for life', into 'A life of jobs', Empowerment in Organizations, *6(6), www.emerald-library.com)*

Creativity in organizations

Rawlinson (1971) believed that there were seven blocks to creative problem solving:

1 Self-imposed barriers.
2 Unwarranted assumptions.
3 One correct answer thinking.
4 Failing to challenge the obvious.
5 Negativity.
6 Pressures to conform.
7 Fear of looking foolish.

So how do people and organizations overcome these blocks?

The creative climate

Creativity works in two ways. First, it comes from the individual's internal psychological climate, and second, from the external climate or environment.

Some organizations kill off creativity by having a negative culture – people say 'it costs too much', 'it won't work', 'it can't be done that way', 'it is not possible'. Other organizations create an open climate where ideas are encouraged, communication is open and structures and strategies are built into the organization to allow the flow of ideas. Reward systems encourage creativity and different types of people are used in the selection process so they get a diversity of views. Leadership behaviour is similarly open. Staff provide role models for younger staff and bring out these values.

In an organization where safety is the mind set, people will not step out of line because it is too risky. They will avoid taking decisions in case they get it wrong. This type of organization is unable to encourage creativity as it is seen as too dangerous.

Innovation and a culture of customer improvement are the result of a complete learning process. This is not something that can be achieved overnight. The organization may well need to approach this change in a variety of ways.

Managing change

Managing change is covered in the module Effective Management for Marketing.

In the meantime you can personally:

1 Stop saying 'Yes, but' and change it to 'Yes, and . . .'.
2 Turn negative experiences into positive ones and make them something you can learn from.
3 Break through your habitual way of thinking and find a new mind-set.
4 Find yourself an idea you would like to develop.
5 Give yourself time to reflect and incubate your ideas. Talk about them to as many people as you can inside and outside the organization and see how they feel.
6 Get the support and resources you need to develop your ideas.

Case study

Image Makers

Image Makers is an American owned, full-service international communications consultancy, providing everything from research to the implementation of campaigns for clients based in over forty countries worldwide. Billings annually from the European Division, with headquarters in Paris, have reflected the hard times faced by the industry generally. These figures have been corrected for inflation and are quoted in $ millions.

Table 5.4 Sales in $ million from European Division

1989	1990	1991	1992	1993	1994	1995	1996 (forecast)
89	95	103	103	99	89	91	91

The agency's sales force in Europe consists of thirty Key Account Managers who are responsible for building and retaining existing business and fifteen New Business Development Executives who operate across Europe from three offices in Paris, London and Rome.

A recent analysis of Image Makers carried out in May 1996 uncovered weaknesses in the organization of its European sales activity. The following findings emerged from this analysis:

- There was no clear 'leader' of the sales activity and no identifiable strategy for this function.
- Although the agency uses English as a common language, the forty-five individuals who make up the operational sales team had little else in common. There were problems with communication between individuals, no evidence of team spirit and very little exchange of information. This situation was worse because the group came from eight different national cultures and opportunities for integration of activities were not being taken.
- Resentment between the Key Account Managers and New Business Development Executives was clearly identified. It was found that both groups thought the other had the easier job and the fact that a sales bonus system was only available to the New Business Development Executives fuelled the resentment further.

- Within the groups there was also tension related to perceptions over 'best' accounts and easier geographic regions.

A customer care survey, carried out by external consultants in the same month showed the company was perceived by clients to be:

- Arrogant in its dealings with clients.
- Unable to communicate internally.
- Uncaring about its public image.
- Falling below competitors on most of the aspects of customer care surveyed.

The survey concluded that Image Makers had only survived because of its recognized reputation for technical excellence.

Brief

You have been appointed as Manager of Client Relations, with responsibility for the Key Account Managers (KAM) and New Business Development Executives (NBDE) as the first step to putting these weaknesses right.

The management team in the USA have asked you to present a report covering the following points:

1 Your proposals for building the Key Account Managers and New Business Development Executives into an effective working team. The management team have indicated that you are free to propose changes which cut across the current organization and remuneration structures. You should include recommendations for improving motivation and team spirit. (25 marks)
2 The actions you recommend to improve customer care for clients of the Image Makers and a timetable for their implementation. (15 marks)

Sample answer

To: US Management Team
From: Client Manager (Europe)
Date: 20XX

Terms of reference:

1 To make proposals to build the KAMs and NBDEs into an effective team.
2 To outline recommended actions to improve customer care for clients.

1 The organizational development programme will take place on four levels – the whole organization, inter-group, group and individual levels.

1.1 The organization
A series of meetings to discuss strategy will be held. This will take the form of workshops in which the macro- and micro-environments will be discussed, a mission statement reformulated to put customers at the centre of our business, objectives set, and strategies for growth considered alongside competitive strategies and core competences. A customer-care programme will be introduced as one of the tactics we will use in our competitive strategy.

Key outcomes:

- A mission placing customers at the heart of our business.
- Action plans to include what this means in each job description.
- The establishment of a customer-care task force.
- Outline ideas on the creation of a customer retention and care programme.
- The creation of core competences and objectives that can then form the basis of future appraisal and management by objectives system.
- The creation of a strategy for growth and the development of sales strategy.

A task force needs to be established to look at key issues on pay. Policies such as the linking of the bonus system to new business and customer retention will allow both KAMs and NBDEs to participate. Managers need to be given discretion in awarding pay increases.

We may also like to think about organizing around customers instead of geographical areas.

We also need to think about how we can go about creating an organizational culture that will override the sense of nationality and the identity people get from their different areas of work.

We should consider the appointment of a marketing director who will act as a unifying figure for both groups and be responsible for customer retention and new business.

1.2 Inter group
Sessions will be run in which each group will be able to reverse roles. KAMs and NBDEs will be able to explore how each group perceives the other.

Entertainment and a fun evening out will give people the chance to mix socially.

Key outcomes:

- Help groups to reach a more realistic idea of what each group does.
- Provide an opportunity to reduce psychological and physical distance.
- Get some understanding of the dynamics of inter-group behaviour.

1.3 Group
A series of sessions will be held by a consultant to help the group to look at the processes taking place within the team in the normal flow of work, meetings, and informal and formal contacts. Of particular relevance here will be individual's own actions and their impact on other people.

Key outcomes:

- An opportunity to discuss cultural differences.
- An opportunity to talk problems out.
- An opportunity to discuss things that may be difficult to talk about under normal circumstances.
- Get some understanding of group behaviour.

Team building
A series of team building days will be held.

Key outcomes:

- Bonding.
- An opportunity to create culture.
- An understanding of how our actions impact on other people.
- An understanding of some of the key skills needed in order to work effectively in a team.

Belbin role analysis

Key outcomes:

- An understanding of team roles.
- An understanding of strengths and weaknesses (our own and the team).
- An understanding of how people behave in different team roles.
- An opportunity to restructure the teams and balance out the team roles.

1.4 Individual

Role analysis
Any failure to fulfil the individual's needs will lead to frustration and an unwillingness to consider change. We should therefore give each individual the opportunity to settle down with a consultant to talk about their role.

Key outcomes:

- An understanding about the motivation of the individual.
- An understanding of weakness where the job is not being done properly and for which training can be arranged.
- The opportunity to talk through career plans.
- The opportunity to ascertain whether the individual is constrained by anything else.

Appraisal scheme
An appraisal scheme must be set up around the key result areas in the job description relating to sales, customer retention and customer satisfaction.

Leadership training
Group leaders should go on a series of team leader workshops.

2 Recommendations to improve customer care for clients.

Month 1
1 Following on from the strategy day we will already have in place:

- A senior director on the group;
- A task group to oversee the customer-care programme;
- The outline of a tactical programme for customer care.

2 A focus group consisting of a mixture of clients, KAMs, NBDEs, and supporting staff should be set up. The subjects under discussion will be competitor service and customers' complaints. A video will be made of these sessions and circulated within the company.

Month 2
3 Following this a list of key areas of performance will be drawn up. Areas such as:

- Telephone answering;
- Time from enquiry to quotation;
- Frequency of client contact.

4 Measures will then be drawn up to enable us to evaluate our success in reaching our targets.

Months 3, 4 and 5
5 Training for staff on dealing with objections, negotiation, handling complaints and creating a good atmosphere will be organized.

Months 3 and 4
6 A promotional campaign will be organized to show our target market that we are happy, polite, efficient people to deal with. This will reinforce this new identity to our employees.

Month 6
7 Customers will be encouraged to visit our sites.

Budgets
Budgets need to be discussed and allocated. However, we first need to establish if these outline proposals are acceptable.

Conclusion
This report covers a wide range of activities the organization needs to consider. The final change that could be considered would be to make the same people responsible for new business and for customer retention. This would need to be done on a group basis so that the client's decision-making unit was approached with a relationship network in mind.

Summary

This unit has examined the critical role played by innovation and continuous improvement in maintaining a customer focus over time. It has addressed the barriers to innovation that may occur in organizations and suggested ways in which such barriers can be overcome. We will now introduce modelling, the concept of attitudes and how attitude modelling can be used to explain behaviour.

Modelling customer behaviour, attitudes and dynamics

In this unit you will be:

❑ Introduced to modelling.

❑ Introduced to the concept of attitudes.

❑ Presented with the different models of attitudes and how they can be used to explain behaviour.

Study Guide

The emphasis in this unit is very much on understanding the principles and techniques behind consumer modelling rather than slavishly learning specific models by rote. The only way to gain a thorough understanding of modelling techniques and their application is to try working examples and relate these to your own purchasing experiences.

Any questions on modelling will require students to know why models are used, how they are designed, and what their benefits are. Most of the qualitative data we collect as market researchers relates to the attitudes of current or potential customers to the product or services we offer. To gain acceptance from customers we must present a favourable image and avoid unfavourable associations. How favourable impressions translate into active endorsements of a product or service is a matter of some conjecture. The attitude theories described in this unit all approach this problem in a slightly different manner.

Consumer decision making

We all make decisions every day of our lives: *'What shall I have for breakfast?' 'What sort of career do I want?' 'What brand of potatoes should I buy?'* We are so used to making decisions that we rarely think about them. In fact, making decisions has become so automatic that we sometimes have difficulty explaining why we made a particular choice!

The aim of consumer decision-making research is to understand why decisions are made. Not surprisingly, this is not always easy. An understanding of the decision-making process requires a knowledge of consumer behaviour. The contents of this unit tie together many of the basic psychological and social processes that have been described in the earlier sections of this workbook.

Ask a friend or colleague (politely!) why they chose the clothes they are wearing. The response may well be '*I just liked them*' or something quite specific. List the reasons they give for each item of clothing (underwear excepted!).

This should give an idea of the range of possible reasons for a buying decision being made.

What is a model?

Definition 6.1

A physical, visual or mathematical ... simplified representation of a complex system.

Macmillan Dictionary of Retailing

A model is an abstract representation of a process or relationship. A simple example, if we believe that raising the price for crossing a toll bridge will reduce the number of cars using the bridge we have expressed a model which can be represented in one of three ways:

1 *Verbally*: 'as price increases – cars decrease'.

2 *Mathematically*: $C = K \dfrac{1}{P}$

   where C = number of cars, P = toll price, K = constant.

3 *Pictorially*: | Price increase | → | Reduction in cars | .

We all hold numerous models in our heads, most of which we give no thought to, but which allow us to make sense of the world and predict the likely course of events. Consider gravity. We all have a notion about gravity – we know that if we let go of something it will fall to the floor. This allows us to predict what is going to happen when we accidentally knock something over, drop-kick a football, or throw something.

It is possible to have totally different models of the same phenomenon. Keith Williams (1990) gives the example of an atlas where one might find the same country on different pages modelled on its topography, climate, geology, population, and zoology.

Models are of assistance in a number of ways:

1 They assist in the development of theories.
2 They aid the understanding of complex relationships.
3 They provide a framework for discussion and research.

We will now turn our attentions to the modelling of consumer behaviour.

Consumer decision models

In this unit, we are primarily concerned with the use of models to understand consumer behaviour. In most cases, what is being modelled is the behaviour leading up to a purchasing decision.

We are most interested in understanding how and why certain decisions are made. As such, our models will usually include consideration of many of the topics in this workbook:

- Attitudes.
- Perception.
- Learning.
- Motivation.
- Social and cultural influences.

In most cases, consumer models are expressed pictorially and in this unit, we will discuss the basic principles underlying consumer modelling as well as looking at several specific models.

Classification of models

In 1974, the Market Research Society presented the findings of a study group which had been established to look at modelling. They agreed a classification system for assessing models which identified eleven dimensions:

1 *Micro or macro.* In a micro-model each individual or unit in the market or database is represented and processed at the individual level. The output may or may not be a result of the aggregation of individual data. In a macro-model the total market is considered as a whole and the model's output is a global market response.

2 *Data-based or theory-based.* Data-based models are the logical outcome of the process of data analysis used. Theory-based models are developed through the application of reason and have their basis in theories adopted from the behavioural sciences.

3 *Low, medium, or high level.* This relates to simplicity or lack of it. At the lowest level simple models can be devised that require few variables but they inevitably have certain limitations because of their narrow coverage. They are better regarded as sub-models or component parts of some larger, more comprehensive model. At the other extreme there are 'grand' models that seek to orchestrate all relevant market variables and represent the full range of marketing stimuli. The medium category lies elsewhere between the two.

4 *Descriptive (historical or current), diagnostic or predictive.* Here the distinction is made between models that describe market behaviour, those that seek to explain or diagnose why consumers behave as they do, and those that set out to predict how consumers will behave under specified circumstances.

5 *Behavioural or statistical.* In behavioural models, reference is made to underlying assumptions about how the individual behaves. They seek to relate to the total process of consumer responses to a given stimulus. With the statistical model there are no implicit assumptions about how or why consumers behave as they do. The internal parameters are hypothesized as a function of the analytical procedures employed.

6 *Generalized or ad hoc.* Here a distinction is made between models that are intended to be, or can be, applied to a wide range of markets and those that are developed in the context of, and for use in, one market only.

7 *Functional or intellectual.* The functional model represents the actual function of the object; it is meant to have real world application. The intellectual model need not be rooted in practicability.

8 *Static or dynamic.* The static model represents a particular system at a given point in time and cannot take account of time effects. The dynamic model is able to represent systems over time. It can take account of changing values of parameters and even changes in basic relationships between parameters over time.

9 *Qualitative or quantitative.* In the case of qualitative models no explicit variables are measured. In the case of quantitative models they are. A quantitative model is therefore more likely to be helpful in predicting behaviour as it should provide an indication of the weighting of importance that should be given to individual variables.

10 *Algebraic, sequential/net, or topological.* In algebraic models summation or other manipulation is independent of the order of the variables. With sequential or net models the order of the variables is explicitly taken into account by the model. Topological models are based upon field-theory concepts involving space and geometry, forces and motion. They are gestalt models, that is they are concerned with the total situation.

11 *Successful or unsuccessful.* These concepts are indefinable. What constitutes success or lack of it will differ among different people. Nonetheless, it was felt to be a useful criterion.

We would all like a simple model which accurately predicts all consumer behaviour under a variety of circumstances. Unfortunately, the perfect model does not exist and the best we can hope for is to be able to understand the behaviour that most people will conform to under a restricted set of circumstances. Nonetheless, this is better than 'whistling in the wind' and, gaining a better understanding of behaviour, does have other benefits as we have seen in earlier units.

Construction of models

Before looking at models in detail, we must identify the variable types which form the 'building blocks' of these consumer models.

Table 6.1

Stimulus	*Response*
These act as inputs to the consumer's behaviour. Examples include: advertising, environmental factors, reference group influence and physiological factors	These are the observable responses of individuals which may be directly due to certain stimuli or arise as a result of internal processes
Internal	*External*
These are variables which arise as a result of either internal physiological or psychological processes. Examples include: attitudes, learning, motivation, hunger and sex	These are variables which arise as a result of external influences. Examples include: economic factors, situational factors and weather
Endogenous	*Exogenous*
These are variables which have a clearly defined effect. These are included in the model.	These are variables which have a poorly defined effect. For example, a change in future circumstances, price changes by competitors and so on. These are usually not included in a model

To these categories we must add intervening variables which act between stimulus and response. They modify the relationship between the stimuli received and the responses made but, by definition, cannot be observed or measured. They are thus exogenous variables which can be both external or internal in origin.

Figure 6.1 illustrates the action of the various variables, the box representing the consumer. In particular, it should be noted how response variables can impact future behaviour and that past and future considerations can be considered as stimuli.

143

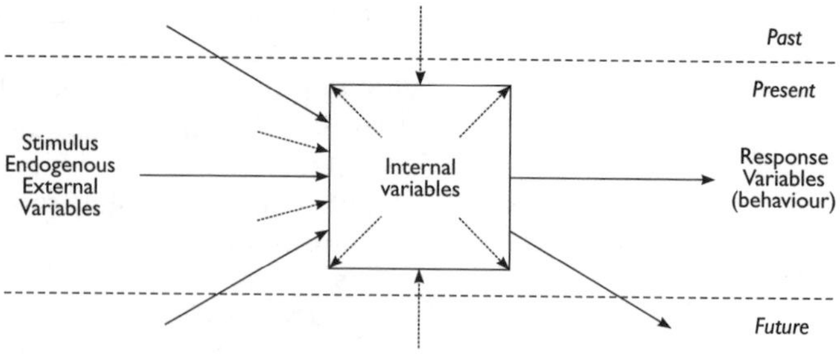

Figure 6.1
Showing effect on consumer of variable types. Dotted lines represent the possible influence of exogenous variables

Evaluating models

Before considering specific models in detail, it is worthwhile to consider the criteria to be used in their evaluation. The following were proposed by Williams (1990) as being indicative of a 'good' model:

1 *Simplicity* – whether the model is of high or low level, it should seek to break down complex behaviour patterns into simple easily understandable components.
2 *Factual basis* – a model should be consistent with the facts as far as they are known.
3 *Logic* – to be plausible a model must make sense and be internally consistent.
4 *Originality* – if a model is to advance knowledge it should be original, either in its basic construction or in the way in which it links together previously separate areas of knowledge.
5 *Explanatory power* – a model should seek to explain how, and why, specified behaviour takes place.
6 *Prediction* – a model should aid the prediction of a consumer's reaction to a given stimulus.
7 *Heuristic power* – this refers to a model's capacity to suggest new areas of research.
8 *Validity* – if a model is to have validity it must be verifiable. This means that it should be possible, at least in theory, to test the relationships proposed between variables.

It would be unrealistic to expect every model to satisfy all these criteria. However, they do provide a useful framework for assessing the importance and significance to be attached to a particular model. If, for example, a model lacked any factual basis, failed to explain observed behaviour and did little to enlighten our thinking, then we would be justified in dismissing it.

Of course, no set of criteria can be comprehensive or pertain to every situation. As with all such problems, a common sense assessment, against the background of a general understanding of the components of consumer behaviour, will go a long way.

Simple models

Simple models of consumer behaviour take a 'broad brush' approach to understanding consumers. In contrast with the comprehensive models to be discussed later in this unit, they consider only the main influences on behaviour. Simple models fall into four general categories:

1 *Black box* – this is the generic name for models which do not consider internal processes but rely solely on directly observable stimulus variables and responses.
2 *Decision process* – these types of models enjoy widespread use within marketing. They illustrate the various decision stages a consumer progresses through to arrive at a particular course of action. An example is the AIDA (attention, interest, desire, action) promotional model.

3   *Personal variable* – these, in contrast to black box models, focus on internal variables. They attempt to model particular internal processes. One example is Fishbein's attitude model.

4   *Hybrid decision/personal* – these attempt to combine the features of decision process and personal variable models. In this unit, we will consider Chris Rice's *PV/PPS* model.

Black box models

Perhaps the simplest black box model of behaviour is the stimulus–response (SR) model which is typically illustrated by the experiments of Pavlov. Pavlov found that when a dog was presented with meat it salivated. In this case the stimulus was the meat, the response the salivation. Simple SR relationships also exist in people. For example, a short tap just below the knee (stimulus) will cause the leg to move in a reflex action (response). The basic SR model can be represented as in Figure 6.2.

Figure 6.2
The simplest black box model

More complex black box models typically consider more variables and more entities (whether they are single consumers or organizations).

Figure 6.3 is an example of a 'consumer-centric' black box model of a consumer's decision environment. It shows the stimuli which can influence purchasing behaviour. Note that some of the influencing variables can themselves be influenced by the consumer resulting in a two-way interaction.

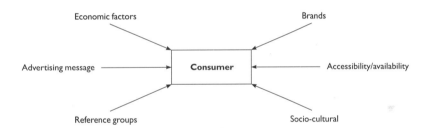

Figure 6.3
Consumer-centric black box model of consumer decision environment

Figure 6.4 shows Kotler's model of the buying process showing inputs and outputs. It presents a more considered view of the buying behaviour. It takes into account more influences and details more of the responses.

As black box models concentrate solely on the action of external variables, they are only useful in the investigation of behaviour where internal variables are not deemed significant. When considering black box models researchers are primarily interested in the relative importance of the stimuli involved.

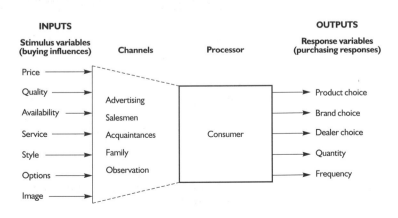

Figure 6.4
Kotler's Model of the buying process. A complex black box model

145

For example, cigarette advertising is banned on British television so, unless a particular consumer is known to be regularly exposed to other sources of advertising (magazines, cinema, etc.), then reference groups, cultural influences and brand experience are more likely to play a part in the brand of cigarettes chosen. Similarly, someone who lives in a big city is less likely to be influenced by accessibility/availability restrictions than a consumer living in a remote village.

Decision process models

Unlike black box models, decision process models represent a process flow. They are derived from the general decision-making/problem solving models of researchers such as Newell and Simon. Figure 6.5 illustrates such a generic model.

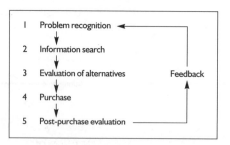

Figure 6.5
The five-stage model

This model allows us to consider buying as a process but it makes various assumptions and has therefore been criticized. It assumes:

- That consumers are rational.
- That decision processes are simple and sequential.
- There are different types of decisions.
- It assumes that customers can receive and order information.
- Many purchases seem not to be preceded by a decision process.

Decision process models occur in many areas of marketing (both with reference to behaviour and other fields) and form the core of most of the comprehensive models.

Problem recognition

The customer recognizes they would like to change the current situation, they have a need. The stimulus could be internal or external (for example, feels in need of a break and/or sees a holiday brochure).

Search for information

The customer looks for information either from external sources or from memory. The more complex the area the more information will be required. The marketer must be able to get the product/service into the consumer's awareness and choice set (Figure 6.6).

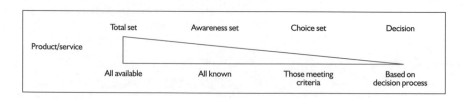

Figure 6.6
The customer awareness and choice set

Alternative evaluation

The customer looks at alternatives from a need-satisfying perspective – they look for benefits.

Purchase

After evaluation the customer buys the preferred alternative or a substitute. The decision to modify or postpone purchase is influenced by the risk they perceive and any anxiety they feel.

146

Evaluation
The purchase is then evaluated against the original criteria.

Risk
When consumers make decisions the outcome may be uncertain purchasing involves risk and anxiety. However, risk is personal and related to the consumer's perception of what they consider to be risky – functional risk (will the product perform?), physical risk (will I be harmed?), financial risk (is it worth the money?), social risk (will the deodorant work?), psychological risk (will it affect my self-image?), time risk (am I wasting my time?).

Managing risk
Consumers may minimize risk by staying with the same brand, buying a well-known brand, purchasing from a reputable dealer, buying a more expensive brand, looking for reassurance (such as money-back guarantees, laboratory test results, prepurchase trial, warranties) and looking for information (such as from family, friends, opinion leaders, consumer reports, testimonials and information found in the media).

Post-purchase dissonance
Often after an important purchase has been made, a phenomenon called 'post-purchase dissonance' is present; this is a feeling of unease that the goods may not represent good value. Consumers frequently rationalize and reinforce their purchase decisions by looking for messages that confirm their past beliefs, or by ignoring the dissonant information by refusing to discuss it or rejecting it. Marketers should therefore reduce post-purchase dissonance by providing reassuring messages, providing after-sales service and general customer care.

Levels of consumer decision making

Extended problem solving and limited problem solving
Not all consumer decision making requires the same degree of information search. The actions at each stage vary and depend on the extent to which customers are engaged in extended problem solving (EPS) or limited problem solving (LPS).

When customers purchase, two factors are particularly useful in explaining how they come to a decision.

1   How involved they are in purchasing the product/service.
2   The difference in their perception between competing brands.

Involvement
The extent to which the customer gets involved in a purchase depends on the individual. Involvement can be transient or enduring especially where the choice is repetitive and past experience produces a brand preference (for example: perfume, cigarettes, magazines and newspapers) (see Figure 6.7).

Figure 6.7
A personal involvement checklist.
Source: Engel, Warshaw, Kinnear, Richard D. Irwin, Inc 1994. Adapted from Edward F. McQuarrie and J. Michael Munson, A revised product involvement inventory: improved usability and validity, in *Advances in Consumer Research*, vol. 19, eds John F. Sherry, Jr., and Brian Sternthal (Provo, Utah: Association for Consumer Research, 1992), p. 111. Used by special permission

For each of the 10 statements, circle the extent to which you agree or disagree. The scale ranges from (1) strongly agree to (6) strongly disagree

1	I would be interested in reading about this product.	1	2	3	4	5	6
2	I would read a *Consumer Reports* article about this product.	1	2	3	4	5	6
3	I have compared product characteristics among brands.	1	2	3	4	5	6
4	I think there are a great deal of differences among brands.	1	2	3	4	5	6
5	I have a most preferred brand of this product.	1	2	3	4	5	6
6	I usually pay attention to ads for this product.	1	2	3	4	5	6
7	I usually talk about this product with other people.	1	2	3	4	5	6
8	I usually seek advice from other people prior to purchasing this product.	1	2	3	4	5	6
9	I usually take many factors into account before purchasing this product.	1	2	3	4	5	6
10	I usually spend a lot of time choosing what kind to buy.	1	2	3	4	5	6

	High-involvement purchase decision	Low-involvement purchase decision
Decision making (information search, consideration of brand alternatives)	Complex decision making (autos, major appliances)	Variety seeking (cereals)
Habit (little or no information search, consideration of only one brand)	Brand loyalty (cigarettes, perfume)	Inertia (canned vegetables, paper towels)

Extended problem solving (EPS)

When customers are highly involved in the purchase and they can see that the differences between brands are significant. High involvement purchases involve a degree of risk, for example:

- They are highly priced (financial risk), e.g. cars.
- Very complex (psychological risk) the wrong decision will cause stress, e.g. computers.
- They reflect self-image (social risk) and peer group approval is important, e.g. clothing, jewellery.

The stages are as follows:

1 *Problem recognition*
2 *Information search*
  Customers will look for information from a wide variety of media sources and personal selling will influence their choice. The decision making may be carried out over an extended period of time.
3 *Alternative evaluation*
  Multiple criteria will be used to evaluate the brand and each brand will be seen as significantly different from each other.
4 *Purchase*
  Customers will travel and visit a lot of shops. Personal selling will influence their choice.
5 *Post-purchase evaluation*
  Satisfaction will increase their loyalty to the brand.

Limited problem solving (LPS)

Customers are not very involved in the purchase, there are minor perceived differences and the problem that needs to be solved is not large. The stages are as follows:

1 *Problem recognition*
2 *Information search*
  The customer is unlikely to look extensively for information.
3 *Evaluation of alternatives*
  When involvement and interest in a brand is low, brand switching is likely to take place. The brand decision is not considered important enough to warrant pre-planning and will often take place in the shop.
4 *Purchase*
  Customers are likely to try the brand out when they come across a purchase trigger like an in-store display, a coupon, a free trial. Point-of-sale display, price and packaging are important aspects of the marketing mix as buying action is also influenced by brand recognition. Customers may switch brands out of boredom, others may buy the same brand again out of 'inertia' because it is just not important enough to give it any thought.
  It may also be better to position these products functionally (see positioning Unit 3).
5 *Post-purchase evaluation*
  Beliefs about the brand may be formed by learning passively about the brand and recalled from memory or the brand may be evaluated after use and beliefs about it formed by experience.

How much information do customers need?

It is generally believed that customers make decisions to purchase on a small number of selectively chosen pieces of information.

It therefore follows that it is extremely important to understand what information the customer feels will help them to be able to evaluate goods and services. In group decision making it is likely that each member of the group may have different needs for information.

| Activity 6.2 |

This process is now considered in more detail and the following activity will enable you to get some hands-on experience of customer decision making. Working with a partner take a recent or planned purchase and work through the five stages answering the following questions.

1 Need recognition
   The customer recognizes they would like to change the current situation.

   - What is motivating the person? (think about basic psychological needs and benefits, these can be driven internally or externally by the environment).
   - Are the needs dormant or can the customer express them?
   - How involved with the product are they? Think about the situation, is it one of extended problem solving or limited problem solving?

2 Search for information
   The customer looks for information either from external sources or from memory to solve the problem. The amount of information that is found will be influenced by a number of factors such as time available, past experience involving ways in which attitudes have been formed and patterns of learned behaviour, and other influences such as social factors which include reference group influence, personal contacts, etc.

   - Do you understand what information they need to proceed to the next stage of evaluation?
   - Do you know where information about the product/service comes from?
   - Do you know what information they have?
   - Do you know if the customer is motivated enough to look for alternative information?
   - What criteria (features, benefits) do they use to assess the information?

3 Alternative evaluation – the customer looks at alternatives from the perspective of need-satisfying benefits.

   - What else is being evaluated at the same time?
   - What criteria (features, benefits) are the competition using?
   - Are there existing customer–supplier relationships?
   - Are the criteria used perceived by the customer as being different or essentially the same?
   - How important are the differences?

4 Purchase
   After the evaluation has been made the customer then buys the preferred alternative or a substitute.

   - Do they have the money?
   - Will the offer have to be adapted in order to clinch the deal?
   - Will the customer go on looking until they find exactly what they want?
   - Will they accept a substitute?
   - Where do they expect to make the purchase?

5 Post purchase evaluation
The purchase is then evaluated against the original criteria. Does it meet the needs and expectations of the customer?

- How satisfied are they and what reasons do they give for their satisfaction/dissatisfaction?
- How does this experience compare with previous experiences with other products/services?
- Have they told anybody else about their satisfaction/dissatisfaction?
- Have they tried to complain? What reaction did they get?
- Will they purchase again or will they use an alternative?

Personal variable models

As noted, these focus on modelling specific internal processes such as attitudes, perception and motivation.

The rise in the 1980s of information processing theory has been influential in the development of personal variable models. Information processing theory is mostly concerned with the mind and the way it is organized. It has provided another perspective on the way in which decisions are modelled and in particular in the area of rule development – the rules used in arriving at a decision where alternatives are being considered. There are four basic personal variable models, classified according to the decisions rule types used within the model:

1 *Compensatory, or trade-off, rule* – this assumes that consumers trade-off products against each other considering all of the features of the products against some hypothetical ideal. The rule implies that sacrifices are made as part of the decision process but that each alternative is considered thoroughly. For example, you may be willing to compromise on the appearance of a new stereo system if the sound quality is good.
2 *Threshold rule* – this assumes that products can be totally rejected on the basis of just one undesirable characteristic – without further consideration. For example, you may reject the purchase of a new set of kitchen pans out-of-hand if their colour clashes with the rest of your kitchen despite the fact that the other characteristics of the pan may have been ideal.
3 *Disjunctive rule* – this assumes that a product can be chosen simply because it excels on one characteristic. Returning to the pans example, it may be that a sub-standard set of pans is chosen simply because they are the 'right' colour.
4 *Lexicographical rule* – this assumes that a product can be selected on the basis of considering just a few characteristics considered in a pre-determined order. Taking house buying as an example, you may have a set of criteria such as number of bedrooms, access to shops, size of garden and so on, which you have prioritized to determine your choice of residence. If these are satisfactory, then you may not bother considering any further characteristics (for instance you may not mind if it does or does not have a garage, how many bathrooms or if it is a maisonette or house).

Hybrid model – Rice's *PV/PPS* model

In an attempt to overcome the weaknesses of the personal variable and decision process models, Chris Rice synthesized the two approaches to develop, what he calls, the perceived value/perceived probability of satisfaction (*PV/PPS*) model.

The central notion in this model is that the subjective utility (*SU*) of a particular decision alternative can be calculated from:

1 The value attached to the outcomes (perceived value or *PV*).
2 The perception of the probability of each outcome occurring (perceived probability of satisfaction or *PPS*).

The formula for calculating SU is:

$$SU = PV \times PPS$$

The model therefore predicts that the highest utility option will be that where the outcomes are valued highly and are most likely to be satisfied.

This can be illustrated graphically as in Figure 6.69, neatly dividing purchases into four categories.

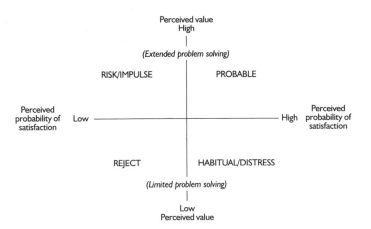

Figure 6.9
Type of purchase analysed in terms of the Rice *PV/PPS* model

The following explanation is adapted from Chris Rice (*Consumer Behaviour*):

The lower right-hand quadrant is concerned with purchases which are of low perceived value in themselves, but which have a high probability of satisfaction. Here an example might be the situation of running low on petrol when travelling down a motorway. Government quality standards ensure that there is little to choose between brands so the car is filled with whichever brand is sold in the next service station. Many petrol companies attempt to increase the perceived value of their brand by offering air miles, tokens or similar. This example could be classed as a *distress purchase*, but a similar process would be predicted in *habitual buying* at supermarkets. Low involvement purchases are often made on the basis that there is little, or nothing, to choose between brands.

The top left-hand quadrant is interesting (high value, low probability) as it may go some way towards explaining otherwise apparently irrational behaviour. An example might be gambling on the UK lottery despite the chances of winning a fortune being extremely small. Here the hypothesis would be that, for many people, the very high value of winning a very large sum of money (with its attendant outcomes of travel, giving up work and being able to afford luxuries), more than compensates for the very low probability of that outcome occurring. This can be classed as a *risk* or *impulse purchase*. The top right-hand quadrant is the marketers dream – high values and high probability of satisfaction – the combination that is most likely to result in *probable purchase*.

Thus, in practical terms this model clearly identifies two key objectives of marketing effort and communication:

1 To raise the perceived value of the outcomes of purchase.
2 To raise the perceived probability of satisfaction following purchase.

An example will illustrate the model. Suppose, we are trying to decide which type of food to purchase on our way home from work. We have two alternatives: either pre-cooked or fresh. However, we are unsure what our partner has planned for this evening. We may be 'watching a video' (in which case we might want something quick and convenient to cook) or we may be having 'a romantic meal' in which case a well cooked, tasty meal

151

is called for. Obviously, a real situation may consider many more characteristics and/or alternatives.

To assess perceived value we could rate the value of each characteristic on a scale of 1 to 10. We might arrive at the results similar to those in Table 6.2. It is important to remember that these are only perceived values and may bear no resemblance to an objective assessment.

Table 6.2 Rice *PV/PPS* model – perceived value table

Food	'Romantic meal at home'	'Watching a video'
Pre-cooked	3	8
Fresh	9	5

We must then assess the probability of each of the conditions occurring. We may perceive that 'watching a video' is more likely and give this a probability of 0.8 (an 80 per cent likelihood of happening). This leaves us with a probability of 0.2 (or 20 per cent) for the 'romantic meal at home' (the complete set of probabilities must add up to 1.0).

To calculate the subjective utility scores (*SU*) we must now multiply each cell in the value table by its perceived probability. Therefore, all the entries in the 'romantic meal' column are multiplied by 0.2; and all the entries in the 'watching a video' column are multiplied by 0.8. Table 6.3 shows the results.

Table 6.3 Rice PV/PPS model – subjective utility scores

Food	'Romantic meal at home'	'Watching a video'
Pre-cooked	0.6	6.4
Fresh	1.8	4

According to *PV/PPS* theory we will act on the outcome that will result in the highest *SU* score. In this example, we are certain to buy pre-cooked food.

In this context, the pre-cooked meal is seen as relatively the most probable purchase – it would thus occupy the top right-hand quadrant in Figure 6.9 in that it has both perceived high value and perceived high probability of satisfaction.

Comparison of simple models

Table 6.4 Comparison of simple models

	Black box	Decision process	Personal variable	Hybrid decision/ personal
Considers internal variables	No	Yes	Yes	Yes
Considers external variables	Yes	Yes	No	Yes
Good for explanation	No	No	Yes	Yes
Good for prediction	Yes	Possibly	Yes	Yes
Good for structuring marketing stategies	No	Yes	No	No
Simple to understand	Yes	Yes	No	No

Comprehensive, or grand, models of consumer behaviour

There are also, so called, grand models of consumer behaviour which attempt to comprehensively explain all those aspects of the buying situation which their creators deem to be significant. These are:

- Nicosia model.
- Howard–Sheth model.
- Engel, Blackwell and Miniard model (which you may see referred to as the Engel, Kollat and Blackwell model – an earlier derivative).

These models are not discussed in this syllabus and are now thought to be rather outdated.

Attitudes and behaviour

Most of the qualitative data we collect as market researchers relates to the attitudes of current or potential consumers to the products or services we offer. To gain acceptance from customers we must present a favourable image and avoid unfavourable associations. How favourable impressions translate into active endorsements of a product or service is a matter of some conjecture. The attitude theories described in this unit all approach this problem in a slightly different manner.

The motivations that drive customers are also important. To provide what the customer needs requires an understanding of their goals and aspirations. Whereas proven theories of customer motivation are thin on the ground, the general theories of motivation that exist provide useful guidance to marketers.

What are attitudes?

> I know what I like and I like what I know
> lyrics from the Genesis album *Selling England by the Pound*

Most of us have at some time been asked what we 'think' or 'feel' about a particular object, issue, activity, or person. Our responses to such questions are an expression of our attitudes. That is, whether we generally like or dislike the object, issue, activity or person under discussion.

Formal definitions of attitude try to capture this notion of 'liking and disliking' but, as much of what we say and do can be interpreted as expressing an attitude, such definitions are often broad and/or uninformative. Examples of the more popular definitions are given below.

Definition 6.2

A learned orientation or disposition, toward an object or situation, which provides a tendency to respond favourably or unfavourably to the object or situation (the learning may not be based on personal experience but may be acquired through observational learning and identification). Rokeach, 1968

Attitudes are likes and dislikes. Bem, 1979

An overall evaluation that allows one to respond in a consistently favourable or unfavourable manner with respect to a given object or alternative. Engel et al., 1990

Characteristics of attitudes

Attitudes are held by individuals. When similar attitudes are held by many individuals they become embedded in that society's culture. The following are generally held to be characteristics of attitudes:

- They can be held about any object, person, issue or activity – referred to as the attitude object.
- They may be strongly or weakly held – an attitude is not simply something that is turned on or off, it is an assessment based on a continuous evaluation.
- They are learned – we acquire attitudes in much the same way we acquire culture, through conditioning and social modelling.
- Attitudes change – they are dynamic. We no longer have the same attitudes as we did when we were younger. We are constantly modifying attitudes based on our experiences and acquiring new attitudes as we encounter new attitude objects.
- Some attitudes are more fundamental than others and more resistant to change – certain opinions stay with us throughout our lives, whilst others change from week to week.

Marketers are most concerned with understanding attitudes (for instance, does a brand have a favourable or unfavourable image), modifying attitudes (to make them more favourable towards certain attitude object and/or less favourable towards others) and turning positive attitudes towards an object into action, usually involving the purchase of the item in question.

Understanding attitudes

An attitude is not a simple entity but is formed from a combination of mental processes and expressed by actions.

Most psychologists agree that, at some level, attitudes contain three components:

1 A cognitive component – the knowledge and perceptions about an object. For instance, its shape, colour, price and so on.
2 An affective component – what a person subjectively feels about the attitude object – whether or not they are favourably disposed towards it. For instance, is the colour of the product a 'favoured' colour?
3 A behavioural component – how a person responds to the attitude object (based on 1 and 2 above).

Suppose we are interested in customers' attitudes to washing powder. The cognitive component to their attitudes may relate to the fact that the powder cleans, that is environmentally friendly and so on. These are what they believe to be the 'truths' about the product. Whether they are favourably disposed to the product overall will depend on how they feel about the cognitive components of the product. If they value both cleaning ability and environmental friendliness highly, then they are likely to feel positive towards the product overall. As a result, of assessing the cognitive and affective components of their attitude they may decide to purchase one brand of powder instead of another (the behavioural component).

Attitudes, beliefs and values

Attitudes are normally thought of as resulting from a combination of beliefs and values.

- Beliefs – the body of knowledge we hold about the world (may be incomplete or inaccurate). These underpin the cognitive component within attitudes. Beliefs are often expressed in sentences where the word 'is' appears. For example, the information that 'Guinness is good for you' was presented as a fact in a clever advertising campaign. Undoubtedly, this view now forms part of many people's belief system.
- Values – these are deeply held views about what is good, desirable, valuable, worthwhile. Unlike beliefs, these are usually ideals to which we aspire and may be expressed in sentences where the words 'should be' appear. For example, 'Health care should be free to all' is an expression of the value of social justice.

The relationship between attitudes and our beliefs and values is a complex one. People typically have thousands of beliefs about the world, hundreds of attitudes although probably fewer than fifty values.

It is interesting to see how advertisers use these values to sell products. Typically, a product is associated with a particular value dimension to give it appeal.

For example, pharmaceutical products are typically sold using the dimension of theoretical (truth). Facts and figures, often in the form of a graph, are shown to demonstrate the effectiveness of the product being sold. It may be that a brand of toothpaste prevents the formation of plaque for six hours or that a shampoo bonds extra proteins to your hair, and so on.

Relationship between attitudes and behaviour

As marketers, we are most interested in being able to predict and alter the behavioural component of attitudes. We want people to like our products but also buy them, remain loyal and recommend the products to others. All these involve action of some sort.

Figure 6.10 represents a simple model of the relationship between attitudes and behaviour. In this simple model positive cognitive and affective perceptions of an object lead to positive behaviours and vice versa.

Figure 6.10
A simple model of the relationship between attitudes and behaviour

Unfortunately, psychological research has found that there is no clear relationship between measured attitudes and behaviour. Perhaps this is not surprising as many of the factors which also influence our behaviour are outside of our own control. It might be, for instance, that we would like to take a three-week holiday in Portugal. We are extremely favourably disposed towards the idea but there are a number of reasons why we might not be able to actually book the holiday. Some examples of outside influences, in this instance, might be:

- We have no money.
- We cannot get the time off work.
- The are no more bookings available for Portugal this year.
- Spain has an air-traffic control strike on at the moment which is stopping flights to Portugal.
- A family member is ill and needs our support.

Some of the apparent difference between what we think and what we do may be due to measurement difficulties. We may observe a person buying a product but are they doing so because they are favourably disposed towards that product or because it happens to be the nearest on the supermarket shelf? Interview is the only way of securing attitudes in isolation from behaviour, but such methods also have their problems.

Some elegant experiments have been undertaken by psychologists and sociologists to try and determine the factors affecting the link between attitudes and behaviour. Perhaps most famous of these is the 'Travelling Chinese Experiment'.

In the early 1930s strong feelings existed against the Chinese in the USA. Around this time Richard LaPiere, a sociologist, took a Chinese couple on a tour of America. The trio stopped at 250 hotels and restaurants during their trip. On only one occasion were they refused entry. After returning from his trip, he wrote to each of the establishments he had visited asking them whether they would accept Chinese patrons. Somewhat surprisingly, of the half that responded to his letter, 90 per cent said they would not.

155

This experiment demonstrates a rather large gap between what the various proprietors said they would do and what they actually did. In other words, their attitudes (as secured by letter) were strikingly different to their behaviour (as demonstrated by LaPiere's visits).

There are a number of methodological problems with LaPiere's informal experiment. For example, had the same person that answered the letter been in a position to refuse service. Nonetheless, the results are strongly suggestive of a real discrepancy between attitudes and behaviour.

Question 6.1

Can you think of any other factors in LaPiere's 'experiment' that may have weakened the link between attitudes and behaviour?

As a result of LaPiere's study and the experiments of others, it is generally agreed that attitudes are only one factor in behaviour. It is said that they are a predisposing factor. In other words, without any other interventions, the attitudes would lead more directly to behaviour. The following intervening factors are said to affect the degree with which attitude leads to behaviour:

- *Unforeseen events* – it may be that unforeseen events lead to a change in behaviour. For instance, you may wish to go to a football match but it starts raining so you reluctantly make alternative arrangements.
- *Elapsed time* – as attitudes are dynamic, the longer the elapsed time between measurement of the attitude and the behaviour you are trying to predict, the less likely there is to be a link.
- *Situational factors* – it may be that the situation you find yourself in precludes action. For example, a consumer may wish to buy a tub of ice cream but the shops have just closed or they may not have enough money to hand.
- *Stability* – a particular attitude may be unstable in that you keep changing your mind. For example, one day you may feel like wearing jeans, the next day more formal wear.
- *Conflict of attitudes* – it may be that more than one attitude is applicable to a certain situation, the resultant behaviour will inevitably lead to a compromise behaviour. For example, you go into a shop to buy a tub of ice cream. You and your partner both want a different flavour. You equally well want to keep your partner happy and you want your favourite flavour. The behaviour you exhibit will be a compromise between these two contradictory aims (the exact compromise will depend how selfish you are!).
- *Strength* – the strength with which an attitude is held can determine behaviour. Also, one attitude can be expressed in many different ways. For example, if you support a particular political party you may or may not become a member depending on the strength of your support.
- *Specificity* – the accuracy with which attitudes are measured also affect the degree to which they are able to predict behaviour. This is discussed in more detail below.

We are left with a more complex view of the relationship between attitudes and behaviour than suggested earlier. Figure 6.11 is more representative of the relationship that exists:

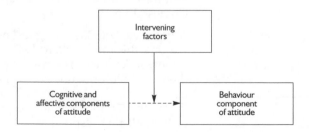

Figure 6.11
Most likely relationship between attitudes and behaviour

Specificity of measurement

Fishbein and Ajzen argue that you can predict behaviour from attitudes if the attitudes you are investigating are measured accurately enough. In other words, you need to ensure *specificity* of measurement. This has implications in the design of attitude surveys. Most importantly, questions must ask precisely about the behaviour you are trying to predict. The pill experiment, carried out by Davidson and Jaccard in the late 1970s, on women's attitudes to the contraceptive pill illustrates this point quite well.

A group of women were asked a question about their general attitudes to birth control. There was found to be a very low correlation between positive attitudes towards birth control and their actual use of the pill.

When the question was changed to something more specific – it asked about their attitudes to oral contraception – the correlation between attitudes and usage was much higher (0.32). When the question was made more specific again – asking about their use of oral contraceptive over the next two years – an even higher correlation between attitudes and behaviour was found (0.57). When measured attitudes are similar to the observed behaviour, they are said to correspond.

Consistency theories of attitude

There are three prominent attitude theories which address how attitudes change and adapt to changing circumstances:

1 Balance theory (Heider, 1958).
2 Congruity theory (Osgood and Tannenbaum, 1955).
3 Cognitive dissonance theory (Festinger, 1957).

These are all based on the assumption that people seek consistency in their attitudes. That is, one cannot simultaneously hold two contradictory beliefs. Suppose, a reliable friend recommends a restaurant which you subsequently visit and find disappointing. In general terms, consistency theories state that you cannot simultaneously believe that both your friend is reliable yet his recommendation was wrong. You would, according to consistency theorists, be 'forced' to either change your opinion of your friend or make some excuse concerning the performance of the restaurant on the occasion you visited.

Summary

In this unit you have learned about:

- Models.
- Attitudes – their characteristics and component parts.
- The relationship between attitudes and behaviour.
- The importance of specificity of attitude measurement.

The motivations that drive customers are also important. To provide what the customer needs requires an understanding of their goals and aspirations. The following unit covers aspects of individual, group and organizational customer behaviour.

The individual, the group and organization as customer

In this unit you will be:

❑ Introduced to the concept of culture and explore its constitutional elements.

❑ Consider the nature of culture – how we acquire it, what membership means, and the cultural consideration required when marketing to different cultures or sub-cultures.

❑ Consider factors influencing the individual's purchasing behaviour.

❑ Be introduced to the concept of motivation, self-concept theory, psychoanalytic role theory, trait factor theories and new application to consumer behaviour.

❑ Look at group influence – how it can occur and its impact on buying behaviour.

❑ Be introduced to the influence of primary and secondary groups.

❑ Understand the difference between consumer and industrial buying.

Study Guide

In this unit you are introduced to influences on buying behaviour arising from social and cultural aspects of the society. You will explore how it influences and shapes buying behaviour and be able to anticipate problems which can occur when marketing across cultures and sub-cultures. You will also understand the importance of group influence in shaping behaviour and how this influence can be used in marketing.

The motivations that drive customers are also important. To provide what the customer needs requires an understanding of their goals and aspirations. Whereas proven theories of customer motivation are thin on the ground, the general theories of motivation that exist provide useful guidance to marketers. Other theories are touched on.

External factors influencing customer behaviour

These are the social and cultural factors influencing the individual's behaviour as a customer. Sociologists use the term culture to describe the physical and social environment which results in shared attitudes and behaviours, a fact which is of interest to marketers.

Culture – The values, attitudes, beliefs, ideas, artefacts and other meaningful symbols represented in the pattern of life adopted by people that help them interpret, evaluate and communicate as members of a society.

Culture can be represented graphically as in Figure 7.1.

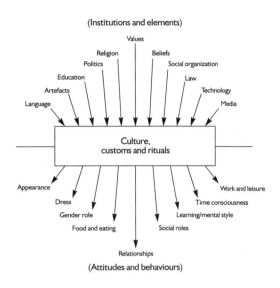

Figure 7.1

Influences from institutions and other elements of society (such as education, politics, and the law) combine in complex ways to provide us with culture, customs and rituals which are expressed as attitudes and behaviours.

Keith Williams (1990) *Behavioural Aspects of Marketing* describes five main characteristics of culture:

1 It exists to serve the needs of a society. For example, most cultures have some form of 'wedding' ceremony.
2 It is acquired socially. That is, we are not born with any cultural knowledge but acquire it throughout our lifetime.
3 It is learned by interacting with other members of the culture.
4 It is cumulative. Culture is transferred from generation to generation with new influences constantly being added to the cultural 'soup'.
5 It is adaptive. Culture changes in response to the needs of the society.

Importance of culture in marketing

By understanding the nature of culture, and the cultural differences that exist in the population, the marketer can do much to prevent potential problems arising when marketing to different cultural groups. A thorough understanding of a particular culture can also be used in a positive way to more effectively market within that culture.

Elements of culture

Culture is exhibited by the customs, language, symbols and rituals within a society. These are the observable elements of the culture:

- Customs are the established 'rules' of behaviour within a society. They define what is, and what is not, acceptable.
- Language and symbols are the means by which members of a particular culture communicate with one another. This communication can be

verbal (using words) or non-verbal (using images which convey directly, or indirectly, ideas).

- Rituals are patterns of behaviour, often quite complex, which a society shares. Ritual behaviours include religious services, attainment parties (eighteenth birthday, retirement, engagement, etc.) and private routines such as the Saturday morning shopping trip or the Sunday walk in the park.

Customs

Williams (1990) defines four classes of customs:

1 Folkways – these are the everyday customs of the culture. Greetings are one such example.
2 Conventions – these are more formally observed folkways, ones which might start to cause more long-term offence if ignored. For example, the sending of Christmas presents.
3 Mores – these are formally recognized rules of behaviour such as respect for your parents.
4 Laws – those mores which society wishes to control are governed by laws.

Languages and symbols

Marketers involved in multi-lingual operations must be aware of the implications of selling their products to speakers whose native language is not English. The use of language in advertising copy also requires attention.

Word-plays are very much surface features of a language. It is also common for language, and objects, to have other meanings and associations other than those that might appear in a dictionary. For instance, a crudely drawn heart (♥) conveys a meaning of innocent love. The phrase 'he fought like a tiger' only makes sense because of the symbolism we associate with the word 'tiger' (courage, cunning, stealth). Such words and objects are said to be 'symbolic'. Symbols add richness to communication within a culture.

Table 7.1 Some common symbols and their associations in European culture

Symbol	Associations
Dolphin	Intelligence
Tick	Correctness
Gold	Wealth
Crown	Superiority
Swan	Grace
Owl	Wisdom

Symbols can be simple and blunt or subtle and complex. The richness of symbolic meaning can be used in marketing to associate certain qualities with your product or convey more complex meanings in a shorthand form (which can thus be understood and absorbed more quickly).

Figure 7.2
Even different typefaces can have different symbolic associations

Rituals

From a marketing perspective, rituals and rites represent a substantial opportunity. In particular, if it is possible to associate an object or other event, known as artefacts, with a ritual then the persistence of the ritual will ensure the continuing use of the artefact.

One example is the red and white Santa Claus costume. This has become so closely associated with Christmas that many people believe it to be historic. In fact, the red and white costume was 'invented' by Coca-Cola as a marketing promotion. It has ensured that the combination of red and white (the Coca-Cola colours) has a continuing positive association with fun and jollity.

Table 7.2 Common UK rituals and typical artefacts

Rituals	Typical artefacts
25-years' service*	Award ceremony, clock/plaque
Friday night at home	Video, take out meal, beer
Saturday night out	Meal, cinema/theatre/disco/concert
Valentine's day	Red rose, card
21st birthday*	Key, card, presents

* indicate rites of passage

Activity 7.1

If you have ever been abroad, think of the things you found strange about the host country's culture. Try to list five things. Were these customs, language/symbols or rituals?

Macro- versus micro-culture – the cultural onion

At any one time we are influenced by many different cultures. A person living in England is most probably influenced by 'Western', 'European' and 'English' cultures. The customs and rituals of these cultures are shared with many other people. Such widespread cultures are frequently referred to as macro-cultures. Imagine peeling an onion. The well-defined outer layers are rather like macro-cultures, with one nesting neatly inside anther. However, if we were to peel the onion further we would find that the layers become less distinct. It is rather the same with culture. As we examine smaller and smaller cultural groups the dividing lines become less distinct. A single individual may well be a 'member' of ten or more overlapping sub-cultures, or micro-cultures, as they are known (see Figure 7.3).

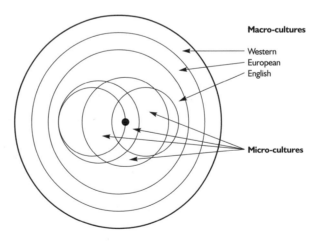

Figure 7.3
The cultural onion. As the size of cultural groups become smaller and smaller the separation between them becomes less distinct. The position of a hypothetical individual is represented by a black dot

There are six broad sub-cultures in the UK based on ethnicity, age, geography, religion, gender, occupation and social class:

1 *Ethnicity* – This includes not only indigenous population groups, such as the Welsh and Scots, but also from those groups that have settled in the UK.
2 *Age* – Within society there are certain values and attitudes which are shared by persons of a similar age. For instance, people brought up

161

during the war years shared some very extreme changes in society such as rationing and life-threatening situations which few persons have since experienced.

3 *Geography* – The physical separation of peoples can lead to the development of distinct cultures in different regions.

4 *Religion* – Those whom subscribe to a particular religion are strongly influenced by its customs and practices. Most religions dictate rules which their followers must abide. These often include dietary, social and ethical requirements.

5 *Gender* – Traditionally, in our culture, women have been considered 'home makers' whilst men have been considered the 'bread winners'. Whilst these descriptions are no longer accurate or relevant, many advertisers perpetuate, or use these stereotypes and other gender differences, to market products.

6 *Occupation and social class* – These characteristics of UK culture are often used interchangeably. Many organizations, such as the Market Research Society, define social class in terms of occupation. Occupation is a product of many things such as the occupation of one's parents, education, intelligence, aptitude and opportunity. People with similar occupations tend to share similar lifestyles and incomes. It is common for insurance companies, for instance, to target specific occupations which have been proven to be of a lower risk. One such occupational group is the police force.

Market segmentation using culture

It is possible to segment a market according to the micro-cultures that exist within the target population.

You might decide to market to women, for instance, to try to increase their consumption of lager. You could get more specific and decide to target businessmen under 35, in the South-East, to increase sales of a new cure for baldness.

Activity 7.2

Think how you might use sub-cultures in the UK to market a new dating service.

Learning culture

As has been stated, all culture is learned. The process of learning one's native culture is termed socialization. The learning of a new culture is called acculturation.

Definition 7.2

Socialization is the process by which the culture of a society is transmitted from generation to generation so that each individual not only understands and follows the 'rules' of their culture but is able to pass these on to others.

There are three main mechanisms by which culture is learned:

1 *Social modelling* – Where a culture is learned by copying an existing member of the culture. It may be that this learning is direct (i.e. from a peer or family member) or indirectly from the media (i.e. from television or a magazine). Fashion, for example, is often adopted from the pages of a magazine and rarely from other members of the family.

2 *Role-playing* – A form of social modelling where imitation is allowed to develop further.

3 *Conditioning* – Whereby certain behaviours are rewarded or punished according to their conformance with the rules of the culture. Eating food without cutlery is likely to be admonished by parents.

Social modelling is the mechanism of most use to marketers in gaining acceptance of their product. Showing a prominent member of a culture behaving in a certain manner (for example, Naomi Campbell wearing a new fashion) can increase the acceptability of this behaviour amongst other members of the culture.

Conditioning can also be used. If purchasers are rewarded for buying a product, through discount vouchers or cash-back offers, the purchasing behaviour is more likely to be repeated.

Dynamic nature of culture

Culture is constantly changing but we are so much part of it that these changes often go unnoticed. It is only when we compare our current culture with that of the past that the differences become apparent.

Marketers should be aware of cultural trends so that they do not get 'left behind' or, conversely, do not miss the opportunity to be the first in the field to market based on an emerging cultural characteristic. Promotions aimed at young people must be particularly careful in this respect.

Cross-cultural marketing

We have already seen how mistakes can be made, and the benefits to be gained from an understanding of the cultural differences between markets.

There are two strategic approaches to cross-cultural marketing:

1 Global marketing – which uses common cultural characteristics of consumers.
2 Local marketing – which makes use of differences in consumers from different cultures.

Local versus global marketing

Figure 7.4 summarizes the sorts of products more suitable for both global and local marketing.

Product types more suitable for global marketing

Products aimed at a specific global micro-culture (e.g. the 'jet-set')

Products which are easy to tailor (e.g. foodstuffs)

Products which are novel (e.g. electronics)

Products which are difficult to tailor (e.g. furniture)

Products which appeal to a specific culture only (e.g. greeting cards)

Product types more suitable for local marketing

Figure 7.4
Product types more suitable for both global and local marketing

In support of the scheme presented here, some marketers label the products most suitable for global marketing as 'high tech' and 'high touch' (Schiffman and Kanuk 1994). By this they mean that high technology products (such as computers and cameras) and high touch products (such as perfumes and wrist watches) are more likely to transcend cultural differences and are thus more amenable for global marketing. In contrast, products which are low technology or low touch are more suitable, it is claimed, for a local marketing strategy.

Measurement of culture

The multifaceted nature of culture necessitates that a range of measurement techniques are used:

- *Projective tests* – These are frequently used to assess motivation and personality.
- *Attitude measurement* – This is frequently used to determine beliefs and values.
- *Depth interviews and group discussions* – These are useful to discover emerging cultural characteristics.

- *Observation* – This can provide valuable insights into the more obscure aspects of culture which may not be amenable to direct questioning. For instance, a consumer may not be aware that certain of their behaviours are ritualized.
- *Content analysis* – As the name implies, this technique uses an analysis of past and present media to identify cultural changes. This can also be undertaken on a cross-cultural basis. Such a survey carried out in the early 1990s found a shift in trends in household furnishings away from greys with primary spot colours towards pastel tones.

The individual as customer

The difference between a brand and a commodity can be summed up in the phrase 'added value'. The added value can be tangible or intangible. In seeking to understand what creates 'added value' marketers need to understand the characteristics of consumers. The understanding of customers and their psychological make up provides marketers with a richer basis for understanding consumer behaviour than do demographics and other mechanical methods of classification that tell the marketer very little about consumers' actual needs.

It is standard ethnographic practice to assume that all material possessions carry social meaning and a main aspect of cultural analysis would be to concentrate upon their use as communicators. Goods have a double role, they provide subsistence and create lines of social relationships. Goods are the medium that links social relations. As Mary Douglas says (*The World of Goods*, Penguin 1980):

> Man is a social being, we can never explain demand by only looking at the physical properties of goods. Man needs goods for communicating with others and for making sense of what is going on around him ... goods make visible statements about the hierarchy of values to which we choose to subscribe.... We need to know how they are used to create an intelligible universe.... There is no mention in utility theory about physical enjoyment, spiritual needs or even about envy.

The modern brand secures an emotional involvement rather than only meeting a functional need. The brand links the consumer through the brand to the supplier and its values and to other purchasers as a member of a connected tribe. Brands define who is in the group as much as who is not.

Branding and the post-modern consumer

Gregory Carpenter and Alice Tybout (Mastering Marketing, *Financial Times*, October 1998), write that we have moved to an era in which brands need to satisfy a greater range of goals than before. They will need to satisfy many goals simultaneously, reconcile conflicting goals or satisfy neglected needs. Many of today's consumers do not see consuming brands as an objective as a previous generation may have done. They see brands as a means to an end.

Classic branded products signalled that one had the money to buy certain goods that were produced to a high standard, the decision making was simplified and that they formed a common bond within the community. The goods were largely defined by a single goal largely determined by the product function. For example, fast food restaurants satisfied one's hunger with the minimum of fuss.

Contemporary brands then moved to creating a broader benefits base and built the brand around functionality and associated benefits. For example Volvo cars protected self and family.

Post-modern brands enable buyers to attain a much broader range of goals but have less time in which to achieve them. This is largely a reflection of the large number of roles post-modern buyers play. Working mothers have more active careers, working fathers play a more active role at home. There is less time, more pressure but there is still the expectation of being able to carry out the roles competently.

Some of the goals people are looking for are timeless: membership of a larger community, intellectual stimulation, spirituality, freedom, recognition and responsibility. Others reflect our changing lives, e.g. status, convenience and stress reduction. Post-modern buyers are willing to turn brands into satisfying many of these goals. People therefore try and satisfy more than one goal at the same time.

Multiple goal satisfaction
Products that enable people to satisfy more than one goal at a time are flourishing. Examples are mobile telephones and laptop computers that help people to use downtime and continue doing more than one thing at the same time.

Resolving goal conflict
Brands can be built to help buyers cope with role conflict. Levi jeans for example encouraged companies to implement the concept of 'Casual Friday'. This blurred the difference between business and leisure and enabled workers to integrate these two goals.

Satisfy neglected goals
As a result of the lack of time and the focus on financial security, social responsibility and social acceptance many people do not have time to develop more internal, self-orientated goals. Brands can be developed that focus on these unsatisfied aspects. For example, Harley Davidson help people to satisfy the desire for individuality and freedom. Jeep and Land Rover introduce an element of adventure into mundane tasks. Volvo is now changing its advertisement to encompass goals of individuality and self-expression, Volvos still protect but also contribute to psychological well being by enabling the person to escape to remote and beautiful settings.

People can be said to live in a double environment, the personal inner world of feeling, emotion and thoughts as well as the outer world of people, places and possessions. If customer behaviour is to be understood it is not possible to solely concentrate on the rational, conscious motivations of individuals who react in a calculated way to their environment. It is necessary to also look at their perceptual processes as well, how customers create a mental vision of the brand in their own minds and the feelings that they associate with that image.

To do this one has to be able to look at the mind as being something dynamic. Not something that is static and fixed. The marketer can create a brand and instigate the branding process as an input, but it is the buyer who forms the mental vision of it and what they create (the branding output) may be very different from what the marketer intended. Consumers are certainly not passive!

Internal factors
Most people do not understand either themselves or others very well, our senses are often flawed and limited and our perception is limited. Selection plays an important part in everything we perceive.

The essential problem of enquiring into what may be in other people's minds is captured in this quote:

> To try and understand the experience of another it is necessary to dismantle the world as seen from one's place within it, and to re-assemble it as seen from his. For example, to try to understand a given choice another makes, one must face in imagination the lack of choices which may confront or deny him. The well-fed are incapable of understanding the choices of under-fed. The world has to be dismantled and re-assembled in order to be able to grasp, however clumsily, the experience of another. To talk of entering the subjective experience of another is misleading. The subjectivity of another does not simply constitute a different interior attitude to the same exterior facts. The constellation of facts, of which he is the centre, is different. Berger and Mohr, 1975.

Any enquiry into what is in the minds of others is not only an exploration of what is consciously expressed by people but it is also about interpreting what is unconsciously believed and felt.

An output process

Successful marketing techniques must be considered in the light of the above. Customers do not receive messages passively. Customers take the message marketers give them and then actively use them to fit into their own internal world and also to give them clues about the brand's capability. It is what customers do with the marketing mix in their minds that needs to be assessed. The marketer has constantly to say 'What is going on in there?'

The brand becomes the consumers' idea of the product/service, not the marketers. It is what customers perceive, interpret and then believe the values of the brand to be. So much so that the brand then acquires a personality that is so well recognized that even products with very little functional difference are seen as being different.

Attention

The term perception implies the use of direct sensory information but it is not only external stimuli which makes products/services stand out, but our attention is also influenced by our interests, needs, motives and expectations.

The person's interests and motives may lead them to positively select certain information from their environment. The processes involved here are selective attention, selective exposure, selective retention, selective vigilance and perceptual organization.

Expectation

Expectation plays an important part in the selection of what we perceive. It refers to the way people respond in a certain way to a given situation or set of stimuli. This may be the result of either known or unknown past experiences.

People often perceive what they expect to perceive rather than the message they do receive. This concept is particularly important in service marketing where people are involved.

Subliminal perception

This is the expression used to describe something that is below the level of perception. There is a great deal of debate in this area as to whether it works and it is legal.

Awareness set

Brand choices do not just depend on brand awareness but also on the consumer's evaluation of the product into distinct groups or sets. Faced with a number of product groups made up of similar brands, consumers will try and simplify their purchase decisions.

Howard and Sheth argue that consumers will select from the brands of which they are aware – the awareness set – a smaller range of brands from which they will make their actual brand choice – the evoked set.

The concept of the evoked set is useful in marketing research as it can help to identify:

- The competitive position of the product.
- What the consumer thinks are the competitive products.
- Strategies which can be adopted to change the way in which the brand is categorized.
- An appropriate marketing mix – such as media advertising, sampling, comparative advertising, redesign of the product – as the marketer will be able to see whether the evoked set or inert set includes their brand or not.

Motivation

> Do not buy what you want, but what you need; what you do not need is dear at a farthing. Marcus Porcius Cato (234–149 BC), *Reliquae*

The study of motivation is concerned with *why* people choose to behave in a certain way. In particular, it is concerned with:

- The most basic human requirements – referred to as 'needs'.
- How these needs translate into behaviours – referred to as 'drives'.
- What these behaviours aim to achieve – referred to as 'goals'.

In an organization context, understanding what motivates a work force is of prime importance to ensuring their continued productivity and satisfaction. In a marketing context, understanding what motivates a consumer is equally important. It enables products to be produced which are both desired and satisfying. An understanding of what motivates is also of use in preparing promotions and can be used for market segmentation purposes.

Certainly, this is a broad area of study. The great psychologist George Miller (1957) described the study of motivation as covering all things 'biological, social and psychological that defeat our laziness and move us, either eagerly or reluctantly, to action'.

At a basic level, our body has a need (hunger, for instance) which translates in a drive (in the case of hunger, this is a drive to obtain food). The goal is to satisfy the need (in this example, to feel full). This can be represented diagrammatically as shown in Figure 7.5. Achievement of the goal satisfies the initial needs thus completing the circle. Of course, next time that need surfaces (if the case of hunger, the next meal time) then the whole circular process will start again.

Figure 7.5

Perhaps the most popular theory which links needs and drives with goals is that of Hull. His drive-reduction theory attempts to explain both motivation and learning. He was mostly concerned with the operation of primary needs but the principles he presents are of general interest. Hull's theory is illustrated in Figure 7.6. As we have discussed, a need gives rise to a drive and corresponding behaviour aimed at reducing the drive and thus the need. According to Hull, this act of reducing the drive (drive reduction) reinforces the drive-reducing behaviour thus making the behaviour more likely to occur again in response to reoccurrence of the need.

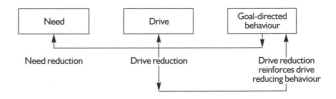

Figure 7.6
A simplified view of Hull's drive reduction theory

Suppose we are on a beach and feel thirsty. We will go to find the nearest source of refreshment, a beach bar perhaps. According to Hull's theory we are most likely to drink a product which has satisfied our thirst in the past, Perrier water for instance. If this is not on sale, we may pick something similar, or try something new, and this (if it satisfies us) is then more likely to be selected next time we are thirsty.

As well as positive motivations (in the above example the drink) we can also experience negative motivations or avoidance of certain items or situation. If we are thirsty, for example, we are likely to avoid salty things, which are likely to make us even more thirsty. To give another example, if we are cold we will avoid situations which will make us colder (avoidance of cold) and seek out situations that make us warmer (approach warmth).

On this basis, we can classify objects as either approach objects (contact with these will satisfy our need) and avoidance objects (contact with these will make our need worse). Let us now look in more detail at needs.

Needs

These fall into three broad categories:

1 Physiological (or primary) needs – these are the needs that sustain life. They include the need for food, air, sex and self-preservation.
2 Psychological needs – these are the needs that relate to our competence to deal effectively with the outside environment, often termed personal competence.
3 Learned (secondary or cultural) needs – we have already seen the influence that culture can have on an individual's behaviour. Learned needs are those needs which arise as a result of our socialization. As the name suggests, they are learned and are dependent on the culture we grow up in. Some cultures value power and status, others humility and a structured life. These are all learned needs.

These different categories of needs are related in complex ways. For example, the food a consumer purchases (a primary need) will depend on secondary needs. If you are hungry at breakfast time in the UK, you are most likely to eat cereal and toast. In the USA you may well satisfy your hunger by eating pancakes or even cake – the culturally acceptable breakfast foods in that country. In addition, psychological needs may play a part – does the food look palatable, pleasant and well presented.

The following are examples of how learned and psychological needs interact with primary needs:

- Donating a kidney to save another life.
- Fasting for the purpose of protest or religious 'cleansing'.
- Giving up one's life for the greater good (such as with the Japanese kamikaze fighter pilots in the Second World War).

Needs arousal

We are aware of our needs only when they are aroused. They can be aroused by four distinct stimuli; physiological, cognitive, environmental and emotional. Table 7.3 contains examples of all four stimulus types.

There at least two prominent theories that address motivation needs which are of use to marketers.

1 Maslow's hierarchy of needs.
2 McClelland's three motivating needs.

Before discussing these we will turn to a description of goals.

Table 7.3

Stimulus type	Example of mechanisms	Need aroused
Physiological	Drop in blood sugar levels	Hunger
	Testosterone release in men	Sex
Cognitive	Remembering a loved one	Affection
	Seeing an advert which reminds you to phone a friend	Social
Emotional	Fear of being burgled	Security
	Chaotic life	Stability
Environmental	Finding a dream home that you can afford	Success
	Walking past a clothes shop and seeing clothes you want to buy	Prestige, self-respect

Goals

As already noted, these are the end-points of motivated behaviour. Goals can be generic or specific. If you are thirsty, you may want any liquid or you may want a specific brand of drink (see Figure 7.7). Some psychologists distinguish between *wants* and *goals*, referring to the specific want as the object of desire (the brand of drink in this case) and the goal as the behaviour required to obtain the specific want.

GENERIC   SPECIFIC

Figure 7.7

Any drink —— Any cold drink —— Any carbonated drink —— Any carbonated cold drink

From the marketer's point of view, we are interested in making goals specific to our products. Different levels of specificity are appropriate to different types of products. For example, many foods are unbranded – potatoes for example. In the case of this food, the Potato Marketing Board presents the purchase of potatoes as a fairly generic goal.

Choice of goal chosen to satisfy a certain need depends on a number of things:

- *Personal experience* – If a particular goal has satisfied a need in the past then it is more likely to be selected again. As we have seen with Hull's drive reduction model, the success of a goal in satisfying a needs actually reinforces its use again. For example, if a particular washing powder has been successful in cleaning our clothes we are more likely to buy that same washing powder in the future.
- *Cultural norms and values* – We have seen in the previous unit how cultural norms and values affect behaviour. To give an example, it may be that we shun the purchase of a new washing machine liquid (as opposed to powder) because using such a product is not the 'done thing' in our culture.
- *Personal norms and values* – Our own personal norms and values, possibly religious or ethical, can also affect the goals we select for the achievement of a particular need. For example, if we are 'green minded' we might choose to select an environmentally-friendly washing powder.
- *Physical and/or intellectual capacity* – It might be some goals are unachievable due to our own personal limitations. Suppose we want to own a cat but are allergic to fur. Our need for companionship must find an alternative goal.
- *Accessibility of goal* – It may be that the goal we select is determined on the basis of accessibility. We may wish, for example, to go to a particular play but the distance of the theatre precludes us going.

Maslow's hierarchy of needs

Maslow categorized human needs in five groups which he arranged into a hierarchy of importance (see Figure 7.8).

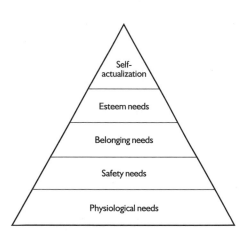

Figure 7.8
Maslow's hierarchy of needs

169

These five groups, arranged from lower to higher importance are:

1 *Physiological needs* – such as hunger, thirst, sex and activity.
2 *Safety needs* – freedom from threat, health but also security, order, and stability.
3 *Social, or belonging needs* – relationships, affection, sense of belonging (identification).
4 *Esteem needs* – such as prestige, success and self-respect.
5 *Self-actualization needs* – the fulfilment of personal potential.

He also introduced other categories of 'enabling' needs which provided the channels through which the five categories of needs could be achieved:

- *Freedom of enquiry and expression needs* – for social conditions permitting free speech and encouraging justice, fairness and honesty.
- *Knowledge and understanding needs* – to gain and order knowledge of the environment, to explore, learn, and experiment.

Marketing applications of Maslow

As a theory, Maslow's hierarchy of needs has proved useful in applying a more behaviour-oriented structure to the market. As such, it has found use in market segmentation and brand/product positioning.

Each product/service has a 'natural' needs category which it addresses. Most products only actually address the very basic physiological and safety needs. For example, all the foodstuffs sold actually only address our physiological need for sustenance. However, it is possible to position products to appeal to just about any needs category which broadens the appeal and can be used to create a brand image.

Table 7.4 provides some examples of positioning by need category.

As already stated, we can also segment a market using Maslow's needs categories. Table 7.5 gives examples of these.

Needs also translate into benefits which form the basis of benefits segmentation. Furthermore, motivation is also used in psychographic segmentation (see Unit 2).

Activity 7.3

In terms of Maslow's categorization of needs (physiological, safety, social, esteem, self-actualization), how would you segment the following products/services:

- Headache tablet
- Cream cake
- Household burglar alarm
- Computer
- Church service
- Wedding ring
- Typing course

For each of the above, think of a way of how you might market position them in at least one other segment. Write this down and explain your decision.

Evaluation of Maslow's hierarchy of needs

Maslow's theory certainly has intuitive appeal. If you are desperate for food you are unlikely to be concerned about social niceties or self-fulfilment. His ideas are also useful in that they consider much of what drives us as individuals. Unfortunately, there are a number of problems with the theory as Rice (1994) explains:

- Lack of empirical evidence to support it. Physiological and safety needs are not always the predominant factor in determining behaviour.
- The absence of money from the list of needs worries some people.
- Self-actualization and esteem needs are likely to be a function of each individual's self-perception.

Table 7.4

Needs category	Products appealing to this category
Physiological	'Ready Brek' breakfast cereal provides you with a protective 'barrier' against the cold
Safety	AA rescue service stops you being stranded at night in a hostile environment
Social	British Telecom adverts – the telephone keeps you in touch with absent family and friends
Esteem	Rolex watch adverts suggesting that ownership of a Rolex is a sign of success
Self-actualization	Adverts for adult education courses encouraging you to further yourself

Table 7.5

Needs category	Potential target groups
Physiological needs	Teenagers eager for sexual experience Old persons worried about health problems
Safety needs	Wealthy people with valuable possessions to protect Families worried about safety of children
Social needs	New arrivals in an area looking for social affiliations clubs, societies, etc. Single parents looking for company
Esteem needs	Recent high income earners eager for outside signs of prestige High status groups, e.g. company directors
Self-actualization	Those in higher education – likely to be looking for additional education Health conscious teenagers eager to conform to perfect body image

Notwithstanding these problems, Maslow's work has provided a framework which is easy and useful to marketers.

McClelland's theory of need achievement

Unlike Maslow, some psychologists, such as McClelland and his colleagues, believe in the presence of just three main needs. Whereas these can be subsumed within Maslow's hierarchy, considered as separate entities they are useful for marketers to consider:

- *Affiliation* – this relates to a desire to belong, to be part of a group and to have friends.
- *Power* – this relates to control over both people and other objects in the environment.
- *Achievement* – this relates to the need to achieve.

Activity 7.4

Think of work colleagues, friends and family that you know. How would you classify them in terms of McClelland's three needs theory? Which need motivates them most?

Other theories of motivation

There are two other theories which are occasionally referred to in a marketing context. A brief explanation will suffice for each of these.

Alderfer's ERG hierarchy of needs

This proposes a hierarchy of just three needs – existence, relatedness and growth (hence ERG). While similar in many ways to Maslow, Alderfer introduces the useful notion of frustration. That is, if a need is not satisfied it results in frustration which may result in other behaviours. In a marketing context, we may find consumers dissatisfied with a particular product settling for an alternative or complaining at what they have purchased. It is important to accept that frustration can occur in any buying situation and to plan for it.

Vroom's expectancy theory

This theory is strongly related to the extended Fishbein model of attitudes. Essentially, the strength of an individual's motivation is based on the expectation that a behaviour will lead to a certain outcome and the preference (or valence) for that outcome. For a worked example see Activity 7.5. From a marketing viewpoint, it is clear that to increase the motivation to buy we must increase the perceived value of our products/ service and raise the expectancy of satisfaction that will result from its purchase.

Activity 7.5

In a previous unit we have discussed probabilities. Working through an example of the use of Vroom's expectancy theory is a good way of exercising this knowledge.

1   List five outcomes that you might expect from going on holiday to the West Indies. To get you started, outcomes 1 and 2 have already been completed:

   1   Feel relaxed
   2   Get a sun tan
   3
   4
   5

2   Now give each of these outcomes a value. This is known as the valence (V). $+1$ if you like them; 0 if you feel neutral towards them and -1 if you dislike them.

3   Estimate the probability of attaining each outcome. You will remember that a probability of 1 is equal to absolute certainty while 0 is equal to no chance at all. For example, 0.5 represents a 50 per cent chance of the outcome being achieved. This value is the expectancy (E).

4   Now place your values in the table provided below and calculate $E \times V$, placing this value in the last column. Now add up the values in the $E \times V$ column. The result is called the F score and relates to the motivational value of the holiday.

Outcomes	Expectancy (E)	Valence (V)	$E \times V$
1 Feel relaxed			
2 Get a sun tan			
3			
4			
5			

You might want to experiment with this technique as a way of comparing the F scores from different product brands.

Measuring motivation

The most popular techniques for motivation research are undoubtedly projective techniques such as those discussed in the earlier unit on primary data, such as word association and thematic apperception tests (TAT).

However, depth interviews and group discussions are also used. Unlike other uses of these methods, the focus is to uncover *why* a particular behaviour took place. The group discussion can yield more information than individual in-depth interviews but is not suitable for the discussion of certain topics such as those that might embarrass, are difficult to discuss in company, or require very individual consideration.

Activity 7.6

Try interviewing fellow students about their motivation for undertaking the marketing course. Start by asking the question:

> Why did you decide to apply for this particular course at this particular college?

Make notes as they answer. After each answer your aim is to ask another why question about some detail of their previous answer. It is likely that a number of opportunities for further questioning will arise, make sure no opportunity is missed. Note each question, returning to it if necessary. If you have a tape recorder available, you may wish to use this to record the interview to ease later study.

> What needs do you identify?

When you try to use ideas from these theories to help you define your customers needs more accurately, it is important to remember that the concepts you are using come from a therapeutic area where they are used to enable people to make some sense of their lives. These are not theories that are cast in stone but are useful as metaphoric models that help us to capture different aspects of experience. There are many conceptual frameworks that are used to enable people to make sense of their lives, only a few are dealt with in this workbook and it is also beyond the scope of this workbook to deal with them in any detail.

Consumer imagery

Self-concept theory

The theory centres around the concept of 'self' which Newcomb (*Social Psychology*, New York: Holt, Reinhart and Winston, 1950) defines as 'the individual as perceived by that individual in a socially determined frame of reference'. This perceived self influences the person's perception of both their environment and their behaviour. The Jungian concept of self is quite different.

Each individual has an idea of themselves as being a particular type of person. Self-concept develops in different ways, from the way we have grown up, from our background and experience. The self-image comes from interactions with other people, starting off from parents and then to other individuals and groups with whom we have contact, including the culture in which we are brought up in – these experiences teach us how to see ourselves. Some people have a high self image, others have a low one.

One of the most important aspects of self-concept is the individual's level of aspiration, and their own self-perception compared with their perception of others. Once developed, self-concept is reinforced by the process of selective perception, this allows the person to maintain and enhance an internally consistent self-image and the person reacts in a way that is consistent with his self-image.

Possessions, brands, people and places have symbolic value for them and are judged on the basis of how they fit with their own personal picture of themselves. There are different types of self-image:

1 *Actual self-image* – how consumers see themselves.
2 *Ideal self image* – how they would like to see themselves.
3 *Social self-image* – how consumers feel others see them.
4 *Ideal self-image* – how consumers would like others to see them.
5 *Expected self-image* – how consumers expect to see themselves at some specified future time.

Studies show that consumers prefer brands which relate to their self-perception and to their subjective images of brands.

The extended self
Consumer possessions can be seen to confirm or extend the person's self image. People identify with them by projecting their own meaning and emotion into them, they also identify with them by taking certain aspects of meaning and emotion from them into themselves – they introject them. This can work both positively and negatively.

It has been proposed by Russel W. Belk, (1989) Possessions and the Extended Self, *Journal of Consumer Research*, 15 September, that possessions can extend the self in a number of ways:

1 By allowing the person to do things that they would otherwise find difficult or impossible to accomplish (e.g. problem solving using a computer).
2 Symbolically, by making the person feel better or 'bigger' (e.g. receiving an employee award for excellence).
3 By conferring status or rank (e.g. status among collectors of rare works of art because of the ownership of a particular masterpiece).
4 By conferring feelings of immortality, by leaving valued possessions to young family members (this also has the potential of extending the recipient's 'selves').
5 By conferring magical powers (e.g. a ring inherited from one's grandmother might be perceived as a magic amulet bestowing good luck when it is worn).

Altering the self
Self-altering products which help consumers to look better, create a new self or maintain the existing self (e.g. cosmetics). Other self-altering products can make a consumer look like another type of person (e.g. create a yuppie look).

Products, dreams and self-concept
The mind also uses product images in dreams as shown in this example:

> The dreamer dreamed about a young woman at work, a single parent, and struggling financially. She wanted to do something for this woman, to show her that there was another side of life and to give her a treat. She decided that she would give her a ride in a Porsche.

One can even go as far as to say that customers are surrounded by a little group of 'friends' and the friends become the medium through which non-verbal communication takes place. They reconfirm the ideas the person has about themselves as they reflect their self-image.

In the same way that products can be owned, services, people (politicians, pop stars and football teams), organizations and places can be owned in the same way – they all become part of the customer's internal world; and in varying degrees this process can be both conscious and unconscious.

Psychoanalytic theory
The structure of psychoanalysis has by far burst the thought boundaries set for it by Freud. He put forward the theory that the human personality system consists of the id, ego and super ego. The id seeks immediate gratification for biological and instinctual need. The super ego representing societal or personal norms that have an ethical constraint on behaviour. The ego mediates between the two.

For example, picture a gorgeous woman next to a car. The car is an extension of male virility and the woman is placed next to the car to emphasize this fact. (The gorgeous woman appeals to the id and the car becomes a phallic extension of the id.)

The sale of insurance on the other hand would appeal to the super ego where it plays to the sense of responsibility. The ego is buffeted between the super ego and id. For example, a family man wants to buy a Ferrari when he turns forty, but super ego realizes that he should put the money in an endowment plan, and the ego makes a compromise between the two. So if the organization selling the endowment policy gave a 'treat' that appealed to the id some compromise could be reached between the two.

Role theory

Historically, individual consumers have been thought to have a single self and to be interested in products and services that satisfy that single self. However, psychoanalytic theory indicates that it is more accurate to think of people in terms of a multiple self and although between the inner and the outer world there is an ego which is a filtering process that screens aspects of the outer world, people are likely to behave differently in different situations within the context of their social roles. In fact, acting exactly the same way may not actually be all that healthy.

Role theory is concerned with the roles people act out in their lives. People's behaviour will change depending on different social groupings in which they find themselves.

Role signs

In many situations people are expected to have a specific appearance or uniform – milk and post deliveries, railway guards, and so on. A uniform is an important role sign and various personal possessions (briefcase, organizer) can be used to reinforce a person's perceived role. A product/ service image can be enhanced by being associated with particular roles. A marketer needs to know the role signs people want to buy.

Activity 7.7	How do you use role signs?

Role relationships and models

Role relationships can very often define a relationship quite specifically. For example, a customer will expect sales assistants to behave in a certain manner. Generally people have perceptions of the way in which the role should be carried out, these would be based on the rules of behaviour (norms established by society) associated with that role. Role models who embody the highest expectations of particular roles can be associated with a product.

Products can be used to indicate the nature of the role relationship, intimate and formal.

Role ambiguity and role conflict

When people have multiple roles problems associated with differing expectations occur. Role conflict occurs when people who have several different roles find that the roles are incompatible. Marketers can provide products that assuage the customer's guilt and sense of inadequacy of not being able to fulfil their different roles. For example, the busy working woman who still wants to cook a proper dinner can use wholesome convenience gourmet foods.

Role conflict can occur between roles, for example having to finish a piece of work and attend a child's birthday party at the same time.

Intra-role conflict arises when there is a conflict arising from different aspects of the same role. For example, a parental role when the parent wants to both love and discipline the child.

Role ambiguity refers to the individual's uncertainty of what is expected in a role, and also to the role sets (the people to whom the role holder is relating to) uncertainty of what is expected in the role.

Brands can be developed to help clarify roles and enable the values associated with the role to be achieved.

Trait factor theory

Trait factor theory puts forward the idea that an individual's personality is comprised of predispositional attributes called traits. These traits are relatively enduring.

Trait theory makes a number of assumptions:

1 Many individuals share the same traits.
2 Traits will vary in intensity between different individuals.
3 Traits are relatively stable in different environments. However, some people believe that personality may be more situational than trait theorists propose.

These assumptions lead then to the belief that traits can be inferred by measuring behaviour.

Trait factor theory is used in marketing personality research to try and find a relationship between purchasing, media choice, risk taking, attitude change, fear and social influence. It is also used in recruitment.

Cattell is perhaps the best known of the supporters of the trait approach to personality. He used the technique of factor analysis to identify what he believed to be the principal factors of personality as set out in Table 7.6.

Table 7.6 Cattell's 16 principal factors (16PF)

Cool	A	Warm
Concrete thinking	B	Abstract thinking
Affected by feeling	C	Emotionally stable
Submissive	E	Dominant
Sober	F	Enthusiastic
Expedient	G	Conscientious
Shy	H	Bold
Tough minded	I	Tender minded
Trusting	L	Suspicious
Practical	M	Imaginative
Forthright	N	Shrewd
Self-assured	O	Apprehensive
Conservative	Q1	Experimenting
Group-oriented	Q2	Self-sufficient
Undisciplined self conflict	Q3	Controlled
Relaxed	Q4	Tense

In addition a number of second order or composite factors are identified which include:

- *Extroversion* – the extent to which an individual is socially outgoing.
- *Anxiety* – the extent to which an individual is habitually anxious.
- *Tough poise* – the extent to which an individual is more influenced by facts than feelings.
- *Independence* – the extent to which an individual is aggressive, independent, daring and incisive.
- *Super ego/control* – the extent to which an individual tends to conform to the rules and expectations associated with their roles in life.
- *Neuroticism* – the extent to which an individual is apprehensive and emotionally reactive.
- *Leadership* – the extent to which an individual appears to have the traits that are commonly associated with leadership potential, such as sociable, relaxed, assertive and self-assured.
- *Creativity* – the extent to which an individual is imaginative and experimenting.

People are asked to complete extensive questionnaires and the responses are subjected to mathematical analysis. The questions are subjective both in formations and interpretation. There is also a tendency for people to answer questions as they think a normal person would, or how the person wishes themselves to be. However, it seems likely that personality traits should have some effect on purchasing behaviour.

Behaviourist theories

Skinner rejected the idea that each person's behaviour is shaped and determined by internal personality factors. He suggested that each person's behaviour can be explained entirely by reference to the individual's reinforcement history and specific behaviour that has been rewarded or punished.

This concept can be used to explain loyalty marketing. Organizations reward customers for 'good' behaviour, and our ultimate aim is for them to learn brand loyalty.

Primary and secondary groups

People in groups

People are naturally sociable. There is a strong desire amongst most people to form part of a group. This group may be a family, a department at work, or a social club.

Definition 7.3	A group may be defined as two or more people who interact together and share some common attitudes and/or behaviours.

This definition is by no means comprehensive. It is perhaps easier to define a group in terms of its characteristics. A collection of people which possess most of the characteristics listed are usually deemed to constitute a group:

- More than one person.
- Sufficient interaction between members.
- Perception of themselves as a group.
- A certain set of agreed/accepted values (called norms).
- Allocation of specific roles (different activities) to members.
- Social (affective) relations between members.
- Shared aims.

Group influence

Most research work by psychologists has shown that groups exert a strong influence on the way we behave.

Undoubtedly, the most quoted experiment performed by Professor Mayo was the drawing office experiment. Chris Rice (1993) explains:

> Here the problem lay in low morale which was blamed on the lighting. Mayo split the department into two – the first group was the experimental group, the second group acted as the control group and their lighting remained unaltered throughout the experiment. When the intensity of the lighting of the experimental group was increased the expected improvement in morale and output occurred. What was unexpected was that the morale and output of the control group rose in exactly the same way. This puzzled Mayo who proceeded to reduce the intensity for the experimental group – output of both groups again rose! His conclusion was that the changed behaviour was nothing to do with the intensity of the lighting, but was a group phenomenon.

Interestingly, culture plays a strong part in the degree of conformance exhibited by an individual. Isolated members of a culture within a group (for example, a white male in a group of black females) are more likely to conform than if they are in a group with members of their own culture.

It also seems that certain cultures are more likely to conform than others. Norwegian students have been found to conform more than the French; similarly Russian children were found to conform more than their Israeli counterparts (Gross, *Psychology*, 1989).

Consumer reference groups

From a marketing perspective, reference groups are useful in that they are influential in the formation of consumer behaviour. A teenager may, for instance, decide to dress in a certain way because of the influence of their school mates. In this example the school mates are the reference group.

There are two general types of reference groups:

1 *Normative groups* – These are groups which shape the basic attitudes and behaviour of an individual. The most prevalent normative group is the individual's family.
2 *Comparative groups* – These are groups which are used to compare and contrast one's existing attitudes and behaviours. In common parlance if you are doing well, in comparative terms, it is often said that you are 'keeping up with the Joneses'. That is, your lifestyle is comparable to others that you perceive to be in the same social class.

Reference groups are frequently categorized on the following dimensions:

- *Ascribed versus acquired groups* – Ascribed groups are those to which an individual naturally belongs, e.g. gender, family unit. Acquired groups are those to which an individual actively seeks membership, e.g. health club.
- *Formal versus informal groups* – A formal group is well defined in terms of its structure and purpose, e.g. parliament. Informal groups are less well structured and exist primarily to fulfil a social function, e.g. a group of drinking 'buddies'.
- *Primary versus secondary groups* – Primary groups are usually small and associated with more personal contact, e.g. close friends, colleagues at work. Secondary groups are usually larger with communication which is generally less personal, e.g. colleges, large work groups.

There are two important reference groups to which an individual does *not* belong:

1 *Aspirational groups* – These are groups to which an individual aspires to joining, e.g. rock musicians, artists.
2 *Dissociative groups* – These are groups which an individual actively avoids membership of, e.g. for some people the Hell's Angels motorbike club might be such a group, others might actively avoid working in the arms industry.

From a marketer's viewpoint, informal, primary groups are of most interest as they are likely to exert the most influence on an individual's consumer behaviour. In addition, aspirational groups are the most important non-membership groups for the same reason.

Activity 7.8

List five reference groups that you belong to. For each of these decide whether it should be classed as a normative group, a comparative group or whether it fulfils both functions.

The influence of reference groups is summarized in Figure 7.9.

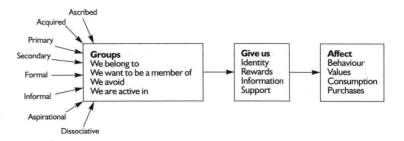

Figure 7.9
Reference groups and their influence

An experiment by Rule et al. (1985) tried to assess the influence that various groups exert. US students were asked to record, both when they felt that someone was trying to influence them and when they were trying to influence someone else. Whereas such experiments are unlikely to be completely accurate (are students exposed to the same influences as others?, would they recognize all attempts to influence them?), they do provide a useful guide. The results are summarized in Table 7.7. Perhaps not surprisingly, immediate family and close friends were perceived as the groups who made the most attempts to persuade. These groups were also those that the student tried most to persuade.

Table 7.7 Groups that US students perceived as trying to persuade them and whom they tried to persuade

	Who tries to persuade you (%)	Whom do you try to persuade (%)
Immediate family	27	35
Extended family	7	5
Close friends	18	24
Occasional friends	7	12
Instructors	13	7
Sales people	11	2
Other professionals	10	3
Trait defined – religious, etc.	5	9
Goal defined – trying to impress them etc.	2	3

Question 7.1

Categorize the following groups on the dimensions: ascribed/acquired, formal/informal, primary/secondary. Note whether they might also be aspirational or dissociative.

- Dance troupe
- Local branch of political party
- Your college class

Group membership – roles and norms

> I would never be a member of any group that would have me as a member. Paraphrased from Groucho Marx

When you join a group you accept certain norms, which govern the behaviour of the group, and take on a certain role (whether it be active or passive).

Norms may apply to any aspect of the behaviour of the group. If you joined Greenpeace, the environmental action group, you would be expected to agree with their 'direct action' method of campaigning. You might also be expected not to buy environmentally-unfriendly products where alternatives were available, to avoid unnecessary car travel, and to vote for the Green Party. As a member of a local Greenpeace group you might also be given, or take on, a number of roles; as organizer of a door-to-door collection, as press officer and so on.

Norms commonly affect the following aspects of the group culture:

- Physical appearance and dress.
- Social and leisure activities (even when these are not the main business of the group).
- Language and gestures used.
- General opinions, attitudes and beliefs.
- The way in which the group carries out its own business.

Roles within a group are decided, primarily, on how we see ourselves and what others expect of us. If we see ourselves as a leader we are likely to try for this role. Alternatively, if others see us as 'leadership material' we are likely to be offered this role.

Within any groups a number of role types commonly exist. Most roles inevitably fall into the first two categories:

- *Task roles* – a member or members concerned with pursuing the goals of the group (often referred to as the members who 'get things done').
- *Maintenance roles* – a member or members concerned with keeping the group operational and efficient (these may be the group administrators or act as emotional supports for the group).
- *Comedy role* – a member who is a joker or the willing butt of jokes.
- *Observer role* – a passive observer of proceedings.
- *Deviant role* – a member who constantly disagrees and challenges the group norms.
- *Specialist role* – a member who is held as being a specialist in the technical activities of the group.
- *Spokesperson role* – a member who communicates the activities of the group to non-group members.

Communication within groups

The way in which group members communicate with one another is important to marketers. The direction and density of communication affects how quickly decisions are made, the satisfaction of group members and the quality of the decision. Study of communication patterns might also help you to market your products more effectively and efficiently.

The sociometric method is the technique most used to determine communication patterns. Individuals are asked where they obtained advice or information on a certain subject or product and whom they provided with advice or information. Lines are then drawn on a diagram between circles representing the individuals involved to form what is called a sociogram. It might be that you wish to know how knowledge of a particular book spread within a community or how consumers found out about a special offer.

When such studies are undertaken, three common sociogram patterns emerge; circle, wheel (or star) and all-channel. These are illustrated below in Figure 7.10 for a five person group. Each line represents a channel of communication, each dot represents an individual.

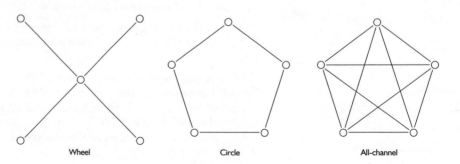

Figure 7.10

Activity 7.9

How do you communicate within your class? Pick a subject which has been discussed at a recent break time and draw out a sociogram. Describe the various structures you discover.

Consumer-referent groups

Marketers have identified the groups which have the most impact on consumer behaviour:

- *Family* – Members in the family take on different roles in the decision making.
- *Peer groups* – Through school, our teenage years and on into adulthood we are constantly surrounded by people of our own age and social class. These are usually informal and often social groups of friends. In conjunction with the family, close friends are the biggest influence on our consumer behaviour.
- *Consumer or lobbying groups* – In recent years consumers who feel that they are getting a 'bad deal' have formed groups with the specific purpose of bringing pressure to bear on manufacturers and service providers. Such groups may address a single issue or provide a more general service as a 'watchdog'.
- *Work groups* – People at work form both formal groups (departments, divisions and so on) as well as more informal groups (company sailing club, after-work drinking 'buddies', office squash league, and so on). The amount of time that people spend at work in the company of their work colleagues provides ample opportunity for influence.

How the mass media uses referent groups

The appeal of certain types of referent groups is used in advertising to influence the consumer. Three general approaches are:

1 *Aspirational appeal* – present the product in a situation, or use a celebrity or type of person, to which the consumer aspires. Examples include showing the product in the context of a beautiful house or using an athletic actor.
2 *Peer appeal* – present the product by a person to whom the consumer can relate. For instance, an advert aimed at selling car telephones to working women may show a business women stranded in the middle of nowhere with a broken down car.
3 *Expert appeal* – the product is endorsed by an expert, who may be known or unknown, with the aim of convincing the consumer that the product does the job for which it was designed. The more trustworthy the expert, the more convincing the appeal. Ex-police officers have been used on several occasions for this very reason.

The benefits of using reference groups in the ways described is that they reduce the perceived risk of purchase and increase product awareness. As we have seen in earlier units, these are two of the most important barriers to successful marketing.

Table 7.8 Some examples of referent group appeal

Appeal element	Product	Type of appeal
Michael Jackson	Soft drink	Inspirational
Exotic locations	Cars	Inspirational
Ex-police chief Markham	Car tyres	Expert
Ex-police chief Stalker	Alarm systems	Expert
Head of company post room	Courier service	Expert
Scientists	Washing powder	Expert
Driver in broken down car in unsafe or remote area	Car breakdown and recovery service	Peer

Family purchasing

The most comprehensive marketing model on family purchasing and decision making assumes that children are growing up in a two parent family structure (Sheth 1974). In reality family structures today include not only married couples with children but also a variety of alternative family structures, including female and male-headed single parent families.

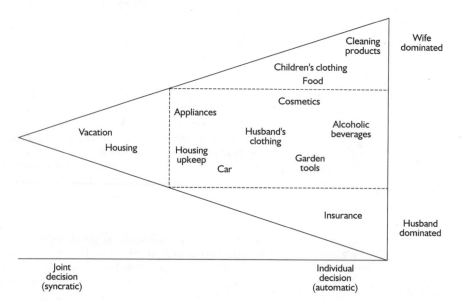

Figure 7.11
Purchasing decisions. *Source:* Adcock, Bradfield, Halberg and Ross (1994)

With family purchasing decisions can be be made autonomously or jointly: on one's own behalf, on behalf of one or more other family members, or for the family as a unit.

The organization as customer

Differences between consumer and industrial buying

- many buyers prefer to deal with suppliers who can offer complete systems
- there are fewer customers than the consumer marketer
- the market is clearly segmented – a supplier may know all potential customers and a potential buyer may know all potential suppliers
- some large organizations have enormous purchasing power
- the practice of reciprocal buying may exist
- the external environment will influence the organization in different ways. For example: the level of primary demand, the cost of money
- many organizational markets have inelastic demand (see Unit 8)
- decisions are made through a group buying process
- buying is often carried out by purchasing professionals
- an unsuccessful decision carries much greater risks than the average customer purchase, a bad decision will affect both the individuals, the groups involved in the purchase and the organization itself
- the buying process is more formal – with written reports, detailed product specifications, and purchase orders
- there is an interlinking customer–supplier chain of dependency and counter dependency
- the demand fluctuates quite widely, a small increase in consumer demand will create a large increase in industrial demand
- much of the purchasing is done on the basis of history and ongoing relationships are of crucial importance. Organizational marketers very often work closely with their customers – they help them to define their needs, customize the offer and deal with the after-sales service
- the organizational culture and structure will influence the buying process and the way decisions are made

- because organizations consist of many people, individual needs will be more varied and need to be taken into account
- no two organizations are the same. Although the standard promotional material may be the same the people who are in direct contact with the customer need to be aware of the differences
- the buying criteria that will be used to judge 'good value' will be much wider. These criteria could include: price/discounts, technical quality, advantage and advancement, after-sales service, reliability and continuity of supply, back-up advisory service, credit facilities.

The organizational buying process

- the type of buying situation will be different but the categorization in terms of low involvement and high involvement purchases made by individuals is similar:

    - routine behaviour or **straight rebuy** where the buyer reorders something without any changes being made. History is a significant factor here and there is an inertia which tends to make it difficult for a new supplier to enter the market – very often price cutting is a way in
    - limited problem solving or **modified rebuy** is where the buyer wants to modify the specification, prices, terms or suppliers
    - extended problem solving or **new buy** is where the buyer is buying something for the first time; these tend to be lengthy as the buying criteria will have to be established and developed from scratch

See Figure 7.12 for some examples

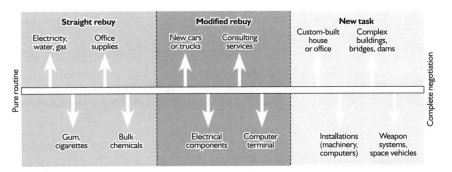

Figure 7.12
Three types of industrial buying situation. *Source:* Enis, Ben, M. (1980) *Marketing Principles*, Copyright 1980, Scott, Foresman and Company. Reprinted by permission

---

Question 7.2

In what way does an industrial buying situation differ from the consumer market? Use an example of your choice.

The organizational decision-making unit: internal processes of the DMU

Gatekeepers
Gatekeepers are often able to acquire power that goes well beyond their formal status. For example, many secretaries exert a special influence by controlling what information comes into an organization, or who is allowed into the organization.

The gatekeeper can very often be a specialist who feeds relevant information into the rest of the DMU, so there is an overlap with other roles.

Initiators
The initiator (the person who triggers off an idea or identifies a problem) may have great ideas but may not have the power within the organization to carry out ideas. It is always important to find the decider in the DMU and to involve them as soon as possible.

Figure 7.13
Major stages of the industrial
buying process in relation to major
buying situations. *Source:* Kotler
(1980), *Principles of Marketing*,
Prentice-Hall International, Inc.,
adapted from Patrick J. Robinson,
Charles W. Faris, and Yoram
Wind, Industrial Buying and
Creative Marketing (Boston: Allyn
and Bacon, 1967), p. 14

		Buying situations		
Stages of the buying process		New task	Modified rebuy	Straight rebuy
1	Problem recognition	Yes	Maybe	No
2	General need description	Yes	Maybe	No
3	Product specification	Yes	Yes	Yes
4	Supplier search	Yes	Maybe	No
5	Proposal solicitation	Yes	Maybe	No
6	Supplier selection	Yes	Maybe	No
7	Order routine specification	Yes	Maybe	No
8	Performance review	Yes	Yes	Yes

Influencers

Influencers are people who influence decision making. They perform the role of informing, persuading or stimulating the decision-making process. They can be inside the organization, for example technical people in research and development. They could be outside the organization, for example, stakeholders, pressure groups.

Deciders

Deciders actually make the decision to buy and have the power to decide on what is required and who will provide it.

Buyers

Buyers do not necessarily make the decision to buy, they do, however, make the purchase. They have formal authority from within the organization to select a supplier and negotiate the terms of purchase. In some cases their role is purely administrative.

Users

Users are the people who actually use the product or experience the service. In many cases, they initiate the buying proposal and help define the product specifications and have a high level of technical expertise. They may or may not be the deciders or the buyers.

Financiers

Financiers are the people who determine and control the budget.

Question 7.3

What roles do people take up within the industrial DMU and what part do each play within the DMP? Relate your understanding to an organizational situation you have some experience of.

Forces influencing organizational behaviour

Activity 7.10

Choose an organization with which your company has a commercial relationship and see how much of the following information you can find out: (if your work does not provide you with the opportunity to carry out this task, work with another colleague). Remember to look at the whole system, not only one aspect of it.

Past history with your organization

- records on: sales visits, purchases made, frequency of purchase, time of purchase, credit arrangements, complaints, etc.
- information on previous relationships they have had with members from your own organization
- information on the current supplier chain within your own organization – who else in your business has contacts with this customer and are these relationships satisfactory and how has history affected them (misbilling, personal friction, late delivery etc.)?

Information on the organization

1   Organizational environment

- how does the macro-environment (PEST) influence their business?
    - Economic, commercial and competitive factors such as interest rates, exchange rates, industrial optimism/pessimism
    - Also the political, legal and social environment such as the green movement, equal opportunities policies, ISO9000
    - Technological change
    - Supplier size and flexibility, financial reputation
    - Co-operative buying.

You will also need to find out about:

- Their customers – information on their customers and how their needs will have an influence on what your organization produces.
- Other competitors – information on any other organizations competing for their business.

2   The organization as a whole

- how does the organization stand commercially?
- can you describe the overall size and culture of the organization? (Don't forget different sub-cultures you need to be aware of.) This will effect the structure of the organization, the reporting relationships, the buying policies, the level of autonomous decision making.

3   The group DMU

- What is the type of purchase (straight rebuy, modified rebuy or new buy)?
- How do they get information?
- What other sources of information are available to them (any other external influences on their purchasing behaviour like other businesses, journals, co-operative buying, etc.)?
- How active are they in the search for alternative information?
- How is the decision-making unit structured and how does it fit into the organizational structure?
    - Is the DMU centralized?
    - Is the decision-making process (DMP) formalized to the extent that rules and procedures are stated and adhered to by members of that organization? Are there any meta rules (unseen rules that govern the rules)?
    - Is the DMU specialized to the degree in which different departments take on different aspects of the decision-making process?
    - How does the DMU function?
        Initiators
        Influencers
        Gatekeepers
        Users
        Deciders
        Buyers
        Financiers
- Is there information on the buying criteria?

Are there any group attitudes to:

- Time pressure?
- Price–cost factors?
- Supply and continuity?
- Risk and their methods of avoiding risk?
- Quality?
- Seeing problems?

What are the relationships between groups?

- Any record of conflict in the DMU between people or departments?
- Any record of functional interests in defining the problem?
- How is conflict resolved (joint problem solving, persuasion, bargaining or politicking)?

4   The individuals

- The names and roles of the people involved in the decision-making unit
- How do they see their problems? Different backgrounds and training will influence the way problems are perceived
- How satisfied are they with previous purchases and why?
- The needs of the individuals in the DMU, how they perceive themselves and the quality of relationship they like to have with suppliers. For example:

   - What is their background (class, age, education and lifestyle)?
   - How much time do they want spent with them?
   - How frequently do they want suppliers to contact them?
   - Do they treat suppliers as peers?
   - What level of intimacy do they want?
   - Will they want to dominate the relationship?
   - Will they want to become dependent on suppliers?
   - Will they be aggressive?
   - What attitudes do they have towards risk? And how does this show in the way they procrastinate and throw up objections?
   - How will sex, race and other forms of difference influence the relationship?
   - How will they play their professional role and what sort of relationship will their professional role allow the supplier to play
   - How is the supplier expected to behave? Remember you have to create an ongoing relationship with them!

Unforeseen factors
These could relate to the internal and external environment. Is there any thing outside the control of the DMU that could affect the decision making (industrial relations problems, cash flow, tax changes, etc.)?

Summary

When you approach an organization it is important to look at the whole system and not only at one aspect of it. You start with what has gone before, past history. You then go on to look at the organization from the outside – external factors affecting it within the macro- and micro-environment (see Unit 4), then the inside of the organization – first as a whole, then the DMU groups within it and lastly the individuals. In any situation possible unforeseen circumstances should be taken into account.

Forces influencing organizational behaviour

1   The selling organization

- Past history

2   The buying organization

External factors

- macro-environmental factors (PEST)
- micro-environmental factors (competitors, suppliers, distributors, customers)

Internal factors

- The organization
- The group
  - what happens in the DMU group as a whole (intragroup)
  - what happens between groups (intergroup)
- The individuals
  - what happens between individuals in the group (interpersonal)
  - what happens in the individuals' minds (intrapersonal)

3 Unforeseen circumstances

Question 7.4

What role do sales people play in helping customers to make decisions? Use the decision-making process as a structure on which to base your discussion. Consider both a retail situation and an industrial situation.

Summary

In this unit we have considered cultural factors influencing customers' behaviour, theories of motivation, consumer imagery, psychoanalytic theory, role theory, trait factor theory and behavioural theory. We have also looked at the influence of the group on organizational purchasing. There are similarities and differences between buyer behaviour towards consumer and industrial goods and services.

Buyer behaviour is influenced in many different ways – the condition of the economy and other environmental factors, products characteristics, the type of market and its characteristics, the product's stage in the life cycle, the degree of market segmentation, the number of competitors, the number of customers and their geographic spread, the psychological factors operating within individuals such as their motives, approach to risk, attitudes and personality and other personal factors that are unique to a person such as their ability and knowledge, demographic factors and situational factors, social factors influencing the buyer decision process such as roles and family influences, reference groups, social classes and culture and sub-culture. The decision-making process (DMP) and the extent of the decision making involved – extended and limited problem solving, routine response buying, impulse buying and the degree of involvement in the purchase and the decision-making process within the decision-making unit.

The following unit introduces you to relationship marketing and you will be able to develop your ideas in a different way.

Relationship marketing

Study Guide

This unit introduces students to the concept of relationship marketing, where the priority has shifted away from transaction marketing to creating ongoing relationships with customers to create life-time values. Relationship marketing is considered in both consumer and industrial markets. Situations are analysed in terms of their suitability or unsuitability to relationship marketing. The benefits are considered and difficulties of relationship marketing are considered.

Creating positive relationships with customers

The rules for business success are changing fundamentally. Forces such as globalization, technological change and the rising power of the customer are stimulating marketers to find new ways to retain, satisfy and work with customers so that their needs can be anticipated and products and services customized more accurately. One of the most reliable indicators of the success of a company is whether it retains its customers. It is estimated that it costs between five to fifteen times as much to acquire a new customer as it does to keep a current one.

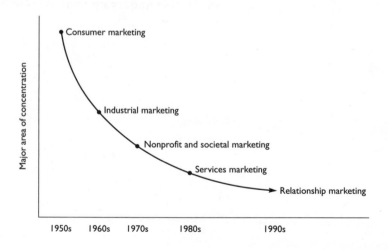

Figure 8.1
Historical applications in marketing

The result of this concern is relationship marketing. Priority is shifting from products to people and processes aimed at creating delighted customers. Companies are now realizing that like every other organism they exist in a feedback loop with their environment. This is the underlying theory of using a systems approach towards organizational behaviour, in recognition that every aspect of the system will have an effect on another.

Marketing is moving from transaction marketing to relationship marketing. Each of these approaches has its own characteristics.

Transaction marketing:

- Focus on single sale.
- Orientation on product features.
- Short time scale.
- Little emphasis on customer service.
- Limited customer commitment.
- Moderate customer contact.
- Quality is primarily a concern of production.

Relationship marketing:

- Focus on customer retention.
- Orientation on product benefits.
- Long time scale.
- High customer service emphasis.
- High customer commitment.
- High customer contact.
- Quality is the concern of all.

Relationship marketing is the process of building and managing collaborative customer and other value chain relationships to increase customer value, retention and profit. The relationship process moves customers up a ladder of loyalty, as shown in Figure 8.2.

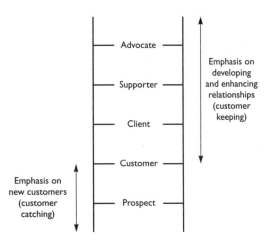

Figure 8.2
The relationship ladder.
Christopher, Payne and Ballantyne,
Relationship Marketing

Collaborating internally

Companies, instead of just being led by their production capability, their technology, or their financial departments, are looking at the needs of their customers and are breaking down walls internally to develop value chains based on relationships. As we have learned communication, empowerment and teamwork are key issues.

These customer-focused companies are thriving on their relationships, or rather the strength of their relationships both internally and externally so that there is a good match between the external and internal environment. Relationship marketing involves taking a broader view of this match.

The key to successfully implementing a relationship marketing strategy is to organize and motivate your organization so they are interested and understand the concept then:

1 Carry out an industry analysis.
2 Carry out an audit of relationship markets (see Gummesson).
3 Analyse internally.
4 Collect information on your customers.
5 Identify customers for RM strategy.
6 Understand individual customer profitability.
7 Market internally and externally.
8 Measure and evaluate the results.

Relationship marketing in consumer markets

Up until recently the idea of relationship marketing was mainly applied to industrial and services marketing, but it may also have some relevance for consumer marketing. This will depend on the characteristics of a market segment and the product field in question. It is important to understand and distinguish between actions that would aim to develop marketing relationships and actions that are interpreted and evaluated as sales promotion and merely create sales in the short term.

Marketing relationships are often initiated by the supplier, but sometimes consumers make the first move and take responsibility for maintaining and developing a relationship. This is termed reverse marketing, good examples are the relationship between a private consumer and a local builder, or the relationship patients may build up with a dentist as they seek further treatment over a lifetime.

It is this trust and confidence that relationship marketing seeks to build with larger groups of customers. Although this one-to-one, individualized marketing communication is more expensive per person to undertake, in the long term it may be less of an expense, if analysed in terms of lifetime value.

The use of technology
Falling IT costs now make it possible to offer customers the recognition that was formerly only possible in businesses where the customer base was relatively small. Organizations are now using refined information about current and potential customers to anticipate and respond to their needs. Continuous relationship marketing now gives marketers a range of information about their customers. It is then possible to rearrange the information in many different ways.

The elements of a marketing relationship – when is it possible?

1 *Time frame*. In considering whether a relationship marketing approach is possible one needs to consider the opportunity for a long-term relationship with the customer.
2 *Differentiation*. The product or service must be able to be differentiated from the competition in some way.

Recognizing a natural RM possibility
It should be clear that some products and services naturally offer the opportunity for a relationship to form, and suppliers in the market place who are unable to satisfy and manage these relationships in a competent way will suffer in a competitive market place.

High involvement products/services
Some products and services offer the opportunity for a personal relationship to develop. For example, a musician may go to a music shop for

advice about instruments. The help and care that the assistant can give is a natural opportunity to create a long-term relationship with that particular customer.

Risk
Purchasing must be considered in terms of generating anxiety and putting the consumer at risk. There are different types of risk: social, psychological, financial, and product failure. It is obvious therefore that customers may prefer to have previous experience of an organization before committing themselves to purchasing. In terms of ongoing purchasing they may be reluctant to change.

The desire to pay for more than just the core product
The essence of marketing is to turn a commodity into a brand. It is in the branding process that the product/service is augmented in such a way that customers are prepared to pay a premium price.

Customization
Some products/services need to be customized. With the growing understanding that customers wish to be treated as individuals, organizations should look at how they can tailor what they give to meet individual needs.

Training
When customers purchase products that are complicated, they may perceive a need for training. This need offers an opportunity for relationship marketing.

Psychological need
A relationship may be sought out by customers for very many reasons. For some it may be loneliness: with the breakdown of family, and the development of home working, some people may not have a large network of people in their personal lives to relate to. Others may wish to attach themselves to various organizations for reasons as varied as status, a better deal, or even the reluctance to look elsewhere. The research done by the Future Foundation indicates that we now live in a wider environment and that many of the values we once treasured in personal relationships we now look for in society and the relationship business creates with its social environment. The language used 'industrial intimacy', 'making corporate love' is suggestive of this.

Regular maintenance and repair – ongoing services
Hairdressing, dress making, accountancy, law, fitness training, massage – there are any number of services where there is an ongoing interaction. A product requiring maintenance or repair throughout its life, or whose ongoing nature engages customers in a relationship with the providers.

Frequency of purchase
The higher the frequency of purchase the higher the opportunities will be to create a relationship.

Differentiation
The more a product or service is adapted to the particular tastes of a customer the greater will be the opportunity to create a relationship. Hairdressing, interior decoration and architecture are good examples.

Inconvenience
The more a supplier knows about a customer and their particular tastes the greater the opportunity for forming a relationship. For example, lawyers hold detailed client histories and clients may be reluctant, or too busy, to have to go through telling another lawyer about their life; the same holds true for accountants.

High switching costs
There may be costs involved in changing a supplier. For example, the new supplier may need to go through some sort of learning curve where

191

mistakes will have to be made. There may be equipment costs where the old supplier has provided the customer with equipment free of charge.

Extended problem solving

Suppliers can add value to products/services which highly involve the customer in an extended period of decision making, where there is a high degree of risk (social, psychological, financial and product failure) and where expertise is valued as a supplier.

Extended problem solving and a high level of involvement in product/ services occurs where there is a perception of high risk and customers have a need to have things explained to them. Suppliers can add to the relationship by showing a real interest in the product area perhaps by visiting a customer, ensuring that the product is being used in the right way and sending invitations to further demonstrations, updates on product information and even a Christmas card.

Even where the level of involvement may not be high, for example in buying a tube of wallpaper paste, the customer may value advice. This in itself gives the retailer the opportunity to build a relationship on an ongoing basis, and then focus on linking these intangible benefits with a tangible benefit as a reward to purchase loyalty.

Role relationships

At all times the provider of the service must be aware that the relationship is based on the financial transaction, and the boundaries that delineate that relationship from one based on personal preference must be considered. The role relationship, and the behavioural expectations arising from a performer of the role, must be analysed in detail. For example, a nurse or a teacher is expected to behave in a particular way. The possibility of relationship marketing must be viewed from both the customer's side and that of the market/product/service field and what is deemed suitable. Further consideration to some of the difficulties involved in relationship marketing, and how to manage them will be given at the end of this section.

Customer and product influences on relationship potential

In approaching consumer markets the traditional categorizations of products and services can be viewed in terms of their 'relationship possibilities'. These relationship possibilities may well be tangible or intangible.

There are thus two different types of incentives:

1 Incentives that offer tangible benefits.
2 Incentives that offer intangible benefits.

Tangible benefits

Tangible benefits attempt to encourage customers to enter into a relationship or to remain in one for a longer period of time. They can include:

- Money or near-money benefits. Examples include the British Telecom 'Family and Friends' scheme, the Air Miles benefits that participants can collect, and product discount-based schemes such as that run by Homebase. All these types of scheme give extra supplies at a better price or other products at a preferential price.
- Access to extra features. Examples include the British Airways Executive club member scheme which gives access to a special lounge, or the special shopping evenings which some shops have from time to time.
- Access to customized products or services.
- Access to special customer service arrangements. For example, ordering by telephone, chauffeur-driven car to the airport, late check-in facilities.

- Extra information. Companies can send existing customers information on special deals or new product information, or produce a leisure magazine containing such information.
- User groups. Common interests create common bonds, the creation of user groups is another way of giving people the opportunity to relate to each other.

Intangible benefits
Intangible benefits could centre round self-esteem, using the relationship to reflect or imply quality, reducing risk such as social, psychological, economic and quality.

Social status, self-esteem and social concerns
Charities and fund-raising offer opportunities to fund givers to improve their social status. Royalty is associated with the voluntary sector and becoming involved may provide the chance to meet the rich and the famous in a well-known place not normally accessible. Charities following this path of fund-raising need to look at sponsorship, or holding events such as operas and recitals where the great and the good are able to display themselves. At the other scale it my mean joining in local activities and finding a sense of community. They also need to send ongoing information in order to keep donors involved and identified with the project.

Raising money for charity or doing something for a particular cause may well give a person a greater sense of self-esteem as well as the opportunity to show to the world that they are doing something. At a more symbolic level it may give the donor the opportunity to work out deep-felt social concerns, and sometimes concerns that they have experienced personally in the course of their lives.

Relationship marketing in organizational markets

Industry and relationship analysis
An industry and relationship analysis including an examination of competitors is an essential step prior to making a decision about your own strategy. In undertaking an analysis of any industry, its characteristics and long-term prospects can be analysed in terms of five dimensions:

1 The nature and degree of competition.
2 The barriers to entry to that business.
3 The competitive power of substitute products.
4 The degree of buyer power.
5 The degree of supplier power.

Through analysis of these five dimensions insights can be gained into relationship with a number of key market areas, in terms of both opportunities and threats, as well as the specific key factors for success in the industry under consideration.

The five forces which contribute to industry profitability are summarized by Christopher, Payne and Ballantyne:

1 *Potential entrants.* Two factors determine how strong this force will be – the existing barriers to entry and the likelihood of a strong competitive reaction from established competitors. The threat of entry tends to be low if barriers to entry are high and/or aspiring new entrants can expect extremely hostile retaliation from the established firms within the industry. If the threat of entry is low, profitability of the industry tends to be high.
2 *Buyers.* The bargaining power of customers (buyers) is high when a number of critical factors are present. These include: the products that a company purchases forming a large proportion, in terms of cost, of its own product; the buyer group is operating in an industry of low

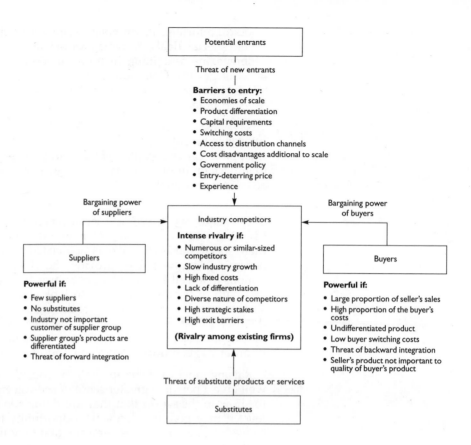

Figure 8.3
The Porter industry analysis model.
Based on Porter, M. E. (1980),
*Techniques for Analysing Industries
and Competitors, Competitive
Strategy.* New York: Free Press

profitability; the products supplied are undifferentiated, making it easy for the buyer to switch between suppliers at little cost; the products being purchased in large volumes; and the buyers having the potential to integrate backwards. Such conditions of high buyer power will result in lower industry profitability.

3 *Suppliers.* Similarly, the bargaining power of suppliers can be high if there are relatively few suppliers; if the industry is dominated by only a few suppliers; if the industry is not an important customer of the supplier group; if the supplier has the potential to integrate forward into the customer's business; if there are few or no direct substitutes for the product, or if the supplier group's products are sufficiently differentiated that the firm being supplied the goods cannot easily switch to another supplier. Conditions of high supplier power lead to reduced industry profitability.

4 *Substitute products.* In many markets it is possible to identify products which can serve as substitutes. In industries ranging from tele-communications to car making, the threat of substitution is present. The higher the threat of substitution, the lower the profitability is likely to be within the industry. This is because threat of substitution generally sets a limit on the prices that can be charged. The factors which influence the threat of substitution include the substitute product price–performance trade-off, and the extent of switching costs associated with changing from one supplier to the supplier of the substitute. If the threat of substitution is low, industry profitability will tend to be high.

5 *Industry competition.* The degree of industry competition is characterized by the amount of rivalry between existing firms. This can vary considerably and is not related necessarily to whether or not the industry is highly profitable. Intense rivalry can exist if there is slow growth within the industry; if competitors are evenly balanced in size and capability; where switching costs are low; where there is a high fixed-cost structure and companies need to keep volumes high; where exit barriers are high such that unprofitable companies may still remain within the industry; and where competitors have different strategies – the result of which is that some firms may be willing to pursue a

strategy that results in considerable conflict within the industry with price wars being a common outcome. A high degree of rivalry depresses industry profitability.

Porter argues that the goal of the corporate strategist is to find a position in the industry where their company can best defend itself against these five forces, or alternatively influence them in its favour.

A complete and balanced analysis of the competitive environment in which a firm is operating would include an examination of barriers to entry, the relative power of buyers and suppliers, the power of substitute, and the degree of rivalry within the industry. This understanding needs also to extend to the relationships that exist between all these players so that the marketer understands that they are not entering an empty playing field. This would lead to a good understanding of the key factors for success, and give managers a sense of the strengths and weaknesses, opportunities and threats within the industry. The power structure in an industry may result in conflicts being structuralized or institutionalized. This may, or may not, be insurmountable and affect the shape relationship marketing is able to take. In some industries it may even affect the relationships the distribution channels have with their customers.

It is also of importance to consider relationships with competitors. The type of relationship with competitors, is often the result of the degree of rivalry and the competitive structure of the industry. Rivalry is usually strong where there are numerous or equally balanced competitors but may also be intense under other conditions. Poor relationships can manifest in deep-seated antagonism between firms in the way they use their resources to attack one another, to their mutual detriment.

Better relationships between two seemingly implacable rivals in a given market sector may restore industry profitability. Porter points to the need to adopt strategies relating to competitors that could be called 'cooperative', and that make the industry as a whole better off. Kevin P. Coyne and Somu Subramaniam (Bringing discipline to strategy, *The McKinsey Quarterly*, http://www.mckinseyquarterly.com) point out that the traditional Porter model needs to be reassessed.

Evert Gummesson (Stockholm University, School of Business, e-mail egdfek.su.se) says, although the frameworks presented in marketing books claimed to be universally valid, they dealt with consumer goods marketing: cola drinks, pain killers, cookies and cars. Contrary to common belief, consumer marketing is the smallest part of all marketing; services marketing and business marketing account for the major share.... Relationship marketing is becoming a general marketing approach and

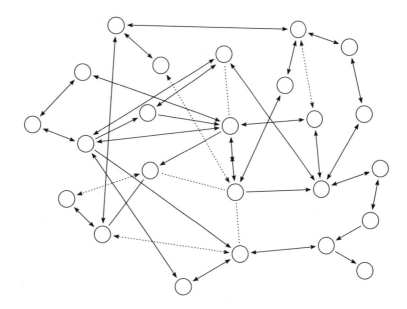

Figure 8.4
Source: Gummesson, E. (1999), *Total Relationship Marketing*, Butterworth-Heinemann

Table 8.1 TRM as a paradigm shift in marketing. *Source*: Gummesson, E. (1999) *Total Relationship Marketing*, Butterworth-Heinemann

Definition	RM is marketing seen as relationships, networks and interaction.
Characteristics	Value for the parties involved – of which the customer is one – is created through interaction between suppliers, customers, competitors and others; the parties in a network of relationships are co-producers, creating value for each other.
Making RM tangible	Specification of thirty relationships, the 30Rs, both operational market relationships, and mega and nano non-market relationships.
Relationship portfolio	As part of the marketing planning process, a selection of focal relationships is made for the planning period in the marketing plan.
Values	Collaboration in focus; more win-win and less win-lose; more equal parties; all parties carry a responsibility to be active in the relationship; long-term relationships; each customer is an individual or a member of a community of likeminded people.
Theoretical and practical foundation	Built on a synthesis between traditional marketing management, marketing mix (the 4Ps) and sales management; services marketing (3Ps); the network approach to industrial marketing; quality management; imaginary organizations; new accounting principles; and the experiences of reflective practitioners.
Links to management	RM is more than marketing management, it is rather marketing-oriented management – an aspect of the total management of the firm – and not limited to marketing or sales departments; the marketing plan becomes part of the business plan.
Links to accounting	The balanced scorecard and intellectual capital provide tools for measuring return on relationships.
Links to organization structure	RM is the marketing manifestation of the imaginary organization and vice versa.
Advantages to a firm	Increased customer retention and duration; increased marketing productivity and thus increased profitability; increased stability and security.
Advantages to the market economy	RM adds collaboration to competition and regulations/institutions; the symbiosis between these three contributes to a dynamic marketing equilibrium.
Advantages to society, citizens and customers	RM is the marketing of the value society and the postmodern society; increased focus on customized production and one-to-one marketing, diminished focus on standardized mass manufacturing and anonymous mass marketing
Validity	By focusing on relationships, networks and interaction, RM offers a more realistic approach to marketing than is currently prevailing in marketing education. In practice, business is largely conducted through networks of relationships.
Generalizability	RM can be applied to all kinds of organizations and offerings, but the relationship portfolio and the application is always specific to a given situation.

customers need to be seen as living within a network of relationships where people enter into active contact with each other. Figure 8.4 illustrates the complexity of relationships and shows how they exist as intertwining networks.

Gummesson suggests that the traditional audit needs to carry additional questions. His definition of relationship marketing is as follows: 'Relationship marketing is marketing seen as relationships, networks and interaction' (Gummesson, E. (1999) *Total Relationship Marketing*, Butterworth-Heinemann).

In his book he outlines thirty types of relationship, and suggests that marketers should look at them and their constituent parts and answer the following questions:

1 Is the composition of our relationship portfolio satisfactory?
2 How well are we handling specific relationships and their parts?
3 Are specific relationships or parts of them crucial for success?
4 Could specific relationships add to our performance if we improve them?
5 Should certain relationships be terminated?
6 Do we measure return on relationship (ROR) in the best possible way?

His framework of thinking adds an additional understanding to the audit and also takes marketing into a wider framework. Gummesson has extended the term relationship marketing to total relationship marketing (TRM) and he says that it represents a paradigm shift in marketing as illustrated in Table 8.1.

Another consideration in relationship marketing is to understand when it is appropriate, and indeed how much of the relationship the customer actually wants. Within the context of business-to-business marketing it is important to understand that:

1 Activities that would create commitment take time and therefore money.
2 Organizations interact with more than one department in the course of doing business. It may be difficult to ensure in a relationship marketing programme that the whole organization is singing from the same song sheet.

In setting up a relationship marketing programme within a business it is important to communicate that the time, effort and cost of carrying it out is probably less than would be spent looking for new business and carrying out discrete transactions.

For relationship marketing in business-to-business marketing, the same question applies as in consumer marketing – does the customer actually want a relationship? Because if the customer does not want one, or is not getting the one they would like, an organization may well waste a lot of money supplying the wrong thing.

Communication

Gummesson in his book *Total Relationship Marketing*, Butterworth-Heinemann (p. 236) says that the 30R approach allows marketers to go beyond supppliers and customers and see marketing relationships as embedded in a network of multiple relationships:

- Classic market relationships (R1–R3) are the supplier-customer dyad, the triad of supplier-customer-competitor, and the physical distribution network, which are treated extensively in general marketing theory.
- Special market relationships (R4–R17) represent certain aspects of classic relationships, such as the interaction in the service encounter or the customer as a member of a loyalty programme.

Table 8.2 The thirty relationships of TRM – the 30Rs

Classic market relationships

R1   The classic dyad – the relationship between the supplier and the customer. This is the parent relationship of marketing, the ultimate exchange of value which constitutes the basis of business.

R2   The classic triad – the drama of the customer-supplier-competitor triangle. Competition is a central ingredient of the market economy. In competition there are relationships between three parties: between the customer and the current supplier, between the customer and the suppliers competitors, and between competitors.

R3   The classic network – distribution channels. The traditional physical distribution and modern channel management including goods, services, people and information, consists of a network of relationships.

Special market relationships

R4   Relationships via full-time marketers (FTMs) and part-time marketers (PTMs). Those who work in marketing and sales departments – the FTMs – are professional relationship makers. All others, who perform other main functions but yet influence customer relationships directly or indirectly, are PTMs. There are also contributing FTMs and PTMs outside the organization.

R5   The service encounter – interaction between customer and the service provider. Production and delivery of services involve the customer in an interactive relationship with the service provider, often referred to as the moment of truth.

R6   The many-headed customer and the many-headed supplier. Marketing to other organizations – industrial marketing or business marketing – often means contacts between many individuals from the supplier's and the customer's organization.

R7   The relationship to the customer's customer. A condition for success is often the understanding of the customer's customer, and what suppliers can do to help their customers become successful.

R8   The close versus the distant relationship. In mass marketing, the closeness to the customer is lost and the relationship becomes distant, based on surveys, statistics and written reports.

R9   The relationship to the dissatisfied customer. The dissatisfied customer perceives a special type of relationship, more intense than the normal situation, and often badly managed by the provider. The way of handling a complaint – the recovery – can determine the quality of the future relationship.

R10   The monopoly relationship: the customer or supplier as prisoners. When competition is inhibited, the customer may be at the mercy of the supplier – or the other way around. One of them becomes a prisoner.

R11   The customer as 'member'. In order to create a long-term sustaining relationship, it has become increasingly common to enlist customers as members of various loyalty programmes.

R12   The electronic relationship. Information technology – telecoms, computers, TV – are elements of all types of marketing today and they form new types of relationships.

R13   Parasocial relationships – relationships to symbols and objects. Relationships do not only exist to people and physical phenomena, but also to mental images and symbols such as brand names and corporate identities.

R14   The non-commercial relationship. This is a relationship between the public sector and citizens/customers, but it also includes voluntary organizations and other activities outside of the profit-based and monetarized economy, such as those performed in families.

R15   The green relationship. Environmental and health issues have slowly but gradually increased in importance and are creating a new type of customer relationship through legislation, the voice of opinion-leading consumers, changing behaviour of consumers and an extension of the customer-supplier relationship to encompass a recycling process.

Table 8.2 continued

R16   The law-based relationship. A relationship to a customer is sometimes founded primarily on legal contracts and the threat of litigation.

R17   The criminal network. Organized crime is built on tight and often impermeable networks guided by an illegal business mission. They exist around the world and are apparently growing but are not observed in marketing theory. These networks can disturb the functioning of a whole market or industry.

Mega relationships

R18   Personal and social networks. Personal and social networks often determine business networks. In some cultures, business is solely conducted between friends and friends of friends.

R19   Mega marketing – the real 'customer' is not always found in the market place. In certain instances, relationships must be sought with governments, legislators, influential individuals, and others, in order to make marketing feasible on an operational level.

R20   Alliances change the market mechanisms. Alliances mean closer relationships and collaboration between companies. Thus, competition is partly curbed, but collaboration is necessary to make the market economy work.

R21   The knowledge relationship. Knowledge can be the most strategic and critical resource and 'knowledge acquisition' is often the rationale for alliances.

R22   Mega alliances change the basic conditions for marketing. The EU (European Union) and NAFTA (North American Free Trade Agreement) are examples of alliances above the single company or industry. They exist on government and supranational levels.

R23   The mass media relationship. The media can be supportive or damaging to marketing and they are particularly influential in forming public opinion. The relationship to media is crucial for the way media will handle an issue.

Nano relationships

R24   Market mechanisms are brought inside the company. By introducing profit centres in an organization, a market inside the company is created and internal as well as external relationships of a new kind emerge.

R25   Internal customer relationship. The dependency between the different tiers and departments in a company is seen as a process consisting of relationships between internal customers and internal suppliers.

R26   Quality providing a relationship between operations management and marketing. The modern quality concept has built a bridge between design, manufacturing and other technology-based activities and marketing. It considers the company's internal relationships as well as its relationship to the customers.

R27   Internal marketing: relationships with the 'employee market'. Internal marketing can be seen as part of TRM as it gives indirect and necessary support to the relationships with external customers.

R28   The two-dimensional matrix relationship. Organizational matrices are frequent in large corporations, and above all they are found in the relationships between product management and sales.

R29   The relationship to external providers of marketing services. External providers reinforce the marketing function by supplying a series of services, such as those offered by advertising agencies and market research institutes, but also in the area of sales and distribution.

R30   The owner and financier relationship. Owners and other financiers partly determine the conditions under which a marketing function can operate. The relationship to them infuences the marketing strategy.

The next two types are non-market relationships which indirectly influence the efficiency of market relationships:

- Mega relationships (R18–R23) exist above the market relationships. They provide a platform for market relationships and concern the economy and society in general. Among these are mega marketing (lobbying, public opinion and political power), mega alliances (such as the NAFTA, setting a stage for marketing in North America), and social relationships (such as friendship and ethnic bonds).
- Nano relationships (R24–R30) are found below the market relationships, that is relationships inside an organization (intraorganizational relationships). All internal activities influence the externally bound relationships. Examples of nano relationships are the relationships between internal customers, and between internal markets that arise as a consequence of increasing use of independent profit centres, divisions and business areas inside organizations. The boundary is sometimes fuzzy; it is a matter of emphasis. For example, the physical distribution network (R3) is part of a logistics flow, concerning internal as well as external customers.

Gummesson has a unique way of looking at relationships. He uses the metaphor of the Russian doll and says that Vandermerve, in her book *From Tin Soldiers to Russian Dolls* (Butterworth-Heinemann, 1993), uses the metaphor of tin soldiers and wooden dolls to describe the management of an emerging service society. The metaphor points to connections and dependencies that must be considered when a company organizes its marketing. The doll becomes a symbol of the imaginary organization where the borderline between organization, market and society is not as clear as in traditional organization theory and economics.

Recognizing a natural relationship marketing possibility

There are a number of factors within organizational markets that may lead to the opportunity for a relationship marketing approach:

1 *Uncertainty.* When an organization feels that the product supplied is not homogenous there will be a certain amount of uncertainty. The uncertainty, or rather the management of risk and spreading of the risk within the organization, will determine the complexity of decision making and the need for relationship marketing.
2 *Unequal power.* In some business relationships one organization may have more power than the other; the weaker organization may then need to appoint people within its own ranks who have influence in the stronger organization.
3 *Environmental uncertainty.* Raw materials may vary in terms of price. A relationship could be developed as a way of handling this so that variability is absorbed.
4 *Legitimacy.* Creating a relationship with a powerful organization and being able to publicize this fact will give an organization legitimacy as far as quality, financial standing, or reliability is concerned to such an extent that other customers may feel they no longer need to check their credentials.
5 *Inconvenience.* A relationship may develop between two organizations because they are tied into each other by the way of shared equipment, shared knowledge or a shared expertise.

Risks involved in relationship marketing

There is a danger of only thinking about marketing in terms of relationship marking. The objective of relationship marketing is to turn new customers into advocates for a company on a long-term basis. Hopefully, this will ensure that they stay with the company and refer other people. Relationship marketing therefore adds an additional concept to customer service and quality to the traditional marketing mix.

Some aspects of role relationships are dealt with on page 15. Other aspects that need to be considered are as follows.

Personal and professional dimensions of role relationships

It is obviously easier for relationships to form if the people concerned get on well together – it is another matter when they do not, or even when they start off getting on well, and for their relationship to deteriorate as a result of some personal or professional disageement.

The question is: how does the organization put in systems to deal with this (like taking a temperature reading) before the situation becomes confrontational? The relationship itself will need to be maintained, and feedback on the functional, professional and the feeling side, to do with the personal relationship that is forming or has formed, needs to be considered.

Creating an atmosphere in which these discussions can take place can only be done in a 'no blame' environment. Human beings are not like machines. Very often things go wrong that, with an opportunity for reflection, we can learn to manage.

Within this context of understanding organizations need to meet on a regular basis to look at:

1 The task elements – is the job going well, are the contractual and legal obligations being met?
2 The feeling elements – how are people feeling? Are the behavioural criteria being met? If they are not it may be time to move key individuals out of the relationship. In a no-blame culture where people are open to discussing the vagaries of human nature it should be possible to do this less painfully than in a blame culture where scapegoating is the norm.

Relationships and innovation in role

Relating in any personal relationship requires people to adapt and be innovative within the relationship. It is truly interactive, the success of the relationship is two way as two people are involved. Relationship marketing involves a fundamental change in the philosophy guiding the organization's behaviour. When there is a change in values and beliefs in an organization a certain amount of discomfort will be created. An understanding of stress and anxiety, role and role relationship will enable this process to be understood.

Changes in role

Relationship marketing and empowerment involve a devolution of power to the front line. However, when an organization changes its philosophy and structure so that more power authority and autonomy reside with the staff in contact with customers, middle managers may feel threatened. Managers need to understand that changes like these will release them from day-to-day tactical responsibilities so they have more time for strategic planning and playing a facilitative role. Conversely, employees who are given more responsibility may feel overwhelmed and will need to be given training in order to enable them to expand their roles.

Membership of a primary group

Sociologists have long said that membership of stable primary groups is essential to the well-being of every society. It is through membership of groups that basic needs for affiliation, security and recognition are satisfied. If we accept this, we can look at organizations as groups of people who come together to satisfy their own psychological needs.

It is these psychological needs that prevent change from taking place within the organization. A customer-centred organization seeks to satisfy the needs of its customers and its employees and tries to create a balance between the two. Nonetheless, there may be some difficulty in adjusting because change affects people in different ways and many employees may feel stressed and anxious.

The outcome of any change process will be determined by the way in which an organization manages these feelings.

Stress and anxiety

The stress that people feel at work is an area that is receiving a considerable amount of attention. Stress on the personal level causes real pain and suffering. On an organizational level it causes disruption and loss of production.

Anxiety arising from stress is a response to perceived danger – the physical symptoms are a pounding heart, sweating palms, rapid breathing and all the other bodily dysfunctions anxiety can produce. Externally, anxiety manifests itself in low productivity, lateness, absenteeism, illness, depression and so on.

External danger will automatically result in a person feeling anxiety; however from within the person unconscious feelings and memories can also cause intense feelings of anxiety.

For example, you may be asked to carry out a new task at work which, by overcoming your anxiety, you are able to complete. However, a different person in the same situation may experience such intense anxiety that they are unable to complete the task.

The new service culture puts many people in touch with customers and expects them to behave in an unfamiliar way, we are being asked to be friendly to strangers. This increased contact, for people who have not been specially recruited with such skills in mind, and who do not like or find it difficult to engage with their feelings with strangers in this way, may lead them to feel under increased pressure when they are asked to expand their roles.

Defences

When people are anxious and stressed they will understandably try to protect themselves from anything that may result in emotional pain.

When individuals suffer from anxiety they externalize their feelings and attribute them to an external cause. Other people or social groups become repositories for these projections.

The conceptual framework that underlies this approach to organizations is based on Melanie Klein (1959) who explained that people divide feelings into differentiated elements. She called this 'splitting'. By splitting emotions people can gain relief from internal conflicts. Projection often accompanies splitting, and involves locating feelings in others rather than oneself.

Projection blurs the boundaries between people because it distorts reality and makes what is inside people appear to be outside them. Their actions are therefore based on an assessment of a situation that is unreal.

These processes can make it difficult for people to open up and create an innovative organization involved in a process of continuous change. This type of reaction creates a blame culture. Organizations can change this by making it acceptable to talk openly about feelings, and by giving people proper real information about the external environment (macro, micro and internal organizational factors) so they can adapt accordingly.

Taking up a role

Adapted from work done at the Grubb Institute by Reed and Palmer.)
The idea of role can be looked at as an idea held in the mind of individuals through which they are able to bring together their skills, knowledge and resources (such as people, machinery and money) in order to deal with an external task. Role training is covered in Unit 4.

The key to the way in which people perform their tasks at work lies in their ability, or inability, to take up and perform their roles.

The subjective psychological aspect of a role relies on:

- The person's ability to understand what the job is in terms of the work that must be done.
- The person's understanding of where they are within a given organizational system (the role relationships).
- The person's realization of how other people expect them to behave (the role set's expectations).
- The person's understanding of the environmental considerations that impact upon an organization externally.
- The reality of the pressures that impact on them from within the organization itself.
- The ability to reflect on their self management within their role.
- An understanding of any intra-role conflict (conflicting demands of the different requirements of the same role – for example, a manager may feel that drinking with the boys will inhibit him from managing).
- An understanding of inter-role conflict (for example a salesperson who is required to travel a great deal might find their work role conflicts with their role of parent, which requires them to be at home)
- An understanding of intra-role conflict when the ethics of an organization conflict with personal values and beliefs.

In order to manage themselves 'in role' people need to understand the feelings they have about their roles, and the reactions they have to the way in which others behave towards them because of their role.

For example, it can come as a total surprise to experience how people change their behaviour towards others when they become part of 'management', or when they have to deal directly with customers.

People will need training to look at their roles, learning to manage their behavioural aspects of a role and understanding how people will expect them to behave so they do not upset people and are able to handle any conflicts inherent in the role itself.

Similarly, the increase in tasks and responsibilities that people are asked to take on may make them very anxious and therefore unable to take on their roles.

When people are unable to make the most of their roles either because of fear, reprobation or risk there will be stagnation on a personal level and on an organizational level.

The understanding of role and the expectations of customers will enable organizations to ensure that customers only meet with people who know how to behave in role. Similarly, the person in role will understand what these expectations are and be prepared for them – for example customers who feel that the role holder should be prepared for aggressive, demanding and infantile behaviour (for example, drunkenness in a pub).

Role management

The role idea is the idea which individuals carry in their minds and which motivates them, and relates them to some inner meaning which helps them to manage their behaviour. The way in which a person manages their role will be influenced by:

- Their own view of their relationships with other people. If a person feels threatened by others the role will be defined more tightly – if the person feels encouraged they may well expand their role.
- Their own assessment of their performance. If a person thinks they are doing well they are likely to expand that role.
- A change in the working environment, or a new colleague either of which can threaten people and thus lead to a redefinition of roles.

203

- Similarly a change in culture may inhibit people or help them to look at the roles in a new way.
- A change in the micro-environment (this includes changes to the primary task or mission of the organization) or macro-environment may frighten people individually and inhibit them from performing their roles.

Role defence – the avoidance of pain

Role may appear to others as an objective reality, but people experience roles as a subjective reality; we do not see roles, we see people doing things. Role involves both a task and a behavioural requirement in the way the task is performed. It also has an imaginative element which depends on the way in which the individual sees, creates and performs their role.

The term role defence is used to describe the way in which the members of an organization protect themselves from anxiety. When individuals face situations that are too difficult, too threatening or too painful to acknowledge, they defend themselves against them. Central among these defences is denial, which involves pushing certain thoughts and feelings and experiences out of conscious awareness because they have become too anxiety-provoking. When attention is brought to them, there is an emotionally charged refusal to accept them – this is called resistance.

Managing and monitoring one's own behaviour and taking feedback is an essential skill for front-line staff. People may well need help in order to be able to do this.

Role relationships

It may be helpful for people to think about their roles as being able to provide them with some protection. For example if we rely on our personal relationships to get things done and then people fall out with each other, work will suffer. However, if people look at each role and the specific tasks that need to be carried out by the holder of that role it is then possible to

Old – Relying on making personal relationships to get things done. If people fall out with each other the work suffers.

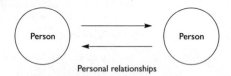

New direction – Using role relations to achieve the task of organization.

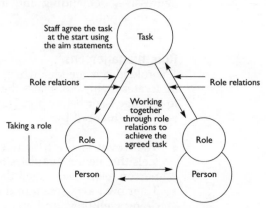

Figure 8.5
Source: Grubb Institute

move into a role relationship and not have only a person-to-person relationship on which to rely on. Although the two can be managed together it of course helps if the people get on as people

Role conflict

Role conflict occurs when two sets of pressures occur simultaneously that make carrying out one aspect of the role more difficult. There may be a great relationship but the service manager may also have to say things that may cause a negative reaction.

Role definition

Role definition covers the degree to which roles are interrelated and the way in which people relate through their roles. The relationship roles need to be defined – in terms of the contractual elements related to the task and also in terms of contact. (See Patching and Chatham (1998) Getting a life at work: developing people beyond role boundaries, *Journal of Management Development*, **17**(5,), www.emeraldlibrary.com)

Role interdependence

Role interdependence is a measure of the information one person must receive from another in order to perform their role, and so that they can perform their roles.

Role ambiguity

This arises when there is a discrepancy between the information available to the person and that which is required to perform the role adequately. It is particularly prevalent in situations where disclosure is necessary to the professional performance of the role.

Role suction

Very often when an organization places people on customers' premises or they get involved with the relationship aspects of managing a customer, supplier, distributor or any other stakeholder, they may be sucked out of their role of representing the interests of the organization who is paying their salary and feel they belong more to the organization they are serving. Obviously, this balance must be carefully considered and employees given the opportunity to discuss what is happening.

Parallel process

Picking up on how the organization feels about issues – if the people working within an organization feel badly about it, customers will tend to feel the same way. If customers feel badly about an organization, the employees will feel the same way as well.

Picking up how customers feel about themselves – people working for an organization tend to pick up the same feelings and dilemmas as their customers. For example, a management school very often practises the worst kind of management. Organizations need to be able to talk about the effect their client group is having on people. If the client group is particularly demanding, for example, in an unemployment office or a customer complaints department, the organization must provide for space and time for these issues to be addressed and allow people to talk about their feelings.

Understanding the dilemmas of other people and organizations

Close business relationships provide opportunities for a greater understanding about how other people feel about the organization for which they are working. It is clear that while remaining empathetic a relationship marketer must be able to manage the boundaries between their own organization and that of the customer/supplier/distributor/stakeholder's organizations.

Summary

This unit has introduced the concept of relationship marketing and its increasing importance in the context of developing sustainable competitive advantage. We have considered where it can be applied in both consumer and industrial markets, and discussed some of the difficulties that can be encountered. The next two units deal with market research.

References

Relationship Marketing in Consumer Markets, R. Christy, G. Oliver and J. Penn, *Journal of Marketing Management 1996*, **12**, 175–187.

Relationship Marketing in Organizational Markets: When is it appropriate? K. Bliss, *Journal of Marketing Management 1996*, **12**, 161–173.

The basic principles of investigative (market) research

This unit introduces you to the basic principles of market research. You will:

❏ Learn about the market research process.

❏ Be introduced to the common experimental design formats.

❏ Find out about the selection of target populations.

❏ Consider the wider framework of investigating customer dynamics.

❏ Appreciate the possible pitfalls with investigative market research.

❏ Learn about cognitive dissonance.

❏ Look at the main means of interpreting and presenting results.

By the end of the unit you will be able to:

❏ Understand the logic of research design and have a basic knowledge of customer dynamics.

❏ Know how to construct testable hypotheses, select suitable populations and pilot test new research designs.

❏ Initially interpret results.

❏ Be aware and take account of the possible problems with investigate research.

Experimental design

Understanding the market research process

The first step in any study is the development of research objectives. These usually arise from the research brief – a description of what information is required – but may be originated by the market researcher. The usual research flow is illustrated in Figure 9.1.

Research briefs often pose questions which are too vague or broad to make good research objectives. For example, 'why are fewer people using high street insurance agents?' It is necessary for the researcher to turn this general question into one or more testable hypotheses (see later in this unit). These may well be initially informed by the intuition, experience or knowledge of the marketer.

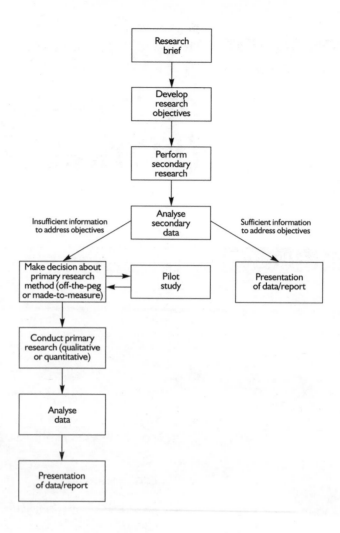

Figure 9.1
Primary and secondary research
process

Prior experience of a similar problem in another retail sector might lead the researcher to first investigate any changes in local shopping habits – for example, are other high street retailers being affected in the same way? Or, it may be that the researcher focuses on issues of market share – is business being won by the new crop of telephone insurers?

Presumably, though not always, the research brief also wants some answers or pointers as to how to proceed. A good research study will always be proactive in identifying next steps.

The research objectives must be clearly stated. There is rarely enough effort put into the early stages of planning a research study which should clearly define at least the following:

- Type of data required.
- What will be done with the data once it is collected.
- Who is the audience for the final report.
- The target population.
- The detailed design of the research process itself.

Once the research objectives are identified, secondary research is undertaken – that is a review of existing data. If this proves sufficient to address the research objectives then it is possible to move straight to analysis and presentation of a report.

If, on the other hand, existing data is not available to address the research objectives then new, or primary research must be planned and executed to collect more data. This can then be collated, analysed and reported.

The various types of primary and secondary research are described in the next section.

Pilot testing

Before embarking on primary research or new testing methodology it is important to undergo thorough pre-testing or piloting. This is best achieved by undertaking a peer review followed by limited testing, on the intended target population (usually referred to as a pilot test).

A peer review is a review by other market researchers, or colleagues, to ascertain their views on the suitability of the research tools and methods being used. It may be that they are able to identify confusing questions and/or bring to bear their experience from similar research that they have undertaken.

A pilot test on the target population is more costly – in time and resources – but is the best way to identify flaws in procedures and tools. A pilot test can be used to check the following:

- Data – Is the data you collect of the correct type and format (this avoids later analysis problems)?
- Analysis – Does your analysis method yield the summary data that you require to address your research objectives?
- Tools – Is the research tool (i.e. questionnaire) easy to comprehend and use?
- Resources – Has the research project been allotted sufficient resources (the pilot provides a good indication of the resources that the full project will require)?
- Time – Has the research project been allotted sufficient time (again, the pilot will give you a feel for how much time the full study will require)?
- Staffing – Are research staff sufficiently trained and experienced enough to run the full project?

It is important that your pilot gives you the confidence that the full study will yield reliable and sufficient data to address the research objectives. If not, then *run another pilot!*

You may wish to share the results of your pilot with the author of the research brief to check your (and their) understanding of the research objectives.

Basic building blocks

At its most basic level experimental design focuses on understanding the relationship between two or more factors. Usually one is manipulated whilst measuring changes in the other(s). For instance, we may pilot test three different promotional pricing structures and measure the effect on sales. In other words, experiments are used to determine if a causal relationship exists (in this case between pricing and sales). Experimental design is a well-established scientific method (see Figure 9.1) with it's own established rules and terminology. Many of these are 'borrowed' for use in a variety of market research applications. The main terms used are described below:

- Hypothesis – This is the 'big question' that your study is aimed at answering. For instance, you might have an intuition that changing the packaging of electric toasters will lead to higher sales? A hypothesis would then be constructed to test this prediction.
- Variables – These are the factors under investigations. For instance, sales and packaging design.
- Independent variable – This is the name for the variable(s) we are manipulating. In the toaster example given, this would be the packaging design but we might also change price, colour, product features and measure the effect on sales. These would also be independent variables.
- Dependent variable – This is the name for the variable(s) we are measuring. In the toaster example given, this would be the sales but we might also want to measure customer feelings towards the new packaging and other aspects of their purchasing behaviour as a result of changing the packaging design. These would also be dependent variables.

- Intervening (or extraneous) variables – These are those unwanted factors that 'interfere' with your research. For instance, you may be trying to assess people's attitude to changes in product price over a period where there are considerable fluctuations in the national economy. In this example, the economy is an intervening variable. Intervening variables contribute to experimental 'noise', that is, unavoidable variations in the study which affect the accuracy with which the effect of the independent variable can be assessed.
- Experimenter – This is the term used to distinguish the researcher from those they are studying (i.e. this would probably be you!).
- Subjects – These are the people being studied (e.g. shoppers, product users and potential purchasers).
- Control groups – These are groups of subjects which are monitored for the purpose of providing a comparison only. For instance, if we are trying to assess the impact of a new mail order catalogue we might monitor two groups of subjects. One group would be sent the new catalogue whilst the other group would continue to receive the old catalogue. The group that receives the new catalogue is called the experimental group. The group that continues to receive the old catalogue is called the control group.
- Field studies – These are studies carried out in the 'real world'. They are the opposite of laboratory studies.
- Laboratory studies – These are studies carried out under controlled conditions such as in a laboratory or other 'mock-ups'.

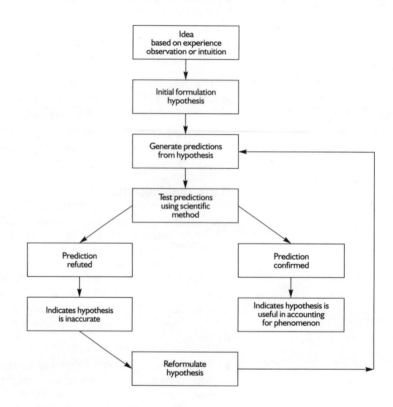

Figure 9.2
The traditional scientific method.
Source: Rice, C. (1993) *Consumer Behaviour*, Butterworth-Heinemann

---

Question 9.1

British Telecom ask you to investigate customer satisfaction towards a new 'cheap rate' service for frequently called numbers which has been given on a trial basis to some of their customers.

In this example, who, or what, are likely to be the:

- Independent variable.
- Dependent variable.
- Experimenter.
- Control group.

Would the study be classified as a field or laboratory study?

Construction of testable hypotheses

There are three main steps in the design of an experiment:

1 *Decide on your hypothesis*
   This must be expressed in a form which can be tested. For instance, 'some pricing structures are better than others' is *not* a good hypothesis. The use of the terms 'some' and 'better' are vague. An improved version would read something like 'A 10 per cent price discount leads to higher customer satisfaction than a 5 per cent price discount'.

2 *Select your dependent and independent variables*
   The variables must be clearly defined and measurable. The more accurately they can be measured the better. The actual variables used will depend upon the hypothesis. In the pricing example, we would probably choose discount level as our independent variable and customer satisfaction as our dependent variable. However, it is not a sufficient definition of the testing design in itself. The exact pricing structure to be used must be clearly specified as should the method that will be used to measure customer satisfaction.

   Care should be taken that nothing other than the discount level is changed. The service delivered must be identical in all other respects. To introduce any other differences would be to risk introducing intervening variables. For example, if one of the discounts was promoted in a slightly more aggressive manner we would not know whether it was promotional change that had affected customer satisfaction rather than the change in discount.

   We may decide to measure customer satisfaction at one particular outlet or across a number of different outlets. We would need to be clear:

   - What was going to be measured. (Whether we are trying to get a more holistic understanding of the effect of pricing structure on customer satisfaction with the service quality or are we just interested in satisfaction with the price. If the former, what aspects of service quality are we interested in?)
   - How this measurement was going to take place (point of purchase, telephone interview, postal survey and so on).
   - The time period over which this measurement was to take place.

3 *Decide on the format that your experiment will take*
   There are a number of alternative experimental designs. The design you choose will depend both on your hypothesis and practical constraints (such as time, cost and other resources).

Analytical constraints on hypothesis development

Whilst the traditional experimental method of hypothesis development and testing is ideally suited for the measurement of associations, for example the link between price and packaging design, it is less suited for the exploration of the less tangible and/or open-ended types of investigation.

The difference is essentially that between qualitative and quantitative research as described in the next section.

Common experimental design formats

Five experimental design formats are described by Chris Rice in *Consumer Behaviour*. These cover most of the designs that you are likely to need. In each case the X represents the event – which is usually the purchase decision or other significant interaction with the customer. The T represents the investigation; the point at which the dependent variable is measured.

211

Case study or survey

An event occurs, such as the purchase of an item, which we later examine by means of a case study or survey. This can be represented diagrammatically as follows (X = the event, T = the study):

$$X \rightarrow T$$

An example would be the purchase of a mountain bike. This popular style of bicycle became unexpectedly popular in the early 1990s. To try to find out the reason for this we may decide to survey those persons that purchased mountain bikes during this period. It may be that the result of such a survey would help us to develop a new bicycle and/or predict futures sales of existing styles of bicycle.

One group pre-test/post-test design

Sometime referred to as a test–retest design, a group of individuals are surveyed, an event occurs such as a change in our method of service delivery, and then we re-test the same group. This can be represented diagrammatically as follows (X = the event, $T1$ and $T2$ = are tests):

$$T1 \rightarrow X \rightarrow T2$$

Suppose we wished to determine customer opinions on how well our new telephone support line is performing. It would be sensible to test opinions of our support service both before and after the introduction of the support line so that a comparison could be drawn.

Time series design or survey

In a time series survey, individuals are repeatedly surveyed before and after an event. This can be represented diagrammatically (for 8 surveys) as follows (X = the event, $T1$ to $T8$ = tests):

$$T1 \rightarrow T2 \rightarrow T3 \rightarrow T4 \rightarrow X \rightarrow T5 \rightarrow T6 \rightarrow T7 \rightarrow T8$$

A common use of time series surveys is in opinion polls. The event may be, for instance, the resignation of an MP due to impropriety or a change of party leader. The aim of a time series survey to understand how responses change over time. The individuals tested may be the same on each occasion, as with consumer panel testing, or different as in the random sampling most commonly used in political polls.

Non-equivalent control group design

This is similar to the one group pre-test/post-test design already described except that two groups are involved. One group, called the experimental group, is exposed to the event, the other group, the control group is not. This can be represented diagrammatically as follows (X = the event, $T1$ and $T2$ = tests):

Experimental group: $T1 \rightarrow X \rightarrow T2$

Control group: $T1 \longrightarrow T2$

By using a control group it is possible to eliminate the effect of many intervening variables. Suppose in our telephone support line example we split our regular customers into two groups. Rather than both groups being given access to the support line we would provide this facility to only one group (the experimental group) whilst the other group (the control group) would continue with the previous support package.

When opinions were re-tested we could therefore be more certain that any difference in opinions was really due to the changes in the support package rather than any other spurious effects such as changes in support needs, differences in the perceptions of the company due to new product developments and so on.

When this control group design is applied to a product, for example a new type of medicine, it is often referred to as a 'blind' or 'double blind' trial. To try and avoid experimental effects (to reduce the number of intervening variables) it is usual to give the experimental group a real medicine and the control group a placebo medicine (a fake made up to look like the real thing). Of course the control group believes that they have been administered the real thing – thus they are 'blind' to the reality. If the experimenter and/or evaluators – in this case the persons administering the medicine and assessing their effects – are also unaware of which group has received the real medicine then the experimental design is said to be 'double blind'.

Problems with this method relate to the matching of the groups. We must be sure that the experimental and control groups are similar in all respects otherwise it may be possible to attribute any changes in the dependent variable as an artefact of the group characteristics rather than the manipulation of the independent variable.

Classic experimental design
This design is similar to the non-equivalent control group design but overcomes the problem of matching groups by randomly assigning subjects to the experimental and control groups at the outset. The experimental format is identical in all other respects to the non-equivalent design.

$$\text{Experimental group (random):} \quad T1 \rightarrow X \rightarrow T2$$

$$\text{Control group (random):} \quad T1 \longrightarrow T2$$

To comply with this design, the respondents in the telephone support line example would have to have been randomly assigned to the experimental and control groups.

Question 9.2

You have been asked to test the effectiveness of a regional TV advertising campaign for private healthcare insurers who have experienced a drop-off in customers. What experimental design(s) could you use. Who would constitute the experimental and control groups?

Question 9.3

You have been asked to make a prediction as to whether New Labour will win the next general election. What experimental design(s) could you use?

Selecting your target population

Determining your sample
In determining your sample you need to decide whom you will survey and how many people you will survey. Researchers often call this group the target population. In some case, when doing an employee attitude survey for instance, the population is obvious. In other cases, such as when prospective customers are involved, determining the target group is more difficult. Correctly determining the target population is critical. A poorly defined target population will result in unrepresentative results.

Suppose we are commissioned to find out opinions of the recent architectural changes to the entrance of the Ashmolean Museum in Oxford. How would we go about determining our target population? If we were looking for a relative appraisal of the changes then we would need to find people who had seen the Museum entrance before and after the changes. If we were only asked to find out visitors general opinions of the new entrance then it would not matter whether, or not, they had seen the original architecture. Clearly, in this example, our survey goal determines the target population.

To decide how many persons need surveying is both a statistical and commercial decision. Surveying more people costs more money but does increase the accuracy, or precision, of the results (up to a point). To increase a sample from 250 to 1000 requires four times as many people, but it only doubles the precision. The statistic issues are dealt with in detail in Unit 7.

Sampling methods

There are two basic types of sampling:

1 Probability (or random) samples – where individuals are drawn in some random fashion from amongst the population.
2 Non-probability (or non-random) samples – where individuals are selected on the basis of one or more criteria determined by the researcher.

Probability samples

Within this category there are four sampling methods which are commonly employed in market research:

1 Simple random sampling – individuals are randomly drawn from the population at large (for example, by selecting from the electoral register).
2 Systematic sampling – individuals (or households) are sampled at intervals based on a random start point. For instance, it might be decided to visit every tenth person on the electoral register starting at number 4. In this case the sampling interval is 10. The individuals that would be sampled are thus numbers 4, 14, 24 and so on.
3 Stratified random sampling – the population is first divided into groups based on one or more criteria (e.g. age, gender, or other affiliation) and, from within these groups, individuals are randomly selected. For this method to be possible the data available on each individual must contain information about the criteria being used to stratify the groups. This is not always the case.
4 Multistage sampling – the population is first divided into quite large groups, usually based on geography. A random selection of these large groups is then selected and sub-divided again. A random selection of groups is again made from the resulting sub-divisions and the process repeated as many time as required depending on the survey requirements. Eventually, individuals are randomly sampled from the small groups arising as a result of the final sub-division.

To select individuals on a random basis it is necessary to construct a sampling frame. This is a list of all the known individuals within the population from which the selection is to take place. Each individual is assigned a unique number then, using random number tables or the computer equivalent, individuals are selected on the basis of the random numbers produced.

Obviously, to list all the individuals within the UK would take forever. Luckily, such a list is already produced by the Government. It is called the electoral roll (or register). Its primary purpose is to record those persons eligible to vote. Unfortunately, the electoral role has several drawbacks:

- Those under eighteen years old are not listed (as they are not eligible to vote).
- Many persons choose not to register to vote and are thus not listed.
- Mobile individuals – such as students – are frequently not registered where they live.
- Newlyweds are not listed correctly – a women's maiden name may appear and, if they have recently started living together, only one name may appear on the register.
- The register may be up to a year out-of-date.

In an attempt to overcome some of these problems, the postal address file (or PAF) is often used. This is the most comprehensive list of addresses in the UK. Addresses are then randomly selected from the list and the interviewer tries to interview one person from each household. Recently, more and more people are failing to register to vote which has led to increased use of the PAF. Unfortunately, the PAF too has several problems:

- There is no way of knowing who lives at the address.
- There is no way of knowing how many people live at the address.

It is thus left to the interviewer to select a person to interview based on an extensive set of rules provided by the research organization. This can result in error.

Non-probability samples

When a sampling frame cannot be established, or would prove too expensive or time consuming, one of the following four non-random methods are usually used.

1 Judgement sampling – the researcher uses their judgement to select persons that they feel are representative of the population or have a particular expertise or knowledge which makes them suitable. For example, business leaders, top scientists and so on. This method is commonly used with small sample sizes.
2 Convenience sampling – the most convenient population is chosen which may be the researcher's friends, work colleagues or students from a nearby college. This method is often used to save time and resources.
3 Cluster sampling – the population is repeatedly divided into groups rather like the process for multistage sampling. However, cluster sampling is different in that all individuals from the remaining small groups are interviewed rather than just a random sample of those remaining.
4 Quota sampling – the researcher selects a predetermined number of individuals from different groups (i.e. based on age, gender and so on). This is perhaps the most popular non-probability sampling method used.

Setting quotas

Rather than randomly selecting individuals, you may wish to enforce balance in your population by setting quotas for certain sub-groups. For instance, if you are surveying for a product that you know will be mostly used by under-thirty-fives you can set a quota for this age group in your survey sample. You may decide as a result that 90 per cent of your sample should be in this age group.

Table 9.1 Comparison of different sampling methods

Simple random	Systematic random	Stratified	Multistage	Convenience	Judgement	Cluster	Quota
Requires sampling frame	Requires sampling frame	Requires sampling frame	Requires sampling frame	Does not require sampling frame	Does not require sampling frame	Does not require sampling frame	Does not require sampling frame
High cost	Moderate cost	Moderate cost	Moderate cost	Low cost	Low cost	Moderate cost	Moderate cost
May not be representative	May not be representative	Representative	May not be representative	May not be representative	May not be representative	May not be representative	Representative
Low likelihood of bias	Low likelihood of bias	Low likelihood of bias	Low likelihood of bias	High likelihood of bias	High likelihood of bias	Moderate likelihood of bias	Moderate likelihood of bias

To give another example, if you are interviewing users about a particular product brand, you may wish (depending on your project goals) to select your sample based on their current brand preferences to approximate current market share. Alternatively, you may decide to interview only those individuals that currently use a competitive brand or those that use no brand at all.

Quotas are usually specified to a research organization in the form of a grid. For example, if we have a requirement to interview fifty shoppers we might specify that:

- 25 of them under forty-five years old.
- 25 aged forty-five or older.
- 15 in the AB social classes.
- 35 in the CDE social classes.

Alternatively, we might specify how many of a particular age should come from each social class grouping:

	AB	CDE
Under 45	13	12
45 or over	2	23

The structure of the sample is therefore fixed by the researcher.

Deciding the sample size for your survey

There are many factors which affect the size of a sample apart from the statistical considerations:

- The survey method used. Large sample sizes are easier to achieve with some methods (i.e. postal surveys and telephone surveys) than with others (i.e. face-to-face interviews and observation).
- Time and resources may be limited. This will involve a trade-off between sample size and the amount and accuracy of the information to be collected.
- Precision required. There is no point using large sample sizes when only a rough estimate of a population mean is required. Decide on the precision you require and use the formula provided for determining the sample size required.
- Number of groups sampled. If you plan to sample a number of groups you may be able to merge the group data to provide a better overall estimate of the population mean.

Investigating customer dynamics

A broader experimental framework

It is important to know not only how to construct an experiment but what to measure and where (and when) comparisons should be made. This section sets experimental design in the broader framework of the investigation of customer dynamics. But first, a brief explanation of why such explorations are important.

In a survey of the UKs 100 leading businesses the most important indicators of future success were reported as 'building long-term relationships with key customers' and 'creating a more customer-centred culture'. Over 90 per cent of respondees reported quality and customer satisfaction to be 'very important' yet these two key aspects of service and product perception are often poorly understood.

The main role of investigative market research into customer dynamics is to understand customer needs so that a product or service can be developed to satisfy these needs and understanding their perceptions of the product or service once delivered as part of a quality management process. The basic cycle of needs analysis and improvement is shown in Figure 9.3.

Quality is concerned with supplying superior benefits in the opinion of the customer. Thus, the pursuit of quality is the pursuit of greater customer benefit (Hooley, 1993).

The principles are the same whether the organization involved is a producer of televisions, a supplier of financial services or a healthcare provider. The key to success is understanding the complex dynamics between customer and organization, the interactions that inform or reinforce customer perceptions.

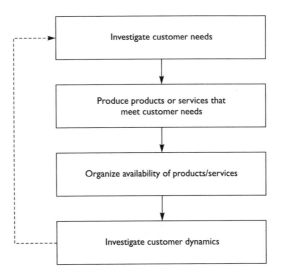

Figure 9.3
The basic quality improvement cycle

Such an approach is variously defined as being customer-focused, market-led or a part of a total quality management process. A useful distinction can be drawn between market-driven and market-led research. The former responds to current customer demand, the latter is led by customer needs. The difference in definitions are subtle but have huge implications for the philosophy of organizations and hence the data they seek to gather and their methods of investigation.

Another significant shift is that towards the measurement of service quality. This has come about partly due to the change in philosophy highlighted above and partly because of the increasing significance of the service sector to global and domestic economies. We are moving rapidly towards an economy where service providers predominate with the consequence that the measurement and management of service quality becomes more pressing. For example, service industries now account for more than two-thirds of gross national product in the USA. Service sector jobs account for three-quarters of total employment.

Service quality can be defined as 'the ability of the organization to meet or exceed customer expectations' (Christopher, Payne and Ballantyne 1991)

Many of the techniques formerly used to assess product performance and perceptions are simply not up to the job of exploring the less tangible dimensions of service quality. For the purposes of investigating customer dynamics, services are different from products in a number of important ways:

1 Production and consumption takes place simultaneously – the service is delivered at the point of use. A healthcare service, for example, is largely delivered by a direct contact between medical staff and customer.

2 Services are largely intangible – they cannot be tasted, touched, seen or heard. Perceptions of an insurance or banking service are based largely on intangible qualities – feelings of security, reliability, confidence and so on.

3 A service is highly dependent on the person (usually) that delivers it. Unlike a product, consistency and uniformity cannot be centrally controlled or guaranteed. For example, a car hire company will have less control over the quality of their customer service than their rental vehicles!

Although service quality is in many ways more difficult to measure than product quality, the tools and techniques suitable for such investigative research are well developed from their application to the field of social science. Both the modern marketer and scientist want to understand and explore the ways in which perception works at an individual and group level.

Principles of service quality measurement – gap analysis

Conceptual model

As we have learned, providing a quality product or service is all about meeting or exceeding customer expectations. Where expectations are met then the customer is satisfied. If expectations are not met then the customer experiences dissatisfaction.

Consider a small, high specification, portable television and a budget wide-screen model. Other things being equal, which is most likely to satisfy a customer? The marketing answer is either one of them depending on the initial customer expectations. If the requirements were for an easily moved unit which could fit in a guest room then the portable TV would probably best meet expectations. If, on the other hand, the need were for family viewing the wide-screen design would probably be perceived as the best choice.

This logic is even more applicable to service provision where there are fewer tangibles. Take, for example, the experience of flying first class. The customer has certain expectations of the level of service that they will receive based, perhaps, on advertising, past experiences or hearsay. Perhaps they expect a separate check-in, a comfortable waiting lounge, personal luggage-handling facilities and so on. When they actually fly they will, consciously or unconsciously, evaluate the performance of the airline company against their expectations. If their expectations and evaluations do not match then there will be a 'gap' leading to satisfaction or dissatisfaction depending on the direction and extent of the gap. Dissatisfaction, so the theory goes, will lead to a perception of poor quality and vice versa. This potential difference between expectations and evaluations is what gap analysis seeks to measure. A basic model of the customer satisfaction gap is shown in Figure 9.4 (Hooley, 1993).

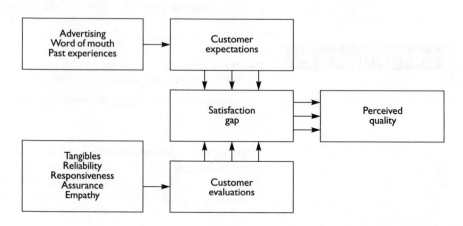

Figure 9.4
From Hooley paper, 1993, p. 321.
(*Journal of Marketing Management*, 1993, pp. 315–35)

The customer satisfaction gap is not the only service quality gap that is said to exist (although it is the key gap directly relevant to consumers). Parasuraman, Zeithaml and Berry (1985) identified five potential gaps in their conceptual model of service quality and more recently Hooley (1993) has suggested that possibly six more could exist. The conceptual model of Parasuraman is presented in Figure 9.5. Gap 5 is the previously mentioned customer satisfaction gap. The other gaps relate more to the work of the organization and marketer.

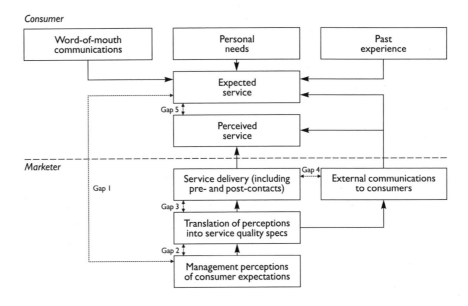

Figure 9.5
Conceptual model of service quality. *Source*: Parasuraman, A., Zeithaml, V.A. and Berry, L.L. (1985). A conceptual model of service quality and its implications for future research. *Journal of Marketing*, **49**, Fall.

Parasuraman (1998) suggests that the customer satisfaction gap, Gap 5 or the service quality deficiency perceived by the consumer, may be a function of the four key internal (i.e. organizational) shortfalls. The four gaps on the seller's side can be defined as follows:

- Gap 1 Market information gap: due to incomplete or inaccurate knowledge of customers' service expectations.
- Gap 2 Service standards gap: arising from failure to translate accurately customers' service expectations into specifications or guidelines for company personnel.
- Gap 3 Service performance gap: occurs when there is a lack of appropriate internal support systems (e.g. recruitment, training, technology, compensation) that enable company personnel to deliver to service standards.
- Gap 4 Internal communication gap: inconsistencies between what customers are told the service will be like and the actual service performance (e.g. due to lack of internal communication between the service 'promisers' (such as salespeople) and service providers (such as after-sales service representatives).

Methods for the measurement of quality service, discussed in the next section, will focus on Gap 5. However, Gap 5 in Figure 9.4 is influenced by the four preceding gaps.

Service quality benchmarking

As well as identifying service quality gaps within your own organization and customer interactions, it is important to understand how you compete with others. You need to know whether, or not, your performance is better or worse than that of your main competitors.

Called service quality benchmarking, performance measurement can be undertaken using a number of methods. Christopher, Payne and Ballantyne favour a five-stage approach whereby the competitive arena is first defined and then the key determinants of customer service identified. Next it is recommended to establish relative weightings for these service

Benchmarks can be created for practically any part of your operation. For example, this list of potential benchmarking categories can help measure your operations against your competitor's.

Advertising
Expenditure
Themes

Sales
Terms
Sales force
• size
• structure
• training/experience
• compensation
• number of calls
• turnover rates

Sales literature
Proposals
• style
• structure
• pricing

Accountability
Cross selling

R&D
Patents
Staff
R&D $/sales
Government contracts

Customers/products
Sales/customer
Breadth of product line
Product quality
Average customer size

Distribution
Channels used
Middlemen

Marketing
Product/brand strategy
Market share
Pricing

Financials/costs
Profitability
Overhead
Return on assets
Return on equity
Net worth
Margins
Cash flow
Debt
Borrowing capacity

Plant/facility
• size
• capacity
• utilization
• equipment costs

Capital investments
Integration level
Quality control
Fixed and variable costs

Organization
Structure
Values
General goals
Expected growth
Decision-making level
Controls

Strategic plans
Short term
Long term
Core business/expansion or stability
Acquisitions

Figure 9.6
Competitive benchmarking checklist. *Source*: Strategic Intelligence Checklist. Cambridge, MA: Fuld & Co. Inc.

elements before actually measuring organizational performance and that of your competitors.

Finally, the benchmarking results can be mapped in a number of ways to identify relative performance, compared with the competition, as well as performance on those aspects of service quality which are perceived as important by the customer. Figure 9.7 shows a profile mapping for a typical set of customer expectations shown in the central column. The line on the left shows the relative importance of these elements; the lines on the right show the performance by the organization and a selected competitor.

Weaknesses can be clearly identified as those where importance to the customer is high and organizational performance is low. In this example, 'order cycle time', 'delivery reliability' and 'frequency of delivery' would seem to need attention. The method can also be used to expose areas where unnecessary effort is being expended where the element is of low importance to customers.

For a detailed description of service quality benchmarking the reader is referred to *Relationship Marketing*, Christopher, Payne and Ballantyne (1991), Butterworth-Heinemann.

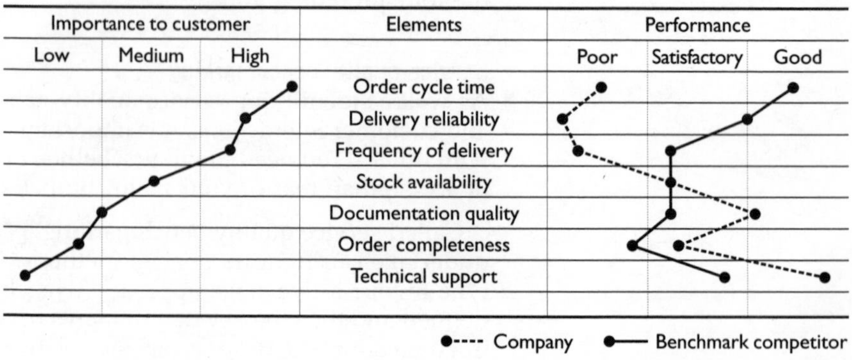

Figure 9.7
Customer service profile

220

Bias in your target populations

If you select a sample population which is not representative then your results may be biased. That is, they will not represent responses in the wider population. For example, if you asked Ford employees whether they preferred Ford cars you would probably get biased results. Totally excluding all bias is extremely difficult but should be the goal in any survey. However, just being aware of bias will allow you to avoid the more obvious sources and interpret certain results more cautiously. There are three main sources of bias:

1 Incomplete coverage – there may be a number of reasons for this:
   (a) Sampling frame is incomplete;
   (b) Certain outlying areas are excluded (it is common in UK surveys to exclude counties north of the Caledonian canal in Scotland);
   (c) The survey method used may place constraints on those that can be sampled, i.e. a telephone survey requires ownership of a telephone!
2 Non-response – low response rates are a problem in any survey. Whether it is a street, telephone or postal survey a significant proportion of those approached will refuse to answer questions.
3 Over-representation – some sampling methods deliberately over-represent certain groups (the non-probability sampling techniques already mentioned). Although this allows detailed examination of a certain sub-group of the population, there is no way of knowing how else the group characteristics might affect the survey responses.

Table 9.2 below shows the ways in which over-representation can introduce bias.

Table 9.2

Sample	Possible source of bias
Existing customers	Customer loyalty may mean that more favourable responses are given
Ex-customers	Possibly no longer customer because of dislike of product/service – may give less favourable results
People in city centre shopping street	Depending on shopping area, may only capture data from certain social classes. May be that only certain members of the family shop
People in out-of-town shopping centre	Unlikely to be used by those without a car or those that have good local shops

Question 9.4

You are asked to gather opinions on a new design of carry-cot for babies. What problems might you experience using your classmates as a convenience sample.

The reliability and validity of customer responses

Questionnaire design

The primary data collection tool is the questionnaire. Whether you are conducting an interview by post, telephone, face-to-face, or even via computer, you will be need to design a questionnaire.

There are two important concepts in the design of measurement methods – reliability and validity.

Validity

If a data measurement tool actually measures what it purports to, then it is said to be valid. For example, time over a 100 metre sprint is not likely to be a valid measure of intelligence. On the other hand, a well-designed intelligence quotient (IQ) test *is* likely to accurately measure intelligence. The IQ test is therefore said to be a valid measure of intelligence.

Poorly designed questionnaires are often not valid measures – they purport to measure things that they do not. For example, the question, how many times a week do you watch television may seem – on the face of it – a valid way of measuring television viewing time. This is not the case. All the question actually does is measure the *number of times* the television is viewed and not the *length of time* it is viewed for. This question would therefore not be a valid measure of television viewing time.

Similarly, surveys on sample populations are said to be invalid if their findings are not to be generalized to the whole population.

Reliability

If a measurement tool consistently measures the same thing then it is said to be reliable. For example, the IQ of a person changes only slowly. Therefore, if we measured it two weeks in a row we would expect it to be approximately the same. A good IQ test would indeed give a similar score week after week. Such a test is said to be reliable. A poorly designed IQ test might give widely differing scores each time it was administered. Such a test is termed unreliable, as it cannot be relied upon to give an accurate answer.

Good questionnaires are both reliable and valid; they measure what they purport to and they do so reliably. Repeat testing of questionnaires, and comparison with other data sources, are methods used to check both validity and reliability.

Cognitive dissonance in the acceptability of research findings

> 'Cognitive dissonance is a motivating state of affairs. Just as hunger impels us to eat, so does dissonance impel a person to change his opinions or his behaviour. . .' (Festinger, 1962).

According to Festinger, any two pieces of information (say A and B) contained in a person's mind can be related in one of three ways:

1 They can be consonant, or consistent. In this case A implies B.
2 They can be dissonant, or inconsistent. In this case A implies the opposite of B.
3 They can be unrelated or irrelevant to each other. A not related to B.

For example, the two pieces of information 'I like cream cakes' and 'cream cakes make me spotty' are dissonant. Presumably, one does not want to have spots yet one wants to eat cream cakes. On the other hand, 'I like Guinness' and 'Guinness is good for you' are consonant pieces of information.

Cognitive dissonance theory states that people seek to reduce the amount of dissonance they experience, which can be considered as a sort of 'mental discomfort'.

The emphasis in marketing is on post-purchase dissonance. That is, when information about an accepted or rejected item is received following a purchasing decision. At this point, positive information about the rejected item will generate dissonance, as will negative information about the accepted item.

Suppose, you have to choose between two alternative summer holiday destinations, the South of France or Portugal. After a lot of thumbing through holiday brochures, you finally settle on the South of France. Just after booking the vacation you meet someone who has just returned from the South of France. A negative report from them is likely to generate dissonance as will a positive report from recent visitors to Portugal.

The magnitude of this dissonance will be proportional to:

- The significance of the decision – if you had spent a lot of money on the holiday or perhaps if it was your only holiday for a number of years, the dissonance would undoubtedly be greater.
- The attractiveness of the rejected alternative – if your decision had been a narrow one then positive information from one of the rejected options is likely to create greater dissonance.
- The number of negative characters of the choice made – if the selected destination was seen to have several things 'going for it' then a disappointing report about the weather, for instance, is less likely to create dissonance.
- The number of options considered – the more rejected choices the greater the dissonance. Trying to choose a holiday destination from ten alternatives makes it more likely that one of the rejected options would have turned out better.
- Commitment to decision – if the decision can easily be reversed and/or no public expression of the decision has been made then less dissonance is likely to result.
- Volition or choice – if the choice is 'forced' rather than voluntary then dissonance is minimized.

As with the other consistency theories considered, a person experiencing dissonance will act to reduce the discomfort. There are a number of ways this can be done. They can:

- Change their decision – this may not always be possible or practical.
- Actively seek positive information about the chosen alternative. This is called selective exposure.
- Concentrate on information presenting the positive features of the chosen alternative and ignore information presenting negative features. This is called selective attention.
- Change their attitudes.
- Actively avoid exposure to information that is likely to cause dissonance. This is called selective avoidance.
- Dismiss or devalue ambiguous information about the chosen option. This is called selective interpretation.

For example, the dissonance resulting from the information that 'I like cream cakes' and 'cream cakes make me fat' can be reduced by one or more of the following. We might:

- Stop eating cakes (change decision).
- Decide that cake eating does not cause spots (change attitudes).
- Convince ourselves that enjoying a cream cake is worth the risk of a few spots (selective attention).
- Question the link between cake eating and getting spots (selective interpretation).
- Eat a cake but then avoid information in magazines and papers which suggests cakes are bad (selective avoidance).
- Eat a cake but then seek information in magazines and papers which suggests cakes are good (selective exposure).

Marketers can use dissonance theory in several ways:

- Post-purchase reinforcement – continue to supply the purchaser with positive information about the product even after purchase thus reducing post-purchase dissonance. This will retain brand and corporate loyalty. This is common amongst car manufacturers who continue to send owners glossy brochures and owner newsletters after the purchase is made. BMW are known to place car adverts aimed solely at existing owners of their cars.
- Try and buy schemes – offering limited trials, reinforced by coupons and gifts will create a commitment and positive attitude towards the product which is then more likely to be purchased (to avoid dissonance when the product is returned). Book clubs are one example of sales organizations that operate in this way.
- Anticipating and addressing dissonance in the adverting message and product branding – a recent advert for cream cakes actually empha-

sized that they were a treat which, perhaps, wasn't the healthiest. The message given was 'Go on – you are worth it'. In the area of product branding, one cigarette manufacturer is actually trying to give a similar message with 'Death' cigarettes. This approach acknowledges the health problems with smoking but promotes a devil-may-care image.

However, dissonance also poses problems for those trying to assess customer satisfaction post-purchase – as occurs during the measurement of service quality. Dissonance theory would suggest that post-purchase dissonance might affect the size of the customer satisfaction gap because of the positive attitude which arises from the desire to reduce dissonance.

Take, for example, a person considering a change in their bank deposit account who might rank their identified needs as the following:

1 Polite counter service.
2 Convenient location of bank.
3 High interest rate.

However, having made the decision to shift bank accounts they may find that their expectations were not met in the case of their highest ranked need – for politeness. However, they may find that they have more money than they bargained for due to a higher-than-expected interest rate (their lowest ranked need). Having gone through the effort of changing accounts they might seek to reduce the dissonance associated with the poor performance on 'politeness'.

As with the cream cake example, their later evaluations could be affected in a number of ways. They might:

- Change their attitudes – decide that polite service is not as important as previously thought.
- Selective attention – convince themselves that the service is polite by attending only to examples of good service.
- Selective interpretation – question the link between good service and high quality banking (this notion might be reinforced by the high interest rates).
- Selective avoidance – avoid using the bank's counter service so that possible negative examples of the counter service are not experienced.
- Selective exposure – go only to those branches of the bank you know to be the most polite.

Results of post-purchase customer satisfaction surveys must therefore be interpreted with caution. The use of a control group in this instance would be highly beneficial in distinguishing between 'real' and 'dissonance-induced' changes in evaluations.

Question 9.5

How would you construct an experiment, using a control group, to ensure that any bias in findings due to dissonance were clearly identifiable.

Answer 9.5

To determine the extent of any cognitive dissonance induced changes in service quality evaluations you should use a control group.

For example, a courier company wants to know which aspects of their delivery service are important to their recently signed-up customers but are concerned that post-purchase dissonance might affect the results. To try and determine whether such dissonance significantly altered ratings they could use a matched control group of potential new customers and compare the rankings.

Evidence for dissonance theory

Post-purchase dissonance has been demonstrated in a study by Brehm (1956) in which potential customers rated the desirability of several household appliances on an eight-point scale. As a reward for participating in the experiment, the subjects were then asked to choose between one of two items to take home.

When customers were asked to re-evaluate the items after their decision, they rated the chosen items more highly than they had previously, and the rejected items less highly. This is consistent with dissonance theory which predicates that post-decision dissonance will act to reinforce the purchase decision.

A review of literature in this area by Fiske and Taylor (1984) found that people do appear to selectively attend to positive information on their selected alternative (selective attention) and positively interpret ambiguous information (selective interpretation) but little evidence was found to suggest that people go out of their way to find positive information (selective exposure).

Activity 9.1

Have you ever been aware of post-purchase dissonance? How have you coped?

Try to think of three examples.

Activity 9.2

Find one or more people who are intending to buy a lottery ticket. Ask them to rate their chances of winning on a scale of 1 to 10 where 10 is high, 1 is low.

After they have bought the ticket – get them to rate their chances again. Has their rating changed? If so, how can this be explained by dissonance theory.

Activity debrief 9.2

Ratings should be higher after the ticket is purchased. Research suggests that the act of committing oneself to a bet creates dissonance and leads to a dissonance-reducing boost in confidence in one's choice.

Interpretation of results

Characteristics of data

Each piece of data you collect, whether it is the response to a question on a questionnaire or the weight of produce purchased by a shopper, is called an 'observation'. Each of these observations has a 'value' associated with it. This may be numerical or non-numerical; 'Yes', 'no', 207, 11 kg, 110 mm and 493 widgets, are all valid values. Sometimes non-numerical responses are converted (or coded) into numbers to make them easier to handle and store. For instance, a response of 'yes' may be converted to the number 1; 'no' may be converted to the number 0.

The observations you collect in the course of a particular study, are called a data set. You may collect one, or more, data sets from a series of studies and compare them for changes in attitudes, buying behaviour and identify trends.

Data which has not been altered in any way (that is, it remains unchanged from when it was collected) is called raw data. In most cases, the raw data you collect will simply be pages of numbers or questionnaire responses. This, in itself, is fairly meaningless. Before raw data can be interpreted it must first be summarized. Three main methods are used to describe and present summarized data:

1 Tables.
2 Graphics.
3 Statistics.

As an example, let us imagine that you have conducted a small survey of ten marketing students to find out how many of the recommended textbooks they have actually read. You find that one student admits to having read only one book, two students admit to having read two of the recommended books, four students say they have read three books, two students say they have read four books and one diligent student claims to have read five books.

Using tables
We could represent the data from the textbook example in tabular form (Table 9.3).

Table 9.3 Number of recommended textbooks read by marketing students

Number of books read	Number of students
1	1
2	2
3	4
4	2
5	1

This sort of table is called a frequency table because it records the frequency with which particular values occur.

Using graphics
We also represent the same books data graphically (Figure 9.6).

This representation of data is called a frequency distribution. Like the tabular equivalent it represents the frequency of unique values found in

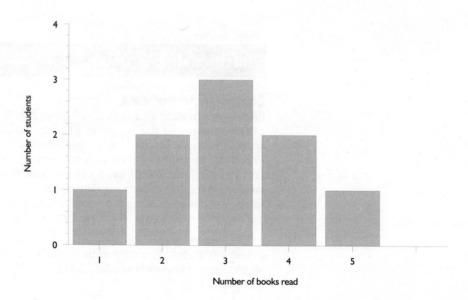

Figure 9.8
Numbers of recommended textbooks read by marketing students

226

the data. You will also notice that this particular frequency distribution is symmetrical around the mid-point. That is, the left- and right-hand sides or the distribution are mirror images of each other. This situation is quite rare in market research but important nonetheless as symmetrical distributions (also called normal distributions) have certain special properties.

Using statistics

Complex data is usually interpreted using statistical methods. These range from simple techniques such as calculating the mean result to sophisticated factor analysis techniques.

It is important to have a basic understanding of the correct use of basic summary statistics although it is outside the scope of this workbook to go into detailed descriptions and present the methods of calculation.

Measures of location

The commonest method of summarizing raw data is to calculate the 'average' response. There are three 'averaging' statistics. These are called the arithmetic mean, mode and median. Collectively, these statistics are known as measures of location. You may well come across these statistics whilst reading market research studies or literature, however, it is not necessary to know how to calculate them for this unit of the course.

Measures of dispersion

In addition to knowing about the 'average' of a distribution it is also useful to know about the 'spread' of values in the distribution. There are three statistics which are commonly used to describe 'spread'. These are called the range, interquartile range and quartile deviation. Collectively, these statistics are known as measures of dispersion.

As with measures of location, you may well come across these statistics but do not need to know how to calculate them for this unit of the course.

Proportions, fractions and percentages

Often it is useful to represent values, not in terms of their absolute numerical 'worth', but in terms of their relative value in comparison with other observations. For example, it is all very well knowing that your product sold 250,000 units this month, but of more interest is how it performed in comparison to the competition. For instance, what market share do you have?

There are three ways of representing such information:

1   As a percentage – for example sales are up 10 per cent.
2   As a fraction – one half (½) of our customers are satisfied with our service.
3   As a proportion – 0.25 of our product retail price goes on the packaging.

All of these are in common usage.

Presentation of findings

Invariably, the presentation of research data requires the writing of a report. This will include the graphical presentation of data as described in the next section along with a description of your research and recommendations for further action.

A report is usually the only full record of your research; the purpose of the work, the sample used, all the results, the method of analysis used, the conclusions reached and so on.

Characteristics of a good research report:

1   Objectives of the research are well defined.
2   Structured and logically ordered. The report should be broken down into sections, each with their own informative title. These sections

should be ordered in such a way as to lead the reader through the research. For example, data should be presented and the analysis method described before any conclusions are presented.

3 Comprehensive (it covers all aspects of the research) but concise (should not be unnecessarily wordy or cover irrelevant areas). A summary or abstract should be provided which summarizes the important findings for casual readers.

4 Accurate, clear and precise language is used throughout (terminology should be appropriate for the intended audience).

These four characteristics can be remembered from the acronym: OSCA (objectives, structure, comprehensiveness, accuracy).

Structure of a research report

In the scientific community, a 'standard' report structure has evolved. Whilst this is not suitable for all purposes, it provides a useful guide under most circumstances.

1 *Title page(s)* This should include the following:

- Title of the report.
- Name of sponsor and/or customer for the report.
- Title of researcher and organization.
- Date of publication.

2 *Table of contents* This should include page references for each heading contained within the report.

3 *Executive summary or abstract* This is intended for casual readers who may not have the time or inclination to read the whole report. This often includes the person that makes the decisions!

It should summarize the whole of the report, including the findings and recommendations. As a rough guide, this should not exceed one-eighth page for each five pages of report. For example, the summary for a forty-page report should be less than a page long. If your paper is added to an electronic database often the only text available to the reader is the abstract. Some systems limit the 'on-line' abstract to 250 words.

4 *Introduction or background* This should include the following:

- Purpose of research (often this is referred to as the 'brief').
- Supporting history and background information (i.e. other relevant studies).
- Any assumptions made.
- Specific aims of research.

5 *Methodology* Should include the following:

- Details of any material used (questionnaires, interview forms, special equipment).
- Sample population (numbers and profile).
- Design of study.
- Procedure used (the sequence in which the study was conducted).

6 *Results and analysis* Should include the following:

- Details of analysis method(s) used.
- Descriptive statistics for raw data.
- Any advanced statistics.
- Tabular and/or graphical presentation of data.

7 *Discussion and conclusions* Should include the following:

- Discussion of research findings.
- Conclusions to be drawn from findings.
- Self-critique of study (e.g. unexpected problems that arose, why not enough people could be surveyed, flaws discovered in a questionnaire).
- Additional graphical presentation of summarized or combined data to support discussion or conclusions.

8 *Recommendations*   Should include the following:

- Actions to take as a result of research.
- Recommendations for future research.

9 *Acknowledgements*   Should include the following:

- Thanks to organizations that have funded/supported research.
- Thanks to individuals that have helped in the preparation of the report (i.e. they may have given useful advice or provided administrative support).

10 *References*   Should include full references for all materials and other research studies referred to.

11 *Appendices*   Should include all information, such as the full questionnaire text, which, if included in the main body of the text, would have interrupted the flow of the report.

Activity 9.3

Find a copy of the *Journal of the Market Research Society*, or one of the many other journals in this field, and examine the structure of three papers. How do these compare with each other and with the 'ideal' structure outlined in this unit.

Report writing tips

The following tips are presented to assist in the writing of a good report and help assess the reports of others.

- Does the report contain enough information to allow another researcher to replicate the work? If not, then the report should contain more detail. This is, of course, unless the writer wishes for certain aspects of their research method to remain secret.
- The introductory sections to a report, should address at least the following questions:
  - Why is this report being written?
  - What does it hope to achieve?
  - Who is this report aimed at?
- The results and analysis sections of a report should not contain any discussion or conclusions only an impartial description of the data.
- Conclusions should be based solely on the data reported combined with the findings from other, fully referenced, studies. A clear distinction should be made between the results themselves, the interpretation of the results (which may be contested), and the recommendations being made.
- Recommendations should be concrete and specific, not 'woolly'.
- Are all the graphs and tables properly titled, clearly presented and referenced in the body of the text?
- Does the summary include all the important information from the report?

Summary

In this unit you have learned about:

- The market research process – including hypothesis construction and pilot testing.
- Common experimental design formats.
- The selection of target populations.
- The principles of investigating customer dynamics.
- Possible pitfalls with investigative market research.
- The main means of interpreting and presenting research findings.

Question 9.1
It is most likely that the:

- Independent variable is whether or not a customer has the 'cheap rate' service.
- Dependent variable is the measure of customer satisfaction. This could be obtained via questionnaire.
- Experimenter is most likely to be you.
- Control group is most likely to be those customers that have not had the service installed. They are the best persons to act as a comparative group.

The study is a field study as the experiment is carried out in people's own homes.

Question 9.2
There are a number of experimental designs that can be used to test the effectiveness of an advertising campaign. The exact choice would depend on financial limits, resource constraints and the broadcast pattern of the advertisement. It is most important to test before and after the advertisement is broadcast and, presuming times series data is not available, you are left to decide between pre-test/post-test, non-equivalent control group and the classical experimental designs. First choice would be the latter which provides more opportunity to eliminate the effect of intervening variables. However, if the advert was on trial in a particular region (as is usually the case) it will not be possible to randomly select people from this region (as some may have seen the advert some may not have). We would thus be forced to use one of the other two designs. Of these, the non-equivalent control group is preferred because of the presence of a control group to eliminate the effects of intervening variables.

Question 9.3
It is certain that time series data will be available from past political opinion polls. In this case all that is required is a single test (case study or survey design) which can be compared with secondary data from previous polls. You could determine from this whether the trend in voting is up or down and thus make your prediction on the likely outcome of the next election (you might also wish to take other historical trends into account which could be picked up from the secondary data). Of course, if the resources were available, you might wish to commence your own time-series survey.

Question 9.4
Your classmates may be a biased sample. Certainly, they are unlikely to be representative of the population in general, and would probably not match any quotas for this sort of survey (which would require a high number of parents as subjects).

Unit 10 ▮ Quantitative and qualitative methodologies for investigating customer dynamics

Objectives

This unit introduces you to a variety of different primary and secondary research methodologies. You will:

❑ Learn about the different types of research.

❑ Explore a wide variety of qualitative and quantitative primary research techniques.

❑ Be presented with an overview of sources of secondary data.

❑ Be introduced to the ethical and legal issues surrounding the collection and use of data.

By the end of the unit you will be able to:

❑ Understand the different types of research.

❑ Know how to go about conducting secondary research.

❑ Choose the primary research technique most suited to your research goals.

❑ Be aware and take account of the possible ethical and legal problems associated with investigative research.

Different types of research

Primary versus secondary

Primary data is information collected for a specific purpose. The process of collection is called primary research. A number of methods of primary research are discussed later in this section.

An example of primary data collection is the research required to identify the market for an innovative new product. It is unlikely that such research has previously been undertaken. Therefore the research is likely to be specially commissioned.

Secondary data is data originally collected for a more general purpose usually by a third party. The process of collection is usually termed secondary research or desk research.

An example is the use of the electoral roll for the purpose of ascertaining, for example, the number of eighteen-year-olds in a city (people turning eighteen in a certain year are marked on the register along with the date of their birthday). This data was obviously collected for the purpose of identifying those eligible to vote but might be of use to a marketer looking at, for example, the best place to site a nightclub aimed at younger people.

Activity 10.1

What primary and secondary research does your organization do?

Internal versus external

The information available within an organization is termed internal data. Internal research is therefore relatively rapid and requires minimal resources. Example of internal data could include:

- Sales, production and distribution records.
- Customer database.
- Historical research reports.

External data is data collected by outside bodies. These might be commercial market research organizations or official bodies such as the Office of National Statistics (ONS).

Examples of external data include:

- Official census data.
- Newspaper polls or surveys.
- Academic research papers.

External data is usually, but not always, secondary data. For example, you may wish to commission a third party to research your corporate image. Similarly, internal data is not always primary data. It may, for example, have been originally collected for a different purpose.

Qualitative versus quantitative

Research is either quantitative (it deals mostly with numerical information) or qualitative (dealing with less tangible data such as interview responses, individual opinions and the outcome of group discussions).

Of course, rarely is a particular piece of research either entirely qualitative or quantitative. It may be, for instance, that you conclude a quantitative questionnaire with an open-ended question seeking further comment. The responses to this would be qualitative in nature.

Also, it is possible to 'code' qualitative responses to make them appear quantitative. For example, if you were interviewing a person about a product and, in the course of the interview, they said that they very much liked the packaging you might later rate their opinion by giving it a coding of '3'. If other persons were interviewed who said that they disliked the packaging you might give them a coding of '1'. People who were undecided about the packaging might receive a coding of '2'. Thus, a crude quantitative scale can be built up from qualitative data.

Qualitative methodologies

There are three basic ways of collecting primary data in qualitative research:

1 Depth interviews.
2 Focus/discussion groups.
3 Projective techniques.

Depth interviews

A depth interview is an unstructured discussion between interviewer and respondent. They are generally lengthy (anything up to one hour) and are best carried out by trained, experienced interviewers.

The interviewing style can vary enormously but the aim is to secure the maximum amount of useful information from the respondent on a particular topic with minimum intervention from the interviewer. The role of the interviewer is therefore to:

- Obtain detailed information on the topic(s) needed within the time available.
- Balance the need for open-ended discussion with the need to address certain topics.
- Avoid biasing the respondent by appearing to favour certain responses or asking leading questions.

The interview is best recorded on audiotape. Recorders which are voice activated are best as they save time when analysing the tape and, of course, save tape. Transcripts are prepared from the tape, suitably annotated to indicate the emotional content of the voice as required, and studied for ideas, useful comments and subjective opinions on the topic under investigation.

The respondents need to be chosen with care. Some people are not as good at expressing themselves verbally as others. It may be that respondents are chosen from those taking part in a larger study as a result of their 'extreme' opinions, particular knowledge or responsibilities within an organization.

Depth interviews are particularly useful during the early stages of a product/brand development when little has been decided and/or new ideas are required.

Focus groups

Focus groups are similar to depth interviews in many ways. The main difference being that the discussion is not one-on-one but involves a group of seven to ten respondents. The main effect of this is that the group forms its own identity, much of the discussion is amongst its members. Under these circumstances the researcher facilitates the working of the group rather than actually interviewing its individual members. These groups are sometimes called discussion groups and the researcher leading the group the facilitator or moderator.

As with depth interviews, the role of the facilitator is to focus discussion on the research topic, directing the group where required but limiting their involvement as much as possible. Certain management of the group is also required:

- The discussion needs to be set in motion.
- Track must be kept of the progress of the discussion (time-keeping, etc.).
- The involvement of all members must be ensured (some people are shy in groups, yet their knowledge or opinions may be just as valuable).
- The discussion needs to be brought to a close in a tidy manner.
- Names and other details of the group members need to be gathered (this may be achieved with a small questionnaire which, of course, must be designed and produced).
- Arrangements for follow-up discussion may also need to be arranged and communicated.
- The practicalities of recording the discussion must be handled (this may involve the use of a flip-chart, tape recorder or videotape).

Focus group members are often chosen to reflect a cross-section of the intended target customers for the product/brand under discussion. In this way, more debate is assured.

The processes that take place in groups, their formation, maintenance, decision making and performance, are called group dynamics. A large number of psychological studies have looked at group dynamics including the roles people play, how groups solve problems and reach decisions, how individual members are affected by their membership of the group and so on. Focus groups are popular amongst marketers because:

- They allow qualitative information from many individuals to be collected in a short period of time.
- They provide a good forum for 'testing the water' with new products/brands.
- The group setting is 'emotionally-charged' in a way that a one-to-one interview can never be.
- They are useful for generating new ideas and, under certain circumstances, problem-solving (suitable techniques are 'brainstorming' and 'synectics').

An advertising executive named Alex Osborn (Osborn, A. F. (1957), *Applied Imagination*, New York: Scribner) was the first to advocate brainstorming as a technique to devise new or creative solutions to difficult problems. His rules for brainstorming are reproduced below:

1 Given a problem to solve, all group members are encouraged to express whatever solutions and ideas come to mind, regardless of how preposterous or impractical they may seem.
2 All reactions are recorded.
3 No suggestion or solution can be evaluated until all ideas have been expressed. Ideally participants should be led to believe that no suggestions will be evaluated at the brainstorming sessions.
4 The elaboration of one person's ideas by another is encouraged.

When brainstorming, it is important that the facilitator write down all suggestions where they can be viewed by all group members. A use for brainstorming might be to devise a new advertising slogan, product name or even a new product. With synectics the aim is to focus on producing creative solutions and to enhance the creative potential of the group, members are usually pre-selected on the basis of their creative abilities and may be recruited from a wide range of disciplines unrelated to the topic under discussion. The problems set before synectics groups are usually of a more complex or technical nature.

Activity 10.2

The year is 1999. You are tasked with finding a new name for a special brew of beer. The beer is to be produced in limited edition to celebrate the eighty-fifth birthday of the brewery owner, a retired man fondly referred to as 'The colonel'. The following information is available about him:

- He is well-known and respected in the brewing industry.
- He has a 'handle-bar' moustache.
- He likes horses (his hobby).
- He was a military man and served in a mounted division.

The following is known about the brewery:

- The popular brews it produces are named with an 'academic' theme.
- The company is well-known nationally but with a strong local image.

Working in a group, set aside fifteen to twenty minutes to try and brainstorm a name for the limited edition brew. Appoint a facilitator who writes down suggestions on a blackboard or flip chart. At the end of the allotted time, take your best three suggestions then, as a group, spend five to ten minutes deciding on your preferred, final, name. For each of the three alternatives, give their advantages and disadvantages.

Projective techniques

These set of techniques are based on those used by clinical psychologists to understand a person's 'hidden' attitudes, motivations and feelings. In a marketing context, these techniques are used to illicit associations with a particular product or brand. Many psychological techniques have been successfully used for this purpose. They include:

Word association

Respondents are presented with a series of words or phrases and asked to say the first word that comes into their head. This is often used to check whether proposed product names have undesirable associations, particularly in different cultures and languages. You might not wish, for instance, to call a new life insurance policy 'Wish' if it turned out to be associated in many people's minds with 'death' (death-wish) although you might if it brought to mind a 'wishing well'.

Activity 10.3

What is the first word or phrase you associate with each of the following:

Insurance –

Ice cream –

Computer –

Mineral water –

Psychology –

Compare your responses with those of your classmates. Are any of your responses the same? Why do you think that is?

Sentence completion

The beginning of a sentence is read out and the respondent is asked to complete it with the first words that come to mind. To probe the ideas which are important to people in selecting an insurance policy you might provide the sentence: 'The kind of people that do without holiday insurance are. . .'

Activity 10.4

Working on your own, complete the following sentences:

People who don't own cars are. . .

Women who dye their hair are. . .

A couple who go on holiday to Spain are. . .

Now compare your answers with those of your classmates. Are your answers similar or different? What information does this technique provide?

Third-person technique

Respondents are asked to describe a third person about whom they have little information. This technique was used by Mason Haire when instant coffee was first introduced in 1950. Two groups of housewives were given a shopping list to examine. The list given to each group was identical except that one contained instant coffee, the other ground coffee. The housewives perceived the writer of the list that contained instant coffee as 'lazy' and 'poor' whereas they perceived the writer of the list that contained ground coffee as being 'thrifty' and generally a 'good' homemaker. This research demonstrated the negative attitudes associated with convenience foods in the 1950s. A later replication of this study in 1970, when instant coffee was more widely accepted, no longer found these negative associations.

235

Activity 10.5

The picture is of a man called Dave Rodwell. He is a lecturer at the Oxford College of Marketing. He teaches 'consumer behaviour' on the CIM Marketing courses run at the college.

Without discussing your thoughts, or your answers, with your classmates please answer the following questions. Do not worry if you feel you cannot answer all the questions.

1 What sort of car do you think he drives?
2 What political party do you think he supports?
3 How old do you think he is?
4 What do you think is his favourite sport?
5 Which country do you think he was born in?
6 What do you think his father's job was/is?
7 What do you think is his favourite colour?
8 What sort of place do you think he lives in?
9 What pets do you think he has?
10 What newspaper do you think he regularly reads?

Once you have answered as many questions as you can, compare your responses with those of your classmates. Are there any similarities? Why do you think that is?

Thematic apperception test (TAT)

Respondents are asked to interpret an ambiguous picture or drawing or fill in a blank 'speech bubble' associated with a particular character in an ambiguous situation. A television recruitment advertisement for the UK police force showed a black man in casual clothes running followed by a white policeman running. The footage was presented in an ambiguous way (was the policeman chasing the man? or were they both chasing a third party?) to highlight the problem of racial stereotyping and the need for a multi-racial police force. The advert was part of a campaign to increase the number of non-white police.

Activity 10.6

In not less than fifty words, describe this picture. Also, what might the woman be saying?

Now list the 'themes' in your response (what is happening, who is speaking, what they are saying etc.). Compare your themes with those of your classmates. What information could this technique provide?

Reperatory grid (rep grid)

A modification of the method first developed by Kelly in 1955 to support his theory of personality, the rep grid is useful as a projective technique in many marketing situations. Respondents are presented with a grid and asked to title the columns with brand names or types of a particular product (i.e. flavours of ice cream, types of car). They are then asked to take three of these products and think of a phrase which describes the way in which any two are different from the third. For instance, a Porsche and a Jaguar might be described as 'speed machines' when compared to a Volvo. This description is then used as a row title and each of the other products/ brands rated accordingly. By repeatedly selecting and describing three items, the way in which an individual perceives the market is found. It might be that an individual perceives the car market as consisting of 'speed machines', 'safe but boring', and 'comfortable' cars. This information can be used in a number of ways for planning a promotion, identifying the attitudes associated with established products and identifying where gaps in the market exist. The rep grid technique is described in more detail in the unit on attitudes.

Suppose we have been asked to investigate the various ice cream flavours in the market place and determine what characteristics any new flavour should have to be successful. We know the sales figures for the various flavours but we do not know what it is about the ice cream flavours that people like. This is where the rep grid technique can help.

A rep grid is a table with the columns as elements and the rows as constructs. If we were investigating different ice cream flavours, the flavours themselves would be the elements. In this example we will limit ourselves to four flavours although, of course, a real study would take into account all the flavours on the market. To start with, our rep grid would look something like Table 10.1.

Table 10.1 Rep grid for ice cream example

Constructs	Elements			
	Nuts and cookies	Strawberry	Roast peanut	French chocolate

To generate the constructs we take any three flavours (elements) and find a way in which any two are different from the third. If we took Strawberry, French Chocolate and Roast Peanut we may decide that the Strawberry is different from the others in that it is 'fruity'. We would therefore write in 'fruity' as a construct and place a tick against 'Strawberry' and any other of the elements which we consider to share the 'fruity' construct. In this example, none of the others would probably be considered 'fruity'. By taking another three elements and comparing them we might come up with the following additional constructs: 'has bits in', 'doughy', 'chocolate-taste' and so on. It must be emphasized that constructs are a very personal thing. No two persons' will look the same. After three constructs are generated, the grid may end up looking something like Table 10.2.

Table 10.2 Rep grid for ice cream example with three constructs added

Constructs	Elements			
	Nuts and cookies	Strawberry	Roast peanut	French chocolate
Fruity		✓		
Has bits in	✓		✓	✓
Doughy	✓			

By comparing the high-selling flavours with others we can determine what constructs are the most popular and use this information to determine what constructs any new flavour should match. For instance, we might decide that it should be 'doughy' and 'have bits in'. From this information we might decide to test cookies and chocolate as a combination.

Role-playing

Respondents are asked to imagine that they are an object (e.g. a fridge or car) or a different person (e.g. a bank manager or supplier) and asked to describe their feelings, thoughts and actions. A variation on this technique is the 'friendly Martian' role play where respondents are asked to imagine that they are a Martian and told to describe what they would do under certain circumstances. For example, the following question could be asked to secure information about the appeal of different supermarkets: 'Imagine you are a Martian who has just landed in a shopping centre close to Sainsbury's, Tesco, Asda and Budgen supermarkets. You need food. How would you decide which supermarket to visit?'

Activity 10.7

Working on your own, answer the following question. Produce at least five ideas (no matter how 'silly' they appear).

Imagine you are a tin of cat food on the shelf at a supermarket. How would you make yourself more attractive to shoppers?

Compare your answers with those of your classmates. What similarities and differences exist? Have any new ideas emerged which could be applied to the selling of cat food (or any other tinned food for that matter?).

Comparison of different qualitative research methods

Depth interviews	Focus/discussion groups	Projective techniques
Very time-consuming to administer	Moderately time-consuming to administer	Relatively quick to administer (depending on technique)
Can only administer one person at a time	Can administer up to ten people at a time	Can administer many people at a time (depending on technique)
Requires trained interviewers to administer	Requires trained facilitators to administer	Requires few specially trained staff to administer (depending on technique)
Danger of interviewer bias	Danger of group being biased towards opinions of stronger members	Low likelihood of bias
Time-consuming to analyse	Time-consuming to analyse	Relatively quick to analyse
Possible to obtain very detailed information	Possible to obtain very detailed information	Information limited by technique used
Indirectly useful for generating new ideas	Can be used for brainstorming new ideas directly	Indirectly useful for generating new ideas

You are asked to gather qualitative information quickly from around 100 customers. You have about three weeks for interviewing and analysis. What technique would you use and why?

Quantitative methodologies

There are two basic ways of collecting primary data in qualitative research:

1 Observation.
2 Surveys and questionnaires (including interviews, telephone, diary and postal surveys).

Observation

We all learn by observing the things that happen around us. Observation, as a market research method, is the formalization and refinement of this process.

We can clearly observe the behaviour of individuals but what observation cannot tell us is what people are thinking or feeling. For instance, we can observe which shoppers buy lottery tickets but we can't distinguish between shoppers who may be thinking, 'If I don't win this week I'll stop' from those who are thinking, 'I'm going to keep buying tickets until I win'. These alternatives are obviously of interest because they will affect future behaviour, but observational techniques are not able to distinguish these two groups of shoppers. Observation is therefore quite limited as a technique but, nonetheless, can be useful under those circumstance where we are more interested in behaviour than in any mental processes.

There are three basic types of observation:

1 Secretive – where the subjects of the study are unaware that they are being observed. For instance, the behaviour of shoppers is observed via a hidden camera or by an experimenter pretending to be another shopper. This may pose ethical problems.
2 Non-participatory – where the subjects of the study are aware that they are being observed but the experimenter takes no part in the behaviour being observed. For instance, shoppers are observed by an experimenter with a clipboard sited prominently, perhaps near the checkouts. It is possible that the presence of the experimenters may affect the behaviour of the subject.
3 Participatory – where the subject and experimenter interact. A shopper might be approached by an experimenter and asked what they are buying and why. This can provide useful additional information but the behaviour of the experimenter may actually change the behaviour of the subject they are trying to observe.

Observations can be carried out in the field or in the laboratory. The latter overcomes many of the ethical problems associated with such studies but risks interfering with naturally occurring behaviours and can appear contrived. It may be, for instance, that meeting friends has an influence on supermarket buying behaviour. This aspect of shopping would be difficult to re-create in a laboratory.

One successful example of the use of observational research was that done by the Postal Service in the USA. They found that most people were on first-name terms with their postmen and women. This led to a successful promotional campaign which prominently featured post deliverers.

Observational data is usually collected using recording sheets. A predetermined set of behaviours are identified and printed on these sheets. The experimenter is then able to mark down quickly the behaviours as they occur.

Suppose we were trying to determine the order in which shoppers visit the various areas within a supermarket as part of a study to re-organize shelving (wet fish, deli counter, fruit and vegetables, tinned food, etc.). In this instance we would be wise to prepare our recording sheet with a list of the various areas in which we are interested. It is then easy to indicate, with a number, the order in which they were visited. It is also good practice to prepare for the unexpected by adding space on the recording sheet for behaviours which were not anticipated. For instance, it might be that a shopper visits an area more than once. You may wish to record which area they re-visited as well as the reason why.

Observations that are difficult to record in 'real time' because they happen too fast or are obscured can be recorded on video for later analysis.

Mystery shopping

One special kind of secretive observation is termed 'mystery shopping'. It is, in fact, one of the least mysterious research methods. Researchers simply pose as customers and report on the nature and quality of the service they receive.

They are normally briefed on the various points that it is important to observe. Examples include:

- The appearance of the store and staff.
- Employee product knowledge.
- Speed of service.
- Whether correct sales procedure is followed.

Mystery shopping provides a welcome opportunity for a business to see itself through a customer's eyes.

The technique is not restricted to personal shopping, it can just as easily be used to assess responses to telephone enquiries, service call-outs, order lines and so on.

One well-known company, Abbey National, uses mystery shopping extensively. Each of its branches is 'inspected' twice a year as part of a broader customer satisfaction programme.

Activity 10.8

Observe students in your college canteen. In what order do they make decisions about what they are going to eat and drink? Are these decisions influenced by the people accompanying them?

When and where do they pick up their cutlery, condiments? Where and how do they pay?

On the basis of the answers to these questions, how might the canteen improve its image and the degree to which it meets the needs of its customers?

Survey methods

A survey is the most commonly used method of gathering quantitative data. It is essential to approach the design and administration of surveys in a structured way to avoid errors, wasted time and poor quality responses. The process of undertaking a survey project is similar in many ways to that for an experiment.

Steps in a survey project:

1 Decide on your survey goals – what you want to learn.
2 Determine your sample – who you will ask.
3 Select interviewing methodology – how you will ask.

4 Design your questionnaire – what you will ask.
5 Pre-test the questionnaire, if at all practical (known as piloting).
6 Administer interviews – ask the questions.
7 Enter the data.
8 Analyse the data.
9 Present the data.

Deciding on your survey goals

The first step in any survey is deciding what you want to know. This will determine whom you will survey and what you will ask them. If you are unclear about what you want then your results will be unclear. Researchers rarely take the time necessary at this stage of the project to properly consider their survey goals. Some general goals could include finding out more about:

- Consumer ratings of current products or services.
- A company's corporate image.
- Customer satisfaction levels.
- Television viewer opinions.
- Employee attitudes.
- Opinions about political issues.
- The potential market for a new product or service.

These sample goals represent general areas of investigation only. The more specific you can make your goals, the easier it will be to get usable answers. Specific goals are usually phrased as questions:

- What do the supporters of the different political parties feel about the level of defence spending?
- What do the employees of UserData Limited feel about the new salary scales?
- Do consumers prefer the services offered by Mercury or British Telecom?
- Which washing powder do customers think washes their clothing best – Persil or Ecover?

Even at this stage, it may be necessary to get clarification on certain concepts. For instance, in the last question, what is meant by 'washes their clothing best'? The person commissioning the research should be consulted on such questions of interpretation. The 'best' in this context may mean 'cleanest' or 'whitest' or may be to do with how the powder handles sensitive or coloured fabrics.

SERVQUAL – measuring service quality

One example of a survey tool widely used to measure service quality is SERVQUAL, developed by Parasuraman et al. 1988. This is made up of a series of questions; twenty-two on expectations and twenty-two on performance.

Each set of twenty-two questions contains items on five basic dimensions:

1 Reliability.
2 Responsiveness.
3 Empathy.
4 Assurance.
5 Tangibles.

These are phrased as statements to which responses are given using a seven-point Likert-type scale.

For example, the pair of questions measuring reliability for a bank could be something like the following:

Question pair	Strongly agree						Strongly disagree
Expectation: Banks should be dependable							
Performance: Anytown Bank is dependable							

There is much debate over the reliability and validity of the SERVQUAL instrument but it remains a popular tool for exploring and measuring service quality and identifying gaps.

For a critique of SERVQUAL read Asubonteng et al., (1996) SERVQUAL revisited: a critical review of service quality, *The Journal of Services Marketing*.

Interviewing methods

Once you have decided on your sample you must decide on the method of data collection. The main methods are:

- Personal interview.
- Telephone surveys including computer assisted telephone interviewing (CATI).
- Computer assisted interviewing (CAI).
- Postal surveys.

Personal interviews

What distinguishes this type of survey is that the questionnaire is administered 'face-to-face' with the interviewee. Such interviews are often categorized according to where they take place. The following examples are given:

- Household survey – The surveyor goes door-to-door, either randomly, or according to some pre-arranged sampling method, and interviews people on the doorstep.
- Home survey – Takes place in the interviewee's home. They are normally arranged in advance. This is obviously time-consuming but guarantees a response. Advantages are that, in the comfort of their own home, conversation is likely to be freer and the interviewee will be more tolerant of a longer interview.
- Hall survey – As its name suggests, these take place in a hall or hired room. Individuals are invited to attend or called in off the street to take part.
- Shop surveys – these take place in shopping centres, inside a particular shop or at the entrance to a particular shop. In many cases a 'stall' is set up for this purpose and/or individuals are approached and asked to participate.
- On-street surveys – Otherwise known as 'clipboard' surveys, individuals are approached in the street. In busy, hectic streets this can be problematic. Surveying at busy times, such as lunchtime, is difficult as many people would rather have something to eat! On-street surveys need to be particularly short and to the point.

The use of a prompt card is common in personal interviewing. These are usually a verbal or pictorial representation of the response choices. For example, an interviewee might be asked for which political party they intend to vote. In this case, the response card would contain a list of political parties. The advantage of the prompt card is that it reduces the bias that can be introduced as a result of the changing voice intonation of the interviewer and, by having a number of different cards with different arrangements of responses, the effect of response ordering can be reduced. A further benefit is that 'wayward' responses are avoided. For example, a response to an unguided voting question might be 'Tony's Party'. The interviewee is probably referring to the Labour Party – a prompt card would help to clarify this without a possible biasing intervention from the interviewer.

Telephone (including CATI)

Telephone surveys are probably the most popular interviewing method. The majority of homes and businesses have a telephone which makes coverage almost complete (although about 10 per cent of people are not on the phone – most notably students and old persons but also those who are ex-directory).

Sampling is easy using a telephone directory. Most libraries carry a full set of telephone directories for the whole of the UK. The telephone also makes the sampling of international interviewees easy.

Increasingly popular is computer assisted telephone interviewing (CATI) where the interviewer reads questions from a computer screen and enters the responses directly in the computer. In this way, results can be analysed rapidly. CATI can also assist the interviewer in structuring their interview by only displaying those questions which are relevant based on earlier responses. Unfortunately, the growth of 'junk' telephone calls is increasing refusal rates amongst potential interviewees.

Computer assisted interviews (CAI)

These are interviews in which the interviewees enter their own answers directly into a computer. They are popular at exhibitions and in large organizations where 'electronic mail' is used to send out the questionnaire. This method is convenient and, as with CATI, no post-survey data entry is required allowing for a rapid analysis. Obviously, CAI is limited by the availability of a suitable computer. The novelty and convenience of CAI leads to moderately high response rates.

Postal surveys

These surveys are generally the least expensive type. Postal surveys are seen as less intrusive than personal interviews and telephone surveys but response rates are generally the lowest of any survey method. More often than not, response rates are less than 10 per cent which provides an opportunity for considerable bias. In an attempt to boost return rates, all manner of offers and incentives are used. One American researcher found that enclosing a one dollar bill massively increased response rates (and no doubt also the cost!).

Low levels of literacy are no doubt one reason why responses are reduced – a good reason to keep questions simple. English is not everyone's first language and, in areas where problems with language are envisaged, it may be worth producing multi-lingual questionnaire variants.

However, much of the low response rate is simply due to the high volumes of 'junk' mail people receive. Try to make your survey look as little like junk mail as possible. Better still, and wherever possible, save some trees and use the telephone!

Comparison of different interview methods

Postal survey	Telephone (including CATI)	Computer assisted interviewing (CAI)	Personal interviews
Respondees can see, feel and/or taste	Respondees can hear	Respondees can see and hear	Respondees can see, feel, hear, and/or taste
Moderately long interviews tolerated	Moderately long interviews tolerated	Moderately long interviews tolerated whilst still novel	Longer interviews tolerated when in comfortable surroundings (i.e. own home) otherwise only short interviews tolerated (on-street).
Long time to receive responses	Quick to receive responses	Quick to receive responses	Quick to receive responses
Analysis time moderately fast when survey is electronically readable, otherwise slow	Fast analysis (CATI)/Slow analysis (non-CATI)	Fast analysis	Slow analysis
Easy to survey random sample	Easy to survey random sample	More difficult to survey random sample	More difficult to survey random sample
Full coverage (including international)	Good coverage (including international)	Poor coverage (have to go out and find individuals)	Poor coverage (have to go out and find individuals)
Requires certain level of literacy	Requires comprehension of spoken language (usually English)	Requires certain level of literacy	Requires comprehension of spoken language (usually English)
Allow respondees to answer at their leisure	Forces respondees to answer at time of call	Forces respondees to answer at time of interview	Forces respondees to answer at time of interview
Low response rate	Medium response rate	Medium response rate	Medium response rate
Virtual elimination of interviewer bias	Possibility of interviewer bias	Virtual elimination of interviewer bias	Possibility of interviewer bias
Low cost	Medium cost	Medium cost	High cost
No special interviewer training required	Special interviewer training required	No special interviewer training required	Special interviewer training required
People more likely to answer sensitive questions	People less likely to answer sensitive questions	People more likely to answer sensitive questions	People less likely to answer sensitive questions

What are the advantages of postal surveys compared with telephone surveys?

What are the advantages of CAI compared with personal interviews?

General Comparison of different quantitative research methods

Observation	Surveys
Time-consuming to undertake	Relatively quick to undertake (depending on technique)
Are restricted in the number of people by the circumstances of the observation	Can administer many people at a time (depending on technique)
Requires trained observers to collect data	Requires no specially trained staff to collect data (depending on technique)
Danger of responses being biased by presence of observer	Generally, low likelihood of bias (depending on technique)
Time-consuming to analyse	Relatively quick to analyse (depending on technique)

Questionnaire design

The following 'fifteen golden rules' are provided as a general guide to the design of questionnaires:

1 Keep the survey short – long surveys are often indicative of poorly defined survey goals. As a rule of thumb, keep the number of questions below forty. Go through each question. If you do not know, or care, what you will do with the result then leave the question out.
2 Design the questionnaire to match the survey method being used – for example, CATI and CAI are able to 'branch' to different questions depending on the responses given to earlier questions which can increase the amount of data collected with the same number of questions and make errors less likely.
3 Keep the questionnaire simple – do not mix topics – for example, combining a survey on smoking with one on political issues simply serves to confuse the interviewee.
4 Do not combine two questions in one – for example, 'How do you feel about John Major and the Government?' should be asked as two questions (a) How do you feel about John Major (b) How do you feel about the Government?'
5 Avoid unnecessary terminology, abbreviations, technical words and jargon – these should only be used where questions are intended for specialist groups that would be expected to understand. For example, 'Have you ever owned a PC 486DX 66 computer?' is probably an acceptable question for a computer buff but not a member of the general public.
6 Do not present biased questions – For example, 'How satisfied are you with your new, super fast, hi-tech Swan toaster?' assumes that people already have a positive perception of the toaster and thus is likely to bias their response. A more correct way of phrasing this question would be to ask 'How satisfied or dissatisfied are you with the Swan toaster?' – a suitable response scale would then be provided.

7 Make sure your questions are grammatically correct – poor grammar can lead to confusion, annoys certain people, and creates a poor impression.

8 Each question should have a 'Don't know or 'Not applicable' response unless you are absolutely certain that you have covered all possibilities. For example, in response to the question 'What make of car do you own?' 'Don't know' and 'Not applicable' response categories should be provided. Some people may not actually know, or care, about the make of their car. Similarly, some people do not own a car. You would rarely want to include 'Don't know' or 'Not applicable' in a list of choices being read over the telephone or in person, but should usually accept them when given by respondents.

9 Provide example questions at the beginning of the questionnaire to demonstrate the method of completion. If a number of different question formats are used, provide examples of each and instructions for completion within the body of the questionnaire to avoid confusion.

10 Be specific in your questioning – 'woolly' questions lead to 'woolly' results. For example, 'Have you recently bought a can of cat food' might be better re-phrased 'Have you bought a can of Possum cat food in the last two weeks?'

11 Always allow for the interviewee to make their own comments at the end of the questionnaire – this will often provide useful leads for follow-up studies or allow you to more accurately interpret the data you collect.

12 Take care when laying out your questionnaire – a neat and tidy layout creates a good impression and reduces error.

13 Take care with the ordering of your questions – make sure that the response on a question is not affected by a previous answer or pre-empts a response to a later question. For example, a question which mentions blue packaging should not be succeeded by a question which asks for preferences on packaging colour.

14 Always start your questionnaire by explaining who you are and what you intend to do with the data you collect. This is polite as well as being ethically correct.

15 Always include a question asking whether the interviewee would mind being contacted further – you never know when a quick follow-up study may be required.

Question 10.3

You are stopped in the street by an interviewer. The first thing they say is 'Good afternoon Sir (or Madam), Where have you come from?' What is wrong with this?

Question types
Researchers use three basic types of questions:

1 Multiple choice – where the interviewee has to select from a set of responses (also called closed questions).
2 Open-ended – where the interviewee is allowed to enter anything.
3 Hybrid – a combination of the above two.

Multiple choice
Which destination would you choose for your ideal holiday? (please tick one response only)

London	❏
Paris	❏
Caribbean	❏
None of the above	❏
Don't know	❏

Sometimes more than one response is required. This needs to be made abundantly clear to the respondee as in the following question example:

Which of the following qualifications do you possess? (please tick *all* the responses that apply)

CSE ❏
O-level ❏
A-level ❏
Diploma ❏
Degree or equivalent ❏

Open-ended
What destination would you choose for your ideal holiday? (please write response below)

_____

Again, it might be that more than one response is required, as in the following example:

Please list the three things you like *best* about your new toaster:

1 _____
2 _____
3 _____

Hybrid
Which destination would you choose for your ideal holiday? (please tick or write one response only)

London ❏
Paris ❏
Caribbean ❏
Other (please specify) _____
Don't know ❏

Comparison of question types

Multiple choice	Open-ended	Hybrid
Easy to analyse	Difficult to analyse	If choices well researched then moderately easy to analyse
Likelihood of bias	Low likelihood of bias	Likelihood of bias
Difficult to design	Easy to design	Difficult to design
Suitable for quantitative data collection	Suitable for qualitative data collection	Suitable for quantitative data collection

Response scales
Depending on the sort of data you are collecting, you may need to use one of following types of response scales:

247

- *Likert scale* – developed in 1932 this scale is perhaps the most commonly used attitude response scale. A series of statements are rated in the following five point scale: *strongly agree, agree, undecided, disagree, strongly disagree.*
- *Semantic differential* – developed by Osgood, Tannenbaum and Succi in 1957 this scale is commonly used where an attitude object rather than a statement is being rated. The semantic differential consists of nine pairs of bipolar adjectives or opposites. Each is given a seven-point scale. The adjectives used vary but typically consist of pairs such as good/bad, active/passive, strong/weak and so on.
- *Rank order scales* – here the interviewee is asked to rank items in terms of some specific property or attribute. Rank ordering can provide useful competitive information and is therefore useful in product positioning.

Likert scale

A number of different formats are favoured for Likert scales. Two examples are given below:

1 Using the scale given indicate how strongly you agree or disagree with the following statement (please circle your preferred response):

I enjoy studying marketing

Strongly agree   Agree   Neither agree nor disagree   Disagree   Strongly disagree

2 Place a cross in the box which best indicates how strongly you agree or disagree with each of the statements given:

	Strongly agree	Agree	Neither agree nor disagree	Disagree	Strongly disagree
I enjoy studying marketing	X				
I enjoy attending college			X		
I think the college canteen food is over-priced				X	

Semantic differential

As noted, various adjective pairs are used as rating scales. Research has found that the scales used fall into one of three categories:

1 Evaluation – examples are good/bad, clean/dirty.
2 Potency – examples are weak/strong, large/small.
3 Activity – examples are active/passive, fast/slow.

Sometimes the scales seem rather unusual when applied to certain objects or ideas but, being able to apply similar adjectives across a range of items is one of the strengths of the technique. One example question is given below. Here attitudes to nuclear weapons are being measured.

Place a cross on one of the seven scale points for each of the adjective pairs given:

Nuclear weapons

Bad	___ ___ ___ ___ ___ ___ ___	Good
Fair	___ ___ ___ ___ ___ ___ ___	Unfair
Clean	___ ___ ___ ___ ___ ___ ___	Dirty
Worthless	___ ___ ___ ___ ___ ___ ___	Valuable
Active	___ ___ ___ ___ ___ ___ ___	Passive
Cold	___ ___ ___ ___ ___ ___ ___	Hot
Fast	___ ___ ___ ___ ___ ___ ___	Slow
Large	___ ___ ___ ___ ___ ___ ___	Small
Weak	___ ___ ___ ___ ___ ___ ___	Strong

You may wish to fill this in yourself.

One of the attractions of the semantic differential is that the results can be graphically represented by joining up the crosses on the scale points. This is called a profile. Figure 10.1 is an example of how this is done.

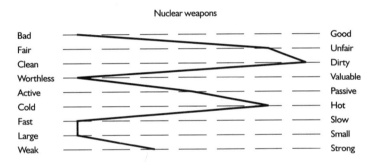

Figure 10.1
A sample profile derived from a semantic differential scale – attitudes to nuclear weapons

Using this profiling method it is easy to compare two 'objects' that have been rated on the same scales. This is particularly useful for brand comparisons. Figure 10.2 shows a profile comparing nuclear weapons with conventional weapons. With more than one line a key is required.

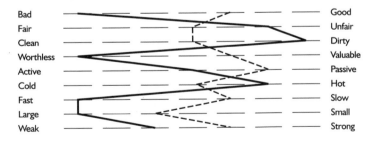

Figure 10.2
Profiles derived from a semantic differential scale: Attitudes to nuclear and conventional weapons

Rank order scale
Rank order scales can be used for rating anything from political parties to chocolate bars. Any number of items can be ranked but it is usual to keep the number below ten, and ideally below seven, to reduce the effort required to answer the question. Figures 10.3 and 10.4 are two examples of rank order questions.

Figure 10.3
Rank ordering political parties by honesty

Rank the following political parties in terms of their honesty. Place a 1 alongside the party you believe to be the most honest, a 2 alongside the party you believe to be the next honest, and so on until all the parties have been ranked.

Liberal Democrat	3
Conservatives	5
Labour	4
Green	2
Plaid Cymru	1

Figure 10.4
Rank ordering washing powders by their ability to clean white cotton clothing

Rank the following washing powders according to their ability to keep white cottons clean. Place a 1 alongside the powder you believe to be the most effective, a 2 alongside the powder you believe to be the next most effective, and so on until all the powders have been ranked.

Persil	_____
Ecover	_____
Tide	_____
Ariel	_____

Figure 10.5
National Savings Survey (excerpt)

No	Question	Answer	Code	Skip to
36	SHOW CARD 5 Can you tell me, very roughly, how much money you have saved or invested altogether in these forms of saving?	£50 or less £51–£200 £201–£500 £501–£1000 £1001–£3000 More Don't know	(69) 1 2 3 4 5 6 7	37
37	In which form of saving do you have *most* money	Only one form held Premium Bonds National savings Certificates Building Society P.O.S.B. Ordinary Account P.O.S.B. Investment Account Bank Deposit Account National Development Bonds Defence Bonds Unit Trusts Stocks and Shares Trustees S.B. Ordinary Account Trustee S.B. Special Investment A/c Local Authorities Other	(70) 1 2 3 4 5 6 7 8 9 0 X V (71) 1 2 3	38
38	SHOW CARD 6 What is this saving for? For any of these purposes (CARD) or for other purposes?	For emergencies For meeting large household bills For holidays, Christmas, etc. For security in later life To provide an income Other	(72) 1 2 3 4 5 6	39
39	Why did you choose that particular form of saving? PROBE!		(73) (74)	40
	IF ONLY ONE FORM OF SAVING, GO TO 41. IF MORE THAN ONE, ASK FOR EACH REMAINING IN ORDER OF SIZE. ASK SEPARATELY FOR ALL OTHER TYPES OF SAVING HELD	(WRITE IN TYPE) Type of saving	(10)	
40a	SHOW CARD 6 what are savings in .... for?	For emergencies For meeting large household bills For holidays, Christmas, etc. For security in later life To provide an income Others	(11) 1 2 3 4 5 6	

To conclude the discussion on questionnaires, it is only right to include one or two examples of questionnaire that are in use. Figure 10.5 is an excerpt from the National Savings Survey which appears in the third edition of the *Consumer Market Research Handbook* edited by Worcester and Downham. This is part of the interviewers sheet. Figure 10.6 is a recruitment advert for a US *Family Circle* consumer panel which appears in *Consumer Behavior* by Schiffman and Kanuk.

Join Our Consumer Panel!

Dear Reader:

We are about to form the 1994 FAMILY CIRCLE Consumer Panel. The 1993 panelists answered two very lengthy questionnaires over the year and received samples of our advertisers' products to evaluate. The 1994 panelists will be asked to do the same – to tell us about yourself, your home, family, work, likes and dislikes.

Please take a few minutes from your busy schedule to answer all the questions below. Although we cannot select everyone who responds, I can assure you that those readers who are scientifically selected will have an interesting and rewarding year. When you've answered all the questions, mail the completed questionnaire by March 1, 1994, to:

FAMILY CIRCLE
6400 Jericho Turnpike
Synosset, New York 11791

Thank you and I hope to hear from all of you!

Jackie Leo, Editor

1. Which of the following do you regularly buy? (Please "X" all that apply.)

Cold/flu/cough remedies (06) ☐1
Hand/body lotion ☐2
Home permanents ☐3
Low-calorie products ☐4
Haircolouring products ☐5
Low-fat products ☐6
Athletic shoes ☐7

Cigarettes (07) ☐1
Feminine hygiene products ☐2
Children's food products ☐3
Children's clothing ☐4
Home fix-it materials ☐5
Jeans ☐6

2. Where do you ususlly buy cosmetics and fragrances?

	Cosmetics	Fragrances
Drug store	(08) ☐1	(09) ☐1
Department store	☐2	☐2
Discount department store	☐3	☐3
Supermarket	☐4	☐4

3. Please indicate below which activities you regularly do.

Bake from scratch (10) ☐1
Cook from scratch ☐2
Watch pre-recorded videos ☐3
Exercise at club/spa ☐4

Cook using convenience foods ☐5
Read romance novels ☐6
Exercise at home ☐7
Buy collectibles ☐8

4. When will your household most likely purchase/lease your next vehicle?

0–3 months (11) ☐1
4–6 months ☐2
7–12 months ☐3

1–2 years ☐4
No definite plans ☐5

5. What will your next vehicle most likely be?

Full size (12) ☐1   Midsize ☐2   Minivan ☐3

6. Do you own a   Dog (13) ☐1   Cat ☐2

7. Do you have children?

Under 6 years (14) ☐1
6 years or older ☐2
No children under 18 ☐3

8. Are you: Female (15) ☐1   Male ☐2

9. Please "X" group that best describes your age.

18 to 24 (16) ☐1   40 to 44 ☐5   55 to 59 ☐8
25 to 29 ☐2   45 to 49 ☐6   60 to 64 ☐9
30 to 34 ☐3   50 to 54 ☐7   65 or older ☐0
35 to 39 ☐4

10. What is your current marital status?

Married (17) ☐1   Widowed ☐3
Single (never married) ☐2   Divorced/Separated ☐4

11. What is the highest level of education you have completed?

Some high school or less (18) ☐1
Graduated high school ☐2
Some college ☐3
Graduated college ☐4
Post-graduate study or more ☐5

12. Are you employed either full-time or part-time outside your home for a wage?

Employed full-time (30 hours or more per week) (19) ☐1
Part-time (less than 30 hours per week) ☐2
Not employed/Retired ☐3

13. Please "X" the box below that best describes your total estimated household income before taxes in 1994 for ALL family members. (Please include your own income as well as that of all other household members. Income from all sources such as wages, bonuses, profits, dividends, rentals, interest, etc., should be included.)

Less than $20,000 (20) ☐1 $40,000 to $45,999 ☐6
$20,000 to $24,999 ☐2 $46,000 to $49,999 ☐7
$25,000 to $29,999 ☐3 $50,000 to $74,999 ☐8
$30,000 to $34,999 ☐4 $75,000 to $99,999 ☐9
$35,000 to $39,999 ☐5 $100,000 or more ☐0

14. Have you participated in a consumer *panel* or *council* in the past 12 months?

Yes (21) ☐1   No ☐2

15. Do you currently subscribe to FAMILY CIRCLE?

Yes (22) ☐1   No ☐2

Name _____

Address _____
_____

Phone # (_____) _____

Figure 10.6 A recruitment advert for a US *Family Circle* consumer panel

Cut out and keep any questionnaires you find in magazines or newspapers. Act as 'devil's advocate' and list the flaws in each. Decide how these flaws might have affected the accuracy of the data collected.

You are working in the marketing department of a large software company. One of the directors has asked that you design a study to find out whether your existing users are 'satisfied' with your new database product which was launched six months ago.

He has expressed interest in finding out about the following:

- Usability.
- Reliability.
- Performance.
- Competitiveness.

Think about the issues that need to be considered and prepare an outline questionnaire design.

Secondary information sources

Sources of secondary data can be placed into one of six categories:

1 Government statistics.
2 Popular media.
3 Technical or specialist publications.
4 On-line and electronic databases.
5 Third party data.
6 Casual research.

Government statistics

In the UK most official statistics are provided by the Government Statistical Service (GSS). The two main organizations within the GSS, the Central Statistical Office (CSO) and the Office of Population Censuses and Surveys (OPCS), merged in 1996 to form the Office of National Statistics (ONS).

Although the GSS existed originally to serve the needs of Government, it makes much of the data it collects widely available to businesses and the general public through the ONS. This data, and the analyses provided, are extremely useful sources for marketers.

The GSS publishes the *Guide to Official Statistics* listing all government sources of statistics. It is more than 500 pages long! The main publications are listed in the pamphlets *A Brief Guide to Sources* and the *ONS Publications Catalogue*.

Those interested in statistics for Northern Ireland should go to the Northern Ireland Statistics and Research Agency (NISRA) rather than the GSS.

Government statistical publications can be broadly divided into nine categories:

1 *Digests* – that is collections of UK and regional statistics.
2 *The economy* – statistics relating to the general economic indicators, financial and companies data, public sector, production industries, housing, construction and property industries and agriculture and fisheries.
3 *Defence* – statistics covering forces personnel and defence expenditure.

4 *External trade* – statistics covering overseas trade within Europe and outside of Europe.
5 *Transport* – statistics covering transport trends, road expenditure, road traffic figures, accidents and casualties, shipping passenger and freight information, and details of air traffic.
6 *Society* – a large category covering labour market, earnings, retail prices, taxation, standard of living, population and household statistics, family spending, education, home affairs, justice and law, health and safety and social security.
7 *Environment* – statistics covering countryside, land use and planning decisions.
8 *Distribution and other services* – statistics covering retailing, wholesaling, motor trade, catering and allied, and service trades.
9 *Overseas* – statistics covering overseas aid and comparisons of European regions.

Altogether, the government regularly publishes over 400 statistical sources in these areas. Included amongst these sources are many regular surveys. Those of particular interest to marketers include:

- *Social Trends* – brings together key social and demographic series.
- *Business Monitors* – summary statistics covering a number of business sectors.
- *New Earnings Survey* – earnings of employees by industry, occupation, region etc.
- *Retail Prices Index* – measures the average change from month to month in the prices of goods and services bought by consumers.
- *National Food Survey* – food consumption and expenditure.
- *Population Trends* – includes a broad range of family statistics (births, marriage, divorce), mortality and morbidity (deaths from various illnesses), electoral statistics and other population data.
- *Family Expenditure Survey* – income and expenditure by type of household.
- *General Household Survey* – continuous sample survey of households relating to a wide range of social and socio-economic issues.

Using government statistics

The chief advantage of government statistics is that they cover the complete United Kingdom. The disadvantage is that they cannot give tailor-made answers to a specific problem. The following list indicates some example marketing uses for these statistics:

- Using the *Business Monitors* you can compare your own performance against general sales trends.
- Those involved in consumer products can gain valuable information on trends and expenditure from the *National Food Survey* and *Family Expenditure Survey*.
- For test marketing, information from the *Population Trends* and *General Household Survey* can provide regional data on consumers.
- General trends in retail prices can be obtained from monitoring the *Retail Prices Index*.

It would take a book a least the size of this to explain all of the published government statistics and their uses. Some useful further contact numbers are contained at the end of this unit.

Popular media

Much information can be gained from keeping an eye on the popular media. Much of this information is not going to be numerical, but may provide leads to previously undiscovered sources of data. The main sources are:

- *Newspapers* – The broadsheet newspapers can provide much useful information. Occasionally, these papers contain regional or national supplements which are especially useful for marketers operating in these specific areas. For financial and business information, try the *Financial Times* or *Wall Street Journal*. For social information, try *The Guardian*. For information on Europe, try *The European*. Local papers can also be a good source of regional business information.

- *Magazines* – There are popular magazines on subjects covering most business and leisure interests. If you are interested in learning about developments in yachting, for instance, you have a choice in the UK of *Practical Boat Owner*, *Yachting Monthly* and *Yachting World* plus several others. Business interests are perhaps most comprehensively covered by *The Economist*, and US titles such as *Business Week*, *Forbes* and *Fortune*.
- *Radio and television* – Current affairs, consumer programmes and news broadcasts are all potentially good sources of information.

Figure 10.7 shows some information gleaned from the *Financial Times* concerning regional house prices. This information might be extremely useful for anyone involved in the construction or allied trades and is of general use to marketers as an economic indicator. Note that the source is shown as the Halifax Building Society. It might be possible to get further information by contacting them.

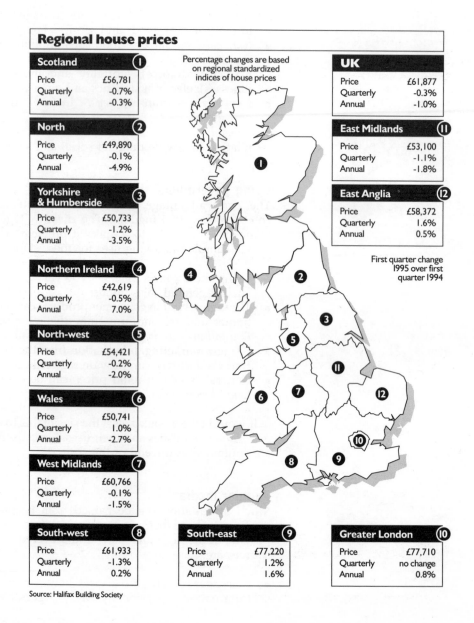

Regional house prices

Scotland ①	
Price	£56,781
Quarterly	-0.7%
Annual	-0.3%

North ②	
Price	£49,890
Quarterly	-0.1%
Annual	-4.9%

Yorkshire & Humberside ③	
Price	£50,733
Quarterly	-1.2%
Annual	-3.5%

Northern Ireland ④	
Price	£42,619
Quarterly	-0.5%
Annual	7.0%

North-west ⑤	
Price	£54,421
Quarterly	-0.2%
Annual	-2.0%

Wales ⑥	
Price	£50,741
Quarterly	1.0%
Annual	-2.7%

West Midlands ⑦	
Price	£60,766
Quarterly	-0.1%
Annual	-1.5%

South-west ⑧	
Price	£61,933
Quarterly	-1.3%
Annual	0.2%

South-east ⑨	
Price	£77,220
Quarterly	1.2%
Annual	1.6%

Greater London ⑩	
Price	£77,710
Quarterly	no change
Annual	0.8%

Percentage changes are based on regional standardized indices of house prices

UK	
Price	£61,877
Quarterly	-0.3%
Annual	-1.0%

East Midlands ⑪	
Price	£53,100
Quarterly	-1.1%
Annual	-1.8%

East Anglia ⑫	
Price	£58,372
Quarterly	1.6%
Annual	0.5%

First quarter change 1995 over first quarter 1994

Source: Halifax Building Society

Figure 10.7
Regional House Prices: Secondary data from the *Financial Times*

Activity 10.9

What popular media do you regularly read? Take a single issue, or pick one of the titles mentioned, and list all references to surveys and other data.

Technical or specialist publications

For in-depth information about a particular field, a visit to a library or bookshop can provide technical and specialist data. The main sources are:

- *Market research and academic periodicals* – such as the *Harvard Business Review*, *Journal of the Market Research Society*, *Journal of Marketing* and *Journal of Consumer Research*.
- *Trade journals* – such as *Campaign*, *Computer Weekly*, *The Grocer* and so on.
- *Specialist books* – these can often provide summarized data along with an opinion on marketing opportunities and operations. Marketing books on Europe are particularly popular at this time.

The disadvantage of such publications is that they may be out of date by the time they are printed. However, they can provide useful information on subjects where change is slow. The Market Research Society, for instance, produce a series of Country Notes with general information, and the data sources available, on specific regions of the world

Activity 10.10

Obtain a copy of one of the research journals mentioned above. What useful information does it contain? How might this information be used by marketers in certain market sectors?

Third party data services

Many market research companies sell data as a major part of the services they offer. Typically, such data comes from consumer panels. Panels exist which monitor a wide variety of purchases, opinions, and activities by gathering data from a group of representative consumers. Such data is collected either continuously or at fixed, regular intervals so that trends can be determined and/or special analyses performed at the request of the data purchaser.

Data is collected either by personal visit, postal questionnaire, telephone or, increasingly, by electronic means. One example of a particularly hi-tech consumer panel is *Superpanel* run by Taylor Nelson AGB, the largest UK consumer panel. Superpanel monitors consumer purchases in 8500 homes. Each house is equipped with a hand-held bar code reader which provides full details of items purchased and brought into the home. Details of the items purchased are retrieved over the telephone system each night making the information available to the data purchaser the next day. This rapid turn-around of data is essential for those monitoring the effects of special offers, targeted advertising, and general economic factors.

A competitor to Superpanel is *Homescan*, run by Nielsen which works in a similar fashion. Figure 10.8 is an excerpt from a typical Homescan analysis that might be provided to a data purchaser interested in the performance of their brand (in this case Brand B).

Activity 10.11

Does your organization use any third party data? If so, what is it used for?

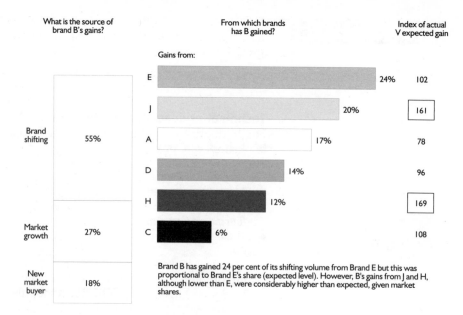

Figure 10.8
A page from an example Nielsen Homescan analysis

Casual research

Much information can be gained by casual research. As its name suggests, this is not formal research nor strictly primary data collection, but occurs 'naturally' in the course of carrying out one's work as a marketer. There are numerous sources of information available to the 'casual researcher' and some of these are listed below:

- Conferences and fairs – these will often highlight previously unknown sources of data and may provide valuable information on competitive products and services via literature or direct contact.
- *Contacts* – friends and associates in the marketing business and other business sectors of interest can provide valuable information. For instance, a solicitor friend may be able to tell you the journal that most solicitors read or a friend in the CIM may be able to tell you where to go for a particular type of data if they have done similar research.
- *Special interest groups* – most societies and associations, such as the Market Research Society, have special interest groups (or SIGs) which can provide a valuable source of information. The MRS has twelve SIG's including postal research, census, international and financial. This category includes persons that subscribe to electronic mail 'news groups' (such as those on the internet) where information is frequently exchanged amongst forum members.

Activity 10.12

How did you first find out about the marketing course you are now enlisted on? What research did you carry out and how would you classify it?

On-line and electronic databases

In recent years, more and more data has become available via computer. A collection of such data is called a database. It is said to be an electronic database if it is available on computer disk or CD-ROM. It is called an on-line database if it is available 'live', usually via a modem (a relatively cheap device which links your computer into the telephone system). Most services in this category are available on the internet.

The ONS, for instance, now provide Databank – a service selling data in an electronic format. This allows you to get the most up-to-date data available and, because this system is so flexible, the ONS are able to offer a broader range of data than is possible in print. Another such service is

StatBase ®. Most of the surveys previously mentioned are also available in a complete or summary form on the internet. See the ONS web site for more details (http://www.ons.gov.uk).

Third party suppliers are also offering data in an electronic form. For example, Dun & Bradstreet International offer a European Marketing Database with information on over three million businesses in seventeen countries.

Most of the publications that are printed are now also available on-line; newspapers, journals, magazines and so on. In this form, information about specific topics can easily be found by searching for 'keywords'. For instance, fairly sophisticated news clipping services are now available whereby you choose the topics you want to read about and an electronic 'newspaper' is automatically assembled for you containing information from around the world according to your chosen 'keywords'. Such a service is the CompuServe 'Executive News Service'. CompuServe, an internet service provider, in their monthly magazine relates the story of one US marketer who uses the service:

> Steven Zahm, who works in his San Francisco home as part of the 'virtual' corporation Prophet Market Research, doesn't own a television. Instead he reads two national newspapers and on-line business and news-wire articles to create what he calls a 'macro and micro news filter'. Without TV, he happily misses 'fluff stories' such as traffic reports and tallies of metropolitan crime. 'I get news of the macro – international crises, national policy changes, social trends' he says ' and the micro – what's the coffee of the week in the shop down the street, or which new movie is in my neighbourhood. (*CompuServe Magazine*, November 1994).

For those with access to a suitable computer, the advantages of on-line and electronic data outweigh all other secondary sources:

- On-line data is immediate and therefore up-to-date – financial prices, for instance, are often transmitted instantaneously.
- Information is global – data is available from much of the world in many languages.
- Open all hours – on-line services never close at night or for lunch.
- Data can be used directly – many statistical and spreadsheet computer packages are capable of loading on-line and electronic data for further analysis or presentation.
- Searching on-line and electronic data is quick and easy – within a matter of seconds it is possible to search the equivalent of more than 1000 conventional publications. This is sometimes cited as a disadvantage. A search on an ambiguous keyword, 'culture' for instance, may return articles covering everything from 'bacterial culture' to the 1980s pop group 'Culture Club'.
- Convenience – most places of work now have a computer capable of reading electronic data or obtaining data on-line. With such a facility, trips to the library and other data suppliers are greatly reduced saving time and resources.

Activity 10.13

Most libraries now have some form of electronic database – usually for finding books or technical papers on certain subjects. Next time you visit a library, or if you are lucky enough to have access to an on-line system, try a search on the database using the keyword 'marketing'.

Does this provide you with useful information? Is there any information which is found that is irrelevant?

Competitive market intelligence

This is the general name given to data collected about your competitors. The information can be obtained in any one of the ways described above. Additional sources can include:

- *Competitive benchmarking* – where your product or service is compared with that of your competitors.
- *Company accounts* – these are lodged annually in Companies House in London and can provide information on the financial performance of your rivals.
- *Patent applications* – these can provide a useful source of information about corporate technology developments.
- *Job advertisements* – these can provide useful information on the skills required by a competitor organization and their growth rate. However, it is not unknown for fake ads to be placed to allay fears about a struggling company!

It is most important to keep a 'watching brief' on the activities of your competitors so that you can spot opportunities, learn from their mistakes and not get caught out by new developments in the market place.

Activity 10.14

What market intelligence does your company have about its competitors? Do you think it has enough information? How might you find out more?

Limitations of secondary data
There are a number of general points to be aware of when using secondary data:

- *Age of the data* – some secondary data is offered for general sale only when it is of no more use to the leaders in the field. Historical data can be of use but only for certain types of research.
- *Survey method used* – not all surveys are well designed or administered. You should be aware of the survey details (for instance number of respondees, geographical sampling and so on) so that you can be confident that the data is reliable and representative for your purposes.
- *Original purpose of data* – the data may well have been collected by an organization with a particular viewpoint which may have led to bias in the collection method used. For example, surveys by the pro-smoking lobby always seem to find no link between smoking and disease!

Despite these limitations, secondary research is still a vital and valuable first step in any research activity. In many cases, it may be all the research that is needed.

Extending Activity 10.3

Cut out and keep any graphs or data tables you find in magazines or newspapers. Look at the 'source' quoted for the data. Make a note of the type of data presented (social, financial, political and so on) and relate this to the source. Is the source private or government? Are the source specialists in this sort of data gathering, or not? If you wanted to find out details about the data not contained in the article concerned, how would you contact the source?

Ethical, legal and procedural issues concerned with the acquisition, manipulation, interpretation and application of customer-dynamic evidence

Ethical responsibilities of interviewers
The Market Research Society publishes a code of conduct which specifically addresses the responsibilities of those carrying out interviews. In summary interviewers shall:

- Be honest and not mislead the interviewee in order to procure information.
- Not use the information collected for any other purpose without the consent of the interviewee.
- Take steps to ensure that interviewees are not embarrassed or adversely affected as a direct result of an interview.
- Carry an identity card or badge including a photograph, name and organization.
- Send a leaflet, card or letter to the interviewee thanking them for taking part in the interview.
- In the case of telephone surveys, at the end of the interview the name of the survey organization a name and contact number should be given.
- Provide a means by which the interviewee may verify that the survey is genuine without incurring any cost.
- Allow an interviewee to withdraw from a survey. Where appropriate, the research organization shall confirm that their data has been destroyed.
- Make no calls in person or by telephone before 9am weekdays, 10am Sundays, or after 9pm on any other day unless an appointment has been made. Those carrying out research overseas should respect the equivalent customs of the host country.
- Only interview children under the age of fourteen with the permission of their parents, guardian, or other person responsible for them (i.e. teacher). The responsible person shall be informed of the general content of the interview before the interview itself takes place.

The various types of research, such as mystery shopping, raise their own ethical issues. It is advised by the MRS, for example, that employees should be notified in advance that their employer intends to undertake mystery shopping. Guidelines also state that the results of mystery shopping research cannot be used for disciplinary purposes.

Data protection and confidentiality – legal issues
Principles of data confidentiality and protection are embodied in a new act of particular relevance to market researchers – the *Data Protection Act 1998*. The following details are extracted from a factsheet which has been prepared by BSI/DISC in conjunction with the Office of the Data Protection Registrar (ODPR).

The new act will implement the EU Data Protection Directive, which has been in effect in the UK from 24 October 1998, and will lay down detailed conditions for the processing of personal data and sensitive personal data, strengthen the rights of the individual, extend data protection to certain manual records and set new rules for the transfer of data outside the EU.

The new act applies to anyone holding data about living individuals on computer or on some manual records. Those holding such personal data (i.e. data controllers) must comply with the eight data protection principles, and, with some exceptions, register with the Data Protection Commissioner (formerly the Registrar).

The new Act contains eight enforceable data protection principles. As previously, personal data must be processed fairly and lawfully. There are important new conditions that must be satisfied for the processing of personal data. Data can only be processed for example with consent or where it is necessary in certain specified circumstances.

- There are stricter conditions for the processing of sensitive data.
- As previously data must be relevant, adequate and not excessive, accurate and up to date and kept for no longer than is necessary. These principles will, however, also apply to manual records.
- The security principle is strengthened with a specific requirement that data controllers have a formal contract with third party processors.
- The new principle restricts exports of data unless an adequate level of protection can be guaranteed.
- The right of subject access to your own personal data has been retained and expanded.

- Explicit rights to object to processing, for example, for the purpose of direct marketing.
- The right not to be subject to purely automated decisions.
- Increased rights to seek compensation for breaches of the act.

Further information on the *Data Protection Act 1998* can be found on the Registrar's web site http://www.open.gov.uk/dpr/dprhome.htm

Principles of data presentation – the use and abuse of statistics

Bias in the presentation of data

Data which is presented in a misleading fashion is said to be biased. Bias can be introduced unintentionally or, in certain cases, on purpose.

The Market Research Society's Code of Conduct states that:

> A member shall not knowingly communicate conclusions from a given research project or service that are inconsistent with, or not warranted by, the data (paragraph B.3).

There are four main ways in which bias can occur:

1 Omission of information.
2 Manipulation of graph axes.
3 Failure to present comparative data.
4 Using an inappropriate presentation method.

Omission of information

Omitting certain important information from a graph is not only bad practice but can mislead your audience. Three examples are given below:

1 *Number of respondees* – Your audience should be told both the number of respondees to a survey and the proportion of those questioned whom responded. Different importance would be attached to a survey where only 20 people where questioned, and one where 2000 people were surveyed. Similarly, if a postal survey of 2000 attracted only 20 replies, we might suspect that the responses represented the opinions of some special interest group only.
2 *Who the respondees are* – Whether your respondees are potential buyers of your product, potential users, randomly selected members of the public, or some other sub-set of the population, may change the interpretation of the results. For instance, comments on price are more relevant if they originate from potential buyers. Other respondees may have no idea of the market value of a particular product.
3 *Scale units* – Your audience can be misled by the omission, or incomplete labelling of, the units used in your graph. For example the vertical axis on a sales graph should be clearly labelled with the units used. It may be that this axis represents some monetary value or unit sales. If monetary, it should be clear whether the figures given represent turnover, profit, or some other financial indicator.

Manipulating graph axes

Sometimes called 'stretching the truth', expanding or contracting the scales on chart axes can make small changes in values seem larger, or smaller, respectively. For example, the following three sales graphs all show the same data, the sales of 'Possum' cat food during the four quarters of 1994. Which do you think looks most impressive?

All the graphs are technically correct but give very different impressions of 'Possum' sales. To avoid misleading your audience, always present your data in a consistent fashion. For example, in the above example, a scale should be used which allows the data from a number of years to be plotted on the same chart. Thus, one could not be accused of exaggerating this year's sales. Also the zero point on the vertical (*Y*) scale should be labelled even if part of the vertical scale is then omitted, as long as this is clearly shown. In such an example, it may be more appropriate not to show absolute sales figures but give an indication of the percentage increase in sales during 1994 or moving averages.

Figure 10.9
Three line graphs, showing sales of 'Possum' cat food, which demonstrate how expanding or contracting scales can mislead

Failure to provide comparative data

Often data can only be accurately presented when a comparison is made with some 'base line' or other comparative data. This may require one, or more, sets of data to be displayed on the chart or the inclusion of a caption.

Suppose we wish to represent the number of shoppers using the 'Shop-Til-You-Drop' (STUD) chain of supermarkets. We would probably use a line graph as shown in Figure 10.10

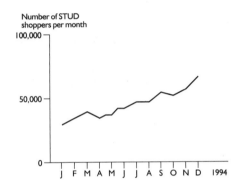

Figure 10.10
Number of STUD shoppers per month during 1994

On the face of it, this increase looks promising. However if, over the same period, the number of shoppers using supermarkets had risen greatly, the increase shown on the graph might actually represent a decrease in market share. Of course, the reverse is also possible. If there had been a general decline in the number of shoppers using supermarkets, the figures shown would indicate that STUD was doing very well indeed 'bucking the trend'. To assist in the interpretation of this data, and to avoid being misled, it is therefore best to provide some comparative data, perhaps the performance of the competition or an indication of the general market trend.

Using an inappropriate presentation method

Using an inappropriate method of presentation can, under certain circumstances, mislead your audience. Suppose a survey is conducted to find out the most acceptable cost for annual tickets to a new leisure centre. Responses fall into a number of categories, the results could be shown with either a pie chart or bar chart:

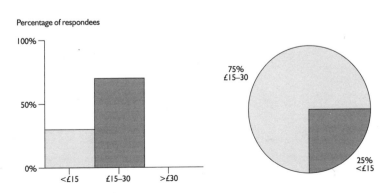

Figure 10.11
Bar chart and pie chart showing responses to survey on leisure ticket cost

The pie chart is, in a sense, misleading because it does not show the response categories where no one responded (in this case none of the respondees thought that more than £30 was an acceptable price). This information is lost in the pie chart presentation but appears, or should do, in a bar chart.

Summary

In this unit you have learned:

- About the different types of research.
- How to go about conducting secondary research.
- How to choose the primary research technique most suited to your research goals.
- The best way to construct a survey tool.
- To be aware and take account of the possible ethical and legal problems associated with investigative research.

Answers

Question 10.1
With limited time, a group discussion is likely to be the most productive technique. It would be possible to gather information from approximately 20 people per day (two groups of 10) so it would take approximately one week to survey 100 people. However, analysis time is likely to take at least another week (depending on the information you require).

Depth interviews will provide more information but take approximately twice as long. Projective techniques may be an option where only a limited amount of information is required allowing use of one of the techniques described.

Question 10.2
Postal surveys are generally lower cost than telephone surveys and the respondee can be sent literature (such as photographs, fabric swatches, perfume samples) which could not be provided over the telephone. Postal surveys also have better coverage than telephone survey (not all people have a telephone), interviewer bias is eliminated, and respondees can complete the survey form at their leisure.

CAI allows more personal questions to be asked than with a face-to-face interview. Responses are also quicker to analyse and interviewer bias is eliminated.

Question 10.3
They broke Rule 14 – by failing to first introduce themselves and the purpose of the survey.

Operational aspects of achieving a customer focus

Objectives

To enable students to understand the benefits to building a customer focus.

❑ To understand the operational aspects of achieving a customer focus.

❑ To explore aspects of outsourcing and partnering.

Study Guide

The benefits of achieving a customer focus are made clear and the operational organizational aspects of achieving a customer focus are considered. First of all, organizations have to find out if, and where, they have a problem. They need then to understand the value of customers and their profitability. Once this has been established organizations need to lock their customers into the business. Once existing customers are locked into the business, the organization can develop ideas about increasing income by increasing sales and improving profit. The use of technology, customization and one-to-one marketing, outsourcing and customer/supplier partnership agreements are explored as a method of decreasing costs and improving customer service.

Key ingredients to achieving a customer focus

The benefits to building a customer focus are clear:

1 *Customer loyalty and retention* Customer loyalty enables the customer and the organization to get to know each other better. This means that the organization is able to match its offer more closely to customer needs and customers are likely to feel greater satisfaction.
2 *Customer satisfaction* Customer satisfaction in turn makes people working in the organization feel as if they are doing a great job and this in turn makes them more motivated to provide better service.
3 *Customer service* Customer service is improved because work becomes a good place to be. Employee stress decreases, absenteeism drops, productivity increases, profits go up, shareholders are happy and don't withdraw their money and the organization contributes more tax and the economy benefits.
4 *Stability* The organization is therefore in a more stable position. We all benefit: society, the economy and you.

The outcome will be:

- Existing customers:
  - Increased loyalty.
  - Increased retention.
  - Lower rates of loss.
  - And, in some cases, higher share of customer spend.
  - Lower levels of complaints.
  - Greater satisfaction in the way complaints are handled.
  - More spontaneous referrals from people who have heard about you.
  - More referrals from customers who when asked, are willing to refer the organization to other people they know.
- New customers:
  - Improved rate of conversion.
- Old/lapsed customers:
  - The improvement in reputation and the return of customers who have drifted away.

The functional/organizational aspects of customer focus

In order to harness the idea of customer focus organizations need to consider the 'how' of getting it done. The following steps need to be considered (adapted from Charles Wilson, *Profitable Customers*, Institute of Directors):

1 Find out if and where you have a problem.
2 Make sure you understand the value of customers and their profitability.
3 Communicate with customers and create relationships where possible.
4 Ensure first class service is provided.
5 Look at increasing income and improving profit.
6 Re-evaluate your distribution channels.
7 Help your customers to save money.
8 Investigate the use of technology.
9 Ascertain if customization and one-to-one marketing is for you.
10 Investigate outsourcing and partnering.

Find out if and where you have a problem

Analysis

Before looking at some of the approaches to solving the problem of quality service, first look at analysing where breakdown in quality can occur. Service delivery must be managed as a whole system, not a fragmented uncoordinated series of activities. Organizations like McDonalds, Disney and IBM pay attention to the design and management of the delivery system and have installed integrated processes and procedures to ensure consistency. However, a balance must be made between maintaining standards, knowledge and skills and allowing for individual expression. This balance will be determined by the organization and its culture and by the context in which it operates.

External analysis

1 *Ask customers* If you are starting from scratch, carry out some market research:

   (a) Old customers – those who have left;
   (b) Existing customers;
   (c) Potential new customers;
   (d) Competitors' customers.

   If you are dealing with an organization you will need to ask people in the decision-making unit or take another slice of the organization consisting of people who are using the service or interact with it in some way.

If potential new customers are dealing with the competition find out from them what they get and what they like and dislike. Find out from old customers why they have left. Market research has been discussed in detail in the previous units. Use your research to find new ways of segmenting your market.

2   *Research other important stakeholders and relationships.*

Internal analysis
Methods of analysis and looking at overall structure have been covered in Unit 3.

1   *Spot problems before they happen* Ensuring that you get customer feedback is one thing, but you also need to ensure that sales and profit are constantly tracked as well. This means that you need a financial system that gives this information. Once you know there is a problem it will be possible to find out whether any decrease in business is due to an internal problem and is controllable or an external problem and therefore uncontrollable. For example, a customer of a customer going out of business.
2   *Make it easy to complain* Most customers hate complaining, they just move their business. If there is a complaint make sure you move quickly. The complaints process needs to be fast, friendly and work with a minimum of administration. Staff should be encouraged to be supportive and to act in a responsive way. Immediate compensation is effective.

Encourage your customers to help you provide a better service
Ted Johns, *Perfect Customer Care* (Arrow Business Books, 1995) provides the following advice:

1   Make it easy to complain: use complaint forms and 0800 (free) telephone numbers. Try video talk back and suggestion schemes.
2   Ask for complaints: seek out customers at random and ask them for their views.
3   Pretend to be a customer.
4   Listen to the complaints without becoming defensive: ask questions, ask for suggestions (what can we do to put it right?), ask what you should have done, ask what the customer expected in the light of the behaviour of other organizations.
5   Act quickly and with goodwill to solve the problem.
6   Replace defective products immediately or repeat the service.
7   Take positive steps to prevent a re-occurrence – don't assume that the first complaint is simply a one-off.
8   Use some imagination in finding ways to secure feedback. If you're in the personnel function you could ring people who come for interview (and who have been rejected) to ask them how they were treated and if they have any suggestions about how their processing could have been improved.
9   Award positive recognition for customer feedback: small prizes for completed questionnaires drawn out of a hat.

You may need to check:

1   Product service failure or performance.
2   Method and efficiency of delivery.
3   Delivery time and frequency.
4   Intensity and effectiveness of promotion.
5   Quality of the sales force and their methods of selling.
6   The after-sales service.
7   The skills and experience of the staff employed.
8   The technology employed.
9   Procedures governing the action of staff.
10   Speed and value of order processing.
11   Mechanisms for dealing with complaints.
12   Employee satisfaction.

Business to business marketing

If you are part of a supply chain, look for weaknesses in the linkages and think about how you can overcome them. Move from being an available supplier to becoming an approved supplier, to a preferred supplier, to a partner agreement. Think about IT links, or look at strengthening the relationship in other ways (see Partnerships).

Think about the future

Close contact with your customers will enable you to understand their vision. This information will then make it possible for you to match your supplies with their needs. If a new product is being developed try and work alongside your customers. Get your R&D people involved with customers – get them close to them so they can listen to real problems experienced by real people.

Make sure you understand the value of customers and their profitability

It is a fundamental rule that if you do not know how much your customers are worth to you, you will not be able to understand how to serve them.

Some organizations take a short-term view of a customer's value, per transaction, others take a longer view. If an activity costing is carried out it will be clear that although customers appear to make a profit in the short term they may not once all the costs are allocated directly to them.

There are four ways to approach calculating the value of a customer:

1 *Acquisition cost* This is the amount that needs to be spent to acquire the customer in the first place. It would include all promotion and sales costs.
2 *Revenue stream* This is the amount of money the customer pays you for the goods/service that have been purchased.
3 *Cost stream* These would include all the costs incurred to provide the goods and services to the customer.
4 *Time* Time is the length of the relationship between a customer and the organization.

Customer value can then be calculated once an estimate of the revenue and cost stream have been calculated. The estimate can then be used to discount back to the present to get a net present value (NPV) estimate of expected profit during the time the customer is with the organization – this is called lifetime customer value.

In order to calculate lifetime value you will need to think about the following:

1 Decide who your customers are.
2 Estimate how you expect them to purchase (frequency, volume spend) over the period of time.
3 Estimate how much your costs will be to retain them.

From this analysis you will be able to work out a marketing strategy that will enable you to target your most profitable customers. This method allows you to create a value based segmentation system. The right level of customer service can then be given to customers who represent a higher lifetime value.

Note: Net present value calculations are covered in the module Management Information for Marketing Decisions.

Alan Mitchell points out, *Marketing Business*, May 1999, that like most great ideas implementing life-time customer value is turning out to be more difficult than enthusiasts first predicted. Many companies still can't identify individual customers let alone individual revenue streams. Loyalty schemes have proved invaluable, but they only scratch the surface. Projecting how current revenues will pan out over a 'lifetime' involves a lot of guesswork, albeit data-driven, educated guesswork.

Table 11.1

Calculation per customer/trade channel	Comment
Annual sales	Sales for the last financial year (including after sales income)
Gross income	(Net sales after discounts – cost of product + overheads but excluding costs to interface)
–	
Costs to interface	Marketing, selling, distribution, service, administration, stock holding, customization, promotions etc. (allocated by customer)
=	
Net customer profitability (NCP)	Gross income – costs to interface
×	
Expected length of relationship	How long will the customer remain loyal?
=	
DCP	£NCP × expected length of relationship (adjusted for internal cost of capital)

Source: Charles Wilson (1996), *Calculating discounted customer profitability*, Institute of Directors/Kogan

Communicate with customers and create relationships where possible

Planning

Before embarking on creating your communication plan you will need to do the following.

Define your relationship target/network

In business to business marketing protect your business with multiple contacts. Develop relationships with your customers by ensuring there are multiple personal links. Look at the interface between the two organizations as a network of exchanges so that personal contacts run between the organizations at many different levels. Think of it as networking into a spider's web. This will make it more difficult for front-line staff to take a customer with them if they leave the organization.

Multiple linkages make relationships more difficult to manage as all the communication linkages will have to be monitored This needs to be thought through on an organizational level to ensure your communications are integrated and ensure that these linkages are maintained and the messages are consistent.

Analyse and define your relationships and networks so that you know who they are and the type of relationship you have with them. Refer to Gummesson's work *Total Relationship Marketing* to help you match them with the context in which the organization is working. A summary of the different types of relationships is shown in Unit 8.

Create a database

It is much easier if all marketing information is on one database. Examples are:

- Trends, opportunities, strategic decisions such as calculating the value of customers, developing profiles and programmes for customer segments and analysing purchasing patterns can all be more easily done.

- Date triggered mailings can be made, responses to various promotions can be coded and respondents identified. Customer awareness can be increased by advising customers of special events or offers, keeping people up to date, rewarding customer loyalty and increasing customer loyalty.
- Customers can be monitored and followed up on an ongoing basis. Special customers can be highlighted in terms of their annual spend and special deals could be offered to them on the basis of their sales history by being able to match your offer with their needs more closely, encourage cross selling.
- Reports can be tailored and analysed on hard facts: such as number of responses, profit, key ratios, customer retention and so on.

Data can be obtained from internal sources:

- Contact name and address and postcode.
- Frequency – how often do they buy from you?
- Recency – when did they last buy from you?
- Amount – how much did they buy from you?
- Category – what type of product or service did they buy?
- Promotion history – when did you promote to that customer?
- Response history – what was the response?

This information is needed to calculate the value of the various customer segments. Once these are classified they can be ranked and contact strategies devised. Tactical activities such as upgrading customers and cross-selling can also be looked at. The customer database is a vital strategic tool which enables organizations to generate high levels of customer retention by using an individually tailored approach.

The organization could also try and increase its database by organizing events in which potential customers provide their names and addresses.

Set objectives
Set your objectives. These will be quantitative and qualitative. Quantitative related to specific measures like the marketing objectives and communication objectives and relationship objectives, and qualitative related to how you want people to think, feel, experience and do with your offer. Objectives will change depending on various factors. For example, customers could be segmented in different ways and objectives will need to be related to market segments.

- Whether they are past, new, existing, potential.
- Where they are in the purchasing cycle before, during, after.
- Where they are on the loyalty ladder.
- Their purchasing history.
- Their total sales, profitability.
- Their geo-demographics, demographics, motivational and psychographic profile.

Information and response
You will need to think through the type of information you want back from them. They may need certain inducements to reply. Confidentiality and security will need to be thought about. Response handling will affect the whole organization.

Method
The suitability of method will depend on the relationship/network targets, the objective and the scale of the response required.

Time
Target market, objectives, information and response, and method will need to be thought through in the context of time – short, medium and long term.

Organizational aspects

The communication will need to be placed within the context of the organization as the response aspect will have an impact on the processes, systems and procedures.

Corporate image

A corporate image doesn't simply refer to the design of a company's letterhead. In reality a corporate image goes much deeper and covers the way a business relates to its whole internal and external social and cultural context. You may need to revise your corporate image so that it reflects your new values.

A corporate image adds value. It is not only brands that customers create a relationship with, but the organization itself. As much as brands become 'in the mind' so do organizations – both for the people working within them and their customers.

Building relationships with technology

David Miller of Miller, Bainbridge and Partners Ltd says that in what might otherwise be considered a delightful coincidence, the growth of the customer who demands to be listened to has gone hand in hand with the growth in technology, which allows brands to listen, understand and respond to customers.

In fact, the move from mass marketing to mass customization is nowhere more evident nowadays than in the new communication channels which technology is opening. Integrating database, call centre and, increasingly, web-site technology means that as marketers, we are able to treat our customers as individuals – albeit, on a mass scale. In the past, we used technology just to talk at people en masse – television being the prime medium. Now we can use technology to listen to our customers – understand what they are saying – and respond accordingly.

So suddenly, brands that had only a mouth, and therefore could only talk, have now been given a set of ears, so now they can listen. We now have the ability to move from talking at customers, to talking with customers.

If brands at their best are commercial friends, then they now can begin properly to behave as friends. They can now listen, understand, as well as talk.

Brands can now begin to come to life in a real way, which the customer can experience – not just as a thirty-second commercial on TV. Impersonal selling is being replaced by personal relationship marketing.

Difficult to do, impossible to copy

Unlike conventional marketing programmes – based for example, on mass media advertising and direct mail – customer relationship marketing programmes are by definition, relatively difficult to execute. They are difficult because you have to have the database, call centre infrastructure and other channels flawlessly integrated before you can even think about beginning to talk to the customer. Then you must add creativity, determine what channels to use and when, and gain permission from the customer to initiate this relationship. You are creating your own private customer communication channels – trying to deliver an outstanding brand experience for each individual customer. Delivering excellence one on one, using a blend of information technology and brand creativity, is not for the faint-hearted – because it's more difficult to achieve, and impossible totally to control. But CRM does not have the great advantage of being almost impossible to copy. Everyone can witness Virgin's latest improvements in customer service or BA's latest brand positioning on TV and choose to fight them if they can. But, a CRM programme is essentially a private affair. Only your customers will know what you do to keep them delighted with your brand – and highly likely to buy from you again.

Understanding and dialogue – the new marketing symbiosis

If we're going to treat customers as special, we have to understand them. If we don't understand them, we can't treat them as individuals. And if we can't personalize our communication with them, then we aren't treating them as special.

The new marketing symbiosis depends on two principal factors – customer understanding and customer dialogue. These two elements are totally inter-dependent. Understanding derives from contact. Better understanding stimulates higher quality, more relevant contact. If both understanding and dialogue progress in tandem, then we have the chance of creating a real virtuous circle.

Customer understanding is facilitated by a continuously updated marketing database – an 'intelligent' database, which records all customer contact, requests and preferences. Importantly both behavioural (what they do) and attitudinal (why they do it) information is collected on customers.

Customer dialogue derives from opening up new channels of communication – not just brand to customer but between customer and brand. If the overall objective of CRM is maximizing customer lifetime value, then the means is by creating a customer-defined, customer-relevant, and customer-valuable dialogue.

Creating conversation

To create real opportunities for conversation or dialogue between customers and the brand, we need to create new and hybrid communication channels – combining the skills of the publisher with those of the adman and the direct marketer. We need to mix brand editorial with offers, incentives and services. And we need to deliver all this in a personalized form.

If 'dialogue' is the goal then there are two other requirements of printed communications – that they should be regular, and that they should give the customer reasons to contact the brand.

We want customers to contact us because we want to be of service, we want their goodwill, and as an ultimate goal, we want to maximise our share of their wallet. The best and most human form of contact is face to face – the practical way of delivering human contact is through the human voice – i.e. a dedicated brand call centre.

The telecentre is key – there is in our book no substitute for the human voice of the brand. People can make you feel special and valued in a way that no piece of direct mail, no television ad or web site ever can.

With a customer file – constantly updated – on the screen in front of the call centre operator there is the capacity to greet the customer personally, fulfil requests personally, offer services which are relevant to the customer in particular, and in the process, gather some new personal data to add to the file.

The customer will come to learn that in volunteering information, they are entering into a value pact with the brand – where information is exchanged for relevant rewards. While recognizing the importance of the call centre we must also be true to CRM concepts and allow customers to choose the channels they want to use. Some customers dislike the telephone and may want to create this dialogue through the internet, mail or even face to face, if possible.

Making the transition

The organization could investigate whether a web site would increase business opportunities. They should bear in mind that at the moment a transition is being made from the use of a basic information bulletin board on the web to value added business applications.

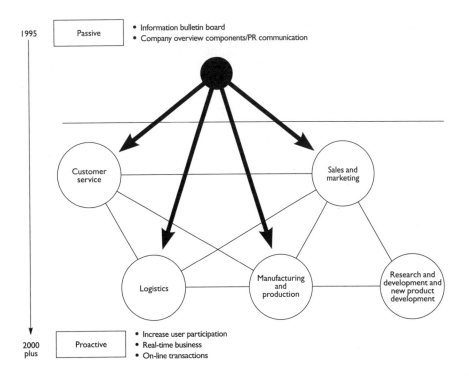

Figure 11.1
Source: Pira International,
http:www.pira.co.uk

Sales promotion

Some promotions, such as price reductions, do not reinforce the belief that the brand is worth paying for and draw particular attention to price as a choice determinant.

Continuous, indiscriminate and badly-executed price cutting is clearly dangerous. However, to ignore the role of normal price and short-term price reduction as a key weapon in the marketer's armoury is equally dangerous at a time when more and more purchasing decisions are being made at the point of sale.

1   With some brands price reductions can *devalue* the brand so as to cheapen its character.
2   A difference must be made between strategic long-term decisions to cut the price in order to undercut the competition (for example, if one wanted to establish a reputation for low prices, or promoting the fact that your store offered the best price in town), and short-term tactical pricing to encourage new buyers or persuade lapsed buyers to return to you.

The role of promotion is to encourage purchase by temporarily improving the value of the brand. Added-value promotions can enhance people's perceptions of the brand, whereas price reductions may reduce it.

Loyalty programmes

Many organizations have developed loyalty programmes. Some of these like the loyalty cards supermarkets use have been said to erode margins and are the equivalent of the old green shield stamps. Other loyalty programmes have a high perceived value but a low actual cost.

When a loyalty programme is chosen make sure it has the following features:

- It bears some relationship to the product/service and customers find it relevant.
- That customers get some choice.
- That the customer finds it easy to use.
- That customers are told what to expect and the results are monitored and the cost and profitability are measured.
- That you choose one that competitors will find hard to copy.

Public relations

Good business is based on achieving good relationships within the environment it operates. Good relationships alter the perceived values. Public relations is a marketing technique which is used to add value not only to a brand but also to the organization. Public relations influences opinion in such a way that people who have a stake in the business are happy to support it – the relationship portfolio (see Gummeson).

Ongoing customer mailings

These could cover the following:

- Customer service updates and factsheets.
- Newsletters.
- Christmas, birthday cards and so on.

Customer service manual

This document and manual outlines the customer service goals. It also goes through the business procedures so that each party knows what they are getting. Documents and facts that could be included are:

- Service objectives.
- Lead times.
- Delivery notes.
- Invoices.
- The names and telephone numbers of key people.
- Hot line services.
- Order status enquiry systems.

Workshops and focus groups

Problem solving workshops can be held on a regular basis to iron out any problems and improve the quality of the services being provided. Role swapping can also be used as a learning exercise.

User groups

User groups or customer groups are groups of people who come together to help each other resolve problems. They communicate via the internet and meet at conferences. They also provide information for new product development and product modifications. They have mostly been used in business-to-business selling, for example in the computer industry but the idea is moving into consumer markets where a club feel can be created. For example, the General Motor launch of Saturn cars, owners were encouraged to come along to barbecues and sports events. The Harley Davidson club is another example.

Football cards and stickers are an old fashioned application of the same principle, children who collected them would join together to swap them.

Other methods of achieving feedback are covered in the section on market research

Ensure first class service is provided (process and people)

Customer service is a serious business. The previous units have given you an idea of the complexity of creating an organization that is focused on customer service. Remember that you will need to keep it going by retraining, giving constant customer feedback, constantly improving procedures, policies and systems, maintaining contact with outside bodies so that you can see what is going on, inviting professional bodies in, benchmarking and keeping the internal marketing going. Recognize your front-line staff as professionals in their own right. They are the ambassadors, the public face of their organization. More often it is the attitude, approach and determination of front-line staff that determines whether an organization will succeed or fail. Encourage them to work towards an Institute of Customer Service award. They do not have an easy job – provide them with training and support and above all respect. Read the Senior Examiner's book – Ted Johns, *Perfect Customer Care*, Arrow Books.

Increase sales income

Market penetration

Sell more to existing customers.
If it is possible you will need to find out how much business they do with other suppliers. Once you have done this you will need to find out what is standing in the way of your acquiring it.

Find more customers in the same market segment
Once you know who your customers are likely to be you will be able to put together a communication plan that enables you to attract more of the same type of person.

Get customers from the competition
If you know what your competitors are providing then you will be able to create an offer that meets the customer needs of the market segment more closely. Suitable tactical competitive measures will then need to be taken.

Market development

New market segments
Marketers should be constantly looking out for new ways to segment the market. This requires a constant updating and understanding of new needs so new people can be brought in. The concept of the product life cycle and the adoption and diffusion curve should give you some perspective on this. New people are constantly being brought into the market – they may have different needs from the customers who first brought from you. You need to keep your market segmentation up to date.

New geographic areas
Think about marketing your product or service in a new geographical area in the same market or overseas.

New distribution channels
The internet offers one new way for organizations to extend.

New product/service modifications for existing customers
Even if you do have a sound relationship with your existing customers you should constantly be monitoring any shifts in their value chain which would entail realigning yours. Looking for improved ways to deliver your offer, perhaps redeveloping it or modifying it in some way is an ongoing process. New product development offers the opportunity to work in tandem with your customers.

Diversification
Diversification can be looked at in three ways – horizontal, backward and forward integration. Joint venture, merger, acquisition and franchising fall into this section.

Improve profits
Income can also be increased by restructuring pricing and terms, by reducing costs and by improving negotiations. Pricing and negotiation are covered in other parts of the Advanced Certificate. A brief summary on pricing is given here.

Pricing
Price is the chief source of revenue for the organization. However, apart from being a simple component of the marketing mix and source of profit, price is a communications channel to the customer in its own right. Correct use of price communicates value derived, and product quality to the customer. It needs to be supported by other elements of the marketing mix.

The future of pricing in the customer relationship
As the development of marketing channels shape the transaction options of the future, many pricing options will be removed. Catalogue selling

over the internet will enable pricing structures to be reviewed and novel pricing methods to cope with this transparency will be developed. Tradable services (those that do not need to be delivered in the customer's premises) and international pricing may lead to some form of bartering or counter-trade system of pricing (see for example, Tofler). Customizing requirements to segments of one, or tailoring products and services for individual customers throughout a customer relationship, will offer different challenges to the price setting structures. What will remain however, is the basic premise that price is a reflection of the value of continually satisfying customers needs and not a function of the delivery cost set in absence of market expectations. (Contributed by Graham Cooper, FCIM, marketer at ICL and lecturer at Oxford College of Marketing.)

The Ansoff growth matrix in Figure 11.2 is a useful model to use for clarifying ideas.

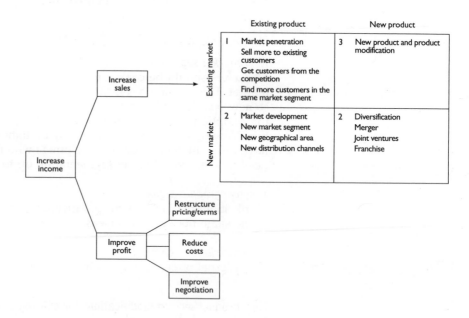

Figure 11.2

Re-evaluate your distribution channels (place)
Re-evaluate your distribution channels to ensure your customers are receiving superior service.

1 Reassess your customers' requirements along your distribution chain.
2 Rethink which type of intermediaries are possible, including direct sale. For example, have you investigated e-commerce?
3 Analyse your costs and establish the following:
   (a) Is it possible to satisfy all your customers' requirements?;
   (b) What type of supplier support will be required to do this?;
   (c) What will the costs be for supporting each alternative channel system?
4 Specify your constraints and outline your objectives and look at your channel system with these in mind. Ensure you think long term.
5 Compare your ideal system, the one operated by your customers, to the feasible one specified by your constraints and objectives.
6 Evaluate the gaps between the existing and feasible systems and consider the impact on your customers and the business.
7 Review all your assumptions and talk to other experts.

Help your customers to save money
Helping your customers to save money does not mean you must cut your price but you can look at ways in which the customer could cut the cost of acquiring a product, possessing and/or using a product/service. Table 11.2 illustrates the routes to reduce total costs for customers.

Table 11.2 Routes to reduce total costs for customer

Customer cost area	Cost/risk	Opportunity for a supplier to help the customer make savings
Acquisition	Cost of goods	Reduce customer wastage/increase product longevity
	Buying cost	Minimize paperwork/buying administration costs
Possession	Storage/obsolescence	Cut customer inventory
	Interest	Offer favourable interest charges
	Handling	Easy to store and handle
Usage	Direct	Simplest, quickest, cheapest to use
	Indirect production costs	Minimal training, back up, administration, etc.
Total		Lowest total cost for customer

Source: Wilson, C. (1996) *Profitable Customers*, Institute of Directors (based on a framework developed by Frank Cespedes in *Concurrent Marketing*, 1995)

Make sure you investigate the use of technology

Recent advances in IT include increasingly powerful microcomputers, sophisticated software packages based on Windows, the information superhighway on the internet, powerful organizational tools (databases/fax/mobile telephones), newly IT educated 'knowledge workers' and new organizational concepts (the remote office and voice responsive computers).

Ascertain if customization and one-to-one marketing are for you

To answer the question of whether to customize or not to customize the Foundation for Manufacturing and Industry, Department of Trade and Industry, IBM Consulting Group 1997 asked organizations to consider their business from two points of view – production and the customer.

Is your production:

- Increasing in range?
- Experiencing both core and cosmetic changes?
- Reducing customer order sizes?
- More specials than standard?
- Shortening life cycle for new varieties?
- Prone to technical and/or fashion obsolescence?

Is your customer:

- Knowledgeable about the capabilities and products and processes?
- Concerned about the latest features and who can provide it?
- Loyal as long as you provide exactly what they want?
- Reluctant to want to pay a hefty price premium for their exact needs to be met?

If the answers are yes – then mass customize.

The study also draws attention to the following issues:

Important issues for businesses supplying consumers

- Innovate in support.
- Customize services.
- Achieve a shorter time to market.
- Provide a higher product choice.

Important issues for companies supplying other businesses

- Innovate in service.
- Customize service.
- Innovate in manufacturing and engineering.
- Customize products.

The organizations in the survey who have customized experienced the following:

- Increase in profitability – 14 per cent.
- Reduction in manufacturing costs – 5.5 per cent.
- Market share increase – 21 per cent.
- Decrease in response time to customer order – 24 per cent.

When not to do it
The study points to three reasons not to do it:

1 Companies in a stable market providing commodity products where individuality is neither needed or valued by the customer.
2 Companies which are not lean manufacturers.
3 Companies unable to contemplate the change required.

Internal organizational barriers to mass customization

1 Factories not flexible enough.
2 Product too expensive.
3 Information systems incapable of supporting customization.
4 Incapable of managing the change required.
5 Insufficient management skills and attention.
6 Problems with understanding what the customer really wants.
7 Suppliers unable to meet the challenge.

It is clear that in order to meet market needs and remain competitive, companies need to customize where applicable and possible and ensure that they customize their services.

Investigate outsourcing and customer/supplier partnership agreements
Managing Service Quality, 8(1) (1998)

Strategic assessment of outsourcing and downsizing in the service market
Donald F. Blumberg says that before taking the decision to outsource organizations need to think about

- The importance of service to the organization's customers and users.
- The market or community's observed perception of the vendor's service quality and responsiveness.
- The current levels of service efficiency and productivity compared to other equivalent service organizations in the market.

Outsourcing has a number of real and perceived benefits, as well as disadvantages.

Outsourcing benefits and disadvantages
Outsourcing can create a number of economic advantages: eliminating investments of fixed infrastructure; allowing for greater quality and efficiency of services; and more significantly, cost savings. However, the concept of outsourcing is not for everyone. There are a number of risks in outsourcing which may create perceived disadvantages. However these disadvantages are mostly of a psychological nature and if managed effectively, do not lead to financial losses. Partnering with a third-party introduces a host of new outlooks, personalities, and demands that can produce new problems. These challenges include a more complicated level of communication, insecurity in the workforce, and the risk of alienating customers. Therefore, systems must be put in place to monitor and evaluate the performance of vendors.

There are a total of eight major classifications of service providers to the general outsourcing market:

1   Computer systems providers including VARs, TPMs and integrators.
2   Office automation manufacturers.
3   Telecommunications providers.
4   Specialist management consultants.
5   Functional support vendors.
6   Facilities management firms.
7   Systems software vendors.
8   Systems consulting firms.

Factors that need to be considered when selecting a partner:

- Breadth and depth of experience.
- Financial solvency.
- Commitment to quality improvement and customer satisfaction.
- Unique service capabilities.
- Understands customer's business and market.
- Commitment to technological innovation.
- Willingness to offer performance guarantees.
- Long-term service commitment.
- Availability of customer references.
- Reputation.
- Skill and experience of service personnel.
- Full range of service portfolio.

Creating a partnership with the supplier could involve a fundamental change in attitude for both parties. The whole idea of having common objectives and sharing some of the risks in order to participate in the rewards may be a little strange for managers too used to working with suppliers on an adversarial basis. This is a critical area for relationship marketing especially when organizations are locked into each other and have to manage irregularities in the market.

As Dull, Mohn and Noren (1995, *McKinsey Quarterly*) state teaming up with suppliers was a first step, marketing's eighth P (partners) is a direct link to strategy. Customers and channels can be partners too, even competitors. They define partnering to be 'when two or more parties agree to change how they do business, integrate and jointly control some part of their mutual business systems and share mutually in the benefit'.

Partnering originated in customer–supplier relationships but many companies have now moved beyond this to intermediaries and/or channels, peer companies and/or allies and also directly with suppliers.

Summary

This unit has focused upon the operational/functional aspects of building a true customer orientation. It illustrates it as a proactive process providing opportunities for profit and savings in cost. The following unit will explore future patterns for segmentation arising from changing demographic and social trends, and e-commerce.

Trends in customer behaviour and expectation and e-commerce

Objectives

❑ To understand how changes in the social and demographic behaviour affect patterns of consumption and market segmentation.

❑ To understand the value and relevance of trade cycles.

❑ To understand how technology can influence a business.

❑ To be introduced to e-commerce and global marketing.

❑ To understand that the delivery of outstanding customer service will form a critical part of tomorrow's business strategy.

Study Guide

This unit introduces you to the socio-cultural factors that influence structures of the market and customer demand. It attempts to give you an idea of the types of market opportunities that can arise from changes in the environment. We also look at the idea of globalization and the growth of e-commerce and examine how the internet can enable exporting.

The future pattern for market segmentation depends on changes reflected in society and their needs. Change will affect their expectations and open up different markets.

We are already experiencing customers whose expectations are putting continual pressure on organizations to increase their quality, service standards, response times, restitution processes and so forth. Some customers are very demanding and understandingly totally intolerant of broken promises and delays. Standards set in one market sector are transferred into another market sector so that all round there has been a greater sense of urgency as customer service becomes more innovative and more flexible.

Bill Gates, *Business at the Speed of Thought*, creates a sense about the expected velocity of change. Customers are also more willing to complain and are willing to do so. Legal enhancements to consumer power and the availability of media outlets makes it much easier to do. Customers are more concerned about ethical issues, about employment conditions and ingredients in food. However, their ideas are not always reflected in their purchasing behaviour (see attitudes to behaviour change, page 153). Sometimes attitude and behaviour do match and when they do customers will stop purchasing as recently witnessed with Nike, genetically modified foods and the beef crisis.

Access to the internet allows customers to call up a vast array of services. Many of the new competitors are coming from outside traditional competitors and are setting new standards of service, quality and speed (for example CD-Now and Amazon.com). Others are redesigning their market interfaces, cutting costs and doing business based on new infrastructures such as Federal Express. Value chains are moving to value networks so that many processes happen simultaneously so that customer service has improved. It is important that marketers keep an eye on the environment.

Market life cycle, product/service life cycles, the process of innovation and diffusion need to be thought about together so that organizations are defining new market segments as an ongoing process. Lazy thinking leads to organizations finding themselves in a mature market selling to laggards where differentiation on price is the sole criteria for purchasing.

Changing customer needs

Changes in the marketing mix
Changes in lifestyle and demographics will create changes in the marketing mix. If this is so, then as culture and values change and people look more to understand themselves, the brands created today already contain the seeds for their own destruction.

Culture is dynamic, it changes and marketers must be aware of changes in society. If and when people change their ideas of who they are the social and political culture will change as well and there will be a demand for different goods/services and the marketing techniques across a whole range of dimensions will need to change as well.

Socio-cultural factors

The demographic environment
Demography studies populations in terms of age structure, geographic distribution, balance between males and females, future size and characteristics. Marketers need to know this for the following reasons.

1 *The demand side* The size, structure and trends of the population exert an influence on demand and the size of market segment. There is a strong relationship between population growth and economic growth, and the absolute size of the population determines potential or primary demand.
2 *The supply side* Labour is an essential resource. For example, in retailing the decrease in young low-paid staff has already led to the employment of older people. Also, the mix of public service, impact of taxation and aggregated spending and distribution.

Changes in population growth are caused by:

- Changes in birth rate and/or fertility rate.
- Changes in death rate.
- Emigration and/or immigration.

Growing populations often require fast economic growth in order to maintain living standards, they need more resources for capital investment, they stimulate investment as the market size increases, they can also lead to greater labour mobility and overcrowding on land and in cities.

Falling populations need to be more productive, they put a greater burden on young people to support an older population; show changes in patterns of consumption and make some scale economies difficult to achieve.

Important trends to appreciate include changes in

- The growth of world population.
- Developed as against less-developed country growth rates.
- The future size of a population.
- The age and gender structure of a population.
- Its distribution by region and locality.
- Migration within and between national borders.

Size of population

The population in the UK is expected to have grown by 1.2 per cent from 56.4 million in 1980 to 57.5 million in 1998. Although this is lower than many countries (the USA is expected to grow by 11 per cent in the same period) there will be other significant changes in the structure of the population taking place during this period. For demographic details search the web.

The population of the United Kingdom has increased since 1991 with the biggest increases being observed in the very elderly age group of 85 and over, in the working population of age 30 and over and in children aged 5–15. The increases of ages 30–64/59 can be traced back to the high birth rates during the sixties and as a result of the post-Second World War baby boom. Despite the overall increase in the population some age groups have decreased since 1991. These are the 0–4, 16–29 and 65/60–74 age groups. The 16–29 age group has declined as a result of low fertility rates during the seventies. The 65/60–74 age group has declined as a result of low birth rates during the thirties.

Geographical shifts in population

In Britain there is a north/south divide which is characterized by different levels of economic activity and employment.

There is an increase of 10 per cent in the number of people living in Cambridgeshire, Buckinghamshire, Dorset and Cornwall in England and Down in Northern Ireland. Other areas which have shown increases include Grampian, East Anglia and the South West.

Find out if your market is likely to be affected by geographical shifts in population?

A country may also suffer from overpopulation in some areas and underpopulation in others. In the UK city centres are facing a fall in population. Other areas, such as the ex-mining towns, are becoming depopulated.

The key marketing factor to emerge from this is the swing from teenagers and young adults to middle-aged marrieds. The increased life expectancy has increased the demand for products and services catering for the elderly, such as entertainment, health products and holidays.

The household as a unit of consumption

Marketers focus attention on the household as a unit of consumption. In household structure several changes have occurred:

- Growth in the number of one-person households. One-person households include single, separated, widowed and divorced. This section has grown over the last few years partly as more people are getting divorced and partly because more young adults leave home early. A UK government forecast expects that the number of one-person households will have increased by 30 per cent in the period 1976–94. At the same time the number of pensioner one-person households is expected to have increased from 2.9 million in 1979 to almost 4 million by the mid-1990s.

- There has already been a demand for more starter homes, smaller appliances, food that can be purchased in smaller quantities and a greater emphasis on convenience products. Other needs for this sector include single bars, physical fitness centres, holiday clubs, radio talk shows, drugs, meditation, adult-oriented television programmes, redesigning of products and services for one person, lifestyle magazines rather than family magazines.
- Rise in the number of two-person cohabitant households. Several sociologists propose that cohabitation is the first stage of marriage. At the same time there is an increase in the number of households with two or more people of the same sex sharing. Married couples with one or two dependent children comprised 30 per cent of households in 1961 compared with 20 per cent in 1991.
- Rise in the number of group households with members of the same sex sharing expenses and living together, particularly in larger cities.
- Dual-income families. Time is now spent working or preparing for work instead of home making and shopping. Purchasing and consumption take place in the evening and weekends. This effects opening hours, home visits to service people, childcare, cooking, cleaning, eating out, frozen dinners. Time matters more and people become quickly impatient and find waiting intolerable. This means that organizations that take time processing will be open to competition by those who solve these problems. Sheth and Ram in their book, *Bringing Innovation to Market*, point out that there is a redistribution of wealth in the community, the middle class is on the decline and is supplemented by a larger affluent class and a larger low-income class. They say the bulge in the middle of the income distribution is being pushed to two ends. As a result there are three distinct market segments: premium (affluent), best value (middle class), and affordable (new poor) products and services in virtually every sector of the economy.

Family structure changes have come about through:

- Later marriages.
- Fewer children.
- Increased divorce rates.
- More working wives.
- Careers for women.

Changing role of women

Sex is important in population studies as the work roles carried out by men and women in different societies vary.

The role of women in the UK has changed with many women working or pursuing further education either on a full- or part-time basis. Women now have more money but less time. The following is a list of trends together with the associated impact on a large retailer's marketing operations:

1   Women becoming better educated and pursuing careers.

- Greater recruitment of professional women into the marketing department to fill emerging skill gaps and take advantage of their comparative skills in interpersonal relationships.
- Demand for a greater geographical variety and quality of product range due to greater travel overseas.
- More environmentally aware consumers impact on green policies, e.g. biodegradable packaging, dolphin friendly tuna.
- Health and fitness consciousness impacts on fat-free products.
- Increased home computer ownership supporting development of home shopping – building on principle of mail-order catalogues.
- Retail marketers may consider home delivery.
- Purchasing products that were within the traditional male domain such as motor cars.

2   More women working pre/post childbearing and later marriage.

- Impacts on demands for convenience foods/in-store preparation.
- Impacts on late/weekend/Sunday opening times/faster checkouts.
- Impacts on car park security/creche/mother and baby provision.
- Impacts on spending power due to second incomes – demand quality.
- Impacts on attraction to one-stop shopping/financial services.
- Impacts on the identity of the decision-maker, choice and the focus for promotional activity.

3   Women require increasing flexibility.

- Impacts on employment conditions for women.
- Impacts on recruitment and retention policies – how the image of the store is marketed.
- Flexitime, flexiyears and career breaks may be the required marketing response.

4   More single parents.

- The rise in divorce and single parenting produces a very different segment.
- Low disposable income suggests value for money ranges.
- Impacts on store location given more frequent visits.
- May impact on the provision of smaller 'metro' type stores.

An ageing population

In 1961, 12 per cent of the population were 65 or over. This will rise to 24 per cent before 2031. Table 12.1 illustrates trends for the age structure of the UK.

Table 12.1 UK population age structure

	Under 16 %	16–24 %	25–34 %	35–44 %	45–54 %	55–64 %	65–74 %	75+ %	Total (millions)
1961	25	12	13	14	14	12	8	4	52.8
1996	21	11	16	14	13	10	9	7	58.8
2011*	18	12	12	14	15	12	9	8	60.9
2021*	18	11	13	12	13	14	11	9	62.2

* Projected

Ageing of the population means that the average age is increasing. Japan, Europe and, to a lesser extent, the USA are facing a sharp increase in the proportion of pensioners as the new millennium approaches. The main causes include falling birth rates but a greater life span. By 2050 there will be some 70 million West Europeans aged 65+, representing over 20 per cent of the population. In Britain there are forecast to be more over-65s than under-16s by the year 2016. This will affect marketing operations in a number of ways:

- The age profile of the shopper and the target population changes. The key resource of shelf space must be redeployed to reflect this changing balance.
- Older customers tend to be more experienced and discerning in their buying habits. They focus on value for money and quality. This needs to be reflected in the marketing mix. Relationship marketing to retain such customers is an obvious strategy. The spread of store and loyalty cards reflects this attention.
- Retailers have tended to rely on younger people for recruitment. The marketing function must turn their attention to the use of 'older' employees to match the customer profile, e.g. B&Q.

- A sports and leisure retailer would have to consider repositioning of its product range. Athletic sports such as squash and football would tend to grow slowly compared to fitness and 'social' sports. Tastes would become more conservative but with a preference for quality and durability. Older consumers may tend to be laggards and resist unreasonable change suggesting fewer layout changes or innovatory new products.
- Ageing brings larger numbers into the 'empty nest' category and significantly higher disposable incomes. Retailers such as Marks & Spencer have already moved to exploit financial services.
- Ageing will impact on the style and facilities of the retailer. Those retiring early will shop during the day and expect restaurant facilities and, in many cases, individual assistance.
- The ageing population will be diverse and segmentable. Retailers must invest in information systems to help identify their changing needs and assist in focusing promotional activity.

The grey market has considerable financial power but this market place is not homogenous and there are large variations within it. It is important to remember that ageing is a process that occurs over a period of time on many levels – biological, social and psychological. According to the Henley Centre, estimates suggest that the over-45s have nearly 80 per cent of all financial wealth, and are responsible for about 30 per cent of consumer spending. Much of this is concentrated in the 55–64 age group. They have higher levels of home ownership and possession of private or occupational pensions.

The future of ageing

- Improvements in healthcare could help to prolong life expectancy even further. Cosmetic surgery and hormone replacement therapy (HRT) will minimize ageing and reduce aesthetic distancing between the generations.
- Cruise and alternative holidays may increase rather than beach holidays.
- We now live in a more liberal society which allows adults to enjoy being young. The older generation will have more in common with their children rather than their parents.
- Durability may replace fashion as key attribute.
- Improvements in technology and the growing movement of the workforce away from the traditional workplace into the home will change work patterns. It will also mean that it is not just the old who stay at home all day.
- If people are unwilling or unable to drive home delivery may intervene.
- Alternative media networks such as the internet, and cable may lead to more dedicated programming for the older consumer by the older consumer.
- A new form of spirituality may emerge to accompany the ageing population. Possibly the development of a post-modern, post-materialist culture will evolve as the older generation seeks to influence society to satisfy this need.
- Social and political groups may emerge to protect the interests of the elderly – organizations that have real political clout.

An increase in health care reflected in services and extending outside this to food, drink, clothing, personal care, appliances, cars, home, creation and leisure. Older people eat less meat so there could be demand for more vegetarian foods. They also drink less caffeine which would lead to tea and coffee substitutes or caffeine-free drinks. They have more capital and are therefore able to start a business and invest on the stock exchange. They are more concerned about safety, security of themselves and their property.

The conventional segmentation that has evolved has been of three groups, with some rough age brands, namely:

- The 'young old' (55–64.
- The 'mature old' (65–74).
- The 'old old' (75+).

Whilst the total population of England and Wales is projected to increase by 8 per cent between 1991 and 2001, the population aged 75–84 is projected to rise by 48 per cent and that aged 85 by over 138 per cent.

Increased middle class

Higher levels of education have created more people who are middle class, this is linked to the slow down of birth in developed nations. Family size is decreasing as many families are only having one child.

Influence of children in family purchasing

Taking children with you to the supermarket can affect what you buy, recent research has shown. Fathers spend on average 13 per cent more when shopping by themselves with their children. Mothers spend less.

Since the number of under-15s will grow by 10 per cent in this decade in the UK, with an estimated disposable income of £9 billion by 1998, this is a crucial influence on buying behaviour.

Education and achievement

It is likely that more and more people will become qualified. In 1977 to 1978, 33 per cent of school leavers left school without any GCE/SCE or CSE qualifications. By 1991 to 1992 this had changed to 12.5 per cent. Fewer girls leave school without qualifications than boys.

There will be a rise in the demand for 'knowledge' workers, which has led to the government expanding vocational and higher education in an effort to avert critical shortages in skills. The trend in university education is that there are more women, more mature students, more from non-conventional backgrounds (for example there are increasing numbers of unemployed doing Open University degrees).

Ethnicity

Aspects of an ethno-marketing environment that could be used to formulate a market segmentation strategy would include demographics, lifestyle, culture, education and employment.

- Demographics 21 per cent of the white population are 60 years and over; the figure for ethnic groups is less than 6 per cent, although this would vary as among the different ethnic groups the ethnic minority population has a younger age structure than the white population. It is being suggested that the minority/majority divide may disappear in many of our cities in the future. For example, ethnic minorities may well make up the majority in half of London boroughs.
- Lifestyle Many ethnic minority groups have a larger average household size with more dependent children than the white population. Although the figure will vary between different ethnic groups the common feature among them is the importance they place on the extended family. The ethnic population is steadily moving up within the British socio-economic hierarchy. Asians, particularly the Indian community, have overtaken whites as the people most likely to have their own businesses and professional qualifications. Their culture that embraces and reinforces the extended family system helps them to get ahead in business. An understanding of the DMP, the DMU and whether it is hard to initiate, influence and to carry out marketing exchanges will be needed by businesses seeking to engage in ethnic marketing.
- Education/and employment The government's labour force survey shows that higher proportions of the young people from India, black and Asian Africa and Chinese origin stay in full-time education after sixteen than their white counterparts. This is now reflected in such professional areas as accountancy, medicine, legal services and computer consultancy.

This means that marketers must question some stereotypes and outdated assumptions.

Healthy living

There is an increased concern for healthy living which has led to a demand for sporting facilities, low-fat products and natural foods.

There has been an increase in vegetarianism, and 'green consumerism' and a concern with 'organic food'. There is an increase in consumption and purchasing.

The increasing interest in health has stimulated the market for sports-related goods. Sporting shoes have become fashion accessories. Some employees are providing gyms and offering help to employees who abuse alcohol.

Employment trends

- Increased numbers of part-time employees.
- More people choosing to work from home as telecommunications improve.
- Flexible working hours – this flexibility is in both employee and business interests. It is underpinning much less standardized lifestyles and demanding a marketing response to cater for three-day weekends, all-night and even all-day entertainment as well as the late-night banking and retailing we increasingly take for granted.
- An increase in the numbers of self-employed people. Ethnic minorities from Asia have higher than average rates of self employment.
- Jobs are no longer 'jobs for life' – increasing numbers of people are employed on short-term contracts which are often renewed at the end of the term.
- The emergence of flexible organizations.
- The rise of the knowledge worker. Since most jobs will require brains rather than brawn in the next century, the government is belatedly expanding vocational and higher education in an effort to avert critical skill shortages from inhibiting high-technology growth opportunities.
- The self-service economy. Non-standard work patterns imply non-standard leisure patterns and more of this leisure time is being absorbed doing tasks which were previously undertaken by business. Interactive computer systems linked to databases offer dramatic potential to transform the way in which many services are currently marketed, sold and performed. Home banking, direct insurance and distance learning are just a sample of leading-edge applications.
- Short-term contracts will need to be reflected by the creation of managers that take into account the needs of a variable work pattern.
- Computers that are aimed at the business/leisure use.
- Financial services for the self-employed.

Changes in lifestyle

Albrecht (1979) has distinguished five major lifestyle changes taking place which have increased the level of stress. These are:

1   From rural to urban living.
2   From stationary to mobile.
3   From self-sufficient to interconnected.
4   From isolated to interconnected.
5   From physically active to sedentary.

Quality of life

There are changes in lifestyle such as, for example, a demand for recycled products, gourmet foods, an increased demand for classical music.

Convenience and self-service

There is an increased demand for convenience such as more ready-to-use products, more convenient sizes and easier methods of payment.

Informality

There is a greater style of informality which has resulted in a demand for more casual clothing, less formal restaurants and less formal furnishings.

Local government

Services which have been traditionally provided by local government employees are having to go out for commercial tender. This has opened up a number of opportunities for the UK private sector.

Pensions

The government is trying to get citizens to take responsibility for providing for their own pensions. This is essential because of the growing number of elderly people.

Private medicine

This area is still covered by the NHS although private medicine has increased. It is unlikely that the majority of people, while they are still being taxed for it, will want to pay for it twice.

Environmental priorities

As Mary Douglas says (*World of Goods*):

> Consumption has to be recognised as an integral part of the same social system that accounts for the drive to work, itself part of the social need to relate to other people, and to have mediating materials for relating to them. Mediating materials are food, drink and hospitality of home to offer, flowers and clothes to signal shared rejoicing, or mourning dress to share sorrow.

We live in a world of goods, but people are becoming more and more concerned about our physical environment. In 1966 Rachel Carson's book *Silent Spring* (1963) drew attention to the possible irrevocable damage being done to the planet and the possibility that we would exhaust the world's resources. The concern was echoed in the coining of the phrase 'eco-catastrophe'. Subsequently pressure groups formed such as the Friends of the Earth who have had a major impact on business practices.

The four major areas of concern are:

- An increasing shortage of raw materials.
- Increasing costs of energy.
- Increasing levels and consequences of pollution.
- An increasing need for government to become involved in the management of resources.

The question facing us is how our need for goods balances with our need to protect our environment, and how this need will be taken up by the rest of the developing world?

Behavioural aspects

Most opinion surveys show a clear growth of environmental consciousness among the public. In the UK, this has been substantiated by research carried out by Market and Opinion Research International (MORI).

Environmental consciousness is an element of the individual's belief system and is part of the social consciousness which is in itself a complex system of values and attitudes. Environmental consciousness would therefore have cognitive, affective and connative components.

The results of surveys only show a change of values on a global level, these are not always reflected in the consumer purchase behaviour.

New judgements, for example, about environmental compatibility, occur only after the consumer has developed an awareness of the inconsistency between values and product choice criteria.

Private and social cost

The costs of production do not solely include rent, rates, labour, material and transport costs – these are relatively simple and easy to calculate. The true costs are not borne by industry, the true costs are the social costs of production.

The costs that businesses impose upon society have included damage to the environment: Global warming, acid rain, depletion of the ozone layer, waste, the catastrophes of oil spillages, nuclear incidents (e.g. Chernobyl), noise, congestion, air and water pollution, industrial pollution, are to name but a few. Businesses therefore need to become increasingly involved in developing solutions for the resource and energy problems facing the nation and indeed the world.

Industrial activity will almost always damage the natural environment. The public's great concern for a non-polluted environment, apart from being absolutely necessary from an environmental point of view, will also create marketing opportunities for companies. New markets can be developed and companies should ensure that customers, employees, other stakeholders and the public are informed about their compliance with environmental standards.

One example would be the growth in renewable energy business, energy conservation and labour intensive repair industries.

A corporate response

Change should not only be driven by law making in Brussels or parliament, by environmental standards, by pressure groups and consumer demand. Businesses should become proactive and make care for the environment part of their core beliefs and values and these should form part of the mission statement. Protection of the environment requires a corporate response that will affect all the areas of a firm's activities.

Environmentalism must be seen as being distinct from a 'fad'. It will not disappear overnight and if it is not to become a corporate burden it must be addressed head on.

Marketing expresses the company's character, environmentalism is now an integral part of the corporate image. Businesses which fail to respond to these changes will be at a significant competitive disadvantage and run the risk of being commercial dinosaurs. People are realizing that pollution is not only a question of 'not in my back yard' but that it is a matter of global concern. Agreements are being reached to do this.

New markets

Green marketing is seen by some as a transparent marketing activity. To many consumers and business people it is not, it is marketing listening to and responding to customers' needs. People buy goods for material welfare, physical welfare and display. We all need recreation and work, to be fed, clothed, sheltered, but we also need peace of mind. Green marketing, taken seriously and with honest intent is part of this process.

A potential market exists for pollution control systems such as scrubbers and recycling systems. Also new ways need to be developed for packaged goods. Demand from consumers is also creating a market for greener products and consumers say they want environmentally-friendly goods and the government is increasingly demanding them.

In order to carry these programmes out businesses will obviously reduce some costs, but will need in some cases to increase prices as plant is changed and products redesigned to create less damage on the environment. Prices will have to be borne by the consumer. All this will involve a cost, marketers need to find out what their competitors are doing and also to establish what consumers will pay for.

Training

Employees working for organizations will also have to change, e.g. work practices. In some cases new technology and processes will result in redundancies and jobs becoming obsolete. This should open up areas for retraining. A major area of training is environmental management.

Carry out this activity within your own organization and find answers to the following questions:

1   How has the environmental movement affected the business?
2   What has it meant to your organization to have to become environment-ally friendly?
3   If changes have been made were they brought about by a change in core belief and values, consumer demand or legislation?
4   Were there any costs involved in making the changes, or indeed any savings?
5   Have the changes been communicated internally and externally?
6   Does your organization only do business with environmentally friendly suppliers?
7   Are any more changes anticipated?

If it is at all possible try and present and discuss your findings in class. It is extremely interesting being able to get some feedback on what other organizations are doing.

Sustainable development

This term refers to the interface between the natural and the economic environment. For development to be sustainable it suggests that any growth or improvement in the standard of living of current generations must not be achieved at the expense of reduced welfare for future generations.

Development which proceeds without regard to the depletion of non-renewable resources or the generation of wastes beyond natural absorptive capacities cannot be sustained and current generations are, in effect, stealing from the future.

High profile examples of non-sustainable development include the depletion of rain forests, fish stocks and nuclear wastes.

Commentary on significance to the marketer:

- Marketers should be aware of rising environmental concerns.
- Consumers increasingly recognize unsustainable behaviour.
- Marketers, such as those at the Body Shop can achieve an edge by promoting an ethical image and taking their social responsibilities seriously.
- Product development should consider designing sustainability into products – consider lifetime impacts.
- Efforts to re-use and recycle materials form part of sustainability. Legislation will eventually enforce compliance.

Pressure groups

There have been sharp increases in membership of consumer pressure groups. Consumers are better educated and have learnt to demand their rights. Retailers have become larger and more remote to the individual encouraging membership of formal and informal pressure groups. Membership of the Consumers Association is a sectional interest group since the member is seeking economic advantage/better value for money. Membership of cause groups is more transitory. Examples include:

- Local people resisting the building of an edge of town store.
- Environmental groups concerned over issues such as animal testing for cosmetics/packaging and recycling/animal friendly foods/ozone free, etc., sustainable products.
- Health and safety causes, e.g. e-coli and BSE.
- Genetically modified foods.

Consumer pressure groups will tend to apply primary pressure on legislators and planners as key-decision makers. These may have an effect on marketing operations as follows:

- Customer orientation means that customer needs must be taken seriously.
- Image and behaviour is important in reassuring customers.
- Codes of conduct might be considered, e.g. Sainsbury's regarding environmental policies.
- Positive steps should be promoted and efforts made to work with serious groups to achieve balanced progress for all stakeholders.
- Pressure to be proactive in terms of recycling and re-use and seek a competitive edge through good practice and clear ethical values.
- Failure to respond to pressures may lead to lost customers and a tarnished image.

Protection of consumer interests

Consumerism is the term used by the consumer movement to describe what they do and is concerned with the protection of consumers' interests. The consumer movement is concerned with protecting the public's interests. These range from:

- Ensuring the availability of product and price information.
- Ensuring the labelling is correct.
- Ensuring that advertising does not misinform.
- Ensuring that products are safe.
- Ensuring that businesses do not indulge in sharp practices.
- Ensuring that businesses abide by the law.
- Encouraging government to intervene on consumers' behalf.

The ethical consumer

Go to www.wdm.org.uk and you can find out about the World Development Movement. Some of the issues they have achieved success in are:

- Convinced Del Monte to allow unions on its banana plantations in Costa Rica.
- Led the fight against the new MAI treaty which would have guaranteed multinationals more power.
- Helped Indian campaigners block P&Os megaport that would have destroyed the local economy.
- Secured a High Court victory to stop the squandering of aid on Malaysia's Pergau Dam.

They are currently campaigning for:

- Persuading big business to put people before profits: such as voicing the concerns of third-world farmers whose lives could be devastated by genetic modification of their staple crops.
- Fighting for government policies that support the poor: such as a fifteen-year battle for an end to the injustice of the third-world debt.
- Justice in the twenty-first century: giving voice to brave and principled campaigners in their struggle against exploitation.

The emergence of the ethical consumer can be traced back to the 1980s when official reports, such as that by the Brundtland Commission (*Our Common Future*, 1987, World Commission on Environment and Development, NY: Oxford University Press; chaired by the Norwegian Prime Minister Gro Harlem Brundtland), started to highlight issues of sustainability. For perhaps the first time this report officially linked social, economic and ecological concerns. For example, depletion of natural resources was associated with poverty and trade with employment conditions in the developing world. This had the effect of boosting the credibility of the established environmental and development-oriented non-governmental organizations (such as Oxfam and Friends of the Earth) and made it more politically acceptable for them to operate on a broader campaign base.

Ethical purchasing campaigns were one beneficiary of these changing circumstances leading to the publication of numerous guides for concerned consumers. Examples include the popular *Green Pages* (Button, J., 1988, Optima) an ethical equivalent of the *Yellow Pages*, and the *Green Car Guide* (Nieuwenhuis, Cope and Armstrong, 1992, Greenprint).

Ethical consumers can generally be considered to be those that make purchasing decisions based on a broader set of criteria than just price. Value to them goes beyond the intrinsic qualities of any purchase (quality, packaging and so on) to the extrinsic taking into account the environmental and social 'life cycle' of the product or service. Thus, they may be willing to buy fairly traded, organic coffee at a premium price, even though the taste might not be totally to their liking, because they perceive that wider benefits will accrue. In this case coffee workers will have an improved quality of life, better working conditions, and fewer harmful chemicals will be used during production.

Ethical consumers are sometimes categorized into 'light' and 'dark greens' depending on the depth and breadth of their beliefs. The latter often eschew consumer culture in favour of a more do-it-yourself, minimalist approach to living. In the United States it has been reported that anything up to 10 per cent of the population have adopted this lifestyle – often termed 'voluntary simplicity'. In the UK and Europe the numbers are likely to be similar, as suggested by the growing number of 'sustainable communities' projects, although little official data exists. One telling trend is the very high membership of social and environmental pressure groups within the UK. Approximately one in nine of the population (11 per cent) is a member of one or more groups which ranges from the Royal Society for the Protection of Birds (RSPB) to Greenpeace.

The ethical consumer is likely to have many of the following ten key values acting on them to varying degrees. (Adapted from several sources including the book *Seeing Green* (Porritt, J., 1984, Blackwell) and the key values of the Green Committees of Correspondence and International Green Parties. A selection of definitions of key values can be found on the web site www.greens.org.)

1 *Social justice* The realization that there is a need to redistribute wealth and provide access to the benefits of society to all the peoples of the world. Thus, it is recognized that, rather than reinforcing exisiting developed-world supply and demand structures, purchasing decisions should aim to encourage and support self-reliance amongst the less fortunate. Thus, companies such as The Body Shop aim to deal direct with local cooperatives in developing countries and link with other initiatives aimed at providing, for example, clean water and education.

2 *Community-based economics* The belief that, in economic terms, 'small is beautiful'. A recognition that buying locally adds financial value to the community and has social and environmental benefits. Examples are the growing number of vegetable 'box schemes' and community farms where residents and local food growers enter into a supply agreement often including doorstep delivery and sometimes in exchange for occasional farm-hand work.

3 *Non-violence* The commitment to resolve disputes at a local, national or global level without resorting to violence. An example is of consumer demand for ethical investment funds which do not invest in companies which manufacture weapons.

4 *Decentralization* The belief that the balance of power should be shifted in favour of local communities rather than being centralized to a national or global level. One example of this is the concerted internet campaign credited with forcing the multilateral agreement on investment (or MAI) out of the European Parliament. The MAI aimed to give more power to multi-national corporations to the detriment of national and local governments potentially denying the rights of local authorities to 'buy local'.

5 *Future focus/sustainability* Thinking in terms of the future. Recognizing the rights of future generations to live comfortably on the planet. This usually manifests itself in a product or service guarantee which claims to offset pollution and replace or recycle the natural resources being consumed. Examples include the many products which use all, or a percentage of recycled materials such as newspapers, plastic carrier and bin bags, and even clothing. Another interesting example is the 1997 concert tour of musician Neneh Cherry where a number of trees were planted to offset the carbon dioxide pollution emitted from the electricity consumed during the tour.

6 *Post-patriachal values* Replacing the traditional ethics of dominance and control with those of cooperation and spirituality. This key value gets to the heart of ethical consumerism. It recognizes that the consumer is not all powerful and has no more rights than any other person in the supply chain. Thus the emphasis is shifted to take account of the needs of those working to grow, manufacturer and distribute products or deliver services. An example is the recent concern over Sunday working which was not just religious but also recognized the need for shop staff to have time off to relax and spend time with their families.

7 *Personal and global responsibility* Taking personal responsibility for the effects of our actions on the whole of society. Again, this key value gets to the heart of ethical consumerism – the belief that individuals should be selfless and consider the impacts of their decisions on other people and the environment. An example of how this has been used is in the selling of paper products where the promise is often made to plant more trees to replace those logged to manufacture the product. This recognizes that consumers perceive the link between purchase and the impact on the natural environment.

8 *Respect for diversity* Honouring cultural, ethnic, racial, sexual, religious, spiritual and biological diversity. Covers a broad spectrum of concerns from the banning of one of Salman Rushdie's books in some countries, on the basis that it was offensive to certain religious groups, to the issue of racial and gender equality and the conservation of endangered animal species. One example is the Worldwide Fund for Nature's link with a range of product manufacturers to ensure a donation to conservation efforts.

9 *Grassroots democracy* A belief that individuals must have the ability to control the decisions that affect their lives. Pertains to consumer issues such as employment rights, human rights and political conditions in country of manufacture. An example of consumer action was the boycott of South African products whilst the country was under minority white rule.

10 *Ecological wisdom* Living within the ecological and resource limits of the planet. Pertains to consumer issues such as energy-efficiency, organic agriculture and waste minimization. An example of consumer action is the pressure for eco-labelling of products and low energy appliances.

The ethical consumer exerts power not only directly – in their choice of products or service – but also indirectly through the political and legislative process.

A related type of consumer is the healthy consumer. There is a strong overlap between what is considered healthy for an individual to consume and what is healthy for the environment. Thus the enourmous public outcry over the introduction of genetically-modified foods brought together those concerned with both the possible effects on the health of those eating GM foods and those concerned at the effect of releasing GM materials into the wider environment. The latter were more concerned with effects such as the development of pesticide-resistant weeds (super weeds) and the impact on wildlife.

In most cases the concern of the healthy consumer revolves around their personal consumption of food. There may be ethical reasons for not wishing to eat certain foodstuffs, for example vegetarianism and/or a desire to eat locally-grown produce, but the healthy consumer is equally as interested in diet. They may seek to avoid certain ingredients, artificial sweeteners, mono-sodium glutamate (MSG), excessive salt, saturated fats, or actively consume others such as vitamins, wholefoods, mineral water and so on.

The healthy consumer may also be seeking to control their weight through their levels of consumption.

The FairTrade mark – A new dimension to shopping

The FairTrade symbol is an independentally-assessed mark awarded only to those products that meet a strict set of criteria including:

- Decent wages.
- Minimum health and safety standards.
- A fair price.
- A long-term trading commitment.
- Good environmental standards.

The FairTrade mark arose as a result of pressure from ethical consumers to assist them in making socially and environmentally-sensitive purchasing decisions. Products with FairTrade marks include coffee, tea, chocolate and cocoa.

The FairTrade Foundation – 0171–405 5942.

World population

Global population has grown exponentially over the last two or three centuries. As industrial economies matured, however, they enjoyed a demographic transition whereby customarily high birth rates fell to levels closer to already-reduced death rates. This process has yet to be completed in many less-developed countries, especially in Africa, meaning that world population will continue to rise, at a reducing rate, at least until the middle of the next century. Less-developed countries account for a steadily increasing proportion of total population. There is an annual and exponential growth rate of 1.8 per cent. The world population will have grown from 4.4 billion in 1980 to 6.2 billion by the millennium. The share of the industrialized countries of this overall total will shrink from 25 per cent to 17 per cent by 2005.

Technology

Marketing research is made easier through the use of analysis packages such as SPSS. The changing technology also affects marketing operations, for example:

- Supply side:
  - Supply chain management;
  - Electronic data interchange (EDI) links suppliers and retailers – enables JIT;
  - EPOS/barcode systems allow automatic reorder;
  - EFTPOS systems to improve cash flow and customer convenience via cash back;
  - Trials with computer linked intelligent trolleys and self check-out.
- Personnel side:
  - Marketing staff have more processing power;
  - Direct marketing is facilitated via loyalty databases;
  - Productivity increases in all areas.
- Demand side:
  - Opens up the potential of home shopping;
  - Product range fine-tuned;
  - Automated telephone ordering systems;
  - In-store secure automated banking services;
  - Sales opportunities.

As Bill Gates says in his book, *Business at the Speed of Thought,* 'if the 1980s were about quality and the 1990s were about reengineering, then the 2000s will be about velocity. About how quickly the nature of business will change. About how information access will alter the lifestyle of consumers and their expectations of business. Quality improvements and business process improvements will occur far faster. When the increase in velocity of business is great enough, the very nature of business changes. A manufacturer or retailer that responds to changes in sales in hours instead of weeks is no longer at heart a product company, but a service company that has a product offering. These changes will occur because of a disarmingly simple idea: the flow of digital information.' For the technically minded, see www.speed-of-thought.com

Changes in technology have an impact on:

- The environment.
- The types of products that are marketed.
- Methods of production.
- The type of work that is done.
- The way in which the work is carried out.
- The way in which human resources are deployed.
- Techniques used for marketing.
- Consumers and society in general.

Economic environment
The economic environment can affect consumer spending and purchasing power. Total spending power includes:

- Current income.
- Savings.
- Credit.
- Prices.

A major determinant of demand income is widely used as a measure of potential demand.

- Net disposable income is all earnings (earned from salaries) and unearned (from investments) health and welfare benefits and so on, less tax.
- Discretionary income is the amount available after all 'essential' (mortgage, rent, food, basic clothing, etc.) expenditure has been met.

Consumer behaviour and marketing strategy will influence whether a product/service falls in the discretionary or non-discretionary sector.

Marketers should be aware of:

1 Patterns of real income distribution.
2 Inflationary and deflationary pressure.
3 Changing consumer expenditure patterns.
4 Changes in the saving/debt ratio.
5 Concern over third-world debt.
6 Different consumer expenditure patterns.

These changes must not be looked at in isolation but be viewed against a background of change in the political/economic balances of power – such as the rise of Japan and South East Asia, the collapse of the Soviet Union, developments in China and major changes in the physical environment.

Economic factors
You should be able to understand how consumer behaviour is affected by economic factors both domestically and abroad. It is important to understand that it is not the objective nature of the economic context but rather the way in which that context is perceived and interpreted by consumers.

Economic forecasting involves looking at the impact and relationship of the following:

- The industrial structure.
- The income distribution.
- GNP per capita.
- Rate of growth of GNP.
- Ratio of investment to GNP.
- Business cycles.
- Money supply.
- Inflation rates.
- Unemployment.
- Energy costs.
- Patterns of ownership.
- Exchange rates.
- Taxation.
- Currency stability.
- Export and so on.

Make sure that you read the quality press and trade and business magazines on a regular basis to keep track of what is happening in your market. Collect articles and put them into your folder. You will be expected to include up-to-date examples in the exam.

The business cycle

This refers to the periodic fluctuations in economic activity that occur in industrialized countries. At times we have economic growth and at other times we have high unemployment and falling production. The word cycle implies that there is something regular about it.

Many different cycles have been identified by various economists, for example Kuznets highlighted a 15–25 year cycle, while Kondratieff identified a 50–60 year cycle. For much of the post-war period most advanced economies have suffered fluctuations of economic activity that last about 4–5 years, these are called business cycles.

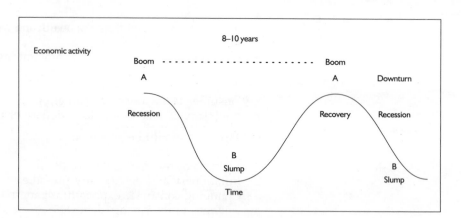

Figure 12.1
Phases of the business cycle

The marketer must be able to try to anticipate fluctuations, especially the stages at which the economy is moving into or out of recessions and booms.

The stage of the cycle will determine the policies you should be pursuing:

- *Downturn* Control stock in line with order slowdown, analyse weak products and channel outlets (Pareto analysis), stop recruitment and further long-term commitments.
- *Recession* Retain skilled core staff and upgrade their skills, order capital equipment for future installation.
- *Recovery* Orders start coming in, start building stock and encourage distributors to do likewise, start hiring and prepare new products for launch.

Forecasting the cycle

Unfortunately no way has been found to do this accurately. However, the marketer can take a careful note of present trends of the following:

- GDP
- volume of retail sales
- level of unemployment
- changes in stocks, and so on.

Surveys of business opinion such as the CBI survey can help. The marketer may also be able to predict trends from changes in statistics. There are a number of statistical trends that are thought to be significant in measuring business cycles – these are called economic indicators. Some react ahead of the trend and are known as leading indicators (housing starts), others lag behind the business cycle (investment and unemployment).

In the UK a range of indicators are published quarterly by the Central Statistics Office in the journal *Economic Trends*.

Globalization

The term 'globalization of markets' refers to (Levitt, 1983):

1 Tastes, preferences and price-mindedness becomes increasingly universal.
2 Products and services becoming more standardized and competition within industries reaches a worldwide scale.
3 The way in which organizations try and design their marketing policies and control systems for global products, consumers and competition on a global scale.

Jean-Claude Usunier writes in *International Marketing*, Prentice Hall (1993):

> Globalization means homogenizing on a world scale. The implicit assumption behind the globalization process is that all elements will globalize simultaneously. A central assumption of globalization is that the mostly artificial trade barriers (non-tariff, regulation, industrial standards, etc.) have kept many markets at the multidomestic stage. If these barriers are removed, which is the aim of 1992, 'insiders' who hold a large market share just in their home market may only be protected from new entrants by natural culture-related entry barriers.

Electronic commerce and its impact on the organizational customer interface

Martin Butler and Thomas Power have very kindly supplied much of this information from their book *The E-Business Advantage* (Martin Butler – www.butlergroup.com and Thomas Power – www.TheEcademy.com).

Martin Butler and Thomas Power are IT and e-business analysts who work closely with Europe's leading companies. They can see clearly that the internet has truly created a new, completely electronic economy. It has unique financial models, strategies, structures, politics, cultures, combatants, regulations, successes, failures, opportunities and problems.

They define e-commerce as the buying or selling of products, goods, information and services over the internet and e-business as the transformation of an organization's internal processes through the application of web technologies.

- E-commerce:
  - Home page;
  - Catalogue;
  - Order taking;
  - Secure transactions.
- E-business:
  - Intranet and extranet;
  - Electronic procurement;
  - Customer acquisition;
  - Catalogue management;
  - Merchandise planning and analysis;
  - Order entry – confirmation and fulfilment;
  - Returns;
  - Shipping and freight;
  - Warehousing and inventory management;
  - Pricing – promotions, taxes, duties, freight;
  - Payments – credit cards, digital cash, bank transfers;
  - Financial accounting;
  - Reporting;
  - Customer profiling and customer relationship;
  - Customer service.

Butler and Power ask why this new market opportunity is causing so much excitement, confusion, fear and denial? The corporate world is divided. Some companies seem able to make business sense of the internet, or at least are willing to try. Other organizations think they've done enough by putting their annual report up on the web. As they say: 'It seems to us that it is the young companies that are profiting from the internet, and the old established organizations that are turning their backs on a very profitable way of doing business'.

This is reinforced by *The Global internet 100 Survey 1998* carried out by Insead for Novell. This study assessed internet usage by 120 of the world's largest companies, all drawn from *Fortune 500* lists. In summing up, the study's leaders, Professors Soumitra Dutta of Insead and Arie Segev of Berkeley, endorse their feelings that most companies, even the best in the world, haven't been able to work out what the internet means for their business.

> Few firms are rethinking their business models to take advantage of the internet's unique interactive capabilities. Most firms remain stuck in the first stage of exploitation: simple electronic publishing of corporate and product information. Few have actually moved onto the next stage of conducting true electronic commerce – only about a third of the companies surveyed currently offer electronic ordering and payment. Even fewer have actively moved into the third and most interesting stage of internet exploitation – business transformation in cyberspace.

Butler and Power put this down to the possibility of IT fad fatigue. However, they draw our attention to the fact that the world's best performing companies from 1995 to 1998 are Microsoft, Dell, Cisco, Intel and Compaq (*Business Week*, 30 March 1998). Cisco Systems conducts 69 per cent of its sales – $11 million per business day – over the internet. The company expects the volume to increase from its current level of more than $2 billion per year, to $5 billion in the near future. By selling through the internet, the company has reduced its annual operating expenses by nearly $270 million. Cisco's managers say the real value of the electronic channel is that it allows the company to provide buyers with a range of advantages – convenience, information, personalization and interactivity – that competitors cannot.

Market growth and market shake-ups

Analysis indicates that the effects of e-business are being felt most keenly in the following industries; computer hardware and software; financial services; travel; retailing; books and cars. Many experts believe that 30 per cent to 50 per cent of automobile sales will be made over the internet by 2004. (Butler and Power believe it could be 80 per cent). Another area is banking. Butler and Power point out that niche internet banking companies attract high value customers. The traditional banks see a loss of margin and have to increase charges, which results in the loss of yet more customers.

Smoothing supply chains

While EDI has played a role in smoothing supply chains, it has limitations: cost, inflexibility and an inability to add anything to the process other than the basic transaction. Increasingly larger organizations will drive their suppliers or partners to integrate business electronically. Guardian Royal Exchange has introduced remote video inspection of vehicles for damage assessment. This has obvious benefits as it speeds up claims, reduces time and cost for the insurance company – but more importantly, the insurer is insisting that body shops adopt this technology

Amazon.com is the most commonly used example of e-commerce. Now GE, the world's most profitable company according to *Business Week*, plans to deal directly with suppliers over the internet and to receive multiple bids for every part and service it requires. Based on early trials, GE estimates that it will shave $500 million to $700 million off its purchasing costs over three years and cut purchasing cycle times by as much as 50 per cent. KPMG, say that the effects of electronic commerce are being felt most strongly in the business-to-business market, specifically in terms of the supply chain. Over 29 per cent of respondents in their survey currently use e-commerce for transactions and this is expected to rise to 70 per cent in three years time (*KPMG Electronic Commerce Research Report 1998*).

Butler and Power say that the e-business battleground is already claiming casualties. There is considerable evidence that many industries and organizations are mortally wounded and don't even know they are. Perhaps the UK booksellers who have lost customers to Amazon.com might have an answer, or maybe the suppliers who haven't connected to the internet and therefore are not bidding for contracts from GE can come up with a comforting analysis.

Phil Dwyer, once editor of *New Media Age* (www.nma.co.uk), now Managing Director of Jupiter Communications (www.jupiter.com) says that travel agents grasp that they are being by-passed by a technology which virtually eradicates their expert status. He also says that intermediaries such as travel agents need to think carefully about how exactly they add value in an internet-based economy. Many feel that physical travel agents will be all but gone as early as 2004. The question to ask is what can you do to differentiate. For example, Thomas Cook uses its web site to provide services and products related to the holiday you are booking – from currency and travel insurance to travel guides.

Developing the ability to move to managing a real-time environment

IT is central to the e-business advantage. As Butler and Power say:

> Unfortunately, the very nature of electronic markets militates against easy understanding and integration into existing organizations. It is a move from a planning-based approach of control and management to a realtime environment. It could be argued that established companies have been successful because they have successfully measured the past to control the present and plan for the future. A realtime market, as demonstrated by the stock market, is quite different. Information flows are virtually instantaneous, and the past has little bearing on current behaviour. There are markets that can still look to the past for guidance about how to behave today, but the best examples of these are local authorities which offer no

real customer choice at all and constantly struggle to appoint and manage suppliers profitably. Organizations that identify themselves with the experience of the stock market will survive and succeed. Organizations that are happy to stay the corporate equivalent of the local authority will not.

Disengineer

Butler and Power recommend that companies disengineer their processes because they believe that organizations are unable to engineer all their work processes to meet every business need and eventuality. They use the example of the fire service and other emergency services as the role models that have the flexibility, responsiveness and creativity demanded of e-business. They say there is no better demonstration of knowing what to engineer and what should be left to the discretion of your people. The core capabilities in e-business are characterized by informality (relying on informal lines of communication), creativity and cooperative working. In a business environment where responsiveness and agility count for everything, management has to learn to let go. Disengineering is the art of removing barriers and restrictions that inhibit skilled workers from doing their jobs in the most effective way. Disengeering means creating an environment where trust, tolerance, cooperation and many other similar values are the currency with real worth.

Developing the ability to understand how to manage a real-time worker

The real-time worker manages the present moment and as Butler and Power point out controlling an e-business is going to be like trying to control the shifting sands of a desert. As they say 'we welcome that, because we never believed that you could control anything anyway. Psychologists, spiritual masters and the best business consultants will all tell you the same thing – the only thing that it is possible for an individual or organization to control is its own response to an outside stimuli. E-business means that the stimuli will be constant, but it also provides the tools, the fitness as it were, to respond well. The most effective e-businesses will ensure that all their people understand how the company makes its money and what its values are, so that they can assess the risks they take by agreeing or not agreeing to a customer's request. In turn, the company has to communicate those things simply and clearly and then trust its people to make the right decision. It is advisable to remember that trust requires toleration of different ways of doing things.

Connectivity

External connectivity

The internet is an open system so you can get to your customer easily and in realtime. Likewise, they can get to you. Your customers can also talk to each other and your competitors. Suddenly, you are in an interactive relationship with everybody who does business with you. Combine your technologically open doors with open processes that can accommodate customer feedback and respond quickly, and you have a winning combination.

On the other hand, if all you've done is opened the door to your customers but turned your back on them when they came calling, then you have damaged an existing relationship and endangered many others. E-business has to be approached cautiously because on the internet everyone can see you get it wrong.

Getting involved with e-business has been likened to starting to do business in a foreign country. This foreign country or battleground is not made of rocks and earth; it isn't static and waiting for visitors. It was created by the technologies that connect everyone and everywhere, and it will come to *you*!

Internal connectivity

Connectivity doesn't just mean having an open channel to customers, it can mean that the way goods get produced or services designed become much more efficient. For example, the Canadian Imperial Bank of Commerce in Toronto will start aggregating orders among departments for greater discounts and sending them electronically to suppliers using an internet procurement program. The bank expects to save almost $100 million on its $1.3 billion in annual purchases.

Ubiquity

Butler and Power use the word ubiquity to describe the internet. According to the *Oxford English Dictionary* ubiquity means 'in several places simultaneously'. That definition certainly describes the internet, but we think that is not really the point. It is the fact that the internet, by connecting everybody anywhere, makes information ubiquitous. The profitability of many industries is dependent upon the difficulty surrounding access to certain types of information. The internet makes this information available to customers, suppliers and competitors. Unless a product or service can be differentiated from the competition, it risks being reduced to a commodity. The InsWeb Corporation, for example, allows customers to compare prices for several different products including health, life and car insurance. A consequence of this kind of site could be realtime pricing, whereby customers tell insurance companies what they are willing to pay for specified cover and ask if there are any takers. How many insurance companies are flexible enough to respond?

Sharing information

Butler and Power point out that success lies in the ability to share the information that you have in order to come up with something better. This applies especially to organizations which have started to use the internet to wring more value from their supply chain. They liken it to fishing. The lone fisherman can have a fun time catching the occasional fish, but it doesn't get commercially viable until there's a whole gang of fisherman working together to haul the net on board.

The personalization paradox and infomediaries

Butler and Power point out that the web has equalized the customer/vendor relationship. Many companies relied on customers not having access to information in order to maintain huge, comfortable profit margins. The web allows a customer to know almost everything about their purchases, their vendors, and their competition; and easily pursue the lowest cost option. Customer share is about meeting the related or ongoing needs of your customers, and designing your business to extract a lot out of each customer, instead of a little out of many customers. Your information strategy is built on how much you know about your customers and the degree to which your products are tailored or standardized.

As Jeffrey Rayport says in an article in *Information Strategy* (October 1998):

> Call it the personalisation paradox. Ask anyone in a first-world economy about what defines quality in services rendered, and you'll discover that consumers invariably celebrate services that are personalised and customised to the individual. But ask any of those same consumers how they feel about companies knowing a lot about them – where they live, what they buy, how they consume – and you're likely to get an equally predictable answer. Consumers adamantly reject the notion that companies should know much, if anything, about their personal lives or behaviours or preferences.

An Infomediary is a company that makes money by bridging the gap between the need for companies to capture detailed customer information and exploitation by companies. What technology makes possible is marketing on an individualized basis to specific customers and households. Infomediary strategies are emerging to provide so-called segment of information. Jeffrey Rayport of Harvard Business School, and John Hagel, a consultant with McKinsey, have defined an infomediary as a business wherein the primary source of revenue derives from capturing customer information and developing detailed profiles of individual consumers for use by selected third-party vendors. This task is not made any easier by government and lobby organizations which seem determined to stop commercial operations finding out about their perfect match in consumer terms. The USA are looking for a voluntary solution, the EU is looking at a legislative one. 'Europeans are concerned with protecting people from companies', says one observer, quoted in the *Financial Times* (8 October 1998), 'the American's priority is to protect them from government'.

Customer demand
Customer demand, not forecasts, drives production. The ability to reach millions of people creates products that couldn't be sold economically before. In addition to this computer controlled factory equipment and industrial robots make it easier to adjust assembly lines. Butler and Power believe that if a company can't customize, it's got a problem (it's like any relationship – if those involved are unwilling or unable to moderate their view or position to take into account something else, then the relationship is unlikely to be healthy or long-lived). Companies must also be on call twenty-four hours a day.

One from one and mass customization
Butler and Power point out that it is not so much as one to one but one from one. The ultimate niche is a market of one. The customer will only share with organizations they trust, feel comfortable with, or want something from so badly that caution is thrown to the wind. The ultimate response to customer feedback is altering the price of a product according to who is buying it, when they are buying and where they are. Some companies are already beginning to do this.

Restructuring
Proctor and Gamble is undergoing a major shift in its organization, moving away from its country-by-country set-up to a handful of powerful departments that supervise categories on a global scale. There will be seven global business units that will develop and sell products on a worldwide basis. P&G wants an international image for its product; retailers want something more tangible – a global price.

The importance of IT and market research
As IT moves into the business mainstream the role of the IT director is changing dramatically. E-business transforms the whole buyer/seller relationship and customer feedback is essential. IT is at the centre of this process.

This cannot be done without a strategically minded IT director in place. A survey of 300 chief executives and chief financial officers across France, Germany and the UK, carried out on behalf of Deloitte Consulting by market researchers, Audience Selection, claims that only 13 per cent of those asked said they have a board-level director with any sort of understanding of computers. Although about three-quarters of the directors in Deloitte's survey admitted that data networks were critically important to the business, 70 per cent relied on someone else, with IT expertise, to explain the strategic and operational importance of the technology.

Leonard L. Berry is a Professor of Marketing, the J.C. Penney Chair of Retailing Studies, and Director, Center for Retailing Studies, Texas A&M University. A. Parasuraman holds the James W. McLamore Chair in Marketing, University of Miami. Berry and Parasuraman believe that companies must ensure that they have multiple perspectives from different customer groups. They advocate a listening system that uses many research approaches in combination to capture, organize, and disseminate information. Four in particular are essential: transactional surveys;

customer complaint, comment, and inquiry capture; total market surveys; and employee surveys. The five elements of the service-quality information system are:

1 *Measure service expectations* Companies frequently measure only customers' service perceptions, when they should be including their expectations about level of service; both what they desire and what they deem adequate. Expectations provide a frame of reference when considering customers' perception ratings.

2 *Emphasise information quality* In evaluating information, companies should ask if it is relevant, precise, useful, in context, credible, understandable, and timely.

3 *Capture customers' words* The system should include both quantitative and qualitative databases. Quantified data is more meaningful when combined with customers' verbatim comments and videotapes.

4 *Link service performance to business results* What impact do service performances have on business results? Companies need to calculate lost revenue due to dissatisfied customers, measure customers' repurchases, and gauge the relationship between customer loyalty and propensity to switch.

5 *Reach every employee* Companies should disseminate customer feedback to all employees. They are decision makers who affect the quality of service at all levels.

Rethink what business you are in

Butler and Power suggest that organizations rethink what business they are in. They ask:

> How do you think your organization is going to realise substantial growth over the next decade? It certainly isn't going to be through the 'let's produce more for less paradigm'. It is going to be through the smart use of information technology and the building of electronic relationships with your customers and suppliers.

They feel that information is a commodity but believe that it is the only thing that organizations can use to guarantee competitive advantage. It is knowing how to use information to reduce uncertainty both for the organization and for customers.

Products have a physical and information component. Companies can differentiate their product through the information that they now have, e.g. service support – railroad and trucking companies offer up-to-the-minute information on shippers' freight (see www.tandata.com). Some products have no physical component at all. The information content of every product is growing. Butler and Power give the example of Federal Express who provide an interactive service through its web site.

Butler and Power have redefined:

- *Customer* – an organization that has decided that your products represent the least uncertainty of all options.
- *Supplier* – an organization that represents the least uncertainty as a source for the products and services you need.
- *Partner* – an organization with which you are willing to share relevant information.
- *Competitor* – an organization with which you wish to share as little information as possible, unless it is misinformation.

Butler and Power say that an information strategy is a plan which optimizes the available information in the market, so that the most profitable relationships can be created between suppliers, partners and competitors.

Don't put customers into solitary confinement

Butler and Power advocate creating a customer community communication strategy. They say you need to establish a sense of place for your customers, and not treat them as if they live in solitary confinement. Customers are looking for assistance, support and social connection.

301

Provide them with the forums to get to know and support each other, and you may be able to convert your customer base into contributors, so that your site becomes a living, continually enhanced destination.

Make sure that your customers feel valued, that you are responsive to their needs, that you listen to what they say. Butler and Power say that you must ensure that your customers see you as a knowledge provider, not just a product or service provider.

Think laterally when you think about promotion
You need to get your web address in different places. For example, a car rental company has made its web page available on BT's internal intranet.

Getting the price right
Butler and Power say:

> Imagine passing a vending machine on a sweltering hot day and noticing a flashing sign that told you that Coke was slashing its price by 10 pence because of the heat of the day. The sign flashes the exact temperature and seems to be calling you to put your money in the slot and buy your bargain can of fizzy sugar water. That's the e-business advantage – even prices can now be responsive.

Some companies are already organized to take the advantage. Coca-Cola is one of them. It is just about to experiment with 'smart' vending machines that hook up to its internal computer network. These machines will monitor local inventory and conditions and alter prices accordingly.

> There's a revolution brewing in pricing that promises to profoundly alter the way goods are marketed and sold. In the future, marketers will offer special deals – tailored just for you, just for the moment – on everything from theatre tickets to bank loans to camcorders. *Business Week*, 4 May 1998

Fluid pricing is enabled through a mix of technical and marketing skill. The technology allows sellers to collect detailed data about customers' buying habits, preferences – even spending limits – so they can tailor their products and prices. It's the marketers who have to take this data and apply it to the customers they have, as well as the customers they want.

Making e-commerce happen in your company
E-Commerce requires a well-developed strategy:

1 *High level support* Companies recognize the need for high level support at board level and a budget. This will need senior management vision and understanding.
2 *Need for an enterprise-wide approach* The organization may have to be redesigned to provide an appropriate customer interface and order fulfilment. Responsibility for e-commerce must be allocated to individuals with cross-business unit responsibilities who report to the board. However, in French companies, for example, e-commerce was more likely to be led by the marketing department and to be a joint venture between departments than in companies from other countries.
3 *Organization* E-commerce is not just about internet-based transactions. It is the creation of a whole way of thinking. A programme needs to be set up that outlines how the whole organization will evolve within the networked economy, embracing the issues of marketing, technology, training and resources.
4 *Integration* The point of customer contact – the web front end – needs to fully integrate with existing systems, sales order processing, purchase ledgers and so on.
5 *Technology* E-commerce demands additional security levels. Authentication and non-repudiation are also areas that need to be thought about.
6 *Payment systems* Ensure that the payment system you adopt is flexible.

7 *Use of designated resource* Even when companies identified that electronic commerce is an enterprise-wide undertaking, they still designated a resource to implement it. The largest companies (in terms of employees) were more likely to rely on the IT department for electronic support.

Improving profitability

There are three areas of potential benefit – improved levels of customer services, increased sales volume and reduced operating costs. E-commerce demands innovation within business. It provides the opportunity to deliver existing products to new markets, new products to existing markets and evolve radical new business models with a completely different underlying philosophical framework.

The future

Web telephones will enable individuals to browse the web using their mobile telephones and considering that, while only one in 10,000 people worldwide has access to a PC, one in four has access to a telephone, the significance of this development is clear. Most commerce experts believe that financial institutions will look to give away these devices in a bid to woo customers to their internet banking services. In addition, set-top boxes that provide internet accesses from standard televisions are also expected to gain widespread acceptance. It is expected that at least 40 per cent of people will access the internet from non-PC devices by 2000 (DTI, *E-commerce-The challenge for UK business*).

The Ecademy (http://www.theecademy.com) can provide you with the knowledge that drives e-commerce. They provide information and courses on a wide range of subjects.

Useful world wide web links

Hear are some web sites that will hopefully provide you with further information, ideas for business opportunities or ideas for web page design:

- http://www.baynetworks.com/Solutions/
- http://www.bt.com/business/
- http://www.eca.org.uk – Electronic Commerce Association
- http://www.ibm.com/e-business/what/how/ns.html
- http://www.isi.gov.uk – Information Society Initiative for Business
- http://www.itforall.gov.uk – IT for all Programme
- http://www.interforum.org
- http://lucent.com/enterprise/
- http://www.opentext.com
- http://marketplace.unisys.com/coolice/index.html
- http://www.microsoft.com/siteserver/commerce/default.asp
- http://www.springboard/solutions
- http://www.sun.com/e-commerce/solutions
- http://www.unisys.com/execmag

Examples of electronic business:

- http://www.buckinghamgate.com – shopping
- http://www.eaglestardirect.co.uk – insurance
- http://wwww.ecn.dk – publishing
- http://www.fs-on-line.com – travel
- http://www.ideal.co.uk – distribution
- http://www.nationwide.co.uk – banking
- http://www.sparbanken.se – banking
- http://www.waterstone.co.uk – booksellers
- http://www.blackwell.co.uk – booksellers

Shift in customer behaviour

The internet is forcing both traditional and new players to get away from the narrow, technology-driven approach of telecommunications to the far more broad marketing-oriented view of electronic tradition and information highways. The internet has seen a phenomenal increase in the number of users.

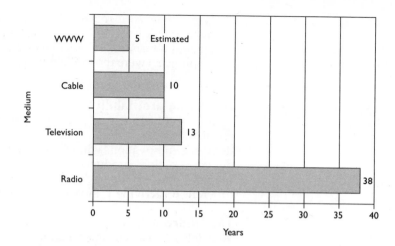

Figure 12.2
Years to reach 50 million users

In 1998, the USA was the top user of the internet with over 76 million users (*Computer Almanac Industry*). Japan was second with over 9 million users, closely followed by the UK (over 8 million users). Other countries in the top ten online countries worldwide were Germany (over 7 million), Canada (over 6 million), Australia (over 4 million), France Sweden, Italy and Spain.

A 1996 study from US motivational behavioural psychologist Bernadette Tracy indicates a real shift in consumer behaviour, set in motion by the internet phenomenon. With rising comfort levels towards the use of the internet, especially amongst the category of users in the twenty-five to forty-nine age bracket, we see a move away from entertainment to information services. In Tracy's study of 500 participants, 81 per cent professed to use the internet to research products and services. The percentages below indicate the number of respondents involved in using the internet for research and ordering products and services.

Table 12.2 Using the information highway. *Source*: Bernadette Tracy/ISSR

Products/services	Researching (%)	Ordering (%)
Computers	84	52
Travel	70	46
Financial services	46	31
Cars	44	0

Research indicated a shift in information gathering from traditional sources to the internet. In 1996 there were 61 million users worldwide, 147 million in 1998. Projections for 2000 indicate 320 million users, rising to 720 million in 2005.

A study among 5000 homes, conducted for America Online by Nielsen Media Research in 1998, has come up with some interesting statistics. The study reports that households with internet or online access are watching

Table 12.3 Shift in information gathering

Activity	Change in behaviour (%)
Watching less TV	64
Sleeping less	29
Reading less newspapers	25
Reading less magazines	24
Spending less time at office	17

15 per cent less television – 8 hours less per week – than non-internet households. In internet homes, daily television usage has decreased by 19 per cent between 4.30 and 6.00pm, by 16 per cent between 6.00 and 8.00pm and by 9 per cent between 11.00pm and 1.00am.

Visa International estimated in late 1998 an increase in global consumer online purchases at a rate of 67 per cent compounded annually over the following five years. In a recent study, the company has considered that by the year 2002 the market value for online purchases could be as high as US$100 billion. Visa has projected that nearly US$15.3 billion will be spent over the internet in 1998, an increase of almost 100 per cent from 1997. Research is ongoing.

Convenience and time-saving motivate internet shopping, plus ease of use and saving money. In the last six months 51 per cent of MSN UK users have shopped online (32 per cent MSN Fr, 73 per cent MSN De). For most, internet shopping is as, or more, secure than ordering by telephone – 70 per cent of MSN UK users are happy to use a credit card over the web (68 per cent MSN FR, 41 per cent MSN De). Goods purchased range from music to books to computers through to a range of financial services and even holidays.

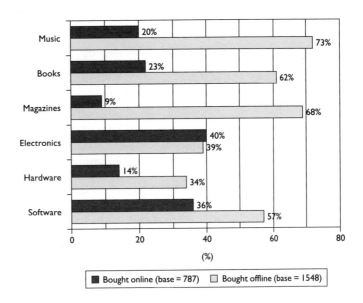

Figure 12.3
Most frequent UK purchases.
Source: MSN

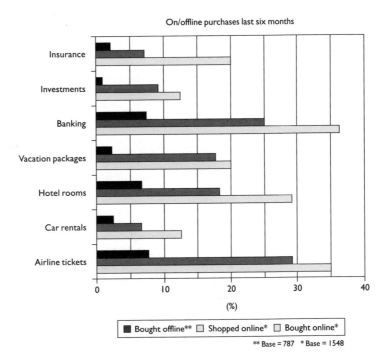

Figure 12.4
Travel and finance purchases

305

The internet allows for impulse buying, informed buying and comparison shopping. BMW find that 55 per cent of their advertising and general leads are generated online and that 8 per cent of these leads are converted by BMW dealers.

In America 13.8 million Americans, or 27 per cent of internet users, use the internet or an online services to make travel plans or reservations. Almost half of them (6.3 million) actually made an online reservation (*Source*: Travel Industry Association Report, taken from *Travel Management Daily*). In 1998 16 per cent of all US trades will be on the web (*Source*: Cyber Dialogue *'Interactive Consumers' Study*). It is estimated (FIND/SVP) that in America in 1998 75 million adults will be on the web, 25 million children and there will be 28 million internet households.

Dell Computers make $14 million sales a day from their web site, of which 10–11 per cent is from Europe. Michael Dell predicts by 2000 50 per cent of total company revenue will be from the web site. Support information is posted on the web, including FAQs (frequently asked questions) and self diagnostic tools and this saves on traditional support costs.

Tesco's have set up a web site, Tesco Direct, designed to reach customers who can't or won't go to a superstore – these are termed 'new customers'. There is a higher average order value than store traffic. It is quicker and cheaper to open 'web stores' than physical ones.

Amazon have set up a web site for the purchase of books over the internet. They offered the idea to Barnes & Noble; they realized their US service wasn't competitive in Europe. They bought local companies in UK and Germany. Delivery and service are now equal and they are outspending UK rivals. Their online catalogue has more than 1.5 million titles.

However despite some success, a significant number of people have doubts about shopping over the internet. These doubts include:

- Worry about iffy retailers (81 per cent).
- Hassle of returning (72 per cent).
- Worry about credit cards (69 per cent).
- Worry about junk mail (63 per cent).
- Want to see and touch what they will buy (62 per cent).

In order to get shoppers to come back for more there needs to be strong brand awareness, brand association and brand interaction. Brand interaction has several components:

- Don't keep your shoppers waiting.
- Don't hide the goods.
- Build trust.
- Don't hide the prices.
- Make human contact.

There is a matching of objectives with online strategy and tactics:

- Brand awareness and traffic generation.
- On- and offline campaign integration.
- Product promotion and customer acquisition.
- Build brand in editorial environment.
- Promote product through event sponsorship.
- Promote product trial and add value via interactivity.
- Build qualified prospect database.
- Distribute product and services.
- Expand into international markets.

Market segmentation

In assimilating internet survey data, PSI Global determined six core consumer segments and their characteristics. These categories and their breakdown of the total surveyed are:

- *Power users* (13 per cent) spend the most time online; have high trust in technology and the safety of online transacting; use the internet for financial transactions, information and entertainment; and are early adopters.
- *Proficient transactors* (20 per cent) have less experience with PCs and online services; are slightly less affluent than proficient transactors; are interested in or use online banking, bill payment and investing; and have less interest in online shopping than the previous category.
- *Online novices* (10 per cent) are the most marginal online group; have low use or interest in online banking, bill payments, shopping and investing; consist of a mix of professionals and blue-collar workers with moderate-income levels; do not have a lot of experience with PCs or online services; and are not very trusting of technology or online security.
- The *disinteresteds* (15 per cent) are similar to the previous category but are much more likely to be professionals; have a higher income and are more experienced with PCs than online novices; have higher interest in online investing than online novices; are concerned about fraud and do not trust current security measures; and have a low use of banking technology such as automated teller machine and debit cards.
- *Entertainment seekers* (25 per cent) use the internet as an entertainment outlet, with low interest in transacting; have an income lower than the US household average; consists of a high number of retired persons, students and blue-collar workers; have a high online time at home but little at work; and have low use and interest in online shopping, banking, bill payments and investing.

V-commerce

The e-commerce world typically extends from the keyboard to the computer screen as transactions are made over the internet. Several companies now are collaborating on an initiative to encourage consumers to make electronic transactions more conveniently over the telephone.

The system, called v-commerce (v = voice), allows users to conduct self-service transactions alternately using the web and the telephone. Heading the charge for this technology is the newly-formed V-Commerce Alliance, which includes Artisoft Inc, Aspect Telecommunications Inc, Brite Voice Systems Inc, Dialogic Corp, Destiny Software, Motorola Inc, Natural Microsystems Corp, Network Engines Inc, Nuance Communications, Periphonics Corp, SAP Labs Inc, Syntellect Inc, SCITEC Ltd, via World Network, Visa International, Voice Integrators and webMethods Inc. These firms are combining speech recognition with products such as application servers, packaged applications and telephony platforms.

The initiative will enable a consumer to make an airline reservation over the web, then later call a specific number to find out the departure gate or to provide frequent flyer account information. This information can be spoken into a voice-recognition program, which in some cases can contain speaker verification technology to ensure a secure transaction. The system eliminates the need to repeat to a customer service representative the information previously keyed in for the reservation over the web.

Companies looking to deploy v-commerce applications have several options of interaction that their customers, business partners or employees might use. These include voice in/out (using a telephone or cellular telephone for low-cost access, various commerce applications, such as brokerage and travel systems) or web in/out (integrating a common web business server with services accessible over the telephone). Another 'futuristic' style is a voice in, web or device out option, which integrates use of voice input and visual output to improve efficiency in completing a transaction.

E-commerce unstoppable

Electronic commerce is rapidly changing the contemporary economy, altering the way businesses operate, as well as how consumers shop. E-commerce is helping businesses communicate with potential customers without relying on traditional and expensive human resources. Because it is both convenient and economically feasible, an increasing number of businesses and customers are turning to the web. E-commerce can help entrepreneurs start up a business with minimal overhead costs. It leverages technology to provide strategic business advantages. E-commerce technology has begun to give small companies a way to compete against the major players.

E-commerce is now making such an impact in certain businesses that we can start talking about an economic revolution. While the internet is still growing, with something like 500,000 new users a month, more important is the fact that those who became involved over the last two to four years are now seasoned internet users – no longer interested in surfing, but well aware of the potential offered by the net.

These experienced users can be roughly divided into two major groups:

1 Children and teenagers, still a very large user group – and it is good to remember that it was this group which kick-started the internet in 1994/1995. Because of limited spending power they have a smaller impact on e-commerce.
2 Young professionals (25–40 years). In this group each individual internet user has now established web sites and activities that they are interested in and in most situations that now includes some form of e-commerce (99 per cent based on credit card payments).

E-commerce activities vary widely. Once again it is important to stress that they are very much based on individual needs and interests. They include business transactions, but also the purchase of groceries (home delivered or picked up at the corner-shop opposite the railway station), clothes and even cars (you look around, select your model then go onto the internet to get the best price).

According to research from the MARC Group over the last six months net clothing sales in the USA have increased by 200 per cent while the average online grocery shopper spends an average of $2,072 per year on groceries. Programs can now put your 'body' onto the internet and you can dress it to see what suits you. The same technology is now used for the doll clothing market, a very lucrative market where tens of thousands of adult doll lovers around the world buy and sell tailor-made dolls' clothing. This market existed pre-internet, but the new technology has greatly increased the business.

While the general consensus is that e-commerce will develop initially in the business market, online retailing could be a wild card. It promises to make it easy for shoppers to compare a wide range of prices and features, a shopping environment that should also lead to lower prices. This is a very powerful benefit to consumers.

We have all heard the story about bookseller Amazon.com. Using sharp pricing that is at least comparable to, if not less expensive than, the alternative and attracting over three million book buyers, Amazon.com is making a strong argument for would-be online-only businesses to jump into the market. The same applies to software, CDs and a variety of information products.

E-commerce servers

Ovum has released in-depth research on how businesses should match their choice of commerce servers to their online business strategy.

Setting up to do business online is a high-risk venture. Businesses who go online are taking part in a very public experiment. For every rising star of online commerce, there are massive dark spaces in between, with no sign of life. As the internet changes from a communications channel to a revenue channel, it will trap many organizations into evolutionary blind alleys of their own making.

The internet and the web create an extraordinary volatility in the value chain. Relationships between organizations, customers and suppliers can be broken, and created, at higher speed, and with greater business impact, than ever before.

In this business environment organizations must be able to quickly learn from experience, and then adapt. The systems which support the business can either assist in this process, or leave companies trapped by their first mistakes.

The market for commerce servers is new. Two years ago it did not exist. According to Ovum:

- This market almost doubled in size in nine months, from $57 million in fiscal year 1996, to $110 million for the first three-quarters of 1997.
- As of the third quarter of 1997, there were 5000 licensed commerce server sites worldwide, serving 15,000 stores.

At present, one of the most striking aspects of the market structure is the indirect competition from 'do-it-yourself' solutions. Ovum estimates that only half the transactional commerce sites on the market today are using a packaged solution. (Information provided by kind permission of Paul Buddle Community Pty Ltd, 1999, e-mail: pbc@budde.com.au, web www.budde.com.au)

For each organization, e-commerce will have an effect on the organizational–customer interface. For example, in the case of higher education, the internet and other national and international networks create environments where intellectual capacity, information and knowledge bases and methodologies are made available to learners anytime, anywhere. A richly interconnected and highly leveraged network of computing resources, tools and information resources that provide students and teaching staff with unprecedented access across disciplinary, institutional and national boundaries has emerged through the use of the information technologies. The evolving national and international network infrastructure allows access by students and teachers to each other and to alternate centres of expertise.

Use of the network for research and learning has aptly been called 'network scholarship'. Researchers are increasingly using it effectively in their scholarly and research pursuits. Bulletin boards, 'virtual laboratories', 'collaboratories' and other means are being used to share equipment, findings and ideas in real time. The network can be a research lab, a forum for debate and a new venue for testing and disseminating information.

This new approach to education will restructure the learning industry:

Table 12.4

Old	New
Competition is other universities	Competition is everyone
Student as interrupting research	Student as a customer
Delivery in a classroom	Delivery anywhere
Multi-cultural	Global
Bricks and mortar	Bits and bytes
Single discipline	Multi-discipline
Institution centric	Market centric
Government funded	Market funded
Technology as an expense	Technology as differentiator

This scenario will require the transformation of higher education. Similarly, technology is uniquely affecting the way that information and money are transmitted. Data has become a principal corporate asset, and the shape of customer relationships are being reconfigured by the internet. Companies are attempting to use technology to reach customers directly and, in some cases, circumvent traditional financial relationships. Traditional risk management strategies in commerce and payments systems are changing, and business-to-business commerce is increasingly relying upon electronic networks that reduce costs and rearrange traditional commercial and legal relationships.

A distinct and continuing movement toward the corporate consolidation of financial services and technology companies will be seen in 1999. This will result in mergers, acquisitions, partnerships, alliances and joint ventures that link financial services companies and the technologies searching for new ways to reach and serve customers in the electronic age with a host of innovative products.

To keep up to date on e-commerce transactions go to www.ffhsj.com/bancmail/bancpage

Summary

Competing in the information age
As you can see we are in the midst of a revolutionary transformation. The combination of globalization, deregulated markets, markets wired together by a converging information highway is being dominated by new and transformed organizations. Customers expect more and are becoming more demanding. This has increased competitiveness based on innovative customer service, and flexibility providing better quality, cheaper products and quicker services tailored exactly to customer needs.

During the industrial age, from 1858 to about 1975, companies succeeded by how well they could capture the benefits from economies of scale and scope. Technology mattered but it was used in a different way – companies would use technology to offer efficient mass-produced standardized goods. Over the last couple of decades market power moved to channels and now market power has moved to the consumer.

Global information and communication resources are becoming available to everyone at extremely low cost. As big business shrinks, small- and medium-sized businesses grow. A new management challenge requires competency to manage alliances with multiple business partners and tie them together into a business network. Companies can use opportunities created by trade deregulation and the internet to make their companies global operations. Organizations can team up with designers in one country, cheap labour in another and take advantage of low tax duties in different countries.

Use the information age scorecard from Futureworld (http://asp.futureworld.co.za/futureworld/quiz.asp) to find out if you have the right vision on life to meet the challenges of the year 2000.

New capabilities
Organizations need new capabilities to be successful. They have to be more capable in managing their intangible assets. For example they may include:

- New market segments need to be identified and served effectively and efficiently.
- Products and services must be designed to meet the specific needs of targeted customer segments and designed and customized at low cost with short lead times.
- Organizations need to try integrating and supplying, production and delivery processes so that operations are triggered by customer orders, and not by production plans that push products and services throughout the value chain.
- Some companies may need to compete globally against the best companies in the world – the competition needs to be redefined.
- As product life cycles shrink companies who compete in industries with a rapid technological innovation need to be able to anticipate future customer needs and be able to innovate product and service offerings very quickly.

- Information technology and databases and systems must be used as the driving force that links many of these ideas together.
- Organizations need to be looked at as whole systems in an open relationship with the environment.

Gummesson says that in the future, less than 10 per cent of the working population of a mature industrialized nation will work on the shop floor. In order to meet customer needs the total offer of goods and services must be made. Services are now key aspects of differentiation and have a strategic marketing role. Internally within organizations, services have been broken up so that very often each section works as a profit centre, with many services being contracted out.

The network approach sees industrial marketing, in a network of relationships between people in the network, accentuate:

- The longevity and stability of relationships.
- The importance of collaboration as a means to an effective market economy.
- The importance of transaction and switching costs.
- The active participation of the parties in the relationship.
- The importance of power and knowledge and how it is managed.
- The importance of technology, procurement and logistics.
- The management of trust, risk and uncertainty.

Currently 80 per cent of business on the internet is business to business, it is expected to extend to consumer markets. Marketing needs to extend itself out of the marketing department to managing an organization that has a marketing focus, where people are seen as an asset, and the key ingredient to success is providing superior service.

The Marketing Customer Interface   3 Hours' Duration

This examination is in two sections.

Part A is compulsory and worth 40 per cent of the total marks.

Part B has six questions, select three. Each answer will be worth 20 per cent of the total marks.

DO NOT repeat the question in your answer but show clearly the number of the question attempted on appropriate pages of the answer book.

Rough workings should be included in the answer book and ruled through after use.

Part A

The PleasureFood Restaurant Group

As the name of the company suggests, the PleasureFood Group operates a collection of fast-food restaurants located principally in town and city centres, shopping malls, leisure complexes, and airports. The Group has expanded from a single cafe/bar opened by the PleasureFood company's owner about 30 years ago; it now has 75 units, some run directly by PleasureFood's personnel, and some operated by franchisees.

The PleasureFood strategy has been founded on organic growth, but it is now contemplating more rapid expansion, if promising lines of development can be found. Some of the major alternatives include: diversification into food 'manufacturing', industrial catering (i.e., restaurants inside office buildings for corporate employees), the creation of branded food products for sale through supermarkets, and entry into overseas markets.

Each of the PleasureFood restaurants is built to a common standard and is intended to provide identical meals and service. Head Office supplies detailed instructions about every aspect of the PleasureFood operation, including portion control, cleanliness and hygiene, the appearance of the staff, the words and phrases used when communicating with customers, and price/product standardisation.

Currently, PleasureFood's principal customer segments are teenagers, shoppers, and families with children. It has around 30 per cent of its chosen market place, its major competitors being McDonalds, Burger King, and a couple of the major pizza companies; the remainder of the competition is occupied by very small, local companies.

The PleasureFood group is a well-managed and successful company. It is in good shape financially. However, the Board consists entirely of people who have spent their careers with PleasureFood, and Board meetings are dominated by the presence of the company's owner.

Question 1

You are a consultant who has been engaged by PleasureFood's Marketing Director in order to offer the company some guidance about the optimal direction which it should pursue in the future. Produce a report initially aimed at the Marketing Director but ultimately intended for distribution to the Board, in which you respond to each of the issues raised by the Marketing Director in her brief, as follows.

(a) Given the fact that the PleasureFood Group has never established a customer database, and has never systematically investigated customer perceptions about its products and service, how could it cost-effectively acquire such a database and also secure definitive information about customer satisfaction?

(10 marks)

(b) What are the major trends in customer segmentation and customer dynamics which could affect the PleasureFood Group's business in the foreseeable future?

(10 marks)

(c) Assuming that one of the options facing the PleasureFood Group is expansion into overseas markets, what are the factors which should be evaluated before such an option is actively pursued?

(10 marks)

(d) How could the PleasureFood Group create competitive advantages for itself against the major threat presented by McDonalds?

(10 marks)

Note. It is permissible to make assumptions by adding to the case details supplied above, provided the essence of the case study is neither changed nor undermined in any way by what is added. You may assume that the PleasureFood Group is located in the UK or in any other country of your choice.

Part B – Answer THREE Questions Only

Question 2

Critically examine the accuracy of each of the following statements which are often to be found in marketing literature:

(a) 'The customer is king (or queen)'

(b) 'The customer is always right'

In what circumstances is it possible that these propositions could be successfully challenged? How accurate are they, for example, when applied to (1) the concept of the 'internal customer' and (2) the 'customers' of a monopoly such as a water utility, municipal authority or taxation-funded central-government department?

(20 marks)

Question 3

What does the term 'customer-centric' mean when applied to the structure of an organisation engaged in **either** financial services OR retailing? Having produced your answer, discuss the features of any organisation known to you which in your judgment is **not** customer-centric, and outline what changes would need to be introduced if the organisation in question were to seek to become genuinely customer-centric.

(20 marks)

Question 4

Debates continue to range about whether mass customisation is (a) a marketing opportunity, (b) a threat, (c) a passing fad, or (d) an illusion. Imagine that you work for a car manufacturer: write a report for your Marketing Manager in which you comment on each of the four interpretations offered above, in the context of the motor industry, and offer a reasoned assessment of the benefits and risks associated with mass customisation so far as your own company is concerned.

(20 marks)

Question 5

You are the newly-recruited marketing officer for either an international airline, a newspaper publisher, or a holiday package-tour business.

Produce a memo for your company's marketing department in which you explore

(a) The future for electronic commerce in general terms;

(b) The implications so far as your own organisation is concerned, and

(c) A reasoned set of actions which you believe your company should take in order to capitalise on the opportunity or prepare itself for the threats.

(20 marks)

Question 6

It has been widely argued that, in the future, manufacturing companies will find it virtually impossible to remain profitable through reliance on manufacturing alone; as a result, they will be forced, whether they like it or not, to achieve competitive superiority (if they can) in such as arenas as customer service and relationship marketing. Why might it be thought that profitability from manufacturing alone is so problematic? In what specific ways can manufacturing companies ensure their continued success through customer service and relationship marketing? Illustrate your answer with relevant examples.

(20 marks)

Question 7

'Customers are becoming more aspirational, more demanding, more litigious and more ethical, all at the same time', you hear someone say at a marketing conference. What do these claims mean, and what evidence could you produce to support them? Assuming that the speaker's predictions are correct, what are the implications of these developments so far as effective consumer marketing is concerned?

(20 marks)

Specimen question paper: outline marking scheme

Introduction

Scripts will be assessed against the five competencies explored in the Tutors Guidance Notes, namely:

- Breadth of familiarity with the subject-matter
- Depth of comprehension and understanding
- Demonstration of a businesslike perspective
- Application capability
- Packaging skills

The precise balance between these five will depend on the priorities within any given question. No specific mark allocation will be made available for 'Packaging skills', but it may be assumed that it could influence about 10 per cent of the assessment (i.e., 2 marks out of 20 for PART B, 4 marks out of 40 for PART A).

Part A

As the question wording itself specifies, 10 marks may be awarded for each of the substantive ingredients within the case-study report. The four separate totals, when added together, may be supplemented by up to a further 4 marks for adherence to the requirement for a business report.

Part B

Question 2

Critical examination of the two statements supplied (10 marks) plus a further 10 marks for comments on their accuracy when applied to 'internal' customers and the 'customers' of a monopoly.

Question 3

Ten marks for exploration of the term 'customer-centric' in relation to structure, leadership, recruitment, reward systems, values, processes geared around customer types or categories, and so forth; a further 10 marks for references to an organisation which is not customer-centric and what it might do to transform itself.

Question 4

Commentary on the four interpretations of mass customisation (10 marks) plus the remaining 10 marks for an assessment of the benefits and risks within the car manufacturer.

Question 5

The future for electronic commerce in general terms (10 marks) plus 10 marks for the specific implications and suggested action programme.

Question 6

Examination of the reasons why profitability from manufacturing alone could be problematic (10 marks), plus 10 marks for the ways in which manufacturing companies can survive through customer service and relationship marketing. Credit will particularly be given for the inclusion of examples, e.g., GE's use of microchips and satellite communications for product maintenance.

Question 7

Discussion of the claim that customers are more aspirational, more demanding, more litigious and more ethical, plus supply of supporting evidence (10 marks), with a further 10 marks for the implications in the field of consumer marketing.

Relationship to the indicative content

Part A

1 Overview, Concepts and Background, *especially 1.2, 1.3.*
2 Managing the Marketing/Customer Interface, *especially 2.1, 2.3 and 2.4.*
3 Customer Dynamics, *especially 3.2.*
4 Investigating Customer Dynamics, *passim.*
5 Customer Dynamics and the Future, *passim.*

Part B

Question 2

1 Overview, Concepts and Background, *especially 1.1.*
2 Managing the Marketing/Customer Interface, *especially 2.2.*
3 Customer Dynamics, *especially 3.1.*

Question 3

1 Overview, Concepts and Background, *especially 1.4.*
2 Managing the Marketing/Customer Interface, *passim.*

Question 4
1 Overview, Concepts and Background, *especially 1.2, 1.3.*
2 Managing the Marketing/Customer Interface, *especially 2.4.*
3 Customer Dynamics, *passim.*
5 Customer Dynamics and the Future, *especially 5.1.*

Question 5
1 Overview, Concepts and Background, *especially 1.2.*
2 Managing the Marketing/Customer Interface, *passim.*
3 Customer Dynamics, *passim.*
5 Customer Dynamics and the Future, *passim.*

Question 6
1 Overview, Concepts and Background, *especially 1.2, 1.3.*
2 Managing the Marketing/Customer Interface, *especially 2.1, 2.3 and 2.4.*
3 Customer Dynamics, *especially 3.4.*
5 Customer Dynamics and the Future, *passim.*

Question 7
1 Overview, Concept and Background, *especially 1.2.*
2 Managing the Marketing/Customer Interface, *especially 2.4.*
3 Customer Dynamics, *passim.*
4 Investigating Customer Dynamics, *passim.*
5 Customer Dynamics and the Future, *especially 5.1.*

The Marketing Customer Interface

Aims and objectives
- To address the marketing opportunities presented through effective interaction between the organization and its customers.
- To equip students with a conceptual framework which enables them adequately to distinguish between different stakeholder groups across a variety of marketing environments.
- To develop a sophisticated understanding of customer dynamics, in which customer behaviour is viewed as an interactive process influencing product/service innovation.
- To acquaint students with the range of methodologies through which customer dynamics may be investigated, measured, analysed and interpreted.
- To examine the stretegic, managerial and operational implications of customer-focused marketing.
- To explore trends in customer behaviour over the foreseeable future, both incremental and transformational.

Learning outcomes
Students will be able to:
- Describe and interpret the significance of the differences between 'customers', 'users', 'consumers' and 'payers'.
- Critically appraise the relationship between customer dynamics and marketing.
- Evaluate the effectiveness of the marketing/customer interface within specific product sectors, and propose cost-effective performance improvements where appropriate.
- Understand the (psychological, social, cultural and economic) factors influencing customer dynamics in particular marketing scenarios and the impact upon product/service improvement or innovation.
- Analyse key issues in customer dynamics including segmentation, relationship marketing, and the behavioural patterns found within the Decision-Making Unit.
- Design and carry out operational investigations into customer dynamics, customer perceptions of product/service performance, and customer satisfaction/delight.
- Develop visionary yet practical strategies for mobilizing customer-focused marketing programmes within defined organizational settings.
- Maximize returns from investments in IT and people within the arena of customer-focused marketing and customer service.
- Comprehend the directions for customer dynamics in the forseeable future and identify marketing opportunities.

Indicative content and weighting

2.1 Overview, concepts and background (10%)

2.1.1 *Terminology and definitions:*
- Identifying 'customer', 'user', 'consumer' and 'payer': Interpretations of customer focus in organizations.
- Assumptions, stereotypes and myths about the marketing/customer interface and customer dynamics.
- SWOT analysis and key issues.

2.1.2 *The emergence of customer power in the new competitive climate:*
- Driving forces and organizational responses.
- Significance for the marketing/customer interface.

2.1.3 *Customer-focused marketing in specific economic sectors:*
- Customer orientation within major profit-seeking and competitive arenas and within not-for-profit organizations.

2.2 Managing the marketing/customer interface (30%)

2.2.1 *The strategic dimension: vision and leadership*
- Corporate strategy, culture and structure; the role of top-down leadership, vision, empowerment and related processes.
- Systems for stimulating customer-focused behaviour within and across organizations.
- Customer focus, customer relationships, retention, and customer service as key ingredients in the drive for sustainable competitive advantage.
- The functional/organizational aspects of customer focus: accountability in the fields of customer focus and customer service.
- The strategic rationale for outsourcing: benefits, risks, applications, goal-setting and monitoring.
- Customer-related measures as part of the corporate scorecard.

2.2.2 *The managerial dimension: mobilizing performances:*
- Key factors in maximizing the corporate benefits from the organization/customer interface: Information Technology and people management.
- Motivational issues and job design for front-line customer-facing roles.

2.2.3 *Creating positive relationships with customers:*
- The features, benefits and costs of relationship marketing.
- Methods of communicating with customers.
- Customer/supplier partnerships and agreements.

2.2.4 *Innovation and the culture of continuous improvement:*
- Sources of customer-focused innovation; barriers to implementation and how to overcome them.
- The role of information-gathering and analysis in generating customer-focused product/service innovation.

2.3 Customer dynamics (25%)

2.3.1 *The holistic perspective of customer behaviour:*
- Modelling customer dynamics: rationale, objectives, applications, limitations.
- Individuals, groups, and organizations as customers.
- Innovation and conservatism in customer behaviour: why new products/services succeed or fail.
- Customer expectations and perceptions: dissatisfaction and delight.

2.3.2 *Classifying customers for competitive advantage:*
- Customer segmentation: rationale, objectives; features of effective customer segments.
- Segmentation systems for individual consumers, customer groups and organizations.
- New approaches to classifying customers.

2.3.3 *The individual as customer:*
- Attitudes and behaviour: relevance to the marketing/customer interface.
- Factors influencing the individual's behaviour as a customer.
- Personality profiling for individual customers.

2.3.4 *The group as customer:*
  – Power, influence and authority within the primary group: targeting the decision-making unit (DMU).
  – Secondary groups: their significance for customer behaviour and implications for national, international and global marketing.
2.3.5 *The organization as customer:*
  – Special features of business-to-business transactions and related customer dynamics.
  – The organizational DMU: characteristics, roles, decision processes and marketing implications.

2.4 Investigating customer dynamics (20%)
2.4.1 *Basic principles:*
  – Systematic techniques for investigating customer dynamics.
  – The creation of meaningful populations (based on market segments).
2.4.2 *Quantitative methodologies for investigating customer dynamics:*
  – Questionnaires, surveys, interviews and other primary methods of data/information collection.
2.4.3 *Qualitative methodologies for investigating customer dynamics:*
  – Projective techniques: features, benefits, risks and applications.
  – Focus groups: features, benefits, risks and applications.
2.4.4 *Secondary information sources:*
  – Sources of secondary data: government statistics, market research agencies, the media, etc.

2.5 Customer dynamics and the future (15%)
2.5.1 *Trends in customer behaviour and expectations:*
  – Enhancement of customer expectations and organizational service standards and performance delivery.
  – Increasing opportunities for customer complaints and legal enhancements to consumer power.
  – Customer concerns about ecological, environmental and ethical issues.
  – Emergent customer attitudes and their impact on (re)purchasing behaviour.
  – Future paterns for segmentation: customized products and services, demographic and social trends, etc.
2.5.2 *Market trends with customer-facing implications:*
  – The global market place and global products and services.
  – Electronic commerce and its impact on the organization/customer interface.
  – Customer service as a sustainable competitive advantage.
  – The decline of manufacturing and the emergence of new service-sector industries.

Glossary

Ad hoc research   Research that has been tailor-made to meet market research needs that cannot be met by standardized surveys.

Adoption   The decision an individual takes to become a regular user of a product.

Adoption process   The mental process an individual goes through from first hearing about an innovation before deciding to adopt a product.

Advertising   Any paid form of non-personal presentation or promotion of ideas, goods or services through the media.

Advertising elasticity   The measure of the extent to which changes in advertising spending affect demand. If a small increase in the amount of advertising spent causes a considerable increase in the demand for a product or service, then the product/service would be called advertising elastic.

$$\text{Formula} = \frac{\% \text{ change in demand}}{\% \text{ change in advertising spending}}$$

Advertising ethics   Ethics covers the moral issues that are raised by the influence advertising has on people's minds.

Advertising objective   The specific outcome that the advertising is intended to accomplish with a specific target audience in a defined period of time.

Advertising strategy   The plan that is used for meeting the advertising objectives. It will cover the target market, the preferred media and frequency, costs, method of evaluation and the overall style of advertising.

After-sales service   The action a firm takes to cover any needs a customer may have once a sale has been made.

Alternative evaluation   A stage in the DMP in which the customer will use information to evaluate other brands in the choice set.

Attention, interest, desire, action (AIDA)   A method of explaining the stages through which advertising should work.

Attitude   The favourable or unfavourable evaluation, feelings or tendencies a person consistently shows towards an object or idea.

Available market   A group of customers who have the money, an interest in and access to a particular product or service.

Baby boom   Refers to the increase in birth rate following the Second World War and lasting until the 1960s. The 'baby boomers', many of whom are already middle aged, represent a considerable target-market.

Barriers to communication   Attitudinal or physical reasons as to why messages fail to be communicated.

Behaviour segmentation   The division of the market into groups of people based on their knowledge, attitude, response to, or use of, a product or service.

Belief   A thought that a person holds about something.

Bench-marking   Standards that are based on the achievements of the most efficient producers within a market place. They are used by companies to set standards by which progress can be measured.

Bias An opinion or influence that favours one line of thought rather than another. For example, the presentation of market research data may be biased to favour a particular viewpoint which is not necessarily borne out by the data.

Blind product test A test in which consumers are asked to evaluate two or more rival products where the brand name is not revealed.

Body language The way in which humans use their bodies either consciously or unconsciously to convey non-verbal messages.

Brainstorming A creative activity in which a group of people are encouraged to express their ideas however bizarre they may appear to be. Once the ideas have all been expressed each idea is considered and evaluated.

Brand A name, sign, symbol, design, colour or combination of these used to identify and differentiate goods and services from their competitors.

Brand image The beliefs that consumers have about particular products or services.

Brand loyalty The consistent loyalty that consumers show in their purchasing habits towards a particular product or service. Brand loyalty can be active in that consumers prefer a particular brand, or passive in that they are used to a pattern of purchasing and cannot be bothered to change.

Brand mapping The selection of key variables that distinguish and differentiate brands within a market and the plotting of the position of each one against the other in order to establish gaps and niches in the market place.

Brand mark The non-verbal elements of a brand name, such as colour, typeface, design, sign or symbol.

Brand name The verbal element of a product or service name.

British Standard 5750 A certification system for ensuring that a firm sets quality targets and then monitors their performance in relation to those targets.

British Standard 7750 A certification system for ensuring acceptable environmental management standards.

Brown goods The term used for goods such as televisions and hi-fis that were traditionally made with wood casings.

Business cycle Periodic fluctuations in economic activity. *See* Unit 9.

Business environment Includes factors outside an individual firm's control such as economic circumstances, changing technology, government legislation and policy, the social environment – commonly referred to as PEST factors.

Business ethics Moral principles that should underpin decision making.

Buyer readiness states Refer to the stages consumers pass through in the decision making process – awareness, knowledge, liking, preference, conviction and purchase.

Buyers Refers to an aspect of the decision making unit (DMU) – the people who make the actual purchase and have formal authority within the DMU to select suppliers, negotiate and contract.

Casual research Research carried out on an informal basis such as might occur from contacting friends, special interest groups, and meeting people at conferences and fairs.

Causal research Marketing research that tests ideas about cause-and-effect relationships.

Cluster samples Respondents taken from a relatively small area and chosen to represent a particular aspect of a product or services target market.

Company culture The shared values and beliefs the people in an organization have about itself and its environment.

Company marketing opportunity The marketing area in which a company would have a competitive advantage.

Competitive market intelligence Data collected about your competitiors.

Concentrated marketing A marketing strategy in which a company goes after one or a few sub-markets.

Concept testing   The testing of new ideas for a product or service with target consumers to establish their appeal.

Consumer durables   Goods owned by households but not consumed by them, examples would include washing machines, cars etc.

Consumer goods   Goods bought by the final consumer for their own personal consumption.

Consumer market   Goods and services acquired by individuals and households for personal consumption.

Consumer panel   A group of consumers chosen from the target market that are regularly consulted for market research purposes.

Consumer profile   A quantified demographic description of an organization's customers.

Consumer resistance   A term given to the reasons why potential customers may decide not to purchase a product or service.

Consumerism   A movement organized by consumers and government to regulate and improve the relationship and rights between purchasers and sellers.

Content analysis   A historical analysis of the contents of one or more sources (usually printed publications) which is used to map changes in culture.

Continuous research   Surveys carried out on a regular basis.

Convenience goods   Goods bought frequently with the minimum of effort and comparison.

Copy testing   The measurement of the effect of a communication before and after it is printed or broadcast.

Corporate identity   The company image that is created for an organization by the use for example of a logo, name, stationery, uniform etc.

Corporate image   The view held of an organization by its stakeholders.

CSO   The Central Statistical Office – now part of the ONS.

Cultural environment   Values, preferences, perceptions and behaviours that exist within different societies.

Culture   Values, preferences, perceptions and behaviours that exist within different societies and are learned by members of that society from the family and other institutions.

Customer value analysis   The analysis an organization carries out to find out the benefits its customers value in relation to offers made by competitors.

Database   Collection of data usually available via computer. This might be in the form of supplied computer disks, CD-ROM or via other means such as over the telephone line.

Delphi technique   Subjective long-range forecasting using expert panels.

Demand curve   A curve indicating the number of units a market will buy at different prices in a given period of time.

Demands   Human wants that are backed by buying power.

Deming, W.E. (b. 1900)   Worked on product quality at Hawthorne lighting plant and asked by the Japanese to help rebuild their industries after the Second World War. Known for his work on statistical process control and is regarded as a founder of total quality management (TQM).

Demographic segmentation   The division of groups of people based on demographic variables such as age, sex, occupation, income, education, religion, race, nationality, family size and family life cycle.

Depth interview   An unstructured, lengthy interview aimed at gaining detailed information from the interviewee about a particular product or service.

Descriptive research   Marketing research that is carried out in order to find out better ways to describe marketing problems, situations or markets.

Desk research   The process of collecting secondary data. Also known as secondary research.

Differentiated marketing   A marketing strategy in which an organization decides to target different segments and to use a different marketing mix for each one.

Duopoly   A situation where there are only two producers in the market.

Economic environment Factors such as taxes, consumer spending, investment and inflation which influence or reflect the state of the economy.

Economic man The assumption about human behaviour based on the idea that s/he is influenced by rational motives such as the desire for financial gain and the fear of financial pain.

Environmental audit A check carried out by firms on their environmental impact e.g. pollution levels, wastage levels and recycling practices.

Experimental research A scientific method of research designed to determine the specific relationship between, usually two, factors. For example, the relationship between price and packaging design.

Focus group technique A group of, usually, seven to ten persons brought together to discuss a particular product or service.

Forecasting The estimation of future demand in the market by anticipating how buyers are likely to behave under given conditions.

Frequency The number of times an average person in a target market in a given period is likely to be exposed to an advertising message. Also a statistical term that refers to the number of observations made of a particular value.

Gatekeeper The role a person within the decision making unit plays in controlling the flow of information from the outside environment.

Generation X The 18- to 29-year-old post-baby boom generation.

Generic brands Products that are unbranded, for example, aspirin, paracetamol, potatoes, milk.

Geographic segmentation The division of a market into different geographical units based on nation, state, regions, counties, cities or neighbourhoods.

Group dynamics The interactions between members of a group such as might occur in a focus or work group.

GSS The UK Government Statistical Service, replaced in 1996 by the Office for National Statistics (ONS).

Hierarchy of needs Categorization of human needs into a 'pyramid' with the basic, survival needs at the base. Theory first proposed by Abraham Maslow in 1954.

HMSO Her Majesty's Stationery Office – publishers of government documents such as those from the ONS.

Human need The state of a felt deprivation.

Human want The form a human needs takes when it is shaped by personality and culture.

Hypothesis A prediction about what a particular piece of research will find.

Idea screening A process of sifting through a number of new ideas in order to drop bad ideas and take advantage of good new ideas.

Impulse purchase An unplanned decision to buy a product or service.

Income elasticity This measures the way in which demand changes when consumers real incomes change.

$$\text{Formula: income elasticity} = \frac{\text{percentage change in demand}}{\text{percentage change in real income}}$$

Index-linked Linking a value specifically to the changes in the retail price index (RPI), which is used as the standard measure of inflation in the UK.

Industrial goods Goods bought by businesses for further processing or used in the process of carrying out a business.

Inelastic demand This is where, for a given percentage change in price, there is a proportionately lower change in demand. For example, if the price of a product rises by 10% and demand only falls by 5%.

Inferior goods A product for which demand rises when real incomes fall. For example, own-label supermarket goods.

Influencers The role carried out within the decision making unit by people whose advice carries some weight within the decision making process.

Information search The stage in the buyer decision process in which the consumer looks for additional information.

Initiator The role carried out within the decision making unit by people who first suggest buying a particular product or service.

Intangibility Services cannot be seen, felt, heard or experienced before they are bought.

Just in time (JIT) The planned flow of resources used in the production process that is designed to minimize the costs of holding stocks of raw materials, components, work-in-progress and finished goods.

Just noticeable difference (JND) The change to a particular stimulus (picture, sound, texture) which is just detectable by our senses.

Kaizen A Japanese term meaning continual improvement.

Kanban The Japanese system of order cards that pull component supplies through a factory.

Learning The process by which people acquire experience and knowledge.

Lifestyle The pattern of living expressed by a person's activities, interests and opinions.

Market The set of actual and potential buyers for a product or service.

Market positioning Ensuring a product or service occupies a clear place in the minds of the target consumer relative to competitor products.

Market saturation This occurs when all the people who want a product already have one.

Market segment A group of consumers who respond in a similar way to a set of marketing stimuli.

Market segmentation The process of classifying customers into groups with different needs, characteristics, behaviour and responsiveness to the marketing mix or groups of products/services with like attributes.

Market share The percentage of all the sales within a market that are held by one brand or company.

Market size The total sales of all producers within a market measured by value or volume.

Market structure A description of all the competitive forces within a market.

Market targeting The evaluation of the attractiveness of each market segment and the selection of one or more segments to target.

Marketing Marketing is the management process which identifies, anticipates and satisfies customer requirements efficiently and profitably.

Marketing control The measurement and evaluation of the results of marketing plans in order to ensure that the objectives are being met.

Marketing information system (MIS) Is a system by which accurate information is gathered, sorted, analysed and distributed on time to people involved in making marketing decisions.

Marketing mix The main variables through which an organization carries out its marketing strategy, often known as the 4Ps – product, price, place and promotion. Three additional Ps are added to cover the service elements – people, place and process.

Mean A measure of location calculated by adding together all raw data values and dividing by the number of values collected. More correctly called the arithmetic mean.

$$\text{Formula: mean} = \frac{\text{sum of values}}{\text{number of values}}$$

Measures of dispersion Statistics which indicate the 'spread' of values in a distribution. The most common measures of dispersion are the range, the interquartile range, the quartile deviation, the mean deviation and the standard deviation.

Measures of location Statistics which provide an indication of the 'average' response. The most common measures of location are the arithmetic mean, the mode and the median. Sometimes called measures of central tendency.

Median A measure of location defined as the 'middle' value in an ordered set of observations. When an even number of observations have been collected then the median is calculated by taking the mean of the two 'middle' observations.

Mode A measure of location defined as the most frequently occurring data value in a frequency table or frequency distribution.

Model A simplified representation of 'real world' processes.

Monopolistic competition A market where many buyers and sellers trade using a range of prices rather than one single price.

Moral appeals An appeal that is used to the sense of what is considered correct.

Motivation Underlying driving force within a person.

Motivational research Qualitative research aimed at uncovering a person's motivations.

Non-durable goods Tangible goods that are usually consumed in one or a few uses.

Observational research A quantitative research technique where data is collected by observation of buying and/or using behaviour, usually in a natural context.

Oligopolistic competition A market in which there are a few large sellers who are sensitive to each other's marketing strategies.

ONS The Office for National Statistics – the main source of government data.

OPCS The Office of Population Censuses and Surveys, now part of the ONS.

Opinion leader A person whose opinions are an important influence on others.

Organization image The way in which people perceive an organization.

Own-label Products branded with the retailer's own name or a name developed by them.

Penetrated market Consumers within a market who have already bought the product or service.

Perception The process by which people create a meaningful picture of the world by selecting, organizing and interpreting information.

Personality The psychological characteristics that distinguish one person from another and lead to consistent responses to their environment.

Political environment Government, the law, political parties influence society and create a particular culture that can either encourage or limit the business interests of certain organizations.

Post-purchase behaviour The stage within the buyer decision process in which the consumer will behave either positively or negatively based on their satisfaction or dissatisfaction with the product or service.

Potential market The group of consumers who say they have an interest in a particular product or service.

Price elastic Where the proportionate increase or decrease in price leads to a proportionately greater increase or decrease in the quantity sold.

Price elasticity A measure of the way the demand for a good responds to a change in its price.

$$\text{formula:} \quad \frac{\text{percentage change in quantity demanded}}{\text{percentage change in price}}$$

Price inelastic Where the proportionate change in a product's price leads to a proportionately smaller change in the quantity sold. These goods tend to have high product differentiation and consumers perceive them as having no acceptable substitutes.

Primary data Data collected by means of primary research.

Primary demand The total demand for all brands of a given product or service.

Primary research Original research carried out to fulfil specific objectives.

Product concept The idea for a new idea for a product expressed in terms that the consumer would understand.

Product position The place in the consumer's mind that the product occupies relative to that of competing products.

Projective techniques A range of Qualitative research techniques designed to provide an insight into consumer psychology (motivation, perception etc.). Examples include sentence completion, Thematic Apperception Tests, and more exotic techniques such as the Repertory Grid.

Promotion mix The mix of promotional methods a company uses to achieve its marketing and communication objectives.

Psychographic segmentation The technique of measuring lifestyle. It is commonly known as AIO analysis – activities, interests and opinions.

Purchase decision The stage within the buying decision making process where the consumer makes the purchase.

Pure competition A market in which many buyers and sellers trade in the same commodity so that no one buyer or seller has much effect on the going market price.

Pure monopoly A market in which there is only one supplier.

Qualified available market The group of consumers who have money, access, and interest in a product or service.

Qualitative research Research which produces data which is primarily non-numerical in nature. Usually the spoken or written word. The three main categories of qualitative research are depth interviews, focus groups and projective techniques.

Quality assurance The attempt to make sure that standards of quality are agreed upon and met within the organization and that customer satisfaction is ensured.

Quality circles A group of people that meets regularly to identify and discuss quality problems, consider different solutions and make recommendations to management.

Quality control The process in which work that is either bought in or newly completed is checked.

Quantitative research Research which produces data which is primarily numerical in nature. Usually the result of answering multiple choice or other coded questions or the classification of behaviours. The three main categories of quantitative research are experimentation, observation and surveys.

Quartile Dividing an ordered distribution of data into four equal parts creates what are known as quartiles. The lower quartile (Q_1) separates out the lowest 25% of observations, the upper quartile (known as Q_3) separates out the top 25% of the observations. The middle quartile (known as Q_2) is equivalent to the median. Interquartile range and quartile deviation are two measures of dispersion calculated using quartiles.

Random sample A sampling method where individuals are randomly selected from a sampling frame.

Range A measure of dispersion defined as the difference between the highest and lowest value observations.

Raw data Unprocessed data; data which is in the same form as when it was collected.

Reference group A group which is used as a reference point by a person in the formation of their attitudes, values or behaviours.

Repeat purchase Occurs when a first-time buyer purchases a product again.

Research 'The collection and analysis of data from a sample of individuals or organizations relating to their characteristics, behaviour, attitudes, opinions or possessions. It includes all forms of marketing and social research such as consumer and industrial surveys, psychological investigations, observational and panel studies' (The Market Research Society).

Response rate   The rate of reply to a survey.

Retail Price Index (RPI)   A single figure economic indicator which measures the change in prices of a 'basket' of products and services over a period of time compared with a 'base' or reference year.

Sample   A group of individuals selected from the target population

Secondary data   Data originally collected for any purpose other than the current research objectives, usually by a third party.

Selective demand   The demand for a specific brand.

Shopping goods   Consumer goods that the consumer will shop around for and compare.

Skewness   A frequency distribtion which is assymetrical is said to be skewed. That is, it has a 'tail' on one side rather than being 'bell-shaped'. If distribution has a longer 'tail' to the right it is said to be positively skewed. A distribution with a longer 'tail' to the left is said to be negatively skewed.

Social grade   The occupational category that shows to which social class each household belongs.

Social marketing   Marketing programmes designed to increase the acceptability of social ideas, causes or practice within target markets.

Speciality goods   Goods which consumers are willing to make a special effort to acquire because of their unique branding or characteristics.

Status   The respect people in society give to a role.

Subculture   Value systems that are shared by a group of people based on their common experiences in life.

Subliminal advertising   Advertising below the level of perception.

Survey research   A quantitative research method, usually using a questionnaire to collect data.

Target market   The segments of the market that the organization decides to concentrate on.

Technological environment   Developments in technology that can effect existing products, create new products and market opportunities.

Test marketing   The stage in the development of a new product in which the product and marketing mix are tested in realistic market conditions.

Third party data   Data collected by an organization other than your own – such as a market research company. Such data may have originated from consumer panels or other regular surveys performed by the organization in question.

Total market demand   The total volume of a product or service that would be bought in a specific geographical area, under specific marketing conditions, in a defined time period.

Total quality management (TQM)   The establishment of a culture of quality within organizations.

Undifferentiated marketing   A marketing strategy in which the organization goes after the whole market with the same marketing mix.

Unique selling point (USP)   The product feature that can be concentrated on in order to differentiate it from the competition.

Users   The role carried out within the decision making unit by the people who actually use or consume the product.

Index

329

Communications, 124–6
  and auditing organizations, 61
  with customers, 267–72
  in groups, 180–1
  and total relationship marketing,
    197–200
Community-based economics, 290
Comparative data, bias and, 261
Comparative groups, 178
Competences, core, 98–9
Competition:
  and auditing organizations, 58
  and customer power, 2–5
Complaints, customer, 57, 265
Comprehensive models of customer
    behaviour, 153
Computer assisted interviews (CAI),
    243, 244
Computer assisted telephone
    interviewing (CATI), 243, 244
Confidentiality, data protection and,
    259–60
Connectivity, e-business and, 298–300
Conservatism, customer behaviour
    and, 118
Constructive feedback, 116
Consumer behaviour, 140–57, *see also*
    Customer behaviour
Consumer goods, 23
Consumer imagery, 173–5
Consumer reference groups, 178–9
Consumer-referent groups, 181–2
Consumerism, 289–92
Consumers, 14–15, 25
  clustering, 39–40
  decision making, 141–53
  ethical consumers, 289–92
  post-modern, and branding, 164–6
  protecting interests of, 289–92
  relationship marketing for, 190
  see also Customers
Continuous improvement, culture of,
    118–39
Convenience, 191, 285
Convenience goods, 23
Core competences, 98–9
Core values, 98–9
Corporate hierarchy of responsibility, 7
Corporate image, 60, 269
Costs:
  for customers, reducing, 274–5
  and human resources, 68
  social costs, 286–7
  switching costs, 191–2
Counselling, 104
Creativity in organizations, 134–5
Cross-Cultural Consumer
    Characterization, 38
Cross-cultural marketing, 163
Cross-functional work flows, 83
Cultural onion, 161–2
Culture, 158–64
  in auditing organizations, 58
  organizational, 73–4, 131–2
    and continuous improvement,
      118–39

and sentient groups, 78
and values, 6, 60
and segmentation, 28
see also Socio-cultural factors
Customer activity cycle (CAC), 83–5
Customer behaviour, 2
  and attitudes, 155–7
  conservatism in, 118
  and culture, 158–9
  and e-business, 303–6
  and environmental consciousness,
    286
  modelling, 140–57
  trends in, 278–311
  see also Consumer behaviour
Customer care audits, 57
Customer care training, 100–1
Customer demand, e-business and,
    300
Customer dynamics, 216–20, 231–62
Customer focus, 8, 263–77
  and innovations, 128–33
  strategy for, 54–94
Customer interface, e-business and,
    295–310
Customer orientation, examples of, 13
Customer power, emergence of, 2–5
Customer satisfaction, 10, 69
  Yellow Pages investigation of,
    104–6
Customer service, 8, 12–13
  and customer retention, 107
  and empowerment, 90–1
  see also Service
Customer service manuals, 272
Customers, 14–16, 19, 25
  analysis of, 264–5
  and barriers to innovation, 126–7
  behaviour *see* Customer behaviour
  in charity marketing, 19
  classifying *see* Market segmentation
  communication with, 267–72
  complaints, 57, 265
  decision making *see* Decision
    making
  expectations, 7–13, 218
  individuals as, 164–77
  internal, 26
  as king/queen, 17
  organizations as, 183–7, *see also*
    Industrial markets
  partnership agreements with, 276–7
  in the public sector, 17–18
  reducing costs for, 274–5
  relationships with, 188–90, *see also*
    Relationship marketing
  retention of, 107
  value of, 266–7
  see also Consumers
Customization, 275–6
  mass, 50–2, 300
  and personalization paradox,
    299–300
  and relationship marketing, 191
Customs, 160
Cycles *see* Business cycle; Life cycle

Data, 225, 259–62
    types compared, 231–2
    see also Information
Data protection, legal issues of,
    259–60
Databases, 256–7, 267–8
Decentralization, 290
Deciders in organizations, 184
Decision making, 25–6
    models of, 140–52, 182
    in organizations, 26, 183–4
    and auditing, 61
Decision making units (DMUs), 25–6,
    183–4
Decision process models, 146–7
Defences, individuals', 202
Demographics, 279–80
    and segmentation, 30–4, 49
    see also Population
Depth interviews, 233, 238
Development:
    and training, 97
    see also Training
Dialogue with customers, 270
    see also Communications
Differentiation, product, 40–3, 191
Diffusion curves, 27
Diffusion of innovations, 119–20
Disengineering, 298
Dispersion, measures of, 226
Dissociative groups, 178
Dissonance, 147, 221–4
Distribution channels, re-evaluating,
    274
Distributors, strategy audits and, 59
Diversification, 274
Diversity, respect for, 291
DMUs (decision making units), 25–6,
    183–4
Dreams, self-concept and, 174
Dynamic nature of culture, 163

E-business and e-commerce, 5,
    295–310
    definitions of, 296
    on-line databases, 256–7
    see also Information technology
Ecological wisdom, 291
Economic environment, 293
Economic factors, 57, 293–4
Economy, the, 5–14, 57
Education, 284
Efficiency, organizational, 69–70
EFQM excellence model, 62–3
Electronic commerce *see* E-business
    and e-commerce
Electronic databases, 256–7
Employees:
    appraisal, 60, 116
    counselling, 104
    empowerment *see* Empowerment
    investment in people, 9–10, 88–9
    and job security, 6
    managing real-time workers, 298
    and motivational issues, 107–13

in organizational analysis, 61
    recognition, 97–8, 130
    recruitment, 10–11, 60, 96–7
    and tests, 97, 99–100
    rewards, 60, 97–8, 129–30
    training *see* Training
    see also Human resources issues;
        Role
Employment trends, 285
Empowerment, employee, 14, 89–91
    five dimensions of, 114
    and self-actualization, 113
    training, 106
Environmental issues, 58, 286–9, *see
    also* Macro-environmental factors;
    Micro-environmental factors
Envy in TQM work, 78
EPS *see* Extended problem solving
    (EPS)
ERG hierarchy of needs, 172
Ethical consumers, 289–92
Ethical responsibilities, data and,
    258–9
Ethnicity, 161, 284
European Foundation for Quality
    Management, 62
Evaluation:
    in decision process models, 147
    of value, 17
Exchange, value in, 17
Expectancy theory, Vroom's, 110–11,
    172
Expectations, 166
    and customers, 7–13, 218
    and role, 16
    in Vroom's theory, 110–11, 172
Experimental design, 207–13
Expert appeal, 181
Expertise, innovation and, 133
Extended problem solving (EPS),
    147–8
    and relationship marketing, 192–3
Extended self, 174
External analysis, customer focus
    problems and, 264–5
External connectivity, e-business and,
    298
External data, 232
External environment, innovation and,
    128
External factors:
    and customer behaviour, 2, 158–9
    and strategy, 57–9

Families, 33–4
    purchasing by, 181, 182, 284
Family life cycle (FLC), 33–4
Family purchase, 26
Feedback, 14, 116
    360° feedback systems, 92
Financial systems, 61, *see also* Costs
Financiers, organizational decision
    making and, 184
Fishbone (Ishikowa) diagram, 85–6
FLC (family life cycle), 33–4

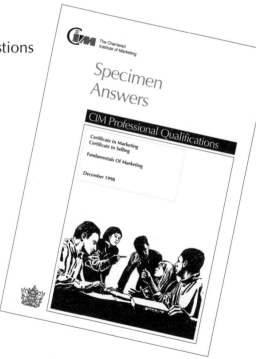